Suffering in Romans

Suffering in Romans

Siu Fung Wu

Foreword by
Todd D. Still

James Clarke & Co

I dedicate this book to my mother

James Clarke & Co
P.O. Box 60
Cambridge
CB1 2NT
United Kingdom

www.jamesclarke.co
publishing@jamesclarke.co

ISBN: 978 0 227 17590 3

British Library Cataloguing in Publication Data
A record is available from the British Library

First published by James Clarke & Co, 2015

Published by arrangement
with Pickwick Publications

Contents

Foreword

FOR ALL OF ITS predictable patterns and outcomes, life is not without surprises. The same is true of New Testament Studies.

When I first turned my attention to the subject of suffering in Romans (5 and 8), I was surprised by the sparse scholarly treatment of the topic.[1] I remember wondering at the time—namely, the spring of 2012—how much longer it would be before a Pauline specialist filled this lacunae in the secondary literature.

I was nonetheless surprised one year later when I was contacted by Melbourne College of Divinity (now University of Divinity) to examine a doctoral thesis entitled "Suffering in Romans" by Siu Fung Wu. And a pleasant surprise it was. In that study, now Dr. Wu treated with clarity and care the theme of suffering in Romans 5–8 with special reference to 5:1–11 and 8:14–39 and persuasively demonstrated the centrality of the subject in that pivotal portion of Paul's magisterial letter to Roman believers.

You need not be surprised, however, as to what lies in front of you in this thesis-turned-monograph. Herein you will find a serious, scholarly study that offers salient insight into a long-neglected topic in an oft-interpreted text. Indeed, it is the most comprehensive and persuasive treatment to date.

Far from surprising, Paul regarded suffering to be part and parcel of both the human condition and of Christian commitment.[2] This investigation of suffering in Romans is made all the more meaningful, at least to my mind, by the fact that Dr. Wu and his family are no strangers to grief and pain. What is more, I harbor the hope that this courageous work will

---

1. The work of J. Christiaan Beker was an exception. See, e.g., his "Suffering and Triumph in Paul's Letter to the Romans," 105–19; and "Vision of Hope for a Suffering World," 26–32. Note now also my "Placing Pain in a Pauline Frame: Considering Suffering in Romans 5 and 8," 73–86, 228–30.

2. See esp. Rom 5:3; 8:17–25. Cf. also Phil 1:29; 1 Thess 3:3–4. Note, too, 1 Pet 4:12–13; James 1:2; Matt 5:11–12.

enable readers to make better sense (of Paul's understanding of) "the suffer-ings of this present time" (Rom 8:18), knowing that not even suffering can "separate us [i.e., 'Christians'] from the love of God that is in Christ Jesus our Lord" (8:39; cf. 5:5).

Todd D. Still

DeLancey Dean and Hinson Professor

Baylor University, Truett Seminary

Waco, Texas, USA

Preface

THIS MONOGRAPH IS A slightly revised version of my PhD dissertation, which was submitted to University of Divinity, Australia, in 2013. It is a daunting task to undertake a project on the topic of suffering. I am deeply aware that suffering is an experiential matter, not theoretical or abstract. Yet my research project was an academic endeavor, and hence by necessity I could not approach the subject in a more pastoral manner. Here I would like to ask my readers for their understanding if aspects of this book fall short of their expectation. Also, I do not for a moment think that I have sufficiently covered the issues around suffering, or that my view is error-prone. My research has enhanced my understanding greatly, but I know that is it only a drop in the ocean in the vast field of study.

There were many challenges during my study. I had a young family when I started my research. I was studying part-time and had a busy job that required a lot of mental and emotional energy. I was able to complete the study because of the gracious hand of God. Not only that he sustained me in my struggles, he also placed people in my life to help me. Here I would like to take the opportunity to thank each of those who assisted me in my journey.

I thank Professor Keith Dyer, my supervisor in the first eighteen months of my study. He played an instrumental role in the early part of the project. Keith is not only a fine scholar, but also a man of grace and kindness. His encouragement over the years is much appreciated. I want to express my sincere gratitude to Revd Associate Professor Sean Winter, my main supervisor for three years. His expertise in Pauline theology and superb supervision skill was crucial to the success of my study. During the course of my research, I had a couple of very difficult years at work. Eventually I lost my employment and regular income. Professor Winter was very supportive during my ordeal. I am grateful to him for his encouragement. I also want to thank Professor Mark Brett, a friend and thoughtful scholar at Whitley College, who read one of the chapters in my thesis and gave me valuable feedback. Mark is one of the most sincere followers of Jesus I know.

I am very grateful to many friends who supported me with their gifts, resources, and prayers. Here I want to specifically mention Hans and Lucia Baars, David and Geraldine Fenn, and our family friends from the 1980s, Dorothy and Daniel Man. I thank them for walking with me and standing by me. I deeply appreciate their friendship and assistance. All of them are exemplary disciples of Jesus.

I would like to thank Professor Todd Still for his willingness to write a foreword for me. I know that it was God who had led me to Professor Still when he informed me that he liked my work and encouraged me to seek publication. It is an honor to have a respected Pauline scholar recommend my work. My thanks also go to Dr. George Wieland, who shares with me the passion for the urban poor and the New Testament. I am greatly encouraged by Dr. Wieland's comments on my work. I must mention another two divine moments during the course of my research. First, I came across Professor Timothy Gombis's blog and his book *The Drama of Ephesians*. His publications gave me plenty of food for thought about participating in Christ's suffering and death. Second, my research project coincided with my work in aid and development. For nearly seven years I sought to walk with the poor, who suffered under the weight of corrupt socioeconomic systems. Their resilience in the face of suffering and oppression gave me valuable insight into how Paul's letter might be read. There is much to be learned from the poor.

The completion of my PhD is a good occasion to remember those who played a significant part in my academic endeavor and faith journey. Johnny and Kim Chan, as well as Irene Chan, taught me to love the Scripture when I was a young Christian in the 1980s, and for that I am grateful. I thank Revd Professor John Nolland and Revd Dr. Kevin Giles for supervising my MPhil thesis. My MPhil provided me with the best preparation for the PhD. Revd Dr. Giles was the one who encouraged me to do an MPhil in Pauline studies. Professor Nolland is a first-rate scholar and a kind man. It was a privilege to study under his supervision.

My most heartfelt thanks go to Catherine, my wife and faithful companion. She has stood by me through many trials and hardships for almost twenty-seven years. I can honestly say that without her I would not have made it through these years of intense studies. I also want to specifically mention my son, Caleb. I have shared with him many research findings over the years, and it is amazing how he is able to absorb the information despite his young age. It has been a delight to share my journey with him. His ability to grasp complex concepts and think outside the box is a special gift from God.

The genesis of my research topic traces back to my childhood when my mother suffered from a heart condition that resulted in a disability. We were garment factory workers in East Asia and had little income. My mother's sickness added a lot of pain and affliction to the family. We experienced many socioeconomic hardships that few people in Australia (my home now) can ever imagine. But my parents showed me that one could persevere in suffering and face it with dignity. I want to thank my father, who taught me that one could stand strong in the face of adversity. But most importantly, I dedicate this book to my mother, who passed away twenty-two years ago. She demonstrated profound resilience and tenacity in her suffering. Not only that she lived with her physical limitations with extraordinary endurance, she also faced the social exclusion associated with her disability with remarkable courage. She was a loyal follower of Jesus.

Finally, I thank God for his unfailing love in the past thirty-three years, ever since I said my first prayer to him. Following Jesus is not easy, and indeed Paul says that the children of God will suffer with Christ (Rom 8:17). But he loved us and gave himself for us (Gal 2:20). So, we are not ashamed, for we know the one in whom we put our trust, and he is able to guard what we have entrusted to him on that day (2 Tim 1:12). I pray that this book will bring glory to the crucified Christ and risen Lord.

Siu Fung Wu
February 2015

Abbreviations

ABBREVIATIONS FOR THE OLD Testament, the New Testament, and the Old Testament Apocrypha and Pseudepigrapha follow *The SBL Handbook of Style* (1999). Other abbreviations are listed below.

ABR   *Australian Biblical Review*

AnBib   *Analecta Biblica*

ANE   Ancient Near East

ANTC   Abingdon New Testament Commentaries

AOTC   Abingdon Old Testament Commentaries

BDAG   Walter Bauer, Frederick W. Danker, W. F. Arndt, and F. W. Gingrich. *A Greek-English Lexicon of the New Testament and Other Early Christian Literature*. 3rd ed. Chicago: University of Chicago Press, 2000.

BCOT   Baker Commentary on the Old Testament

BECNT   Baker Exegetical Commentary on the New Testament

BHT   *Beiträge zur historischen Theologie*

Bib   *Biblica*

BSac   *Bibliotheca Sacra*

BZ   *Biblische Zeitschrift*

CBQ   *Catholic Biblical Quarterly*

CIL   *Corpus inscriptionum latinarum*

CTR   *Criswell Theological Review*

DJG   *Dictionary of Jesus and the Gospels*

DLNTD   *Dictionary of Later New Testament Development*

DNTB   *Dictionary of New Testament Background*

DOTP	*Dictionary of the Old Testament: Pentateuch*
DOTWPW	*Dictionary of the Old Testament: Wisdom, Poetry, Writings*
DPL	*Dictionary of Paul and his Letters*
EKKNT	Evangelisch-katholischer Kommentar zum Neuen Testament
EvQ	*Evangelical Quarterly*
ExpTim	*Expository Times*
FoiVie	*Foi et Vie*
FRLANT	Forschungen zur Religion und Literatur des Alten und Neuen Testament
HBT	*Horizons in Biblical Theology*
HTS	*Teologiese Studies/Theological Studies*
ICC	International Critical Commentary
JBL	*Journal of Biblical Literature*
JL	*The Journal of Religion*
JSNT	*Journal for the Study of the New Testament*
JSNTSup	*Journal for the Study of the New Testament: Supplement Series*
JSPL	*Journal for the Study of Paul and his Letters*
JTI	*Journal of Theological Interpretation*
JTS	*Journal of Theological Studies*
L.A.E.	*Life of Adam and Eve*
LBL	*Loeb* Classical Library
LNSM	Louw, J. P., E. A. Nida, R. B. Smith, and K. A. Munson, eds., *Greek-English Lexicon of the New Testament: Based on Semantic Domains.* 2nd ed. 2 vols. New York: United Bible Societies, 1988, 1989.
LNTS	Library of New Testament Studies
LSJ	Henry George Liddell, Robert Scott, and Henry Stuart Jones. *A Greek-English Lexicon.* 9th ed. Oxford: Clarendon, 1996.
LXX	The Septuagint
MT	Masoretic Text
NCC	New Covenant Commentary
NIB	New Interpreter's Bible
NIBC	New International Biblical Commentary

NICNT	New International Commentary on the New Testament
NIGTC	New International Greek Testament Commentary
NovT	*Novum Testamentum*
NSBT	New Studies in Biblical Theology
NT	New Testament
NTS	*New Testament Studies*
OCABS	*The Journal of the Orthodox Center for the Advancement of Biblical Studies*
OT	Old Testament
OTL	Old Testament Library
PNTC	Pillar New Testament Commentaries
PSB	*Princeton Seminary Bulletin*
QSS	Dead Sea Scrolls
SBL	Society of Biblical Literature
SHBC	The Smyth & Helwys Bible Commentary Series
SJT	*Scottish Journal of Theology*
SNTSMS	Society for New Testament Studies Monograph Series
SNTW	Studies of the New Testament and its World
TDNT	*Theological Dictionary of the New Testament*. 10 vols. Edited by Gerhard Kittel and Gerhard Friedrich. Translated by Geoffrey W. Bromiley. Grand Rapids: Eerdmans, 1964–76.
THNTC	Two Horizons New Testament Commentary
THOTC	Two Horizons Old Testament Commentary
WBC	Word Biblical Commentary
WMANT	Wissenschaftliche Monographien zum Alten und Neuen Testament
WUNT	Wissenschaftliche Untersuchungen zum Neuen Testament
ZNW	*Zeitschrift für die neutestamentliche Wissenschaft und die Kunde der älteren Kirche*

ANCIENT SOURCES

Epigraphy collection

CIL   *Corpus inscriptionum latinarum*

Aelius Aristides

Or.   *Orationes*   Orations

Alexander of Aphrodisias

Mixt.   *De Mixtione*

Caesar

Bell. Civ.   *Bellum Civile*

Cicero

Off.   *De officiis*
De Or.   *De oratore*
Fam.   *Epistulae ad familiares*
Flac.   *Pro Flacco*
Tusc.   *Tusculanae disputationes*

Demosthenes

Phae.   *Against Phaenippus*

Gaius

Inst.   *Institutiones*

Homer

Il.   *Ilias*   *Iliad*

Horace

Carm.   *Carmina*   Odes

Juvenal

Sat.   *Saturae*

Livy

Hist   *History of Rome*

Ovid

Fast.   *Fasti*

Philo

Fug.   *De fuga et inventione*

Plato

Resp.   *Respublica*   *Republic*
Tim.   *Timaeus*

Polybius

Hist.   *Historiae*   *Histories*

Seneca

Ep.   *Epistulae morales*
Helv.   *De Consolatione ad Helviam Matrem*
Nat.   *Naturales quaestiones*

Suetonius

Claud.   *Divus Claudius*

Virgil

Aen.   *Aeneid*
Georg.   *Georgica*

1

Aim and Approach of Study

AIM OF STUDY

THE THEME OF SUFFERING occupies a significant place in Paul's letter to the Romans. It appears prominently in at least two passages, namely, 5:1–11 and 8:14–39. These are situated at strategic locations within Romans, for they bracket the central section of the letter: 5:1—8:39. There are more than fourteen terms representing different forms of suffering, with a concentrated enumeration of trouble and distress in the affliction-list in 8:35.[1] But, surprisingly, there is no major monograph that specifically studies the theology of suffering in Romans.

The aim of our inquiry, therefore, is to determine the theology of suffering in Romans from the perspective of Paul's first audience. The approach of our study will be audience-focused, paying special attention to how a first-century audience in Rome might have interacted with the rhetorical strategy, the literary construct, and the use of Israel's Scripture of the letter.

Because of space limitations, our study will focus on Rom 5–8, with exegesis of 5:1–21 and 8:1–39. There are good reasons why Rom 5 and 8 are chosen. First, the most prominent passages that explicitly refer to suffering are 5:1–11; 8:14–17; and 8:18–39, and they obviously require our

1. These fourteen terms occur sixteen times in Rom 5–8, compared with, say, eighteen occurrences of the δικ- word group in the section. If we consider the whole letter and include other terms that allude to suffering, we find about thirty-eight occurrences of all those terms in Romans. On the other hand, the δικ- words appear fifty-five times in the whole letter. See Appendix A for a list of the terms.

attention. In order to capture the rhetorical strategy of the pericopes within which these passages are located, the entire argument of 5:1–21 and 8:1–39 will need to be examined. Second, as will be argued, the section 5:1—8:39 constitutes a distinctive section of the letter, and the fact that 5:1–11 and 8:17–39 bookend this section makes the study of Rom 5 and 8 a fitting choice.

In the current chapter we will first outline why an audience-focused approach should be taken, and how this will work in our exegesis. We will then discuss how the letter's use of Israel's Scriptures will be useful to our inquiry.

AUDIENCE-FOCUSED APPROACH: REASONS, THE TERM "THEOLOGY," AND SOME SIGNIFICANT STUDIES

In a traditional author-focused approach to Romans, the interpreter seeks to determine Paul's *intention* for the letter. That is, the interpreter asks: What does Paul intend to convey to his audience through the text? In this approach, one may try to work out the apostle's intended purpose in writing the letter, and how his own suffering might have influenced his teaching. Our approach, however, is audience-focused.[2] That is, our question concerns how the audience might have heard the letter as they interacted with the text, given their experience of suffering in first-century Rome. As mentioned, there are substantial references to affliction in Romans. Implicit in these texts is an audience that is suffering, to whom the letter speaks and provides comfort, encouragement and instruction. Indeed, these texts serve to invite the audience to identify with the letter's description of and teaching on suffering, and to respond by taking appropriate action. By analyzing the functions of these texts, we can gather information about what the letter might have conveyed to the audience and how the audience might construe a theology of suffering.

---

2. In taking this approach, I do not intend to undermine the value of author-focused approaches. (In fact, a good grasp of the audience's understanding of the text will provide valuable information for determining the author's intended meaning.) I will soon outline my reasons for taking an audience-focused approach. It should be noted that there are diverse ways of applying this approach in scholarship. As Fowler, "Reader-Response Criticism," 127, observes, while reader-response criticism is now recognized as a legitimate approach in biblical studies, there is no agreement on what a standard methodology of the approach looks like. Cf. Pearson, "Literary Criticism," 251. One of the purposes of this chapter is to outline the particular methodology that we will use in our exegesis.

Having said that, we are aware that the lived experience of affliction of the audience in ancient Rome would have had an impact on the way they understood Romans. The existential nature of suffering means that the experience of the audience most likely played an important role in their understanding of the texts that speak of affliction. Although we cannot reconstruct the "real" audience of Paul, we nonetheless have access to historical information about life in first-century Rome. In the following I will argue that, in order to achieve a fruitful study, we need more information about the "audience" than the one that is "exclusively implied" by the letter. We need to describe the audience in light of the socio-historical situation of first-century Rome, so that the theology of suffering we seek to determine is not unconnected with the experience of the members of the house churches in Rome.

Also, we need to note that we do not use the term "theology" to denote a systematic account of faith and belief, for rarely do ordinary members of a first-century audience develop an orderly system of doctrine. Neither can we assume that after hearing the letter the members of the audience will formulate a well-thought-through belief system concerning suffering. Instead, "theology of suffering" refers to the audience's perspective on suffering in light of what they hear from the letter and their lived experience of pain and affliction—a perspective on life that provides purpose, direction, comfort and practical resources in the face of trouble and distress. In other words, the "theology of suffering" we try to determine concerns the audience's understanding of suffering as they interpret the texts of Romans. We will soon outline how this audience-focused interpretation of Romans will work in our exegesis, but before that we will first discuss why such an approach might be preferable to an author-focused one.[3]

Why an Audience-Focused Approach?

divine calling

First, and importantly, an audience-focused approach allows us to be sensitive to the existential and experiential nature of suffering. By asking the question of how an audience would have understood the letter, we have a

---

3. For discussions on reader-focused interpretation of the NT, see Lategan, "Coming to Grips," 3–20; McKnight, *Post-Modern Use*, 167–272; Fowler, *Let the Reader*, 1–58; Vanhoozer, "Reader," 259–88; Pearson, "Literary Critism," 251–55. The early influential works on reader-response criticism include Iser, *Implied Reader*; Iser, *Act of Reading*; Fish, *Is There a Text in this Class?* It is recognized that Iser thinks that the reader plays a role in interpreting the text, but at the same time the text shapes and controls the reader's reading. Fish, on the other hand, places great emphasis on the authority of the interpretive community.

tool to explore the relationship between the text and human experience. That is, it allows us to explore how the letter can assist its recipients in their times of need and encourage them as they experience pain and sorrow. An audience-oriented approach may shed light on our inquiry in ways that otherwise would not be possible.

Second, an approach that asks how the audience interacts with the text allows us to determine their understanding of suffering even though the purpose and the main themes of Romans are not primarily related to the experience of suffering. There is no consensus among scholars concerning the purpose of Romans, although Paul's mission to Spain and the intra-communal disharmony within the house churches are commonly recognized as Paul's reasons for writing the letter.[4] But none of the main proposals of scholars understands suffering to be the primary purpose of Romans. Likewise, even though the theme of suffering is prominent in Romans 5–8, rarely do scholars see it as a matter that has significant theological implications for understanding the letter. Yet an audience-focused approach can legitimately ask how the audience would have understood the letter's references to suffering and how as a consequence they may have hope in times of pain and hardship.[5]

Third, an audience-oriented approach helpfully limits the scope of our inquiry to a manageable size. By focusing on the audience, our question is not so much about Paul's overall theology of suffering. If it were, then we would have to frequently cross-reference other Pauline letters where the apostle's exposition of suffering, hope, and endurance is present (e.g., 2 Corinthians, Philippians, and 1 Thessalonians). Also, we would have to carefully work out how Paul's view of suffering should be placed within his overall theology in the letter, which is in itself a subject of enormous scholarly debate. This would have meant a much larger research project.

Fourth, an approach that focuses on the interaction between the text and the audience is not hampered by the likely mismatch between the types of suffering experienced by Paul and the audience. Persecutions by members of the Jewish communities, for example, would have constituted a significant part of Paul's affliction.[6] But there is no evidence of widespread

---

4. See Wedderburn, *Reasons for Romans*, 1–21, 140–42; Das, *Solving*; Jewett, *Romans*, 80–91. See also the essays in Donfried, *Romans Debate*, for detailed discussions.

5. As we shall see in the exegesis, this does not mean that the audience's understanding of suffering is independent of Paul's message in the letter. But an audience-oriented approach allows us to be more focused, and not to get lost in the complex and multilayered theology of Paul.

6. See Acts 13:42–52; 14:19–20; 17:5–9; 21:27—24:27; 2 Cor 11:24.

persecution of Christ-followers in Rome at the time,[7] let alone persecution by the Jews.[8] But despite that absence of evidence, the affliction-list in 8:35, for example, is often interpreted through Paul's own suffering, especially via the use of similar terms in other Pauline letters.[9] While this helps us to understand Paul's theology of suffering, it does not inform the interpreter of how such an important text would have impacted on those who experience hardship in Rome.[10]

Fifth, an audience-focused approach can be fruitful even though Paul does not have a close relationship with the Roman believers. As far as we know, Paul did not establish the church in Rome. Nor had he visited them at the time of writing. Whatever Paul's own theology of suffering, he was not speaking to an audience who had substantial fellowship or any shared experience of suffering with him (as opposed to, for example, Phil 1:5–7; 1 Thess 1:6; 2:8–9).[11] But Romans can still provide resources for the audience in their suffering, regardless of Paul's lack of close relationship with them. This takes place via the letter's rhetorical strategy and by virtue of its frequent use of the language of suffering, hope and endurance.

Finally, it should be noted that other scholars have profitably employed audience-oriented approaches in interpreting Romans. Even though one might not agree with all their conclusions, few would disagree that they have made fresh contributions to scholarship. It is worth surveying some of these scholarly works so as to highlight their significance and the way an audience-focused approach is incorporated into their exegesis.

7. It is unlikely that the expulsion of the Edict of Claudius constituted widespread persecution against Christ-followers. According to Suetonius's biography of Claudius, the emperor expelled Jews from Rome, not followers of Jesus (*Claud.* 25.4).

8. I follow most scholars in dating the letter some time between 56–58 CE, and very likely in 57. See Matera, *Romans*, 5; Johnson, *Reading Romans*, 4; Witherington, *Romans*, 7; Jewett, *Romans*, 21; Moo, *Romans*, 3. Byrne, *Romans*, 9, thinks that it is between late 54 and early 59 CE.

9. For instance, Kruse, *Romans*, 362; Jewett, *Romans*, 543–48; Moo, *Romans*, 543.

10. To interpret Rom 8:35 and other affliction-related texts in Romans *purely* in terms of Paul's own suffering will need to assume that the apostle did not write those texts in view of the suffering of his audience.

11. Here we refer to Paul's relationship with the audience as a corporate entity. Paul might have a close relationship with a very small number of individuals, such as, Prisca and Aquila.

Previous Audience-Focused Studies of Romans

The following survey will highlight the importance of the audience in understanding Romans. The most notable recent work that focuses on the audience is Stanley Stowers's *A Rereading of Romans*. Stowers highlights the inadequacy of the traditional historical-critical method.[12] He emphasizes the importance of "the audience in the text," who are explicitly stated to be Gentiles (1:5; 11:13).[13] For Stowers, there is an encoded implicit reader that may be called an "ideal" reader.[14] With this in mind, Stowers goes on to suggest a rereading of Romans that seriously takes into account the rhetorical strategy of the letter.[15] The result is a fresh reading that truly pays attention to the interaction between the text and the audience.[16] For our purposes, we note that the notion of an implied audience in Stowers's approach provides an effective way to explore the relationship between the text and its recipients, and how the text may influence the attitudes and life patterns of the audience. In our analysis we will pay attention to how Romans is heard by its implied audience—although, as will be shown, our "audience" is somewhat different from a "pure" implied audience.

12. Stowers, *Rereading*, 22–33. Stowers specifically challenges the assumption of Jewish elements in the audience.

13. Ibid., 21–22. Like Stowers, Das (*Solving*, 6, 53–114, 261–64) argues that Paul writes to an all-Gentile audience. For our purposes, the ethnic composition of the audience of Romans is not the primary concern. It is because, as it will be seen, the "audience" we are interested in consists primarily of those who suffer in imperial Rome, regardless of their ethnicity. We will, however, make some brief comments on Das's *Solving the Roman Debate*. His argument for an all-Gentile audience is notably forceful, and his scholarship is commendable. Yet, although Das should be applauded for his contribution to the debate, it should be noted that the commentators after his monograph are still not convinced that the Roman audience consisted of Gentiles only. See, for instance, Kruse, *Romans*, 2–3; Longenecker, *Introducing Romans*, 75–84; Hultgren, *Romans*, 9–11; Keener, *Romans*, 11–13. (Both Hultgren and Keener refer to Das's monograph.) Space limitations do not allow me to interact with Das in detail, but I agree with Matera, *Romans*, 7, that "although Das has made the strongest case to date for a purely Gentile audience," Paul's call for his audience to welcome one another in 15:7 and his "description of Christ as a minister to Jews and Gentiles (15:8–9), suggests that even if Paul's audience was composed predominantly of Gentile believers, it included some Jewish Christ-believers as well."

14. Stowers, *Rereading*, 21.

15. Ibid., 36–41. Another significant (earlier) monograph that takes seriously the rhetoric of Romans is Elliott, *Rhetoric*, 60–68, who, while not primarily focusing on the audience, helpfully says that the letter is intended to move the "audience *toward* the adherence to" its "theses or values" (60; emphasis original).

16. This is regardless of whether one agrees with Stowers's conclusion.

Like Stowers, Heil has written a commentary on Romans that focuses on the implied audience.[17] He says that the "audience we meet in Romans is not a real or actual Roman audience but an implied or intended epistolary audience created and established by the author through the text of the Epistle."[18] Heil's commentary is brief, but it is probably the only commentary that uses a "reader-response" approach.[19] The following summarizes Heil's methodology.

> Calculating the responses of this implied audience, then, is . . . controlled by rhetorical analysis of the text. The implied audience or reader is also distinguished from ourselves as actual contemporary readers. We are called upon and challenged to assume the position of the implied audience of the text if we wish to fully experience the emotional, attitudinal and mental persuasions the Letter is intended to communicate. By experiencing its desired rhetorical effects we can better comprehend and appreciate the Letter's message.[20]

Here Heil highlights the advantage of the approach in detecting the experience of the audience, which is particularly useful to our inquiry because of the existential nature of suffering. Our approach will be similar to Heil's, except that in our case a "strictly pure" implied audience is somewhat restrictive. For the purposes of our inquiry, we have to take into account the social and historical sources contemporary to Paul. As we will soon discover, we need a more nuanced and socially engaged description of the audience.

Like Stowers and Heil, in his *Arguing from Scripture* Christopher Stanley attempts to determine how Paul's audience responds to the rhetorical strategy of his letters, although Stanley's interest lies specifically in Paul's scriptural citations. For our purposes, we note that Stanley recognizes that there is a difference between the implied and actual audiences. As a result, he devises a method to explore "the rhetorical effectiveness of Paul's strategy of using explicit biblical quotations to support the argument of his letters."[21] The first step of Stanley's study is to analyze the rhetorical strategy of each

---

17. Heil, *Romans*, 1–11.

18. Ibid., 10.

19. The subtitle of the commentary states this approach. There are commentaries (see below) that take note of the audience's reception of the text, as an integral part of their overall methodology (which is not audience-focused), but Heil's commentary uses a reader-orientated approach consistently.

20. Heil, *Romans*, 10.

21. Stanley, *Arguing*, 65.

cited Scripture.[22] The second is to "estimate how audience members with varying degrees of biblical literacy might have responded to Paul's biblical argumentation."[23] In other words, Stanley attempts to determine *how different types of audience* would have heard the texts. In doing so he takes care to note the "dialogue between the reader and the grammatical, literary, and rhetorical codes embedded in the text, whether intended by the author or not."[24] Like Stanley, we recognize the importance of examining the dialogue between the audience and the text, and like him, we realize that there is a discrepancy between the implied and actual audiences. Although (unlike Stanley) we will not specifically identify different types of audiences, we will define the "audience" in terms of their likely living conditions and socioeconomic situations.

To assist in this task, we will draw on Peter Oakes's insights found in his *Reading Romans in Pompeii*. Oakes provides a fascinating study of the social profile of a first-century audience in Rome and suggests a reading of the letter from the perspective of people in that audience. Using the archaeological evidence in Pompeii, Oakes carefully reconstructs a plausible description of a model craft-worker house church in Rome.[25] He then proposes a fresh reading of specific passages and themes in Romans in view of this audience.[26] What Oakes is trying to do, as I understand it, is to determine the audience's social location using all the data available. In this way he paints a good general picture of the audience's life, without claiming that the actual audience can be identified. He then reads Romans by asking how such an audience would have heard the letter given their particular social location.

Oakes's work demonstrates that an audience-focused approach to Romans can be fruitful even though his constructed "audience" is somewhat different from the implied audience. Indeed, in a moment I will argue that the "pure" implied audience, albeit useful in instructing our reading of the text, will not yield the best result for our particular inquiry. In Chapter 2 we will discuss a plausible social location for the audience in relation to their suffering in Rome, in order to better ascertain the type of audience Paul speaks to in his letter. Our intention is not to identify the real recipients of

22. Ibid., 64.

23. Ibid., 65. Stanley defines three types of audiences according to their different levels of scriptural competencies, namely, "informed," "competent" and "minimal" audiences (68–69). He later studies several explicit citations of Scriptures in Romans and identifies how different audiences might have responded to Paul's argumentation (136–70). We will interact with Stanley further below.

24. Ibid., 70.

25. Oakes, *Reading Romans*, 1–97.

26. See ibid., 130–49.

the letter, but rather to provide a more nuanced social description of the audience that can enrich our exegesis.[27]

The above not only demonstrates the benefits of reading Romans from the perspective of the audience, it also highlights the fact that an audience-oriented approach is often used in conjunction with rhetorical analysis, as well as the tools available in literary, grammatical and socio-historical analyses. The approach taken by this study will be similar. The above survey has also shown that there is a difference between the implied and real audiences, which is a matter that we will recognize in our methodology. Now we are ready to outline the approach of our exegesis.

THE AUDIENCE-FOCUSED APPROACH IN OUR EXEGESIS

Audience or Text?

As mentioned, our exegesis will be audience-focused. We will also explore how the audience might have heard the letter as they interacted with the text, given their experience of suffering in first-century Rome. This approach takes note of the fact that any account of the audience's understanding of the text cannot be independent of the text itself. But this raises the question of where does "meaning" lie? Does it lie in the audience or in the text? That is, does meaning exist in the text independent of its reader? Or is it the audience that determines how the text should be understood? In an essay on intertextuality, Moyise challenges the assumption behind the historical-critical method that texts have only one single meaning,[28] and in particular the presupposition that "a text taken from one context and transposed into another will result in a single resolution."[29] Moyise alerts us that meaning is always "bought at a price" and "meaning can only result if some interactions are privileged and others are silenced."[30]

27. Some recent commentaries have incorporated aspects of the audience-oriented approach in their analysis of Romans, albeit often in relatively small ways. See Johnson, *Reading Romans*, 2–3; Jewett, *Romans*, 1, 3, 53–55.

28. See Moyise, "Intertextuality, Historical Critism," 24–34. While Moyise's concerns are around the use of Scripture in the NT, they are applicable to any exegesis of a text. And since our exegesis will pay specific attention to the use of Scripture in Romans, Moyise's concerns are particularly relevant.

29. Ibid., 25.

30. Moyise, "Intertextuality and the Study of the Old Testament in the New Testament," 18. Paulien, "Elusive Allusions," 65, summarizes Moyise's concerns well—that is, he "is concerned about arbitrary and totalizing interpretations based on overconfidence

What this highlights is the fact that there is always an interaction between the audience and the text. The text plays a crucial role in how the audience perceives the meaning of its message, but at the same time the audience will read the text in light of their life experiences. It also underlines another benefit of an audience-oriented approach for our inquiry, in that we do not neglect the voice of an audience that has firsthand experience in suffering. Our purpose here, however, is not to resolve the question regarding where exactly meaning lies. Yet we know that there is an implied audience in the text of Romans, without whom the meaning of the text exists in a vacuum. The text has the function of assisting this audience to acquire an understanding of suffering, and we can attempt to find this understanding in the text by examining its rhetorical strategy and literary construct.

Also, since suffering is an experienced reality and since the text has been written within a particular historical context, we must be more specific in describing who the "audience" is, so that we can ask specific questions about how they would have heard the letter in relation to their experience of affliction. At the same time, we need to have a reasonable understanding of the symbolic universe shared between the text and the audience, so as to be successful in determining the communication between the letter and its audience. As Lategan says, there have to be "shared convictions" between the text and the audience, in order for the text's "directives" to work and for the readers to "actualize the text."[31] In other words, communication takes place when the text and the hearers share the same worldview.[32] By "symbolic universe" we mean, borrowing from Byrne, "a comprehensive system" of knowledge "expressed in language, symbol and myth, serving to define, legitimate and give meaning to institutions and individual identities and to social interactions between them."[33]

We know that the audience in our analysis cannot be Paul's original audience, for we do not have access to them.[34] But we do have fairly good access to the historical situation in Rome and are able to determine the social systems, political realities, and worldview that the letter and the audience

in having attained the author's authoritative intention."

31. Lategan, "Coming to Grips," 9.

32. The shared worldview does not mean that the communication will automatically yield its desired outcome. The audience may choose not to accept the argumentation in the text. But the shared worldview enables and facilitates effective communication. See, e.g., Fowler, *Let the Reader*, 27–31; Lategan, "Coming to Grips," 8–9, for a discussion about the audience being a "reader" and/or "critic."

33. Byrne, *Romans*, 6–7.

34. Nor can we become the audience that Paul originally intended. See Lategan, "Coming to Grips," 8.

share. We can, then, define the audience within a particular socio-historical context with a certain level of precision, without claiming that we are speaking of the real audience. In this way, the description of the audience is more nuanced than the "ideal" implied audience—in the sense that we are carefully placing the audience in a particular socio-historical situation, namely, that the audience consists of followers of Jesus who live in first-century Rome and are familiar with suffering. In other words, we are still primarily interested in the implied audience, but at the same time we are aware of the reality that an overemphasis on the *ideal* implied audience will somewhat limit the value of our investigation.

So, both the text and the socio-historical situation of the audience are important as we explore the theology of suffering in Romans. Indeed, the interaction between the text and the audience (as the latter engages in the interpretive process) is also important. It is in light of this that we ask the question throughout our exegesis: *How might the audience have heard the letter?*[35] With this in mind, we will proceed to define the letter's audience.

The Audience in Our Inquiry

As mentioned, the text of Romans, especially in 5:1–11 and 8:14–39, implies an audience that experiences suffering, to whom the letter gives encouragement and instructions. For example, the hope of glory in affliction is mentioned in 5:2–5. Implicit in the text is the assumption that the audience in Rome does have experiences of suffering. Likewise, the affliction-list in 8:35 infers that the Romans audience has experienced some of the trials in the list, and the text serves to affirm that no hardship can separate the audience from God's love. Thus, at the most basic level, the "audience" in our inquiry consists of anyone in first-century imperial Rome who experienced affliction at the time when the letter was delivered to them in the early reign of Nero (around 56–58 CE). Although the affliction-list in Rom 8:35 specifies a wide range of suffering, it seems best to see the items as non-exhaustive but representative of many possible types of suffering (see the exegesis in Chapter 7). In other words, it is preferable to treat the audience as a community of believers who experienced a range of hardships and afflictions. The *actual* existence of an audience living with hardship is not without historical

---

35. Although this is outside the scope of our study, it should be noted that this question should help to determine Paul's intended meaning of the text. Since he was most likely aware of the general social location of his audience, his letter, arguably, would have been shaped by that awareness to some degree. At any rate, the question is important for the interpretation of the text.

evidence. In our next chapter we will examine the social location of Paul's audience in first-century Rome, where I will argue that they experienced socioeconomic hardship and religio-political injustice. This general picture of the audience and their social world will assist us in our exegesis.

To reiterate, at the most basic level, our interest lies in how *an audience familiar with suffering in Rome* would have understood the letter. We can be fairly confident that the suffering of Paul's first audience included socioeconomic hardship and religio-political injustice, and this *general profile* will assist our inquiry. It is with this "audience" in mind that we will carry out our exegesis.

How Will the Exegesis Work?

As we examine each relevant passage in Romans, we will ask in what ways the text evokes images of affliction, and how it generates ideas and concepts that relate to suffering. For example, the language of hope in affliction may invoke images of the audience's present hardship in Rome, as well as providing them with hope for a better future (5:1–5; 8:24–25). We will also ask how the text provides the audience with resources to understand the purpose of their suffering. How does the text help them face the reality of pain and sorrow? For instance, the Spirit's intercession is a resource for the audience to face injustice and trials, despite their hurt and agony (8:26–27). We will also ask whether the text invites the audience to respond to its instruction. If it does, what does it ask them to do? For example, the letter exhorts the audience to hope and endure (5:3–5; 8:24–25), which requires them to take heed and persevere in suffering despite the pain.

Throughout the exegesis we will pay attention to how the socio-historical location of the audience might have influenced their understanding of suffering. For instance, we will ask how socioeconomic hardship might influence their understanding of the notion of "hope of glory," for being poor would not be glorious in Greco-Roman culture. Another example would be how the audience might understand the language of peace in Rom 5:1, given the fact that members of the Christ-community might have been sold into slavery as a result of successful Roman conquests. Their daily experience would have been incompatible with Rome's propaganda of the *pax Romana*.

These questions will be asked as we carry out a careful study of the text that employs the appropriate analytical tools at our disposal. Our discussion will investigate the rhetorical strategy and literary construct of the letter. For example, Rom 5:1—8:39 is bookended with the repeated theme of hope of glory in suffering. This serves to persuade the audience that the purpose of suffering is glorification. Our analysis will also pay attention to any narrative structure that is present in the text. As we will see in Chapter 3, we do not assume that Paul is telling stories in his letter, but that narrative structures may be constructed from the information available in the text, which consists of certain characters and a trajectory of events.[36] For instance, as will be argued, the story of Adamic humanity is implicit in Rom 5:12–21, where sin and death entered the cosmos, with implications for suffering in this world. In each case, our exegetical task will involve the question of how the audience might have heard the letter.

To recap, our exegesis will be audience-focused. We will investigate how the audience interacts with the text by utilizing the tools of rhetorical, literary, narrative and socio-scientific analyses.[37] Having said this, we mentioned earlier that special attention will be given to the use of Israel's Scripture in Romans. We will now look at this aspect of our methodology.

USE OF SCRIPTURE IN ROMANS: SIGNIFICANCE AND AUDIENCE COMPETENCY

Significance

The important role of Israel's Scripture in Romans is unquestionable. There are about fifty-five scriptural citations in the letter. The fact that there are in total about ninety-two quotations in the undisputed letters of Paul shows the important place of Scripture in Romans.[38] Significantly, the role of Scripture is highlighted at the beginning and the end of the letter. Romans starts with the declaration that God promised beforehand the gospel διὰ τῶν προφητῶν αὐτοῦ ἐν γραφαῖς ἁγίαις (1:2). This invites the audience to

---

36. See Adams, "Paul's Story," 19–24, for a similar way of understanding the narrative dynamics in Paul. Also, by "narrative structure," we mean the pattern of elements of a story, with events taking place in a recognizable order. Cf. the definition/description given by Stamps, "Rhetorical and Narratological Criticism," 230–31.

37. My approach is, in broad terms, similar to the so-called socio-rhetorical method. But I am not using the *formal* methodology employed by, e.g., Robbins, *Exploring the Texture of Texts*, 7–131; and Witherington, *Romans*, 1–25.

38. As a rough guide, on average there is one direct citation of Scripture in every ten verses in Romans, as opposed to one in twenty-one, thirty-six, and forty-two in Galatians, 1 Corinthians and 2 Corinthians respectively. These figures are derived from Silva, "Old Testament in Paul," 631. Silva lists at least fifty-five citations in Romans. His figures are primarily based on the works of Michel, *Paulus und seine Bibel*); Ellis, *Paul's Use of the Old Testament*; and Koch, *Die Schrift als Zeuge des Evangeliums*. A reference is included as a citation only if at least two of these scholars agree. See also Stanley, *Arguing*, 142n14.

consider the Jewish Scriptures to be a highly significant resource for their understanding of the letter. Towards the end of the letter Paul quotes Ps 68:10 LXX with the citation formula καθὼς γέγραπται, and then says that ὅσα γὰρ προεγράφη, εἰς τὴν ἡμετέραν διδασκαλίαν **ἐγράφη**, ἵνα διὰ τῆς ὑπομονῆς καὶ διὰ τῆς παρακλήσεως τῶν **γραφῶν** τὴν ἐλπίδα ἔχωμεν (15:3–4; emphasis added). Indeed, Paul finishes the letter by saying that his gospel is now disclosed through the γραφῶν προφητικῶν (16:26).

The reference to Scriptures, hope, and perseverance in 15:4 is particularly noteworthy, for the terms ὑπομονή, ἐλπίς/ἐλπίζω appear in 5:2–5, and 8:19–25 twelve times, where the passages speak of suffering. This indicates that God's people can find hope in the Scriptures as they seek to endure in their times of need.[39] In light of these intertextual links between 15:3–4, 5:2–5 and 8:19–25, it seems that the Scriptures play a vital role in comforting and encouraging the afflicted.

The above not only highlights the important role of Scripture in strengthening the argument of the letter, they also show that the audience is alerted to its significance. This is especially important given the fact that Paul did not establish the church in Rome, and hence does not necessarily exercise an apostolic authority over the house churches there. Scripture functions as an authoritative sacred text that underpins the argument of the letter,[40] especially within an ancient worldview where deities and their revelations (through the prophets) were revered with honor.[41] In short, studying the use of Scripture in Romans provides a valuable resource for our inquiry.

---

39. Recent scholarship tends to see that the two διά clauses in Rom 15:4 are independent, so that they may be translated as "with endurance and by means of the comfort of Scriptures . . ." See Dunn, *Romans 9–16*, 839; Byrne, *Romans*, 427. But see Jewett, *Romans*, 880–81, for an alternative view.

40. See, e.g., Stanley, *Arguing*, 21. Later Stanley adds that citations "from sacred and authoritative Jewish Scriptures were an important weapon in Paul's rhetorical arsenal" (183).

41. Given this worldview, although believers in Rome are mainly Gentiles, the Jewish Scriptures still provide an authoritative voice—as long as they have given their allegiance to Christ, the anointed king. Having said that, Ehrensperger, "Paul and the Authority of Scripture," 318–19, rightly suggests that the "authority" of Scripture used in Paul's letters should not be understood in terms of power and domination, but of empowerment and encouragement. In her own words, "To relate to this authority implied that one was called to respond as a response-able member of the [Christ-] movement." This fits in well with Rom 15:4.

Scriptural Competency of the Audience

But does a largely Gentile audience have the scriptural competency to realize the full impact of the use of Scripture?[42] Indeed, in the case of scriptural echoes and allusions, are they able to detect the source texts? These are good questions. At one level, we note that Romans invites and encourages its implied audience to realize the important role of Scripture in its argument, and in doing so, it anticipates that its audience either already knows the Scripture well or will get to know it. In other words, the explicit statements about the Scriptures and prophetic writings (1:2; 15:4; 16:26) and the frequent direct scriptural citations imply that Paul expects a significant level of competency on the part of its audience.[43]

But, at another level it is valid to ask whether the disjuncture of scriptural knowledge between the implied and real audiences is so big that the latter cannot benefit from the use of Scripture at all. In a moment I will argue that the letter's audience did have a reasonable level of scriptural competency. But here we will highlight two aspects of our methodology that serve to ease this concern. First, the majority of the analysis of the letter's use of Scripture will be performed at the end of the exegesis of individual pericopes rather than during the analysis of individual verses, so that our inquiry will primarily focus on the rhetoric and argument of the letter itself. In the case of possible scriptural echoes, this method will avoid the alleged echoes distracting from the analysis of the text. In the case of an explicitly cited Scripture, we will initially examine the function of the cited text within Romans and how it supports the rhetorical strategy of the letter. Then at the end of the pericope we will examine the context of the source text and any correlation between it and the letter. In this way, any interruption to the exegesis of the letter is minimized. In other words, our first task is to find out how the audience might have heard the text in each pericope in Romans, and our second task is to determine whether the Scripture assists the audience to understand suffering. Simply put, our interest in the use of Scripture lies in how it provides *additional resources* for the audience to construe a theology of suffering.[44]

---

42. Stanley, *Arguing*, 43–46, raises this question on the ground that most people in the population were illiterate.

43. Cf. Stowers, *Rereading*, 21. Even Stanley, *Arguing*, 140, admits that in Romans, as opposed to his other letters, Paul assumes a broader knowledge of Scripture.

44. One may say that our interest lies in exploring the audience's reception of Scripture *within the context* of Paul's rhetoric. Thus, our *first* task is to examine the rhetorical strategy of the letter and how the audience might have heard the text.

Second, while our analysis will show that the letter's use of Scripture provides valuable information for our inquiry, it acknowledges the fact that one cannot claim absolute certainty about scriptural echoes, and that at times there is a degree of tentativeness about an alleged scriptural allusion. Every effort will be made to provide ample evidence for any claim regarding the audience's detection of Scriptures, but the level of certainty will be nuanced according to the amount of evidence available and how credible it is.

To reiterate, it appears that the implied audience is expected to have a level of scriptural competency. At the same time, our methodology has built-in features to ensure that our exegesis does not overly depend on the audience's scriptural knowledge. But having said that, it is reasonable to assume that the first-century audience in Rome did generally have a level of scriptural competency. We will first outline how this assumption has been challenged, before turning to provide reasons for its validity.

Stanley believes that the literacy rate in the ancient world was about 10–20 percent, and normally no more than 10 percent.[45] If these figures are correct, it appears that the majority of Paul's first-century audience would have limited knowledge of the written texts of Israel's Scripture. Indeed, their ability to critique Paul would be limited by the fact that access to the physical scrolls was difficult and expensive.[46] In light of this, one may argue that there is little use in studying any echoes or allusions, or even unmarked citations, for few among the audience would have detected them.[47] Similarly, there is no need to look into the original context of any alluded or cited source text, because most of Paul's audience would not have the competency to do so anyway. But these concerns are not as valid as they seem, if we take into account the following.

First, the focus on literacy rates underestimates the oral and aural abilities of the audience. In a culture where communication was mainly oral, audience competency should not be gauged simply by literacy level.[48] As Tsang notes, according to Cicero, "writing in his [Paul's] society was meant primarily for the ear and not the eye (*Fam.* 2.4.1)."[49] Second, one must realize that the unavailability of printed books and electronic media means that

45. Stanley, *Arguing*, 44–45. Here Stanley refers to the findings of Harris, *Ancient Literacy*, 272; Gamble, *Books and Readers*, 4–5.

46. Stanley, *Arguing*, 41–42, 52–54. Stanley follows the views of Harris, *Ancient Literacy*, 193–6, who argues that there were "practical inconveniences" for the readers in the Empire, including the high cost of papyrus and wooden tablets.

47. That is, citations without any introductory remarks, such as the standard "it is written."

48. Cf. Horsley, *Performing the Gospel*, ix–x.

49. Tsang, "Misreading," 219.

the ancients had much greater ability to memorize sacred texts than moderns. Indeed, memory, rather than written scrolls, played a major part in the ancient world.[50] As Tsang says, "Paul's society was thoroughly rhetorical . . . Memory and spoken words were intertwined . . . As in ancient Hebrew culture, Roman society relied on memory much more thoroughly than many modern societies."[51] Also, ancient texts were written with attention to how they could influence an illiterate audience, with its use of literary devices. Punt puts it well,

> The constructive role of texts in the ancient world, and in the Roman Empire in particular, requires attention to the way they influenced their audiences, even when, for the most part, they would have been heard rather than read. Even functionally illiterate people valued literacy in imperial times.[52]

Third, as Lincicum remarks, Stanley's sweeping conclusions about audience competency should be questioned, "given that we know so little of what early Christian worship services actually entailed."[53] As Fisk says,

> There is also reason to suspect that the prevailing patterns of synagogue worship, including the public reading and study of Torah, influenced and shaped the culture of early Christianity in Rome. . . . In light of what other sources [outside Romans] tell us about synagogue practice, however, and given the lack of evidence that Rome's Christian community had uniformly severed its ties with the synagogue, it does not appear unreasonable to think that many of those who first read or heard Paul's letter would have enjoyed considerable prior, and ongoing, exposure to a number of the scriptural passages Paul cites. Paul's best guess about his readers' competence may not be far off.[54]

In fact, the assumption that a largely Gentile audience implies very limited scriptural literacy is invalid. Even Andrew Das, who advocates for an

50. Greenspoon, "By the Letter?" 10–23, provides a good discussion on Paul's memorization of Scripture.

51. Tsang, "Misreading," 219.

52. Punt, "Identity, Memory, and Scriptural Warrant," 33. Punt continues to argue that the "Scriptures of Israel were the primary, though not the sole, constituent artifacts in Paul's cultural memory" (49).

53. Lincicum, review of *Arguing with Scripture*, 429–31. H. H. Drake, review of *Argument with Scripture*, also thinks that it may be possible that "Paul's audiences were more than 'competent.'"

54. Fisk, "Synagogue Influence," 184–5. That the synagogues in Rome were the natural context of the emerging Christianity in Rome and the source of knowledge of Israel's Scripture is proposed by, e.g., Dunn, *Romans 1–8*, 1.

all-Gentile audience of Romans,[55] acknowledges the fact that the "content of
Paul's letter clearly reflects the influence of the Jews and their synagogues in
Rome,"[56] and that the knowledge of Scripture of the audience (as expected
by Paul) "could only be accounted for if at least some of the members of the
Roman audience of Paul's letter had been in contact with the synagogues, in
which they had been instructed in the septuagintal translation of the Jewish Scriptures."[57] Das goes on to argue that the letter's audience "included
current or former God-fearers alongside non-Law-observant gentiles."[58]
Whether Das's view on the ethnicity of the audience is right or not, one
should recognize the likelihood of a significant level of scriptural competency on the part of the audience (because of the presence of God-fearing
Gentiles and/or some Jews, as well as their current or former association
with synagogues).[59]

Fourth, our analysis does not require the entire audience to have an in-
depth knowledge of Scripture, beyond what might be reasonably well-known
to the earliest followers of Jesus.[60] Although Stanley is suspicious of the ancient
audience's scriptural competency, he affirms that Paul thinks that the Roman
believers know the stories of Adam, the patriarchs and Exodus, and that "the
Roman Christians will understand his many allusions to Jewish beliefs . . .
and practices."[61] Importantly, as mentioned above, we understand the role of
Israel's Scripture as being an avenue of *providing resources* for the audience
to understand the letter. Although Scripture will significantly enhance their
understanding of the letter's argument, *they need not have detailed knowledge
of the context of the source text of every citation to benefit from it.* Nor do they
have to detect every single echo of the Jewish sacred text in order to gain

---

55. See our earlier mention of Stowers's and Das's work under our discussion on
previous audience-focused studies, where we briefly looked at the suggestion that the
audience of Romans consisted of Gentiles only. As mentioned, my view is that there
were at least some Jewish believers in the audience.

56. Das, *Solving*, 82.

57. Ibid., 83.

58. Ibid., 113.

59. See also Wagner, *Heralds*, 33–39, who says that "from the demands Paul's argument places on the hearers, one can infer that these are Gentiles who have more than a
passing acquaintance with Jewish practices and beliefs and who have a fairly good grasp
of Israel's scriptures" (35). Wagner goes on to say that perhaps Paul "crafted his rhetoric
in Romans with an eye toward people not explicitly encoded in the letter. Though his
rhetorical strategy addresses Gentiles explicitly, Paul may well have intended his arguments to be *overheard* by Jewish Christians in the Roman congregations" (35–36).

60. For a general review of the current state of scholarship regarding the audience's
biblical literacy, see Stanley, "What We Learned," 327.

61. Stanley, *Arguing*, 138–40.

a thorough understanding of the letter's argumentation.[62] What is required, rather, is that there are sufficient signposts in the letter to guide them so that they may benefit from a citation or echo of Scripture.

In short, given the predominantly oral culture and the possible prior knowledge of Scripture (of at least some in the house churches), it is reasonable to see its use in Romans as a valuable additional resource for the audience to understand the letter, as long as we are careful not to overplay the evidence we gather.

ANALYZING THE USE OF SCRIPTURE IN OUR EXEGESIS

Now we are in a position to outline how we will analyze the use of Scripture in Romans. We will first describe the approach we will use, and then discuss the version of Scripture we assume the audience knows.

A Combination of Proven Approaches

Our analysis of the letter's use of Scripture will utilize a combination of proven techniques used in recent scholarship. There have been three main approaches to Paul's use of Scripture.[63] The first focuses on intertextual evidence between the letter and the cited/echoed text. This approach is famously employed by Richard Hays, who lists seven tests to detect echoes of Scripture in Paul's letters.[64] It has been adopted (with modifications) by scholars like Wagner, Keesmaat and Shum in their major studies on Romans.[65] But while this approach has gained substantial acceptance, some are concerned about (a) whether, in the case of an explicitly cited Scripture, Paul and his audience are conscious of the context of the source text;[66] and

62. It is also likely that the bearer of Romans was charged with the responsibility to help the audience to understand the letter. Furthermore, it is probable that the house churches heard and reheard the letter multiple times and had opportunities to be further impacted by the rhetorical strategy of the letter and even to investigate the Scriptures that are cited or alluded to by the letter. See Wagner, "Heralds of Isaiah," 38–39, for a discussion.

63. Here I follow the categorization used by Moyise, *Paul and Scripture*, 111–25. The three approaches below are categorized in terms of their primary emphases. They do overlap one another and are not necessarily mutually exclusive.

64. Hays, *Echoes*, 29–32.

65. Wagner, "Heralds," 9–13; Shiu-Lun Shum, *Paul's Use of Isaiah in Romans*, 6–11; Keesmaat, *Paul and his Story*, 51–52.

66. In a publication that marks the end of the six-year SBL seminar on Paul and

(b) what degree of certainty one can have regarding the detection of an unmarked echo.[67]

The second is a narrative approach. Here the interpreter determines whether a narrative substructure is present in a Pauline letter, and whether it reflects a story in Israel's Scripture. One can do this by looking for key words and themes in the letter that reflect a well-known story in Scripture or a tradition that is based on a significant scriptural narrative. For Romans, N. T. Wright proposes that Paul has in mind the Exodus story, and that a corresponding narrative substructure can be traced in Rom 3–8.[68] Likewise, Sylvia Keesmaat detects the Exodus tradition in Rom 8:14–39, and argues that Paul transforms it in light of God's salvific act in Christ.[69] The main challenge for this approach is to establish a convincing case for the presence of a narrative substructure in the letter.[70]

The third approach focuses on the way that Scriptural citations serve Paul's rhetorical strategies. Stanley is a major proponent of this approach,

---

Scripture, Stanley, "What We Learned," 324–25, remarks that there seems to be no consensus on whether and to what degree Paul divorces a cited text from its original context. See the discussions by Moyise, "Does Paul Respect the Context of His Quotations?" 97–113, and Kim, "Respect for Context," 115–27, on this matter. Our concern, however, is not so much Paul's intention, but the audience's reading of the texts.

67. Stanley, "What We Learned," 323–24, suggests that the general agreement is that "the burden rested upon the interpreter to convince others that an unmarked allusion or echo was indeed present, and that scholars could legitimately disagree over the validity of such an argument."

68. N. T. Wright, "New Exodus," 26–35.

69. Keesmaat, *Paul and His Story*, 54–154. As mentioned, Keesmaat embraces Hays's method of detecting intertextual links between Romans and Israel's Scripture. But Keesmaat goes further. She argues that Paul recalls, reinterprets and retells the Exodus narrative in Romans, and in doing so he transforms the Exodus tradition but at the same time remains faithful to it (153–54). The essay by Fisk, "Paul among the Storytellers," 56–89, is another example of a narrative approach, although his focus is Paul's rewriting of Scripture and his storytelling.

70. See a similar point made by Stanley, "What We Learned," 324. Witherington, *Romans*, 92–93, strongly disagrees with Wright regarding the echo of Exodus in Rom 3–8. Here I would also like to mention the work of Watson, *Paul and the Hermeneutics of Faith*. While Watson carefully examines the interactions between Paul and the narratives in Exodus, Leviticus, Numbers and Deuteronomy, he thinks that Paul does not retell those stories but reinterprets them in light of divine saving grace. Cf. Watson, "Is There a Story in These Texts?" 232. I hesitate to put Watson's approach into one of the categories I mention here, for his careful reading of Paul disallows us to restrict his method to a narrowly defined category. But his attention to the texts suggests that his approach is probably "intertextual." As he says, "It is scripture that shapes the contours of the Christ-event . . . Pauline thinking is thus intertextual theology: explicit scriptural citations are simply the visible manifestations of an intertextuality that is ubiquitous and fundamental to Pauline discourse" (17).

and has applied it to Romans.[71] He concludes that Paul uses the Scripture to advance his thesis that God has acted in Christ to incorporate both Jews and Gentiles alike to become his chosen people.[72] This approach's focus on Paul's rhetoric is important, but it would be enriched when used with other techniques.

As mentioned, our exegesis will employ a combination of all these three approaches, for the obvious reason that each of them has proven success and that each one has limitations when applied on its own. We will pay attention to how the letter uses the Scripture as part of its rhetorical strategy to persuade its audience. As we do so we continue to ask how an audience familiar with affliction would have heard the texts (the text of the letter and the cited/echoed source text). For example, how does the citation of Ps 44:22 in Rom 8:36 advance the argument concerning God's abiding love in Rom 8:35–39? What additional resource does the citation give the audience as they suffer? We will also investigate whether there are intertextual links between the letter and the surrounding texts of the source text. Are there verbal and thematic features to suggest further relationships between the letter and the associated Scripture? Likewise, in the case of a suspected echo of Scripture, we will examine whether there are thematic and linguistic links between it and Romans? Is the presence of these links strong enough to warrant an echo? What are the implications for the audience's reading of the texts?[73]

Last but not least, we will also investigate whether a narrative structure can be detected in Romans, and whether the narrative reflects a story in Scripture. For example, can we detect a narrative of Adamic humanity in Rom 5:12–21? If so, does this narrative reflect the story of Adam in Genesis? And how might the connections between these stories assist the audience to understand the letter's argument? In short, a mixture of rhetorical, intertextual and narrative approaches will be used when we study the use of Scripture in Romans.

Version of Jewish Scripture

A brief discussion about the version of Scripture we use in our analysis is in order. In scholarly studies on the use of Scripture in the New Testament, two questions are often asked. First, did Paul use the LXX or the Hebrew text,

71. Stanley, *Arguing*, 136–70.

72. Ibid., 170.

73. I will not repeat the seven tests advocated by Hays here, for they are already so well known. But by and large I will primarily use three of them, namely, volume, thematic coherence, and recurrence. See Hays, *Echoes*, 29–32, for definition.

or even the Aramaic one?[74] Second, should there be a reconstruction of the *Vorlage* of the Greek translation of the Hebrew Bible?[75]

For the first question, our decision in the case of an explicitly cited text is determined by which text (LXX, MT, or other) the citation seems to refer to. As to scriptural echoes, we will, unless otherwise stated, use the LXX in our analysis. Since our approach is audience-focused, and since the audience was mainly Gentile (and hence primarily Greek-speaking), it makes sense to use the Greek text in our discussion, for that is most likely the Scripture they were familiar with. Also, among the fifty-five citations in Romans, thirteen of them (closely) follow the LXX but not the MT, with only four following the MT but not the LXX. This indicates that the letter prefers the LXX to the MT. There are twenty-three citations that adhere closely to both the LXX and the MT, which is because the LXX translates the MT more or less verbatim. The rest of the citations do not follow the LXX or MT, which indicates that either Paul decided to change the wording or that he used different versions of the Scriptures. Unfortunately we have little access to the apostle's version(s) or the reasons why he modified the texts. (See table below for reference.[76]) While these statistics concern explicit quotations, they suggest that the LXX provides the best available text for our analysis of scriptural echoes, because it seems to be the preferred version of the letter.

The text the letter uses	Number of occurrences
Romans = LXX = MT	23
Romans = MT but not LXX	4
Romans = LXX but not MT	13
Romans = nether LXX nor MT	15
Total	55

As to which version of the LXX we should utilize, again we do not have access to the version(s) that the first-century audience used, and it seems that we can only refer to the version available to us today.[77] Fortunately, as it

74. Indeed, did Paul use more than one variation/version of the LXX, Hebrew texts, and/or Aramaic texts?

75. For a good and concise discussion on Paul's use of different textual witnesses, see Wagner, "Heralds," 5–10. My approach differs from that of Wagner's largely because of the audience-focused nature of my study. See also Greenspoon, "Letter," 16–18, regarding Paul's use of the LXX and its variations.

76. The figures in the table are derived from Silva, "Old Testament in Paul," 631, which is in turn based on the works of Michel, Ellis, and Kock. Some may dispute certain details here, but minor adjustments to the figures do not affect our argument.

77. We will use the LXX text from Rahlfs, *Septuaginta*.

turns out, there are usually plenty of thematic and verbal links between the letter and the Scripture in the passages that we examine in our exegesis, and indeed, often we are aided by the presence of similar narrative structures between the letter and the source text. This means that the lack of knowledge of the exact version that the audience used does not constitute a major problem for us.

SUMMARY

In sum, the aim of our study is to determine a theology of suffering in Rom 5:1—8:39 from the perspective of an audience familiar with suffering in first-century Rome. By "theology of suffering" we do not mean a systematic or logical account of belief on the part of the audience, but a perspective life and suffering developed as a result of interacting with the letter. Our approach is audience-focused, with careful attention to the rhetorical strategy of the letter and how it serves to assist the audience in their daily experience of pain and affliction. We will also use the tools available in narrative, literary and socio-scientific analyses to aid our inquiry. Although our study is primarily interested in the implied audience, we know that it is also important to study the viewpoint of an audience that had a shared worldview and socio-historical symbolic universe with the letter. We are also interested in how this audience interacted with the letter to derive their understanding of suffering. At the most basic level, the "audience" in our study consists of those in first-century Rome who experienced suffering. Our socio-historical analysis in Chapter 2 will provide a general picture of the types of suffering they had. This analysis, as we will see, will show that the audience suffered from socioeconomic hardship and religio-political injustice. With this information, we will be able to define our audience with greater clarity and precision.

Towards the end of our exegesis on an individual pericope, we will examine whether Israel's Scripture provided extra resources for the audience to understand the letter's theology of suffering. We will utilize a combination of techniques in this part of our analysis, which include rhetorical, intertexual and narrative approaches. Our main question here continues to be audience-focused though. That is, we are interested in how the audience would have understood the scriptural citation or echo in terms of the implications for their understanding of suffering. The bulk of our analysis will consist of an exegesis of Rom 5:1–21 and 8:1–39.

2

Social Location of the Audience and Ancient Worldviews on Suffering

INTRODUCTION

Since suffering is an existential reality, the challenge for modern interpreters of Romans is to read its references to affliction in terms of the experience of the first-century audience. It is, therefore, important for a study of the letter's theology of suffering to include a survey of the social location and worldview of the audience as a corrective to our own assumptions.

In this chapter we will explore the historical evidence available to us, and outline, in general terms, the kinds of suffering members of the house churches in Rome experienced. In particular, we will discuss the socioeconomic hardship that first-century Roman believers suffered, as well as the types of religio-political injustice that they experienced. We will discover that hardship and injustice were intertwined, and were often embedded in the interconnected social, economic, religious and political systems and structures of the Roman Empire. The audience's suffering should, then, be understood in the context of a web of interrelated systemic disorders in the world. Finally, we will examine ancient worldviews in relation to suffering, which will provide background information about the symbolic universe shared between the letter and its audience. Special attention will be given to perspectives on the educative value of suffering, the notion of retributive justice, and the suffering of the righteous.

Before we start our discussion, some clarifications regarding our terminology are in order. The term "socioeconomic" is used to express the fact that social and economic realities are intertwined. Hence, those who had a low social status would often experience economic scarcity. A beggar, for example, was not only economically poor but also socially inferior, and these two realities reinforced one another. Conversely, abundant possessions often reinforced social superiority. Likewise, the terms "religio-political" and "socio-political" highlight the fact that politics, religion, and social systems were interconnected in the ancient world. Caesar was the supreme political leader, and his rule was considered to have the blessing of the gods. And of course the way he ruled had significant impact on the social life of Rome's inhabitants. In fact, religio-political and socioeconomic systems were often intertwined, for the divinely sanctioned Caesar ultimately controlled the social and economic systems of the Empire. Further, we need to avoid misunderstanding "injustice" by viewing the term narrowly through modern lenses. When we speak of "injustice," we do not necessarily refer to the injustice done to people in a flawed judicial system (though this could well be the case). Nor is it only about economic inequality between the rich and the poor (though this may be included). Instead, religio-political or socioeconomic injustice, for the purposes of our discussion, refers to the oppression and exploitation caused by those in positions of political, religious, social, and economic power.[1] For example, slaves might be exploited by their owners because of their social status, and their slavery would have resulted from a political and economic system in Rome that was built on the Empire's military conquests.[2] With the meanings of these terms clarified, we are now ready to survey the types of hardship and injustice suffered by the audience in Rome.

SOCIOECONOMIC HARDSHIP AND INJUSTICE

Socioeconomic Profile of the Christ-Community

There has been a renewed debate concerning the economic situation of the Pauline house churches in recent scholarship.[3] The emerging evidence

1. Cf. Morley, "The Poor," 36, who recognizes the interconnectedness between poverty, political, social, and legal structures in ancient Rome.

2. Our way of defining "injustice" does not, however, mean that exploitation always happens when there is a power imbalance between the socially/economically/politically powerful and powerless. A slave owner, for example, can be kind and generous to his/her slaves.

3. The study of poverty in ancient Rome is no simple matter. The following survey

indicates that a large proportion of the earliest believers lived at or below subsistence level. We will briefly discuss the debate and outline a possible economic profile of believers in first-century Rome. After that we will look at the profile of a model craft-worker house church, which will provide further information about the social and economic life in ancient Rome.

For years, many scholars believed that the Pauline churches consisted of a cross-section of urban society, with a preponderance of artisans and traders, who were relatively wealthy.[4] As Schmidt says, "[in Pauline churches] there may have been very few who were poor by first-century standards."[5] But this view was disputed by J. Justin Meggitt in 1998. For him, the "Pauline Christians *en masse* shared fully the bleak material existence which was the lot of more than 99 percent of the inhabitants of the Empire."[6] The skilled artisans, although being relatively wealthy among the common people, struggled daily to earn enough to avoid starvation.[7] All free workers, both skilled and unskilled, lived in constant fear of unemployment.[8]

Meggitt's proposal generated robust responses from Dale Martin and Gerd Theissen.[9] But although Martin is very critical of Meggitt, he agrees that it is misleading to speak of a "middle class" in the Roman world.[10] Likewise, Theissen agrees that undoubtedly "the majority of the Christians were common and low people."[11] As the debate continues, it has become fairly

---

is by no means comprehensive. Space limitations prevent us from entering into the complexity of the issues. The goal of the survey below is to provide an overall description that is generally accepted, with sufficient details to paint a picture of the "audience" for our later analysis. See Morley, "The Poor," 21–39, for a good discussion on poverty in Rome.

4. It should be noted that urban poverty was more severe than poverty in rural poverty. In fact, urbanization and poverty went hand in hand. See Morley, "The Poor," 37–38.

5. Schmidt, "Riches and Poverty," 827. This is set in contrast to Deissmann, *Ancient East*, 144, 246–7, who believed that the earliest Pauline churches consisted of people primarily from the lower classes. The most significant work on this matter is that of Meeks, *First Urban Christians*, 51–73. More recent discussions on the social and economic life of early Christians can be found in Still and Horrell, *After the First Christians*; Longenecker and Liebengood, *Engaging Economics*.

6. Meggitt, *Paul*, 99.

7. Ibid., 54–55.

8. Ibid., *Paul*, 58.

9. See Martin, "Review Essay," 51–64; Theissen, "Social Structure," 65–84, and Meggitt's response in Meggitt, "Responses," 85–94. See also Theissen, "Social Conflicts," 371–91.

10. Martin, "Review," 53. By "middle class" here, I refer to the meaning of the term in the West today.

11. Theissen, "Social Structure," 75.

clear that while earlier scholars such as Meeks are certainly right that "a Pauline congregation generally reflected a fair cross-section of urban society,"[12] Meggitt's research serves as a strong reminder that the majority of that society lived at or below subsistence level (the minimum economic level required to sustain life). At the same time, Longenecker rightly points out that the deficiency of Meggitt's economic model is its binary nature, with the tendency to draw a sharp distinction between the elite and non-elite.[13] It is true that this distinction is embedded in the rhetoric of Greco-Roman literature, which "served elite purposes to relegate all who were not among the elite to the category of 'the poor' indiscriminately."[14] But it should not blind us to the fact that a broad economic spectrum existed among the first hearers of Romans. Recently Friesen and Longenecker have provided us with very informative economic profiles, using social and historical data from various sources.[15] The profiles they have derived are fairly similar. The table below is a summary of Longenecker's model,[16] which is more conservative than Friesen's in terms of the percentage of people living in poverty.[17]

12. Meeks, *First Urban Christians*, 73.

13. Longenecker, *Remember the Poor*, 40–44.

14. Ibid., 43. Cf. Morley, "The Poor," 29. As Aelius Aristides says, "the existence of inferiors is an advantage to superiors since they will be able to point out those over whom they are superior." (*Or.* 24.34; cited by Longenecker).

15. Friesen, "Poverty," 340–47; Longenecker, *Remember the Poor*, 295–6. The economic modeling used is admittedly beyond my skill. But there is no need to attain absolute accuracy here. For our purposes, the main question is *roughly* what proportion of the audience lived at subsistence level or below. It should be noted that while Welborn, review of *Remember the Poor*, is critical of Longenecker's failure to see Paul's deconstruction of Roman social relations and his intention to transform the class system of Roman society, he does not seem to specifically raise issues with Longenecker's economic profile.

16. Information extracted from Longenecker, *Remember the Poor*, 294–6. Note that both Longenecker and Friesen say that the figures are rough estimates.

17. See ibid., 53, for a comparison. For instance, Friesen's figure for those living at or below subsistence level is 68 percent for the *general population*, compared with Longenecker's 55 percent. I have chosen Longenecker's profile to show that even a more conservative model demonstrates that the majority of the audience were quite poor.

Economic scale (ES)	ES1–ES3	ES4	ES5	ES6–ES7
Description of economic scale(s)	Excess economic security (The elite)	Not without economic risks, but with significant level of economic security	Minimal economic resources	Subsistence-level existence
Percentages within population	3%	15%	27%	55% (30% ES6; 25% ES7)
Percentages for an urban Jesus-group	0%	10%	25%	65% (35% ES6; 30% ES7)
Numbers in this urban Jesus-group (Out of 50 people)	0	5	12	33
Composition of members of the group (number of persons)		An ES4 family of four—which comprises the heart of this household group (4) An artisan (1)	Two ES5 families (9) Two artisans (2) One ES5 merchant (1)	Four family-groups border on subsistence level, usually managing to survive but occasionally dropping precariously below survival standards (18) Three servants in the ES4 family (3) Two servants in the ES5 families (2) Ten at subsistence level existence or below, unprotected from household structures—some could be destitute (10)

According to this model, roughly 65 percent of Paul's audience in Rome lived at or below subsistence level. Just under half of these (30 percent) would be struggling significantly, and they included the unskilled day laborers, widows, orphans, or people with a disability. About 25 percent would have some minimal economic resources, but they "would clearly have been conscious of their economic vulnerability and their proximity to poverty."[18] Within this group there would be some artisans and merchants. Roughly 10 percent would have a moderate surplus, although "not without economic risk."[19] Although these figures are not beyond dispute, it is safe to assume that the majority of people in the Christ-community in Rome were subject to economic risks, with possibly more than half of them living at or below subsistence level.[20]

In a study independent from the economic profiling of Bruce Longenecker and Steven Friesen,[21] Peter Oakes provides a profile of a model craft-worker house church in Rome. Oakes' approach differs from those of Longenecker and Friesens in that it is a social model, rather than an economic one. Here is the profile provided by Oakes.[22]

Oakes' social description of the model craft-worker house church in Rome (30 people)
A craft-worker who rented a fairly large workshop
His wife, children, a couple of (male) craft-working slaves, a (female) domestic slave, a dependent relative
A few other householders
Their spouses, children, slaves, and other dependents
A couple of members of families whose householder was not part of the house church
A couple of slaves whose owners were not part of the house church
A couple of free or freed dependents of people who were not part of the house church
A couple of homeless people
A few people who were renting space in shared rooms (e.g. migrant workers separated from their families)

18. Longenecker, *Remember the Poor*, 55.

19. Ibid., 295.

20. The accuracy of the figures suggested by Friesen and Longenecker—and indeed their methodologies —will be debated, but the point is that a high proportion of the house church members in Rome had to live with some form of economic hardship and/or vulnerablity. See also Appendix B for a brief discussion of the social location of certain people listed in Rom 16.

21. Friesen, "Poverty," 340–47; Longenecker, *Remember the Poor*, 295–6.

22. Oakes, *Reading*, 96. Oakes' significant contribution is his space-distribution modeling using archaeological data in Pompeii. It is beyond our scope to compare and contrast different methodologies for socioeconomic analysis. But see Oakes, "Methodological Issues," 9–36, for a detailed discussion.

It is noteworthy that the makeup of this profile bears some resemblance to Longenecker's profile. The craft-worker and other householders would have a moderate surplus. A few others would have reasonable resources to make ends meet (e.g., some householders).[23] Others, including skilled and unskilled workers, widows, and beggars, lived at or below subsistence level, with various degrees of vulnerability. Although it would be unwise to translate this social profile into an economic one, it does support the view that a high proportion of Paul's audience suffered from socioeconomic hardship in some way.

Living Condition, Sickness, Life Expectancy, and Hunger

As mentioned above, economic life and social reality in ancient Rome were inseparable. It will, therefore, be helpful to consider briefly the daily experiences of people living in Rome, so as to better appreciate what subsistence-level living meant in practice.

According to Jeffers, the wealth of ancient Rome was not surpassed by the Western world until the 1800s.[24] There were massive public buildings with marble facades. Huge temples portrayed the greatness of Rome's gods. There were hundreds of private homes on the hills of the city.[25] In contrast, Rome's poorer residents often lived in the upper floors of multi-story apartment blocks (*insulae*),[26] or small ground-floor domiciles at the rear of the shops (*tabernae*).[27]

It is believed that "[t]he rooms [of an apartment] were small, damp, dark and cold, except in summer, when they were hot and stuffy. Privacy was virtually impossible, and the sounds of the city often made a good

23. It should be noted that householders who owned slaves would not necessarily have financial security, for slave ownership did not mean economic prosperity. Poor free and freed people could have slaves working in their businesses. See Watson, "Roman," 1002. Cf. Rodgers, *Roman World*, 226; Jeffers, *Greco-Roman*, 221, 223.

24. Jeffers, *Greco-Roman*, 59.

25. Ibid., 59. See also Suetonius' *Lives of the Twelve Caesars* 28.3. Building structures remaining today include Aqua Claudia, Aqua Anio Novus, the Theatre of Marcellus, and the Temple of Mars Ultor in the Forum of Augustus. (Unless otherwise stated, references to Greek and Latin classical works follow the translations in the Loeb Classical Library. Cambridge, Harvard University Press.)

26. Jewett, *Romans*, 53. The wealthy also lived in the lower floors of these buildings in the better parts of the city.

27. See ibid., 53–55, for a detailed analysis. Jewett uses the term "tenement" to refer to the apartment blocks in Rome. But Oakes, *Reading*, 91, is somewhat wary of the term, for it seems to connote "a fairly uniformly shabby block of consistently poor housing." First-century apartment blocks were typically more diverse.

night's sleep difficult . . . Living behind the shops was no better . . . "[28] According to one estimate, the population density was three hundred per acre in the residential areas of Rome, which is more than twice that of twentieth-century Calcutta.[29] The overcrowded and unhygienic conditions probably contributed to the plagues that swept through Rome regularly.[30] The poorest had no housing at all and had to sleep in the open air.[31]

Such poor living conditions and the lack of modern medicine help to explain why the average life expectancy is estimated to have been between twenty to thirty years of age. Infant mortality rates were high,[32] with possibly a quarter of children not surviving the first year of life.[33] Life was indeed full of sorrow for the urban poor in Rome.[34] Hunger was either a constant fear or reality for them. Food crises were common in the Mediterranean region.[35] About 150,000 adult males in Rome received the monthly grain dole (*frumentatio*). But it should be noted that women, children, slaves, non-citizens and the most recently arrived citizens were excluded from the dole. This demonstrates the immense poverty faced by the inhabitants of Rome.[36]

28. Jeffers, *Greco-Roman*, 59–60. Cf. Rodgers, *Roman World*, 88. See also the vivid description by the satirical poet, Juvenal, *Sat.* 3.190–211.

29. Jewett, *Romans*, 54; cf. Meggitt, *Paul*, 71n174.

30. Jewett, *Romans*, 54; cf. Meggitt, *Paul*, 71. Meggitt provides examples of the sanitary conditions of urban life. In a collection of jokes dating about 200 BCE, there is a notice put up by someone just moved into a new house that says, "ANYONE WHO DUMPS EXCREMENT HERE WILL NOT GET IT BACK" (*Philogelos* 85; cited by Meggitt). And Juvenal, *Sat.* 1.131, warns people against urinating at the image of a great man.

31. Ibid., 63.

32. Obviously high infant mortality rate and short average life expectancies are interrelated.

33. Those who survived childhood diseases and lived beyond age ten could expect to live for another thirty-five to forty years on average. See Garnsey and Saller, *Roman Empire*, 138.

34. This is especially so for the poorest of the poor, since "the state did not provide for the needs of the aged, widows, orphans, the disabled or the sick," as Jeffers, *Greco-Roman*, 189, notes. Cf. Meggitt, *Paul*, 67–73.

35. Garnsey and Saller, *Roman Empire*, 100.

36. Meggitt, *Paul*, 51–52. It should be noted that the dole might not reduce the number of poor, and it might in fact attract more poor migrants. See Morley, "The poor," 39.

Social Divisions and Injustice

Ancient society was intensely hierarchical. This social structure ensured that the poor remained poor. Indeed, it would have exacerbated their poverty. A brief look at the social framework will help us understand the social injustice people experienced in Rome.

Social divisions in the Empire were maintained by the legal and coercive power of the state.[37] Apart from the imperial family, the upper class consisted of three orders *ordo senatorius* (senators), *ordo equester* (equestrians of Rome) and *decurions* (provincial aristocracy). These were the small minority in the population. At the top of the rest of the social hierarchy were owners of small businesses and artisans, such as bakers, butchers, dyers, and tanners.[38] They probably belonged to ES4 or ES5 in the economic scale above.[39] Then there were the "free poor," who were freeborn Romans. Probably about one third of Rome's population belonged to this category.[40] They might be socially better off than the non-Romans, but economically they were often poor. Then there were ex-slaves and slaves.[41]

"Roman society was obsessed with status and rank," according to Garnsey and Saller. "[A] Roman's place in the social hierarchy was advertised in the clothes he wore, the seat he occupied at public entertainments. . . . There were significant status variations within the same ranks at all levels."[42] Social interactions took place through the traditional patron-client relationships. The patron owed the client protection, while the client owed the patron respect and honor. This type of reciprocal relationship displayed the superiority of the elite over the common people.[43] A patron's social status was measured by the quantity and status of their clients.[44] For example, clients showed honor to their patrons by forming crowds at their doors for

37. Garnsey and Saller, *Roman Empire*, 199. We will discuss Rome's coercive power further below.

38. By no means did they form a "middle class" (as we know it today), however, because the gulf between their living standard and that of the upper class was so great. See Watson, "Roman," 1001.

39. Cf. Meggitt, *Paul*, 54–55.

40. Watson, "Roman," 1001.

41. Ibid., 1001.

42. Garnsey and Saller, *Roman Empire*, 199. Even among the slaves there were differences in terms of their occupations and economic resources.

43. The patron-client relationship did not necessarily lead to exploitation, but often did.

44. Jeffers, *Greco-Roman*, 192. Cf. Walker, "Benefactor," 157.

the morning *salutatio*.[45] In return, they could expect small food hand-outs or invitations to dinner.[46]

Cicero thought that the work of the artisan was vulgar, and that nothing was noble about a workshop.[47] The elite saw poverty as "ugly and dishonorable."[48] It is with this ideological and social mindset (together with the network of personal relations between the imperial family and the elite) that the Empire maintained the political and economic gulf between the upper class and the common people.[49]

The above not only illustrates the highly hierarchical nature of society in Rome, but also the fact that socioeconomic hardship was reinforced and exacerbated by the social attitudes and systems embedded in the fabric of society. Even though the socioeconomically inferior may not have been exploited directly, the social structure ensured that they remained relatively powerless and vulnerable to abuse. Roman residents might have considered these realities as social norms, but they nevertheless experienced harsh living conditions on a daily basis.

It should be noted that believers in Rome almost certainly shared similar social backgrounds with the general population. Using Rom 16 as the main source data, Lampe proposes that Paul's audience in Rome shared a similar social profile with that of the rest of society.[50] As Jeffers argues, as with other non-Romans, "they were confronted constantly with the differences between themselves and the Roman elite in terms of language, education, wealth, power, and honor."[51] Thus, Christ-followers would have experienced the same social divisions and injustice as other residents in Rome.

---

45. Garnsey and Saller, *Roman Empire*, 151.

46. Ibid., 151 The grain dole in Rome was probably the result of benefactions of patrons. See Walker, "Benefactor," 158.

47. *Off.* 1.42. Cicero continues to say that "all mechanics are engaged in vulgar trades . . . Least respectable of all are those trades which cater for sensual pleasures: 'Fishmongers, butchers, cooks, and poulterers . . . '"

48. Jeffers, *Greco-Roman*, 193. MacMullen, *Roman*, 119, cites a Pompeiian inscription that says, "*I hate poor* people. If anyone wants something for nothing, he's a fool. Let him pay up and he'll get it." (*CIL* 4.9839b)

49. Horsley, *Imperial Order*, 16. Another good example of social division is gender inequality. See Appendix B for details.

50. Lampe, "Romans 16," 227–29. Lampe also thinks that Rom 16 implies a high proportion of immigrants in the Roman church (227).

51. Jeffers, *Conflicts*, 9.

Foreigners, War-Captives, and the Jews

Rome was a multicultural society, with plenty of ethnic tension. But the associated social injustice was complex and not restricted to racial discrimination. These tensions and injustices exacerbated the sorrow and pain experienced by the socioeconomically poor.

In Paul's day foreigners and their descendants made up a significant part of the Roman population. Many resident foreigners came involuntarily from the East as prisoners of war, and would, as a result, possess the lowest legal status.[52] Indeed, Romans were known to have killed and enslaved tens of thousands of war-captives in their military campaigns.[53] Some of the slaves might be able to gain citizenship later in life. But since they were of non-Roman stock, they would still have a lower social status than that of freeborn Romans.[54] At any rate, foreign residents in Rome experienced racial discrimination. Africans were reportedly despised, and even Greeks received slurs.[55]

Jews comprised one of the larger ethnic groups in Rome, with about 15,000–60,000 of them in Paul's day.[56] Given the fact that some synagogues were located in the more economically depressed areas, not a few of them would be quite poor.[57] Many would have come from Jerusalem, as a result of the sieges by Pompey (63 BCE) and Sosius (37 BCE). Sources indicate that a significant number were expelled from Rome under Tiberius (c. 19 CE).[58] Many would have been deported after the Edict of Claudius (49 CE). This included Prisca and Aquila (Acts 18:1–3), who returned to Rome later, probably after the Edict lapsed in 54 CE. Even though the Romans granted the Jews special rights (such as permission to meet in synagogues and to live according to their own customs), like other foreigners they were not respected by most of the Roman elite. For example, Cicero called Judaism

52. Note that free persons outside Rome were allowed to relocate to the capital city, and they brought their means of livelihood with them. But they were often discouraged by the lack of employment due to the abundance of free slave labor. See Jeffers, *Conflicts*, 7.

53. See Joshel, *Slavery*, 55. Appendix B provides further information regarding the number of people killed or enslaved by Rome.

54. Jeffers, *Conflicts*, 6–8.

55. Edwards, "Rome," 1014. See Cicero, *Tusc.* 2.65, and *De Or.* 1.105, regarding contempt for Greeks, and Livy, *Hist* 20:12.18, regarding Africans.

56. Jewett, *Romans*, 55. Jeffers, *Conflicts*, 10, thinks that forty to fifty thousand Jews lived in Rome. Again, the exact figure is debatable, but the point is that there were may of them.

57. See Appendix B for a discussion on the economic situation of the Jews in Rome.

58. Jeffers, *Conflicts*, 10.

"a barbarous superstition."[59] Thus, although some Jews like Prisca and Aquila might have enjoyed a level of economic stability (because they were artisans), they would have suffered from other forms of discrimination that foreigners in Rome typically experienced.[60]

In sum, there were many foreigners in Rome, particularly war-captives and their descendants.[61] Often they were economically poor and suffered from various forms of social injustice. The economic hardship and oppression experienced by many Jews is a good example of the harsh living conditions many foreigners endured in Rome.

Slaves

The plight of slaves is very important for our inquiry. The foregoing discussion already implies that many inhabitants of Rome were slaves or of slave origin.[62] In fact, the Greco-Roman slave system was an integral part of every aspect of life,[63] and the economy depended on it. Byron provides an excellent summary of the debates around slavery in recent decades.[64] For some time "scholars tended to portray slavery in the Greco-Roman world as a benign form of mass employment for the under classes as well as an effective means of integrating foreigners."[65] But the reality is that slavery was a relationship of domination, and an example of "the powerful exploiting the powerless."[66]

Archaeologists have unearthed objects relating to slavery, "such as the Roman whip (*flagellum*) whose thongs had pieces of metal attached to them

---

59. Ibid., 10. See also Cicero, *Flac.*, 66–69, and Edwards, "Rome," 1014.

60. Their deportation from Rome following the Edict of Claudius is an example of that discrimination. Forman, *Politics*, 124, thinks that it "is possible that the Jewish exiles returning to Rome (after the ban had lapsed) had previously suffered the confiscation of their property and now faced restrictions on gathering together, homelessness, and the difficulty of obtaining kosher food."

61. Of course, there were migrants who went to Rome voluntarily. See, e.g., Morley, "The Poor," 37, 39.

62. There are diverse views regarding the number of slaves in Rome. For our purposes, it is be safe to assume that about 25 to 40 percent of Rome's population consisted of slaves. See discussion in Appendix B.

63. Rupprecht, "Slave," 881; Rodgers, *Roman World*, 224–27; Jeffers, *Greco-Roman*, 221–26.

64. Byron, "Background," 116–39. See also Byron, *Recent Research*, 1–35.

65. Byron, "Background," 116. This view will be disputed below. See Appendix B for further information against this view.

66. Ibid., 133.

in order to make deep wounds into the flesh."[67] It is true that Roman law removed the owners' right of life and death over their slaves, regulated the punitive sale of slaves, and prohibited the use of private prisons in which slaves were kept in chains. But the law also classified slaves as chattels and a "speaking tool" (*instrumentum vocale*) that could be bought, sold and punished by their masters at will.[68] Moreover, as Jennifer Glancy points out, "Sexual access to slave bodies was a pervasive dimension of ancient systems of slavery. Both female and male slaves were available for their owners' pleasure."[69] Sexual use of female and young male slaves was widespread.[70] In light of this, one can hardly say that slavery was a benign form of mass employment.[71] Two further aspects of the Roman slavery system should be mentioned.

First, the practice of self-sale. It has been suggested that some sold themselves into slavery in order to relieve themselves from debts or seek improvement of quality of life. However, only rare cases of self-sale can be found in ancient sources.[72] Also, "[r]eferences to self-sale in the Roman jurists indicate that individuals who sold themselves into slavery had not only given up their inalienable right to freedom, but also brought shame upon themselves and their family."[73] Slavery was not an attractive option.

Second, the claimed possibility of upward mobility.[74] It is suggested that the socioeconomic prospect of some slaves and ex-slaves were better than the poor freeborn.[75] This is because in some cases a favored slave gained from wealthy masters the training and even sufficient capital to engage in commerce and manufacture upon manumission. This generalized prospect of upward mobility has, however, been challenged. It is true that

---

67. Harrill, "Slavery," 1125. Cf. Cohick, 260.

68. Garnsey and Saller, *Roman Empire*, 116.

69. Glancy, *Slavery*, 21. See also Cohick, *Women*, 268.

70. Glancy, *Slavery*, 23.

71. It should be noted, however, that not every slave was brutalized, and some slaves in the urban setting received better treatment. (See Byron, "Background," 133.) In fact, it was to the masters' advantage that they take care of their slaves' physical needs because they were a financial investment for them. It would be fair to say that the slave system provided some form of protection for the enslaved at least in some instances. Byron concludes that "not all forms of slavery were considered to be undesirable. But the *vast majority* of them probably were" (134; Emphasis added).

72. Byron, "Background," 134.

73. Ibid., 134. See also Glancy, *Slavery*, 80–85, against Bartchy, "Slave," 1099.

74. See, e.g., Martin, *Slavery as Salvation*, 30–42.

75. Garnsey and Saller, *Roman Empire*, 124.

a few manumitted slaves enjoyed upward mobility.[76] There were also imperial slaves and freedmen who held considerable power, such as members
of *familia Caesaris*, and the Roman procurator of Judea, Felix, who was an
imperial freedman of Claudius (Acts 24:22–27).[77] But it is likely that this
represented the exception, not the norm.[78] Most likely the majority of slaves
were not upwardly mobile. It should also be noted that the ruling class took
measures to prevent the upward mobility of slaves. Freed slaves were legally
obliged to provide services to their former masters, as long as they were able
to earn their own living at the same time.[79]

In light of the above, Garnsey and Saller's comment remains valid:
"The psychological oppression associated with lack of freedom, the threat
of the whip, of the break-up of slave families and of sexual abuse, continued
unabated."[80] This sums up the daily reality of life as a slave in Rome.

Given the large number of slaves in the population, it is almost certain
that there were slaves within Roman house churches, and that everyone
would have regular interactions with them. For example, in his model craft-
worker house church (see above), Oakes considers that there were roughly
six to seven slaves out of a thirty-member gathering (20–23 percent).[81] It is
likely that slaves in the house churches experienced the same social realities
that characterized the lives of other slaves in Rome. According to Oakes's
model, there were a number of slaves who did not belong to the householders within the house church, and it is probable that their owners were not
Christ-followers. We can assume that their daily sufferings would be similar to that which has been described above. We would hope that the slaves
owned by members of the Christ-community would have received better
treatment (but they appear to have remained enslaved, Paul's exhortations
in Philemon notwithstanding). Yet we must also bear in mind that there
may have been discrepancies between what believing masters were encouraged to do and what they actually did, especially when the slaver-owners

76. Harrill, "Slavery," 1126. For example, the Latin poet, Horace, was born to a
freedman.

77. Ibid., 1126. Bartchy, "Slave, Slavery," 1099.

78. See Byron, "Background," 121, 135. As Horsley, "Slave Systems," 57, says, "The
experience of the vast majority of slaves cannot be mitigated by focusing on the unusual
influence or atypical mobility of a 'select few.'"

79. Jeffers, *Greco-Roman*, 232, who summarizes their ongoing obligations this way:
"They owed continued reverence, duties and payments to their former masters. The
senate considered requiring freedmen to wear a special uniform so any dodging of duty
would be noticed" (233).

80. Garnsey and Saller, *Roman Empire*, 116.

81. Oakes, *Reading*, 96.

were new converts. At any rate, many slaves were familiar with hardship and injustice, both in their past and present experiences.

SOCIO-POLITICAL INJUSTICE AND ROMAN IMPERIAL ORDER

As mentioned before, politics, religion, social and economic systems and structures were intertwined in the ancient world. We have already seen how social and economic realities are linked. But a closer look reveals that they are also connected with Roman political structures. Here we will highlight those connections by briefly looking at socio-political injustice in Rome and the Roman imperial order, especially in terms of how those in positions of power used social and political systems to exploit others.

Although imperial oppression was not the only reason why people suffered, the repression and cruelty of the Empire would contribute to or increase the suffering of the common people. Food shortages, for instance, were a consequence of a famine, yet often (as mentioned above) the poor suffered much more because of the uneven distribution of available food in favor of the ruling class. The Roman system of property acquisition and transmission ensured social and economic inequality. The Roman law of property rights favored Roman citizens. In an economy that depended on agriculture, the Roman system ensured that the elite maintained their socio-economic superiority and the poor stayed poor. As Garnsey and Saller say, "The direct exploitation of labor by rich proprietors was a central feature of Roman imperial society . . . Wealth was generated for members of the propertied class to a large extent by the labor of their personal dependents."[82] The patronage system of relationships was Rome's way of maintaining public order and control over its subject people.[83] This system took advantage of the "honor and shame" social convention to ensure that the imperial family and the elite were at the top of the social pyramid.[84]

Public rhetoric was an important way by which the Roman imperial order maintained control. Roman rhetoric assumed the function of legitimizing slavery and the suppression of women's social status, in accordance

---

82. Garnsey and Saller, *Roman Empire*, 110–11. More examples of Roman economic exploitation can be found in Elliott and Reasoner, *Documents*, 163–71.

83. Horsley, *Imperial Order*, 14–16.

84. See Malina, *New Testament World*, 27–57, about the honor-and-shame society of the ancient world. But note the warning of Crook, "Honor," 592–611, against a binary view of honor and shame.

with the interests of the slaveholding and patriarchal upper classes.[85] Public speeches were often delivered by figures of power. A common theme in the oratory of the Empire concerned the peace established by Caesar throughout the whole world.[86] The reality, of course, was that the *pax Romana* was possible only because of imperial conquests and oppression. Perhaps the most overt form of oppression carried out by imperial Rome was their military brutality. As mentioned, there were numerous war-captives and their descendants in Rome. Imperial triumph was the cause of their subjugation, loss of property, loss of dignity, geographical displacement, slavery, and degradation.[87]

Political oppression and socioeconomic injustice were, therefore, interconnected. The Roman imperial order ensured that the social and economic systems worked in favor of those in positions of socioeconomic and political power.

Imperial Cult and Caesar the Chief Benefactor

As mentioned, in the ancient world religion and politics were inseparable. Pharaoh was perceived as the true offspring of the sun god, Re, and his kingship was secured by this divine attribute.[88] We find a similar kind of divine rulership developing in the Roman Empire.

The Caesars' claims to divinely sanctioned rule vary, and are best demonstrated by the terminology used concerning their reigns. In Rome the Julio-Claudian emperors did not receive explicit divine honors until after their deaths. But, as Wright says, "being hailed as the son of the newly deified Julius was an important part of Augustus's profile, and that of his successors."[89] Therefore it is not surprising that the title "son of the deified" was inscribed on Roman coins.[90] In the *Res Gestae* (34), the emperor says that he has exceeded everyone else in power after the legal recognition given to him by the senate and the people of Rome because of his achievements.[91] As the chief benefactor of the Empire, Caesar deserved the *fides* (loyalty,

---

85. Horsley, *Imperial Order*, 17–18.

86. That is, the Empire provided security against external attack. See ibid., 18.

87. Ibid., 11–14.

88. Strawn, "Pharaoh," 633.

89. Wright, "Paul and Caesar," 175; Wright, *Resurrection*, 56–57.

90. See Elliott and Reasoner, *Documents*, 141–45, for records of the deification of successive Caesars in ancient documents.

91. Cf. Horsley, *Paul and Empire*, 15.

faithfulness to treaty obligations) of its people because of his *auctoritas*.[92] One of the four personal and moral qualities attributed to Augustus in *Res Gestae* 34 is justice (*iustitiae*).[93] According to Wright, "Rome claimed to have brought justice to the world; indeed, the goddess *Iustitia* was an Augustan innovation, closely associated with the principate."[94] All these were designed to support the claim that Caesar's rule enjoyed the blessing of the gods.

The imperial cult was an expression of the Roman subjects' loyalty to the emperor, since his gifts matched those of the gods.[95] In many Greek cities Augustus and his successors were "compared to and made into a god among traditional gods."[96] Not only was the emperor an object of veneration, he was also the chief priest of the Roman world, *pontifex maximus*. Coins often featured the portrait of Caesar with titles like *divi filius* and *pontifex maximus*.[97] The imperial cult also included a cult for Rome itself. Augustus refused to have any temple consecrated to himself unless it was done in tandem with the goddess *Roma*. The ideology behind this claimed is that "Rome was chosen by the gods to rule the world" and lead them to a Golden Age.[98] According to deSilva, "Rome's power meant order and security, and the cult of the *Augusti et Roma* became an important expression of loyalty to that sheltering power."[99]

Were followers of Jesus in danger of religious persecution? We know of no widespread persecution in Rome at the time Paul wrote the letter. But we should not see "religious persecution" in modern terms, for in the ancient world religion and socio-religious realities were inseparable. Believers' non-participation in pagan festivals would put them in danger of persecution, or

92. Georgi, "Upside Down," 149; Horsley, *Paul and Empire*, 15. The term *auctoritas* refers to the general prestige and influence of a person.

93. The four attributes are courage, clemency, justice and devotion. See also Georgi, "Upside Down," 149.

94. Wright, "Paul and Caesar," 176; See also Georgi, "Upside Down," 149, for a similar view.

95. deSilva, "Ruler Cult," 1026; Rodgers, *Roman World*, 172–3. Cf. Ferguson, *Backgrounds*, 195.

96. Horsley, *Paul and Empire*, 20.

97. deSilva, "Ruler Cult," 1027. Cf. Rodgers, *Roman World*, 172–3; Ferguson, *Backgrounds*, 194–5.

98. deSilva, "Ruler Cult," 1027. Cf. Rodgers, *Roman World*, 172.

99. deSilva, "Ruler Cult," 1027–8. Also, in Italy the imperial cult took the shape of the traditional religion of the *genius* (the guardian spirit of the head of the household). In Rome, rites were offered in private homes to Augustus' *genius*. Thus, through the cult Caesar's reign was the power behind Roman peace and stability. For another good discussion on the imperial cult and Rome, see Jackson, *New Creation*, 68–71.

at least social isolation.[100] Indeed, Elliott and Reasoner list fifteen instances of religious intolerance in Rome, from the prohibition of certain sacrificial rites in 429 BCE to the (first) executions of Christians in 64 CE, with actions against Judaism in recent memory (19, 41, 49 CE).[101] In light of this, Christ-followers had reason to be concerned. It is argued that actions against "foreign" religions were due to Rome's suspicion of any social-religious practices that might engender civic disorder. This is especially the case when a "foreign" religion was perceived "as especially attracting slaves and women."[102]

In short, the allegedly divinely sanctioned rule of the Caesars provided legitimacy for imperial rule and its associated oppression by taking advantage of the patronage system and the social convention of honor and shame. This religio-political system ensured the socioeconomic hardship experienced by the audience of Romans would remain and there was little they could do to overturn the injustice embedded in the system. Importantly, since the gods were thought to be involved in this system, it would be perceived by the ancients that cosmic powers were ultimately behind the power and authority of Rome. As a result, socioeconomic hardship and socio-political injustice would also be understood as connected to the cosmic forces that supported the system. This may come as a surprise to moderns, but it would have appeared as an obvious reality in the ancient world.

THE "AUDIENCE" IN OUR EXEGESIS

The above survey has painted a picture of the daily realities faced by members of the house churches in Rome, and provides the necessary socio-historical background for our exegesis. In particular, the portrayal of the interconnections between socioeconomic and religio-political realities will be crucial to our analysis. But the goal of our socio-historical analysis is also to describe a plausible audience in our exegesis. In Chapter 1 we mentioned that at the most basic level the "audience" in our exegesis consists of all those who were familiar with suffering in Rome. In this chapter we have established that within the first-century house churches the majority of the members would be familiar with socioeconomic hardship and religio-political

100. Commenting on early Christianity in general, Green, *1 Peter*, 9, says, "Failing to associate themselves with these religiocultural activities, their behaviors would have been perceived by the general populace as atheistic . . . they would have been charged with bringing upon their communities the disfavor of the gods."

101. Elliott and Reasoner, *Documents*, 280, document resources for all fifteen instances. For ancient documents regarding troubles experienced by the Jews from the time of Claudius, see pages 206–18.

102. Ibid., 279.

injustice, or at least they regularly interacted with people who experienced hardship. In light of this, we can say that the "audience" consisted of those who understood what it meant to live at or below subsistence level; people who experienced poor living conditions; families who were familiar with high infant mortality rates; foreigners who were involuntarily relocated because of Roman conquests; and those who were enslaved. Indeed, some members of the "audience" may have been destitute, if they happened to be beggars, the chronically sick, or homeless.[103] We will refer to this audience throughout our exegesis, and ask how they would have understood the letter's argument and its references to suffering.

With this audience in mind, we can then ask the relevant questions during our exegesis. For example, how would those living below subsistence level in the audience understand the term θλῖψις in Rom 5:3; 8:35? What would the terms λιμός and γυμνότης in 8:35 mean to the beggars and the destitute? What does the notion of a hope of glory in 5:2-3 mean to the slaves in the audience, given the fact that their social status and daily existence were less than glorious and honorable?

ANCIENT WORLDVIEWS ON SUFFERING

Before moving on to the text of Romans, an outline of some relevant aspects of the ancient worldviews on suffering is needed. This is a vast subject, and much can be said about it.[104] What constitutes suffering? What are the causes? What is the purpose of suffering, if there is one? How should people deal with it, and what should their attitude be? Can one prevent it? Is there value in suffering? If so, what is it? But space limitations disallow us from undertaking a comprehensive study here. Since our interest lies in how the audience would have *interacted with the text of Rom 5-8*, we will specifically survey aspects of Greco-Roman and Jewish worldviews that are relevant to our exegesis.

Educative, Training, and Disciplinary Values

Both Greco-Roman and Jewish writings share the view that suffering has educative value.[105] In his detailed study, Croy asserts that the "view that suf-

103. In Oakes' model craft-worker house church of thirty people, there are a couple of homeless people. See Oakes, *Reading*, 96.

104. See Talbert, *Learning*, 9-23; Croy, *Endurance*, 77-161; Fredrickson, "Paul," 172-8; Smith, *Seven Explanations*, 9-200; Fitzgerald, *Cracks*, 47-116.

105. See Fredrickson, "Paul," 175-76; Talbert, *Learning*, 9-21; Smith, *Seven*

fering was salutary or educational was widespread among Greek writers from the mid-fifth century on."[106] In fact, the Tragedy genre seeks to educate people to develop their capacity to endure hardship.[107] In a letter to his enemy, Pompey, Julius Caesar says that they should consider that the losses both sides have already sustained should serve as lessons and cautions, and that both should consider laying down their arms.[108] The educative value of suffering is often spoken of among Stoic philosophers. Seneca thinks that those who suffer from great misfortunes will eventually be toughened.[109] Epictetus also thinks that pain and suffering lead to moral improvement.[110] Croy summarizes this Greco-Roman perspective on suffering as follows,[111]

> Whatever its origin, suffering was a "given" in human affairs, and its potential for benefitting the sufferer was axiomatic for several Greco-Roman authors. Stoics of a later period (most notably Seneca) saw in suffering the means by which the gods exercised, tested and trained persons.[112]

Jewish writings also speak of the training and disciplinary value of suffering.[113] In the midst of severe affliction, the author of Lamentations says, "Let us test and examine our ways, and return to the Lord" (3:40).[114] Likewise, Eliphaz says to Job, "How happy is the one whom God reproves; therefore do not despise the discipline of the Almighty"[115] (Job 5:17). Elsewhere it is said that God tests the righteous through suffering so that they may be found worthy (Wis 3:4–5). Jubilees 17:17 looks at the testing of Abraham in Gen 22 and says that the patriarch is faithful in all his afflictions.[116] The author of *Psalms of Solomon* says that, in the process of God's testing, the righteous are required to endure so that they may be shown mercy (*Ps. Sol.* 16:14–15). Sometimes sickness is seen as an instrument through which

---

Explanations, 59–78; Croy, *Endurance*, 139–56.

106. Ibid., 139.

107. Ibid., 141–42.

108. *Bell. Civ.* 3.10.

109. *Helv.* 2.3.

110. See Fredrickson, "Paul," 175.

111. Of course, there are those who see that pain should be avoided. The Epicureans think that emotional pain should be avoided, because their goal is tranquility and grief is the opposite of that. See Fredrickson, "Paul," 174.

112. Croy, *Endurance*, 157.

113. See, e.g., Smith, *Seven Explanations*, 59–78, 134–39.

114. NRSV.

115. NRSV. Cf. Ps 84:12.

116. Cf. Smith, *Seven Explanations*, 135.

people can turn from wickedness (Sir 38:9–10), and in the case of Tobit, an angel said that he was sent to test him and heal him (Tob 12:13–14). Thus, suffering is seen as God's way of testing his people so that they may be approved by him.[117] It has educative and training value. It is likely that Rom 5:3–4 reflects this educative value, for Paul says that affliction produces perseverance and character. We will discuss this further in our exegesis.

Retributive Justice

Suffering is very often understood to be retributive or punitive. That is, it is the result of the punishment of the deities, and actions need to be taken to avert their wrath. In the ancient world people believed that the gods punished humans when they were offended, or when not enough was done to please them. This was common within the Greco-Roman worldview. The gods either caused human suffering when they were offended, or prayers and offerings had to be made to them for deliverance from calamities. The earthquake at Sparta in 464 BCE, for example, was thought to be caused by an earlier violation of a sacred site by the Spartans.[118] Sailors would offer prayers and libations to deities for safe voyages.[119] Sacrificial festivals were held throughout the agricultural year of the Greeks in order to ensure that the gods were pleased. The deities kept mice and locusts away to ensure good harvests.[120] Sickness was a major threat to humanity where life expectancy was short, and the gods were called upon for deliverance and healing.[121]

There is ample evidence in Jewish writings that suffering was considered retributive. That is, suffering was seen as God's punishment for human rebellion, and in the case of Israel, suffering was the result of covenantal unfaithfulness. In the primordial story of Gen 3, the curses on Adam and Eve were the result of their disobedience. The lists of covenantal blessings and curses in Deut 28 are vivid examples of God's retributive justice. Israel's disobedience would lead to fear, oppression by enemies, agricultural disasters, crop pests, famine, illness, harm from wild animals, infertility, and

---

117. Ibid., 139.

118. Croy, *Endurance*, 136.

119. For example, The twin sons of Zeus (Castor and Pollux; Διόσκουροι) that are found in Acts 28:11 were found on the rigging of ships in the Greco-Roman world. Cf. Burkert, *Greek Religion*, 266–67.

120. Ibid., 265.

121. For example, the sanctuary of the Temple of Apollo Epikourios at Bassae was probably dedicated as the thanksgiving for the deliverance from the plague in 429 BCE. Asklepios, popular in the NT period, was known as the god of healing. See Jeffers, *Greco-Roman*, 93.

eventually exile.[122] Their obedience would lead to a population increase, agricultural bounty, health, prosperity, and return from exile.[123] Numbers 16:45–50 and 2 Sam 24:1–25 tell stories where plagues started because of human sinfulness but were stopped when atoning sacrifices were made.[124] A careful reading of the Jewish Scripture will find that a significant concern of Israel's prophets was the people's unfaithfulness. Their condemnation of idolatry and social injustice is arguably a warning against covenantal curses in Deuteronomy.[125] As Croy says, "The prophetic texts presupposing a causal relationship between sin and human suffering could be multiplied almost endlessly."[126] There is no doubt that a retributive view of suffering is present in Jewish thinking. This view of suffering makes Rom 8:31–39 fascinating reading, for it speaks of God's election and justification in the midst of the suffering of believers. In our exegesis we will ask how the audience would have understood the periscope, given the ancient conception of retributive justice.

Suffering of the Righteous

While evidence of retributive/punitive suffering abounds, there are voices that challenge the notion that every instance of affliction is caused by people's wrongdoing. In fact, recognition of the educative value of suffering is often the result of the fact that people do suffer innocently. Plato, for example, questions whether evil can come from god,[127] and thinks that suffering can be seen as divine chastisement *with beneficial effect* on those who suffer.[128] Likewise, the examples in *Psalms of Solomon* and Tobit cited above concerning God's testing and training are applied to the suffering of the righteous (*Ps. Sol.* 16:14–15; Tob 12:13–14).[129] In the following we will

122. Deut 29:19–24; 31:17, 21, 29 contain further examples of retributive justice expressed in the Torah.

123. Stuart, *Hosea-Jonah*, xxxii–xxli, provides a summary of covenantal blessings and curses.

124. See Num 8:19 for another correlation between atonement and plagues.

125. See Deut 28:15–68; cf. Lev 26:14–46; Deut 32:1–43. As Stuart, *Hosea-Jonah*, xxxii, argues, the prophets know that YWHW uses them to call "his people back to obedience to the covenant he had given them many centuries before . . ."

126. Croy, *Endurance*, 87.

127. Plato says, for instance, that god cannot be responsible for everything, and that we must look for some other factors (other than god) as the cause of evil (*Resp.* 2.379b).

128. Croy, *Endurance*, 139.

129. There are places in both Israel's Scripture and later Jewish literature that speak of the suffering of the righteous. Smith, *Seven Explanations*, 9–200, identifies seven

outline three types of "suffering of the righteous" that are, as we will see in our exegesis, particularly relevant to our inquiry because of the intertextual links between Romans and Jewish writings.

First, the authors of the Psalter and Wisdom literature wrestle with the notion of retributive justice in suffering. In their prayers and wisdom sayings they speak of the suffering of the righteous. The preacher in Ecclesiastes observes that life is absurd because the righteous perish in their righteousness while the wicked live long (7:15), and they all share a common destiny (9:2). While Ps 1 clearly speaks of YHWH's retributive justice, there are lament Psalms in which the psalmists complain and protest because they see their suffering as undeserved. Also, Job's friends assume that his sufferings result from God's just judgment on his wickedness. But Job is innocent, and YHWH's answers at the end provide no clear explanation for his affliction. These instances challenge the notion that suffering is purely the result of human sinful acts. The lament and protest of the suffering righteous in these writings are particularly useful for our study of the citation of Ps 44:22 in Rom 8:36.

Second, the suffering of the Servant in the Isaianic Servant Songs provides another prime example of innocent suffering.[130] The Songs are remarkably found in a prophetic book where warnings against unfaithfulness abound. Admittedly the Servant suffers because of the sins of others, but the Servant himself/herself is innocent. There are several passages in Rom 5–8 that seem to echo the Servant Songs, which will be discussed in our exegesis.

The third area of interest in Jewish thought is the eschatological vindication of the suffering righteous in apocalyptic literature, as well as the martyrdom theology found in 2 Maccabees. Jewish apocalyptic literature often speaks of the hope a sufferer finds in God's faithfulness in spite of Israel's unfaithfulness. The sufferer is determined to be loyal to Israel's God and believes that he will vindicate those who suffer innocently. A good example is found in Dan 9:17–19, where the prophet (and his companions) suffer as faithful righteous sufferers in captivity.

> Now therefore, O our God, listen to the prayer of your servant
> and to his supplication, and for your own sake, Lord, let your

---

categories of the suffering of the righteous in the Jewish and Pauline literatures, which are essentially non-retributive. They are: suffering resulting from persecution; remedial suffering; suffering as salvation-historical necessity; probationary suffering; the effect of the sin of the first human; pedagogical suffering; and suffering as participation in Christ. (The last category is only found in Pauline letters, according to Smith.)

130. The Isaianic Servant Songs are found in Isa 42:1–9; 49:1–13; 50:4–11; and 52:13—53:12.

face shine upon your desolated sanctuary. Incline your ear, O my God, and hear. Open your eyes and look at our desolation and the city that bears your name. We do not present our supplication before you on the ground of our righteousness, but on the ground of your great mercies. O Lord, hear; O Lord, forgive; O Lord, listen and act and do not delay! For your own sake, O my God, because your city and your people bear your name![131]

Set in a context where Daniel and his friends seek to remain faithful in the face of severe oppression by a hostile political power, the prophet confesses the sins of his people and asks God for deliverance for his own name's sake. This reminds us of the eschatological suffering of the righteous found in *The Thanksgiving Hymns* in the Dead Sea Scrolls. For example, in 1QH 9:1–11 the author speaks of their hope in God's loving kindness in the midst of pain, slander, desolation, and the threat of death.[132] It also calls to mind the theology of martyrdom in 2 Macc 6:1–7:42—the faithful are exhorted to trust in God in the midst of suffering with the hope of his ultimate vindication and deliverance. It is believed that the calamity of Israel is the result of their sins, but God does not forsake his people (6:16). The martyrdoms of Eleazar, the seven brothers and their mother demonstrate that belief. Their hope is that their suffering will bring an end to the wrath of the Almighty (7:38). They put their whole trust in the Lord (7:39).[133] This particular Jewish understanding of suffering is an interesting backdrop to the texts in Rom 8:18–23 in our exegesis, where apocalyptic language is found.

Cosmic Dimension of Suffering

It is important to note that embedded in our discussion of ancient worldviews is the cosmic dimension of suffering. Whether it is the suffering of individuals (e.g., sickness), nature (e.g., famine), or socio-political oppression (e.g., battle defeat), the ancients believe that suffering and cosmic powers

131. NRSV.

132. For further discussion, see Croy, *Endurance*, 116–23.

133. See Kleinknecht, *Der leidende Gerechtfertigte*, 123–26, for a discussion on the tradition of the suffering just in 2 Maccabees. See Pobee, *Persecution and Martyrdom*, 13–46, for a discussion on the theology of martyrdom in Judaism. For a critique of Pobee's interpretation of Paul, see Gorman, *Cruciformity*, 82n15; Lim, *Sufferings*, 8–9. As our exegesis will show, Gorman is right in saying that Paul's understanding of suffering goes beyond a theology of martyrdom. Our interest, however, does not lie in whether Paul's theology of suffering borrows from this particular tradition in Judaism. What we are saying here is simply that 2 Maccabees provides a helpful background for our exegesis.

are interconnected. The Greco-Roman literature, for example, refers to the ancients' belief that cosmic powers and human affliction are interlinked. There is a causal relationship between sacrilege and suffering (as mentioned above).[134] Homer thinks that all things, good and evil, can be traced back to deity,[135] and indeed, Seneca says that everything happens according to god's will.[136]

The cosmic dimension of suffering is clearly found in the apocalyptic visions of Dan 7–12, which are good examples of the Jewish worldview that cosmic forces hold sway over human affairs, including the rise and fall of human kingdoms.[137] Political and social systems, as well as the associated suffering of God's people, are closely connected with the cosmic powers in the visions. The battles between God and evil powers are depicted with vivid imagery. There is a strong sense of *hope in God's final triumph over evil powers*, with the appearance of a "Son of Human" (υἱὸς ἀνθρώπου) as the figure for that hope—whose kingdom and dominion (ἐξουσία) over the peoples (ἔθνη) will last eternally throughout the ages (αἰώνιος) (7:13–14).

Indeed, the assumption in Israel's Scripture is that cosmic powers are behind human suffering. Not only is God the ultimate cosmic power, evil forces are mentioned not infrequently. In primordial history, the serpent represents the cosmic evil force that caused the first humans' disobedience. The serpent is identified as Satan in the Christian apocalyptic literature of Rev 20:2. Satan is, of course, depicted in Job 1–2 as the evil figure behind Job's multifaceted suffering, which includes sicknesses, a storm, loss of life, and loss of properties. Satan is also the one who incites David to count the people of Israel (1 Chr 21:1). A plague on Israel starts as a result, which is halted when David offers a sacrifice as a burnt offering and peace offering. Satan is also the accuser of the high priest Joshua in Zech 3:1–2.[138] Indeed, the term "Satan" (σατανᾶς) is used frequently in early Christian writings, including Romans (16:20), and represents the cosmic power behind all sorts of evil.[139] The Exodus story (not least the ten plagues) is not only about the

134. For instance, Horace says that the neglect of temples and shrines has caused the gods to send defeats and misfortunes in Rome (*Carm.* 3.6). See also Croy, *Endurance*, 156.

135. Croy, *Endurance*, 134.

136. Seneca, *Nat.* 3.12. See also Croy, *Endurance*, 147.

137. I am indebted to Beker, *Suffering and Hope*, 55, for his insights here.

138. The term σατανᾶς also appears in Sir 21:27 in the LXX, and διάβολος in 1 Macc 1:36; Wis 2:24.

139. The term σατανᾶς appears fourteen times in the Gospels, seven in the undisputed Pauline letters, seven in Revelation, and three in the rest of the NT. The term διάβολος appears thirty-seven times in the NT.

liberation of slaves, but also, for the ancient audience, the cosmic battle between YHWH and the Egyptian gods that stood behind the political powers
in Egypt.[140] In fact, Israel's faith hinged on the belief that YHWH is greater
than all other gods, and hence was able to protect them from evil cosmic
forces (e.g., Pss 95:3; 96:4; 97:9; 135:5; 136:2).[141] In short, cosmic powers
transcend all human affairs—social, religious, and political—and indeed,
the entire created order. We may, therefore, say that they are the ultimate
forces behind suffering.

Summary

In sum, suffering is an integral part of a web of interlocked cosmic powers,
socioeconomic and religio-political systems. In both Jewish and Greco-
Roman literature, suffering is often understood to have educative value. But
it is also widely thought that suffering is retributive or punitive. That is, it is
the result of YHWH's/the gods' punishment for human wrongdoings. Libations and prayers are often demanded for the alleviation or prevention of
suffering. Although this view of hardship is very common, there are voices
that speak of the suffering of the innocent. We find these voices in both
Jewish and Greco-Roman writings where they speak of the training value
of suffering. But they are more prominent in Israel's Wisdom literature, the
Isaianic Servant Songs, and the apocalyptic literature, as well as 2 Maccabees. Finally, it is clear that the ancients see a cosmic dimension in suffering.
In fact, cosmic powers, socio-political injustice, and all manner of affliction,
are interconnected.

CONCLUSION

In this chapter we have studied the social location of the first-century audience of Romans. While we do not have access to Paul's real audience, our
socio-historical analysis has given us a general picture of the social world of
Rome. We have discovered that affliction and distress were embedded in a
network of interconnected social, economic, religious, and political systems

---

140. See Enns, *Evolution*, 43–44. Indeed, according to ANE literature, the kingship of Pharaoh is not only political, but also religious and cosmological. As, Strawn,
"Pharaoh," 632, says, "Pharaoh was lawgiver, judge and, in theory at least, the only true
priest to the gods. . . Yet this centrality was not only political or religious . . . it was also
cosmological. Kingship was introduced at the time of creation: the creator-god was the
first king, and according to the Memphite theology Horus was the king of Egypt."

141. See Enns, *Evolution*, 44–45.

in Rome,[142] which were in turn inseparable from the cosmic forces in the world. We have found that a large portion of the letter's audience suffered from various forms of socioeconomic hardship and religio-political injustice. This picture of suffering will be used in our exegesis when we consider how an audience familiar with affliction would have heard Romans. Our study of the ancient worldviews of suffering has found that suffering was considered to have educative value. Having said that, it was often perceived to be retributive. But there were also alternative voices that spoke of the suffering of the righteous. In addition, most likely cosmic powers were considered to be the ultimate forces behind suffering. With this background in mind, we are in a position to read the references to suffering in Romans from the perspective of the letter's audience. We are ready to embark on our exegesis now.

142. Morley, "The Poor," 33–36, helpfully highlights three characteristics of poverty in Rome: vulnerability, exclusion, and shame. Morley recognizes that not everyone was poor by every one of these. But, "poverty in one respect might well lead to another, as shame contributed to social exclusion and social exclusion reinforced vulnerability, since the outcast could not rely on networks of reciprocity or patronage in times of crisis" (36).

3

From Adamic Humanity
to a New Humanity in Christ

INTRODUCTION

As stated in Chapter 1, the aim of our inquiry is to determine the theology of suffering in Romans from the perspective of Paul's audience. Implicit in the texts of Rom 5 and 8 is an audience that faces affliction and hardship. We have just discussed in Chapter 2 the social location of the audience and painted a general picture of the types of suffering they were familiar with in first-century Rome. In the following five chapters we will examine the key pericopes in 5:1—8:39.

Given the vocabulary of ἐλπίζω/ἐλπίς in 5:2, 4, 5; 8:20, 24, 25, it is common for commentators to recognize the theme of hope in Rom 5–8.[1] But an audience familiar with daily hardship and injustice would appreciate the significance of suffering as the backdrop to this hope in a way that others might not. In fact, hope is almost always mentioned together with affliction, groaning or weakness in these chapters (5:2–5; 8:18–23, 24–27), which indicates that 5:1—8:39 is about hope of glory *in suffering*. Indeed, Rom 5–8 contains the most significant references to suffering in the letter (in 5:1–5; 8:14–17, 18–39), with no fewer than fourteen terms representing different forms of suffering.[2] Within this section, Rom 8:14–39 offers the

1. See Byrne, *Romans*, 162; Kruse, *Romans*, 224; Moo, *Romans*, 290.

2. As mentioned, if we include other related terms like ματαιότης, ἀσθένεια, σφαγή, then there are about twenty-nine references to suffering in Rom 5–8, and thirty-eight

most substantial treatment of the hope of glory in suffering, and a thorough analysis will be provided in the forthcoming chapters.

In this chapter, however, we will first outline the key matters in Rom 5–8 that will assist our inquiry. We will then discuss 5:1–11 and 5:12–21 in relation to the theme of suffering and the argument of Rom 5–8. After that we will examine in what ways Gen 1–3 sheds light on our study. As we close our discussion we will suggest some ways in which the audience might have understood Rom 5 in light of Rome's propaganda of the *pax Romana*.

More specifically, I will argue that Rom 5–8 speaks of the formation of a new humanity out of Adam's humanity. The textual basis of this idea is in 5:12–21. Adamic humanity is under the cosmic powers of sin and death. But through Christ's death and resurrection believers have been set free from these powers. This deliverance of God through Christ is in fact his way of accomplishing his purpose of reconciling Adamic humanity to himself, which is the key point of 5:1–11. Reconciliation and peace with God mean that believers are no longer his enemies and are, ultimately, the basis for hope despite their present affliction. I will suggest that Gen 1–3 is the main scriptural background for Rom 5–8. Genesis provides valuable textual resources to explain how suffering and pain entered the cosmos, and why God's creation needs to be renewed. This, in turn, gives the audience hope even though there is chaos in the cosmos. This message of hope and reconciliation, in turn, provides an alternative narrative to Rome's propaganda of the *pax Romana*.

ROMANS 5–8 AS A DISTINCT SECTION IN THE LETTER

Our analysis begins with an overview of Rom 5–8. We will discover that 5:1—8:39 is a distinct section in Romans, with many distinguishable themes and literary features. We will highlight the fact that this section of the letter speaks of the formation of a new humanity out of Adamic humanity, which is accomplished by the death and resurrection of Christ. We will also outline the identifiable narrative structures in Rom 5–8 which concern Adamic humanity, Christ, and the children of God.

With a few exceptions, recent commentators have identified Rom 5–8 as a distinctive section within the structure of the letter.[3] Indeed, back in

---

in the whole letter (compared with the fifty-five occurrences of the δικ- word group in the entire letter). See Appendix A for details.

3. See, e.g., Moo, *Romans*, 33; Schreiner, *Romans*, 26; Wright, *Romans*, 410; Jewett, *Romans*, 534; Byrne, *Romans*, vi–vii; Matera, *Romans*, 16; Heil, *Romans*, 11; Hultgren, *Romans*, 197; Kruse, *Romans*, ix; Grieb, *Story*, vii. The exceptions are: Dunn, *Romans*

1999 Richard Longenecker said that "most scholars today view 5:1—8:39 as a distinguishable unit of material."[4] The alternative views are well known, and only a brief outline is needed. Following Fitzmyer, Harvey lists the four main views: (1) Rom 5 is an isolated unit; (2) Rom 5 concludes the section started from 1:16; (3) 5:1–11 concludes the preceding section while 5:12–21 introduces the subsequent section; and (4) Rom 5–8 comprise a major section.[5]

Option (1) is unlikely because there are obvious links between 5:1–11 and other parts of the letter, especially 1:16—4:25 and 5:12—8:39. Dunn skillfully highlights the verbal and thematic links between Rom 5 and the preceding section. Two good examples of those links are the δικ-words and the vocabulary of salvation (σῴζω, σωτηρία) that started in 1:16–17 and is developed in 3:21-26.[6] But as the discussion below will show, similar links are also present between Rom 5 and the subsequent sections, and so the arguments for (2) and (3) have to rely on building a case that 5:1–11 or 5:1–21 is the conclusion of the flow of thought from the preceding section.

It makes the best sense, however, to see Rom 5:1–11 as part of the section 5:1—8:39. What is decisive is that: (a) there are clear verbal and thematic links between Rom 5:1–11 and 8:18–39, which are highlighted by the repeated occurrences of the terms ἀγάπη, δικαιόω, δόξα/δοξάζω, ἐλπίς/ἐλπίζω, θλῖψις, σῴζω, ὑπομονή in both passages;[7] and (b) the repeated use of the confessional phrase διὰ τοῦ κυρίου ἡμῶν Ἰησοῦ Χριστοῦ (with minor variations) in 5:1, 11, 21; 6:23; 7:25, and 8:39. The former shows that the two passages (5:1–11 and 8:18–39) bookend the section, constituting a "ring composition."[8] The latter is a rhetorical marker to assist the audience to detect the flow of argument in the section. Since hope of glory in affliction is a key theme in both 5:1–11 and 8:18–39, the fact that Rom 5–8 is a distinguishable section of the letter suggests that it performs a significant role in speaking to an audience living with hardship.

Romans 5–8 also has distinctive vocabulary and themes. These not only affirm that 5:1—8:39 constitutes a distinguishable section, they are also important for understanding the theology of suffering in Rom 5 and 8. (Refer to Appendix A for the statistics of the occurrences of key terms.) The frequent language of πίστις/πιστεύω and Ἰουδαῖος/ἔθνος/Ἕλλην elsewhere in

---

1–8, viii–ix; Witherington, *Romans*, 24–25.

4. Longenecker, "Focus," 64.

5. Harvey, *Listening*, 124.

6. Dunn, *Romans 1–8*, 242–44.

7. Cf. Harvey, *Listening*, 125–26; Moo, *Romans*, 292–94; Hultgren, *Romans*, 198.

8. See Harvey, *Listening*, 125–26; Longenecker, "Focus," 65; Moo, *Romans*, 294.

Romans is rarely found in chapters 5–8. The δια- word group is found less frequently in Rom 5–8 than in 1–4, and the term Χριστός is more commonly used in 5–8 than any other section in the letter, which in turn points to the highly christological character of the section. The language of ἀγαπάω/ ἀγάπη most often occurs in the sections 5–8 and 12–15, and in the former it is specifically used in association with suffering. Notably, the language of Adam, death, life, Spirit, rule/reign, and slavery dominates Rom 5–8. Whereas in Rom 1–4 and 9–11 the δια-words often (though not always) have something to do with faith/faithfulness and the law, in 5:1—8:39 it has much to do with the *life* and *death* of Christ and his followers. While in Rom 1–4 and 9–11 the sinfulness of humanity and Israel is expressed in terms of their idolatry and disobedience in history (e.g., 1:18–32; 10:16, 21),[9] in 5–8 human rebellion is expressly caused by the *reign of sin and death*, which came as a result of Adam's disobedience.[10] Lastly, the vocabulary of suffering occurs mostly in Rom 5–8. As our discussion will show, these distinctive features are essential components of the argument that underpins Rom 5–8, and would have contributed to the audience's understanding of suffering.

Significantly, the prominence of Son/children/Father language in Rom 5–8 is striking. It is the only section in the letter that explicitly mentions the fact that believers are God's children. Also, apart from the salutation and thanksgiving in 1:1–15, Rom 5–8 is the only place where God's Father-Son relationship with Christ is mentioned (5:10; 8:3, 29, 32). In fact, the terms for both of these relationships appear mainly in 8:14–30, where the language of suffering is also found. Throughout our discussion we will explain how this unique feature of Rom 5–8 assists us in understanding the theology of suffering in Romans. (See Appendix A for a full list of the key terms in Romans concerning filial relationship.)

A careful look at Rom 5–8—with an awareness of the above distinctive features—reveals that the letter speaks of the formation of a new humanity from Adamic humanity as well as the transformation of humanity through Christ and the Spirit.[11] To assist our forthcoming discussion I would like

9. Cf. Longenecker, "Focus," 63.

10. In addition, Longenecker, "Focus," 63, observes the following concerning the "form of address." (1) "[Paul] speaks directly and consistently to his readers by the use of the pronouns and verbal suffixes 'we,' 'you,' 'yourselves,' and 'us'—addressing them also as 'brothers' in 7:1, 4 . . . " (2) "[T]he style of these two sections [1:16—4:25 and 5:1—8:39] shifts from being argumentative, particularly in the diatribes of 2:2–11 and 2:17—3:8 and the rhetorically structured presentation of God's oneness and impartiality in 3:17–31, to being more "confessional," cast as it is in 5:1—8:39 in the first person plural." Cf. Matera, *Romans*, 121–22.

11. This is well recognized by scholars, even though their emphases are different. E.g., Hultgren, *Romans*, 221, says that Adam and Christ are the heads of two humanities,

to suggest that the argument concerning the formation of a new Christ-humanity can be expressed by three underlying interconnected narratives in Rom 5–8. By "narrative" I do not mean that Paul is deliberately telling a story or that we can identify a story in his mind. Instead, I use the word "narrative," or "story," to refer to a reasonably identifiable narrative structure that can be constructed from the text of the letter. This narrative structure consists of certain characters, a trajectory of events, and possibly a plot (the main event or climax). An identified narrative in the text can be used as a tool to trace the theology and argument in the text that actively interacts with the audience.[12] In Rom 5–8, three interdependent narratives can be detected.[13]

The first is the story of Adamic humanity. Here Adam and the human beings after him are the actors in the narrative. Adam's one act of παράπτωμα/παρακοή brought about κατάκριμα and made many sinners (Rom 5:16, 19). Consequently, all human beings in Adam are under the reign of sin and death (5:12, 14).

The second narrative is the story of Christ, the Son of God. The death of Christ and God's raising him to life are repeatedly mentioned throughout Rom 5–8. Romans 8:3 speaks of the sending of the Son by the Father as a "sin-offering" (see the discussion in the next chapter regarding this translation of περὶ ἁμαρτίας in Rom 8:3; cf. 5:9–10), and 8:32 refers to God's not sparing his Son and handing him over to death. In 8:34 Paul mentions the exalted Christ being at the right hand of God. The trajectory of events thus consists of: The Father sending (and not sparing) his Son; the suffering and death of Christ; the Father raising the Son from the dead; and Christ's exaltation.

The third is the story of a new humanity (the children of God in Christ). It seems clear that a new humanity was created out of Adamic humanity through the work of Christ (5:17, 18, 21; 6:4, 22, 23). This new

---

with Christ's humanity surpassing that of Adam's; and Matera, *Romans*, 123, speaks of humanity's solidarity with either Adam or Christ. See also Wright, *Romans*, 524; Byrne, *Romans*, 268–9, 272–73; Dunn, *Romans 1–8*, 288, 378–87, 457, 464, 467, 485, 495.

12. See Adams, "Paul's Story of God," 19–24, for a similar way of using narrative as a tool. Interestingly, although Matlock, "Arrow," 44–54, is critical of the narrative approaches used by N. T. Wright and Richard Hays, he is by and large happy with Adams' methodology.

13. I do not expect these three narrative structures to be universally accepted as the only and best identifiable stories in Rom 5–8. Instead, they are reasonably detectable and hence can be used as a (not *the*) tool for our investigation. I find the stories constructed by Adams, "Paul's Story of God," 26–39, and Campbell, "Story of Jesus," 102–13, well constructed, although their details differ from mine. Cf. Grieb, *Story*, 56–57, who also briefly talks about the stories of Adam and Christ.

humanity participates in Christ's crucifixion, death and resurrection, and they have been baptized into Christ (6:1–10). They are set free from the reign of sin and death, and come under the reign of δικαιοσύνη (6:11–23). Through Christ, the eschatological Spirit dwells in them (8:1–13). By the Spirit's leading they are children of God, and they are to suffer with him and be glorified with him (8:14–17).[14]

More will be said about these narratives, especially in terms of their interrelationships. But suffice it to say that there is a common thread of the life and death of humanity, and the association of death with suffering. These stories will assist our analyses in the forthcoming chapters. But now, an analysis of Rom 5:1–11 and 5:12–21 is in order.

ROMANS 5:1-11

Romans 5:1–11 functions as an introduction to the argument in 5:1—8:39. The verbal marker "through our Lord Jesus Christ" brackets the pericope in 5:1, 11.[15] Thematically, 5:1–11 introduces the topics of suffering and love, which have not been explicitly mentioned before. These two topics are interwoven with the themes of perseverance and the hope of glory, as well as the work of the Spirit—all of which have only appeared infrequently in the letter so far. These interconnected themes will appear again in detail in 8:18–39.

The pericope is not unconnected with the previous section though. Romans 5:1–11 begins with a statement affirming the believers' right standing with God by πίστις (5:1), a notion that has been developed in 3:21—4:25. Terms like δικαιόω, αἷμα, σῴζω, and ὀργή in the current passage (5:1, 9, 10) link to the various themes in 1:18—4:25.[16] More specifically, 5:1–11 affirms the fact that believers' right standing with God is effected through the death of Christ, through which they will be saved from wrath (1:18; 2:5; 3:21–26; 5:9). It seems that 5:1–11 attempts to introduce new concepts without re-

---

14. These are, of course, only sketches of the narratives. That is, the above does not represent the narratives in every detail. Instead, they are frameworks that can be used as tools for our analysis of the text. There are, for example, multiple events in the narrative of the new humanity, which a simple linear schema cannot represent. For instance, dying with Christ seems to be a process, and there are events that may occur multiple times.

15. See above regarding the significance of this verbal marker in Rom 5–8.

16. The term αἷμα is used in Rom 3:15, 25; 5:9; σῴζω/σωτηρία in Rom 1:16; 5:9, 10; 8:24; δικαιόω in Rom 2:13; 3:4, 20, 24, 26, 28, 30; 4:2, 5; 5:1, 9; 6:7; 8:30, 33; and ὀργή in Rom 1:18; 2:5, 8; 3:5; 4:15; 5:9. See Appendix A for the distribution of these terms throughout the *whole* letter.

ducing the significance of these previously argued notions. In the following we will examine the subunits 5:1–5 and 5:6–11 in turn, and discuss the relationships between the evidently new themes of hope of glory in afflictions, peace with God and reconciliation.

Romans 5:1–5

Paul says in 5:1 that, having been justified by πίστις, we have peace with God.[17] It appears, then, that the "peace with God" in 5:1 is based on one's right standing with God. But, at the same time, this anticipates the notion of reconciliation in 5:10, 11.[18] Reconciliation means making peace;[19] believers are no longer God's enemies because they have been reconciled to him (5:10).[20] For an audience living with hardship and injustice in Rome, the term εἰρήνη most likely carries some connotations of safety and security, which comes with a peaceful relationship with God. This fits in well with the Hebraic notion of *shalom*, which refers to the wellbeing and wholeness that a community has when it enjoys a good relationship with YHWH, who has in turn blessed them with peaceful relationships within the community and with their neighboring communities.[21]

17. I take the indicative reading of ἔχω in Rom 5:1, instead of the subjunctive. See Dunn, *Romans 1–8*, 245, for a discussion regarding the textual evidence. See also Byrne, *Romans*, 169, and most English Bible translations.

18. Haacker, *Theology*, 45–53, makes a good point in saying that "the proclamation of peace with God aims at the root of this universal chaos and promises not only to establish an adequate relationship between human beings and their creator but also to heal all sorts of private relationships and social systems from destructive tendencies" (45). We will discuss the cosmic dimension of sin and death in our analysis, which has implications for social relationships in the world.

19. Cf. Dunn, *Romans 1–8*, 246–47. Dunn places emphasis on the Hebraic notion of peace. For recent discussions on reconciliation, see Kim, "Origin," 360–84; Martin, "Reconciliation," 43–48; Constantineanu, *Social Significance*; Porter, "Paul's Concept of Reconciliation," 131–52. The survey of Pauline scholarship by Constantineanu is most helpful (25–39). See also our discussion of Rom 5:10–11.

20. The conflict and enmity between humans and their Creator were mentioned in Rom 1:21–25, 28–32. In Greco-Roman literature the language of reconciliation, as Jewett, *Romans*, 365, says, is drawn from "the spheres of conflict, in which warring groups, quarrelling citizens, or alienated marital partners make peace."

21. The Jewish eschatological expectation of Ezekiel's covenant of peace (*shalom*) in Ezek 37:24–27 provides a helpful background here. The covenant of *shalom* is associated with the promise of a Davidic king (37:24) who will restore Israel's relationship with YHWH (37:28). It is also associated with the outpouring of the Spirit promised in Ezek 37:11–14, which coincides with the mention of the Spirit in Rom 5:5. We will discuss this further in chapter 4.

Paul often uses the term θλῖψις (5:3) to refer to the distress brought about by external circumstances.[22] The audience has already heard the term in 2:9, where it was used to refer to punitive suffering because of God's judgment on evil deeds (see 2:6). But here the punitive connotation is not applicable, because the audience has already been justified, as was explicitly stated at the beginning of the pericope (5:1; cf. 5:9).[23] That is, believers need not take action (e.g., offering sacrifice) to escape wrath or keep themselves from punishment because they already have a right standing before God. Instead, the mention of δοκιμή and ὑπομονή in 5:3–4 points to the educative value of suffering,[24] which is well known in both Greco-Roman and Jewish thought.[25] Suffering disciplines believers so that they learn to endure hardship, which in turn builds character.

But the fact that ἐλπίς brackets the string of items (namely, θλῖψις, ὑπομονή, and δοκιμή) in 5:2–5, and is placed at the end of the series of ἡ δέ constructions, highlights the significance of hope in the argument. Paul goes beyond the educative value of suffering and asserts that it will ultimately produce hope (5:4–5). Indeed, believers boast (καυχάομαι) in their afflictions (5:3), as well as in the hope of the glory of God (5:2).[26] This points to the Jewish eschatological hope where God's people are called to trust faithfully in YHWH's eventual deliverance and vindication in their suffering.[27] As mentioned, the apocalyptic visions in Dan 7–12, for example, speak of hope in God's deliverance through a divine human agent, and 2 Macc 7:38–39 outlines the hope of martyrs that their faithful trust in their

22. See Dunn, *Romans 1–8*, 249; BAGD 362. Romans 5:2–5 does not tell us what type of affliction is in view. We have to wait till 8:17–39 for more information.

23. In fact, the first word in Rom 5:1 is δικαιόω.

24. The term ὑπομονή denotes a strong sense of steadfastness in enduring severe suffering. See, e.g., Byrne, *Romans*, 170.

25. This is noted by commentators—see e.g., Dunn, *Romans 1–8*, 251; Jewett, *Romans*, 354; esp. Talbert, *Romans*, 134–8. See chapter 2 for the educative value of suffering according to ancient worldviews.

26. The term καυχάομαι is used in a positive and commendable sense here. It is unlikely to carry the common individualistic usage used among the Greeks. Rather, it probably refers to a sense of corporate pride (of a community or nation), as indicated by the first person plural use of the verb. Cf. Dunn, *Romans 1–8*, 249. Importantly, the prevailing social attitude in Greco-Roman culture is that boasting is oriented toward the glorification of oneself or one's family/social group. As mentioned in Chapter 2, social conventions in Rome were characterized by honor and shame. This means that the boasting in affliction in Rom 5:3 is strikingly counter-cultural. See Jewett, *Romans*, 351–53; cf. Judge, "Conflict of Educational Aims," 38–39.

27. See discussion in Chapter 2. For similar observations, see Byrne, *Romans*, 170; Dunn, *Romans 1–8*, 255–7. For a concise description of apocalyptic hope, see Beker, *Suffering*, 54–56.

God in their suffering will bring an end to the wrath of the Almighty. The eschatological nature of this hope is highlighted by the use of καιρός in Rom 5:6 and νῦν in 5:9 and 11,[28] as well as by the fact that the term θλῖψις is used in apocalyptic literature and the early church to refer to the tribulations of the last days (Dan 12:1 LXX; Matt 24:9, 21, 29; Mark 13:19, 24). From the vantage point of Paul and his audience, however, the visitation of God has already taken place through the death and resurrection of Christ (5:6, 9–10). Christ's suffering and death has ushered in the new age already.[29] But the affliction of his followers still abounds. As they live in this already-not-yet reality, they boast in their hope of glory, awaiting God's final deliverance and glorification.[30]

The subunit 5:1–5 finishes by saying that hope does not put us to shame (καταισχύνω), because God's love has been poured out into believers' hearts through the Spirit. In a society where honor and shame underpin social interactions, shame is about the loss or lack of public honor.[31] The mention of "shame" in 5:5, then, is set in contrast to the "glory" in 5:2–3. For the slaves, the war-captives and their descendants in the audience, their social condition would be viewed as a cause for shame within the intensely hierarchical society of Rome.[32] The same applied to the economically poor among them, which were not few in number. What did 5:5 mean to them? It seems that the use of καταισχύνει here is best understood in terms of the usage in the Psalms and the Third Isaianic Servant Song, where the sufferers claim that they are not ashamed of their suffering because their hope is in the eventual vindication of YHWH (e.g., Pss 21:6; 24:2, 3, 20; 70:1 LXX; Isa 50:7).[33] The mention of the Spirit probably reinforces the eschatological nature of hope in the subunit, for the outpouring of the Spirit in Israel's Scripture is often associated with God's visitation and deliverance (e.g., Isa 66:1; Ezek 37:11–14).[34] It is this sure hope of God's deliverance that reas-

28. See Dunn, *Romans 1–8*, 254–5, 257. Moo, *Romans*, 307, provides a good discussion on the eschatological use of καιρός in Rom 5:6.

29. Note that Christ's death is mentioned in Rom 5:6, 9, where καιρός and νῦν appear.

30. Since "glory" is a main theme in Rom 8:14–17, 18–39, I will defer the discussion of the term δόξα until later.

31. Cf. Malina and Pilch, *Social-Science Commentary*, 370; deSilva, "Honor and Shame," 518–19.

32. According to Malina and Pilch, *Social-Science Commentary*, 397, "slavery was always bad, since it thoroughly deprived a person of honor." This is despite the fact that a slave may have a relatively higher status if his/her master has a high social standing.

33. See Dunn, *Romans 1–8*, 252. Note the use of the "shame" language (καταισχύνω, αἰσχύνω, αἰσχύνη, αἰσχρῶς, αἰσχρός) in these passages.

34. This will become clearer when we study Rom 8:1–13.

sured the audience that they would not be put to shame. The ἀγάπη τοῦ θεοῦ and the διὰ πνεύματος point to the experiential nature of suffering. Suffering and shame are existential realities that require the comfort of God's love and the power of the Spirit to overcome. Romans 5:5 does not say more about the relationships between God's love, hope in suffering, and the Spirit, and we have to wait till Rom 8 for further information.

Romans 5:6–11

The γάρ in 5:6, 7, 10, and the rhetorical marker "through our Lord Jesus Christ" in 5:11 indicate that 5:6–11 provides a series of explanations for the preceding subunit, which culminates in v. 11. The significance of Christ's death can hardly be missed here, since ἀποθνῄσκω appears four times and θάνατος once, and they are all used in relation to the death of Christ.[35] The καιρόν in 5:6 and the νῦν in 5:9 specifically refer to the death of Christ,[36] which indicates that his death is seen as the turning point in history that inaugurated the new age.[37] Romans 5:1–5 has just spoken of the eschatological hope of glory in the midst of suffering. Now v. 6 starts to explain how that is possible by saying that Christ died for the godless/impious (ὑπὲρ ἀσεβῶν) at the right (eschatological) moment (καιρός).[38] Verses 7–9 clarify 5:6 and connect back to 5:5 by stating that God has shown his love for us by means of Christ's dying for sinners.[39] Verse 9 says that believers have been justified by the blood of Christ. The use of δικαιωθέντες echoes the believers' right standing with God in 5:1, which indicates to the audience again that their hardship is not the result of God's punishment according to the principle of retributive justice.

Romans 5:10–11 draws the pericope (5:1–11) to a conclusion. Verse 10 says that believers were reconciled to God through the death of his Son. The "Son" in v. 10 is the first reference to Christ as the Son of God since 1:9. This may catch the attention of the audience, as Christ's being God's Son was prominently announced in the opening statement of the letter (1:3–4). The next mention will take place in 8:3, and we will revisit the significance of *the Son's* death in Chapter 4.[40] The three occurrences of καταλλάσσω/

---

35. In Rom 5:7, the verb ἀποθνῄσκω does not directly refer to Christ, but is used to describe the type of death he died.

36. Romans 5:9 speaks of the blood of Christ, which is about his death.

37. Cf. Moo, *Romans*, 307; Dunn, *Romans 1–8*, 254–5; Byrne, *Romans*, 171.

38. Note that v. 6 has the first γάρ in Rom 5:6–11.

39. Note the second γάρ in Rom 5:6–11 in v. 7.

40. One of the things that emerges through the mention of the Son in Rom 5:10; 8:3,

καταλλαγή in these two verses, the γάρ in 5:10,[41] the "peace with God" in 5:1, and the "through our Lord Jesus Christ" in both 5:1 and 11, suggest that reconciliation is the main theme that the pericope drives towards.[42] As already mentioned, "peace with God" in 5:1 anticipated this theme because reconciliation is about making peace. Since the basic usage of the terms ἐχθρός, καταλλάσσω, and καταλλαγή in 5:10–11 denotes the hostility and reconciliation between states, parties, or individuals,[43] the reconciliation in 5:10–11 would refer to the end of conflicts and enmity between God and humans.[44] Their relationship has been restored through the death of Christ (5:9, 10).[45]

29, 32 is the notion that Christ suffered as a righteous sufferer, which probably stems from the Isaianic tradition of the suffering Servant. Cf. Kleinknecht, *Der leidende Gerechtfertigte*, 348–9, who sees in Rom 5:5, 10 an example of God not abandoning those who are his own, which is in accordance with the tradition of the suffering righteous. We will discuss this in the forthcoming exegesis, when the audience has heard more about the work of the Son in Rom 8.

41. So also the γάρ in 5:6, 7.

42. See Constantineanu, *Social Significance*, 25–42, for a thorough survey of recent scholarship on reconciliation in Paul. I find Constantineanu's analysis of Rom 5–8 refreshing (99–143). Constantineanu argues that reconciliation in Romans has a strong social dimension. To argue for his case, Constantineanu draws our attention to the "we" and "us" pronouns in Rom 5–8, as well as Paul's call for the Christ-community to participate in the story of Christ (140–3). The social dimension of reconciliation is in line with what we will discuss later regarding the all-encompassing cosmic nature of God's salvific purposes.

43. See Dunn, *Romans 1–8*, 259; Jewett, *Romans*, 365 nn. 206, 207.

44. This in turn has profound implications for the intra-communal relationships of the house churches in Rome, an issue that Rom 12–15 will deal with. Regarding the ἐχθροί in Rom 5:10 (and its relationship with reconciliation in 5:10–11), there is a debate among scholars. Kruse, *Romans*, 236–7, Moo, *Romans*, 312, and Cranfield, *Romans I–VIII*, 267, understand that Paul speaks of a mutual enmity between God and humanity. Jewett, *Romans*, 364, however, disagrees. Jewett says that the notion that God is hostile towards humans is absent in Rom 5, and that the "atoning death of Christ did not aim at assuaging divine wrath." I doubt whether there is enough information here in Rom 5:9–10 to resolve the matter, but in my view the hostility is ultimately between God and anti-God powers, namely, the cosmic forces of sin and death (note 5:12–14). Scholars have rightly noted the cosmic dimension of reconciliation. (See, e.g., Byrne, *Romans*, 172.) That is, Christ has become the Lord of the cosmos by his death, and has set believers free from the evil forces that have previously controlled them. Since they are no longer under the reign of sin through Christ's death, they have been reconciled to God. (See discussion below.) Martin, "Reconciliation," 43–48, has made a good case for the cosmic dimension of reconciliation through a close examination of 2 Cor 5:18–21 and Col 1:15–20.

45. Commentators debate whether there is a distinction between reconciliation and justification in Romans. Given the fact that in Rom 5:9 and 10 both justification and reconciliation are said to effect salvation, there seems to be an overlap between them.

The final statement in 5:1–11 is highly significant, for it seems to link reconciliation with the hope of glory in suffering. It says, "we boast in God through our Lord Jesus Christ, through whom we have now received reconciliation" (5:11b). The threefold usage of καυχάομαι in 5:1–11 has a rhetorical effect that prompts the audience to see the connections between the messages in 5:2, 3 and 11. The notion of boasting in God can be found in the LXX in Deut 10:21; Jer 9:23–24; Pss 5:12; 105:47, where Israel declares their confidence in God's character and mighty deeds.[46] Within the context of 5:10–11, the "boasting" is about the believers' confident claim and trust that God will ensure that "we will be saved" (σωθησόμεθα), by means of the reconciliation that has been accomplished by the Son's death.[47] The audience has just heard that they can boast in their afflictions (5:3) and the hope of glory (5:2). Putting the boastings in 5:2, 3, 11 together, the boast in the hope of glory is based on God's future consummation of the audience's salvation, in which believers will be glorified at the resurrection (cf. 8:18–30).

Boasting in present afflictions, then, is based on the fact that there is a hope of glory despite current shameful suffering. This is, of course, remarkably counter-cultural given the contemporary social attitude towards honor and shame.[48] All of these boastings are, of course, grounded in the reconciliation that has been accomplished by Christ's death *and* life—that is, his resurrection. If there is enmity between them and God, there cannot be hope in suffering. But as it stands, they have peace with God and hence can boast in their hope.[49] Lastly, the highly christological character of the pericope is highlighted by the repeated reference to Christ and the fact that the phrase "through Jesus Christ our Lord" is associated with the "peace with God" and "reconciliation" in the first and last verses of the pericope.

Hence I think a *sharp* distinction between the two is not necessary (cf. Dunn, *Romans 1–8*, 259–60). What is likely is that Paul uses the notion of reconciliation to incorporate the renewal of cosmos (2 Cor 5:19–20), and hence the shift of vocabulary to reconciliation just before his mention of Adam in 5:12–21 makes sense.

46. Byrne, *Romans*, 169. Interestingly, Ps 5:12 LXX has the three words ἀγαπάω, ἐλπίζω, and καυχάομαι, which reflect the themes in Rom 5:1–11. There is a clear Jewish notion of boasting in God because God's people can put their hope in him.

47. Note that the participle is used (καυχώμενοι) in Rom 5:11.

48. Cf. Jewett, *Romans*, 366–67.

49. Kleinknecht, *Der leidende Gerechtfertigte*, 324–25, says that Rom 5:1–11, together with 8:18–39; 15:1–6, gives a certain outline of how Paul understands suffering, although suffering is not Paul's primary interest in these passages. From the perspective of an audience familiar with affliction and pain, however, suffering is definitely an important topic.

Hope in suffering that is based on reconciliation is entirely dependent on Christ's work.[50]

In short, Rom 5:1–11 speaks of the character-forming and educative value of (non-retributive) suffering, as well as a clear emphasis on eschatological hope in suffering. This hope is about the future realization of salvation that is based on the believers' reconciliation and peace with God, which, in turn, has been accomplished through the death of Christ.

ROMANS 5:12–21

Rhetorically there are two reasons why Rom 5:12–21 is significant for an audience living with hardship.[51] First, it immediately follows a pericope (5:1–11) that has the first explicit mention of suffering, so the audience would still be on alert for any further exposition of suffering. Second, the διὰ τοῦτο in 5:12 guides the audience to the important role of 5:12–21. Commentators often translate the διὰ τοῦτο in 5:12 simply as "therefore."[52] But I find the analyses of Matera and Moo helpful. In his detailed study, Moo says that the transition at 5:12 should be understood as something like: *In order to accomplish* what was said in 5:1–11, the measures in 5:12–21 need to be taken.[53] Matera says that 5:11–21 is not so much the result of the argument in 5:1–11, but the *ground* for it.[54] In other words, the material in 5:21–21 will show how reconciliation is accomplished, which is in turn the basis for the believers' hope in suffering.[55]

---

50. I note that καταλλαγή is referenced in Rom 11:15, where it says that God reconciles the cosmos through the rejection of Israel. This means that God's project of reconciliation is about the gathering of a Jewish-Gentile community, but it may also imply the renewal of the cosmos. Space limitation does not allow us to study Rom 11:15 specifically, but our exegesis of Rom 8:18–23 will show that God will indeed renew the whole creation.

51. The theological importance of this passage is recognized by scholars. See Moo, *Romans*, 314; Matera, *Romans*, 136.

52. See Kruse, *Romans*, 240; Wright, *Romans*, 523, regarding the inadequacy of the translation "therefore" for διὰ τοῦτο.

53. Moo, *Romans*, 317–18. Moo has surveyed the usage of διὰ τοῦτο throughout the NT and the LXX. While my understanding of the phrase is the same as Moo's, we differ on the interpretation of Rom 5 on certain other matters (despite Moo's fine exposition of Paul's letter overall).

54. Matera, *Romans*, 136.

55. The third reason Rom 5:12–21 is important for the audience is that it links to Rom 8:18–30 in many ways, which is a major pericope about suffering. See discussion in Chapter 6.

We will examine Rom 5:12–21 by tracing its arguments in the three subunits, namely, 5:12–14, 5:15–17, and 5:18–21. The first subunit (5:12–14) begins by stating that sin entered the cosmos (κόσμος) through one person (Adam), and through sin death—so that death spread to all humans because all sinned.[56] The exact mechanism through which death spread is debatable.[57] But what is clear is that sin and death are forces in the cosmos that reign over Adamic humanity (5:14, 17, 21).[58] As we will discuss later, sin and death are the ultimate cosmic powers behind human suffering. These forces were at work even before Moses (5:13–14). Verse 14 says that Adam is the τύπος of the one (Christ) to come, which sets the stage for the multiple comparisons between Adam and Christ in 5:15–21.[59]

There are sharp contrasts in the second subunit (5:15–17). While *the many* (οἱ πολλοί) died through Adam's trespass (παράπτωμα), God's grace (χάρις) and the gift (δωρεά) of Christ abounded unto *the many* (5:15). That is, death's dominion in the world caused the death of humankind. But God's

56. Here I follow the majority view to translate ἐφ' ᾧ in Rom 5:12 as "because" (NRSV, NIV, NKJ, ESV), but I think the suggestion of Matera, *Romans*, 136, is possible. That is, ἐφ' ᾧ means "with the result that" (cf. CEB). The other possible option is used by Jewett, *Romans*, 376–77, who translates the half-sentence as "death spread to all so that all sinned in the sphere of the world." See the comprehensive discussion by Byrne, *Romans*, 183.

57. Most major commentaries cover this debate. See, for instance, Kruse, *Romans*, 242–4.

58. That sin and death in Rom 5:12–21 are cosmic powers is recognized by many scholars. See Dunn, *Romans 1–8*, 272; Jewett, *Romans*, 374; Matera, *Romans*, 136–37; Moo, *Romans*, 319; Adams, *Constructing*, 171–74; Gaventa, "Neither," 270. Cf. Heil, *Romans*, 62, who says that sin and death are "evil apocalyptic powers," whose origin traces back to the primeval Adam. de Boer, *Defeat of Death*, 179, puts it this way, "The crucified and resurrected Christ has unmasked the fact that death is a cosmic and cosmological power, embracing all human beings and reigning over them. Sin, death's partner and cause, is to be understood in the same way." Or in the words of Black, "Pauline Perspectives," 421, death is "a personal and cosmic power who demonically reigns in this age (5:14, 17; cf. 1 Cor 15:25–26) . . . we see Paul employing the mythological language of apocalyptic to characterize a biological and ethical phenomenon as a cosmological tyrant." One may not totally agree with de Boer and Black, but their view that sin and death are depicted as cosmic power in Rom 5 is valid, in my opinion.

59. There has been much debate about Paul's view of the origin of sin in Rom 5:12–21. (See the discussions by Matera, *Romans*, 126–27, 143–44; Dunn, *Romans 1–8*, 291.) My sense is that, for Paul, Adam's disobedience opened the door for the entry of sin and death into the world as cosmic powers (largely in light of 5:12, 18, 19). Because of these forces all humans after Adam have sinned. Likewise, death is experienced by all humanity because death reigns in the cosmos. It is important to note that human beings are not personally accountable for Adam's trespass. The crucial and ongoing roles of sin and death (as cosmic powers) in influencing humans must also be noted. As our discussion on Gen 1–3 will suggest, anti-God forces have been against God since the beginning.

grace has been made available to humanity, effectively forming a new human race. The judgment (κρίμα) on Adam's sin and trespass brought condemnation (κατάκριμα). But God's free gift has brought δικαίωμα (5:16).[60]
Death reigns through Adam's trespass. But much greater is God's abundant
grace and gift of δικαιοσύνη that reign in life through Jesus Christ (5:17). The
items in these contrasts highlight the destructive powers of sin and death
through Adam, as well as the superiority of God's grace through Christ,
which effectively undoes the effects of Adam's trespass.

The ἄρα οὖν at the beginning of the third subunit (5:18–21) probably
signals that the superiority of God's grace has been sufficiently established.[61]
But the contrasts continue in 5:18–21 with repeated comparisons between
Adam and Christ.[62] These contrasts, again, point to the reversal of the effects
of Adam's disobedience, and the formation of a new humanity out of Adam's
humanity. While Adam's trespass has brought about condemnation to *all*,
Christ's one δικαίωμα leads to δικαίωσις of life for *all* (5:18). Just as through
Adam's disobedience (παρακοή) *the many* were made sinners, through
Christ's obedience (ὑπακοή) *the many* will be made righteous (5:19).[63] In
other words, Adam's disobedience—working through the cosmic power of
sin—has made humankind sinners. But through Christ's obedience, God
has created a new humanity that has been made righteous. Verse 20 says
that sin increased after the law came, which indicates that sin continued to
reign after Moses. But grace abounded all the more. The concluding verse of
the pericope (5:21) states that sin reigned in death, but grace reigns through
δικαιοσύνη to eternal life "through Jesus Christ our Lord."

After hearing Paul's argument about the hope of glory in suffering in
5:1–11, the audience would be wondering what he has to say in 5:12–21.
The compact statements in 5:12–21 speak of the reign of sin and death in
the cosmos, as well as the disobedience and death of Adam and humankind.
The pericope also says that, by overcoming sin's power through Christ and
hence undoing the effects of Adam's disobedience, God has created a new
humanity. As the διὰ τοῦτο at the beginning of v. 12, 5:12–21 sets out *the
ground for* 5:1–11. This means that God's creation of a new humanity explains how God has accomplished the saving act of reconciling humanity.

---

60. For a discussion on the meaning of δικαίωμα in Rom 5:16, see Kirk, "Reconsidering Dikaiōma," 787–92, who argues that the term should be read in light of the
Adam-Christ antithesis in its context and it does not refer to a "justifying verdict" but
"the just action that allows the judge to justify the defendant" (790).

61. Byrne, *Romans*, 185.

62. Note that Christ is mentioned at the end of each of the subunits in 5:12–14 and
5:15–17. But in 5:18–21, the Adam-Christ pair appears in 5:18, 19 and 21.

63. The ὑπακοή in Rom 5:19 most likely refers to Christ's death (Phil 2:8).

Since the audience has been reconciled to God, they can boast in God and be confident of the hope of glory despite their hardships. Once again, the thoroughly christological character of the passage must be noted. The surpassing grace of God has been given through Christ and is the basis for hope in suffering.

The logic of this argument presupposes that there is a link between suffering and the cosmic powers of sin and death, for otherwise their defeat does not bring hope to those who suffer. But does such a link exist? The answer, I think, hinges on the ancient worldview that cosmic forces and suffering are inseparably interconnected. To this our analysis turns now.

THE COSMIC DIMENSION OF SUFFERING

Romans 5:12–21 seems to provide a primordial historical background for the existence of evil in the cosmos (κόσμος in 5:12, 13), and hence explains why there is suffering. Sin and death are portrayed in 5:12–21 as personified cosmic forces that entered the cosmos. That is, they are powers that hold sway over the world and cause chaos.[64] I suggest that, given the symbolic universe shared between Paul and his audience, it is the powers of sin and death that are the ultimate reasons behind the chaos and distress in the cosmos. If these powers are defeated, then the problem of suffering is also dealt with and the notion of hope in suffering is viable. Here a survey of ancient cosmology is in order.

We have already pointed out in Chapter 2 that, according to the worldviews of the ancients, there is a cosmic dimension to suffering. There is a causal relationship between sacrilege and suffering. Both Homer and Seneca think that all things can be traced back to the gods, and many offer prayers to deities for healing and safety.[65] But more fundamentally, the cosmos, in its original form, is thought to be characterized by order, unity, and beauty, and is free from age and sickness.[66] Importantly, as Adams says, "human beings are microcosmically related to the κόσμος, not only individually but also collectively. There is a natural connection between the order of the κόσμος and the order of human *society*."[67] The extension of this is

---

64. The term ἁμαρτία in Romans predominantly refers to a (cosmic) power—see discussion above. For instance, in 3:9 humans are said to be under sin. The plural usages in 4:7; 7:5; 11:27 refer to sinful actions, and it seems that the vast majority of the occurrences of the singular refers to sin as a power. See Jervis, *Heart of the Gospel*, 79n5.

65. *Il.* 24.468–551; *Nat.* 3.12; Croy, *Endurance*, 134, 147.

66. See Adams, *Constructing*, 64–66, for a good summary.

67. Ibid., 66–67. The microcosmic and macrocosmic relations between humans and the cosmos can be found in Plato's *Timaeus*. For instance, the shape of the universe and

that social, economic, religious, and political relations are defined by cosmic order.[68] There is a "microcosmic-macrocosmic scheme" where the world is ordered by the gods through the agency of the ruler of the state.[69] The ruler, in turn, orders institutions of kinship and the entire society according to divine arrangements.[70]

This cosmology suggests that there is peace and prosperity when such cosmic order is in place. Conversely, suffering and pain are inevitable when the cosmos is in chaos. With this in mind, the pericope in Rom 5:12–21 provides the ultimate reason for the audience's suffering. There are cosmic powers, namely, sin and death, that introduce evil and chaos into the cosmos. The social, economic and political power relationships are not orderly, but infiltrated by anti-God powers.[71] Viewing the reign of sin and death in this way, suffering is not only about the consequence of the sins of individuals, but also the outworking of disorderly and destructive socioeconomic and political systems and structures.[72]

---

the human head and limbs are interconnected (44d–47e).

68. Sociologists are aware of the interconnections between society, religion and the cosmos. For instance, Berger, *Sacred Canopy*, 3–28, begins his chapter on "Religion and World-Construction" by stating that every human society is "an enterprise of world-building," and religion "occupies a distinctive place in this enterprise" (3). The relevance of this way of understanding ancient societies to the earliest Christ-communities can be found in, for example, Esler, *First Christians*, 6–12.

69. The interconnectedness between the gods, the rulers of the state, and, hence, politics can be seen, for example, in the establishment of ruler cults in the Hellenistic period, when the politics of the cities are no longer independent. Since Alexander the Great, Hellenistic rulers were granted divine honors. See Aune, "Religion, Greco-Roman," 923. Cf. Ferguson, *Backgrounds*, 185–97.

70. I have borrowed the phrase "microcosmic-macrocosmic scheme" from Adams, *Constructing*, 70–71, who says,

> The microcosmic-macrocosmic scheme validates the whole institutional order of a society from the state to the institutions of kinship and family. It provides the ultimate sanction for the political and power structure of the day. The governing authority is conceived of as an agent of the gods; to obey the ruler is to be in "a right relationship with the world of the gods." And it integrates the institutions of kinship into the life of the universe . . . Moreover, "cosmization" grounds the stratification of a society in ultimate reality. Socio-economic divisions, social positions and the distribution of power are concerned as part of the rational ordering of the world, the very divine arrangement of things.

71. Gaventa, "Neither," 271–2, alludes to these anti-God powers in her brief discussions on peace, reconciliation, and the slavery language in Rom 5.

72. As Jewett, *Romans*, 374–75, recognizes. In his study on the language of "powers" in the NT, Wink, *Naming*, 99–100, concludes that "powers" are "both heavenly and earthly, divine and human, spiritual and political, invisible and structural," and that they are "also both good and evil" (emphasis original). While some details of Wink's

The Jewish worldview offers further insights. We have already mentioned in Chapter 2 the interconnectedness between cosmic forces, socio-political powers and suffering from a Jewish perspective. From this general point we must now turn to how Adam specifically appears in Jewish literature.[73]

The author of Wisdom of Solomon speaks of the life and attitude of the godless (1:16–24; see the ἀσεβεῖς in 1:18), and that God created (ἔκτισεν) human beings for incorruption, and made them in his own image (εἰκών), but through the envy of the devil (διάβολος) death entered the cosmos (κόσμος) (2:23–24). Here it seems that the wickedness of Adam and the godless are ultimately caused by the entry of death into the cosmos through the devil's scheme. In 2 Bar. 48:42–43, Adam is seen as responsible for his descendants' corruption, and it is said that Eve listened to the serpent.[74] Although the first humans were responsible for the corruption of humanity, the serpent appears to be the ultimate cause. In 4 Ezra, the angel Uriel says to Ezra that evil, sorrow, toil, dangers, and hardships are the manifestation of God's judgment of Adam's transgression (7:11–12),[75] and that this present age is full of sadness and infirmities, and the righteous are not exempt from the plight (4:26–28; 7:17–18).[76] It seems that, according to 4 Ezra, Adam's disobedience opened the door for suffering and pain to enter the world. But

---

findings are debatable, his observation here is correct. This is in line with the observation on Paul's letters by Tamez, *Amnesty of Grace*, 107, who says

> [T]he power of structural sin that enslaved all humanity and, in a dialectical relationship, the impossibility for human beings to do justice, because it had been imprisoned in injustice. As a consequence, in the social, economic, and political reality to which Paul was responding, the poor and weak were completely abandoned to the perverted logic of injustice.

73. There are various voices in Jewish literature about Adam, Eve, and the entry of evil into the world. Scholars often wonder which Jewish tradition Paul follows, or even whether Adam is always viewed negatively. See Dunn, *Romans 1–8*, 272–3; Enns, *Evolution*, 99–103. Our interest, however, is not so much about identifying which tradition Paul follows, but a plausible reconstruction of the general worldview concerning Adam, cosmic forces, and suffering.

74. *Second Baruch* 48:42–43 says, "And I answered and said: O Adam, what did you do to all who were born after you? And what will be said of the first Eve who obeyed the serpent, so that this whole multitude is going to corruption? . . . " Also it is said that because of Adam's sin, death was decreed to be against humans (2 Bar. 23:4). (All quotations of the Pseudepigrapha of the OT are from Charlesworth, *Pseudepigrapha*.)

75. *Fourth Ezra* 7:11–12 says, "For I made the world for their sake, and when Adam transgressed my statutes, what had been made was judged. And so the entrances [or 'the ways'] of this world were made narrow and sorrowful and toilsome; they are few and evil, full of dangers and involved in great hardships."

76. Cf. Smith, *Seven Explanations*, 142–3. Smith also refers to 2 Bar. 23:4; 48:42–43; 56:6 to illustrate a similar point.

4 Ezra continues to say that the righteous will be vindicated at the final judgment (7:75–101). Several things are clear from these diverse perspectives on evil and suffering in primordial history. Cosmic forces—labeled or named as the serpent/devil—were at play when Adam/Eve sinned. These cosmic powers seem to be the ultimate cause of death, pain, and toil in the cosmos, although human disobedience has a part to play too. The outworking of evil or death is wide-ranging, including all manner of toils and dangers. But at the same time, there is a sense of apocalyptic hope of the vindication of the righteous.[77]

This survey of ancient cosmology provides a plausible framework within which the audience would associate their present afflictions with the entry of sin and death into the cosmos in Rom 5:12–21.[78] There is chaos in the world. This chaos was introduced from the time of Adam in primordial history.[79] Sin and death as cosmic powers are the ultimate forces behind socioeconomic hardship and religio-political injustice, because cosmic powers and suffering are interdependent.[80] In other words, sin and death would sound like metonyms that stand for the cosmic powers behind all chaos, pain, and dehumanizing interpersonal behavior and socio-political

---

77. I do not assume here that *4 Ezra* and *2 Baruch* are evoked in Rom 5:12–21, although that may be the case. What I propose here is that there is evidence in Jewish literature that cosmic forces are behind the chaos in the world, and that the evidence includes references to Adam. For our purposes, these Jewish texts are different from, for example, Genesis, in that they are not included in the LXX or the Hebrew Scripture. We will soon examine the possible evocation of Genesis in Rom 5–8 on the ground that in Romans Paul speaks of the important role of Israel's Scripture in his argument. It is the explicit mention of Scripture in the letter that makes Genesis (as opposed to *4 Ezra* and *2 Baruch*) particularly important for our inquiry.

78. Adams, *Constructing*, 172, arrives at a similar cosmological-apocalyptic character of Rom 5:12–21, although his interest is in cosmology rather than suffering.

79. Again, one must note that cosmic forces—represented by the serpent—were already at play when Adam disobeyed. (Having said that, I am not proposing that the cosmic figure "serpent" represents *the* origin of suffering. The "origin of evil" is outside the scope of our study.)

80. Likewise, Jervis, *Heart of the Gospel*, 79–83, thinks that sin is a power, and both believers and non-believers suffer because of this power. For Jervis,

> Sin is the root of human suffering—whether the darkness of physical death or the destructive experiences of our existence. . . . The power of sin trades in instruments of decay, which include disease and natural disasters. Turmoils of illness and natural calamities are evidence of sin's capacity and concern to destroy God's good creation (79–80).

> For Paul, both believers and nonbelievers undergo and trade in the troubles that attend human existence: being victims and perpetrators of social violence, experiencing the terror and loss of the decay that shrouds creation, facing physical death . . . (83).

systems in the world, but there is hope because the eschatological visitation of God has taken place through the death and resurrection of Christ. Since Christ has overcome the dominion of sin and death, the ultimate cause of suffering has also been dealt with. This explains why the audience can boast in the hope of glory in the midst of affliction and pain.[81]

It should be noted, however, that there is still suffering even though sin and death have been defeated. The letter makes no claim that Jesus' triumph over sin and death argued in 5:12–21 means that suffering has been removed from the cosmos. The effects of Adam's trespass have been undone in terms of the removal of condemnation, but not suffering. The explicit mention of suffering and evil in 5:2–5; 8:17, 18–39; 12:9–21 makes it clear that hardship and affliction are still the experience for those who are in Christ. In fact, the list of (mostly) cosmic powers in 8:38–39 shows that evil forces are active. The audience, however, has to wait till 8:14–39 before Paul explains how they can have hope in suffering.

ADAM'S STORY IN GENESIS AND THE STORY OF ADAMIC HUMANITY IN ROMANS

Given the emphasis on Israel's Scripture in the opening paragraph (1:1–4) and the frequent citations of Scripture throughout the letter, it is surprising that there is only one explicit citation of Scripture in Rom 5–8 (see citation in 8:36).[82] The reason seems to be that the core underlying theme of the section is the creation of a new humanity out of Adam's humanity, which has a message that transcends ethnicity and is relevant to all human beings. This in turn means that Scriptures concerning, for example, Israel and its faithfulness (which are frequently cited in Rom 9–11), are not directly relevant.[83] This does not, however, mean that there are no scriptural allusions in Rom 5–8. I will propose a number of them in the course of our study. In the meantime, let us consider the relevance of Gen 1–3.

---

81. This understanding of sin, death, and suffering indicates that reconciliation has a cosmic dimension. It also means that the categories of physical and spiritual death that Kruse, *Romans*, 242–3, uses cannot sufficiently explain the nature of death in Rom 5:12–13.

82. Rom 7:7 probably refers to Exod 20:17/Deut 5:21. But the use of Ps 44:22 in Rom 8:36 is the only explicit citation (with the citation formula καθὼς γέγραπται) in 5:1—8:39.

83. Rom 7:7 is the only exception. Ultimately we do not know the reason for the sparsity of direct scriptural citation in Rom 5–8. We can only speculate.

Not uncommonly commentators mention Genesis in their interpretation of Rom 5:12–21,[84] but few, if any, link the echo of Genesis to suffering. In my view, Gen 1–3 plays a highly significant role in Rom 5–8 and the audience's understanding of suffering. A sustained argument for this will be provided at the end of the exegesis on Rom 8:18–30. However, in preparation for the forthcoming analysis of Rom 8, I will provide a summary of that argument here, with a focus on 5:12–21 in particular.

There are two interrelated reasons for the high likelihood that Gen 1–3 is evoked in Rom 5–8.[85] First, these passages share similar vocabulary and themes. Notably Rom 5:12–21 and Gen 1–3 share the rare use of the term Ἀδαμ. It appears frequently in Gen 1–3 but infrequently in the rest of the LXX.[86] Likewise, it is seldom used in the New Testament, and only three times within the undisputed Pauline corpus (outside Romans).[87] But it appears twice in Rom 5:14 together with multiple occurrences of εἷς in 5:12–21 that also refer to Adam. One should also note the use of κόσμος in Rom 5:12, 13 and the concentrated occurrences of κτίσις in 8:19, 20, 21, 22, 39. These provide a thematic link to the creation account in Genesis.[88] Given the fact that they are located in the early and closing pericopes in Rom 5–8, they also provide an overarching thematic connection between this distinctive section of the letter and Gen 1–3.

84. Hultgren, *Romans*, 221–6; Wright, *Romans*, 525–26; Byrne, *Romans*, 176.

85. See Adams, *Constructing*, 152–5, for a comprehensive survey of the echoes to Gen 1–3 in Rom 1–11, especially in Rom 5–8. My survey will differ significantly in terms of its emphasis and structure. At this point I also need to mention that Gen 1–3 does not consist of one single story in the Hebrew Bible. Genesis 1:1—2:4a and 2:4b—3:24 present different accounts of primordial history. Our focus, however, is how the text of Rom 5–8 might have evoked the Genesis accounts. We have little access to the audience's view of the sources and traditions in the Hebrew Bible. Also, it was likely that they used the LXX, and we cannot be certain about their view regarding how Gen 1–3 LXX was interpreted.

86. But the rare reference to Adam does not mean that Genesis was unknown to the audience. See Lincicum, "Genesis in Paul," 93–94, esp. nn. 2, 3, for a good discussion on the important place of Genesis and the Torah in Judaism and early Christianity. (I am grateful to Dr. Lincicum for sending me an early version of his essay, so that I could work on it before its publication.)

87. The term Ἀδαμ appears twenty-six times in Genesis (chapters 1–5 only), and seven times in the rest of the LXX (scattered over Deuteronomy, Chronicles, Tobit, Sirach). Compared with, say, Δαυίδ, Ἀδαμ appears infrequently. It also appears eight times in the NT outside Romans.

88. Interestingly κτίσις is not found in Gen 1–3. But note that κόσμος is used in Gen 2:1; and οὐρανός occurs sixteen times in Gen 1–3 and γῆ forty-six times. Also, κτίσις, κτίζω, and κόσμος appear in Rom 1:20, 25.

According to Gen 3:16, 17, pain (λύπη) and groaning (στεναγμός) entered human life after the first humans had disobeyed God.[89] (See table below for selected verses in Genesis relevant to our discussion here.) Likewise, as discussed above, Rom 5:12–13 implies that evil and suffering entered the cosmos at Adam's disobedience. Interestingly, the frequent language of groaning, suffering, and affliction in Rom 8:17, 18, 22, 23, 26, 35 occurs near the term κτίσις in 8:19, 20, 21, 22, 39.[90] In fact, the text says that humans groan (στενάζω) just as creation groans. Thus, both Genesis and Romans see a shared experience and destiny between humans and creation. The terms ἔχθρα and ἐχθρός are found in Gen 3:15 and Rom 5:10; 8:7. In Genesis, there is enmity between the offspring of Eve and that of the serpent. In Rom 5:10; 8:7 there is enmity between God and humankind. While the types of enmity are different, their shared outcome is chaos and disharmony in relationships. Genesis 3:16 speaks of Adam's domination over Eve,[91] which symbolizes the end of harmonious and peaceful relationship between humans. This could be interpreted to be part of the "death" that they were warned of before they disobeyed (2:17; 3:3, 4).[92] In Rom 5–8, the language of death abounds, and is a matter that our discussion has covered—and will continue to cover.[93] Significantly, our discussion above has suggested that the entry of death into the world as a cosmic power in 5:12–13 most probably implies the entry of suffering as well. This resembles the account in Gen 3, in that disobedience leads to death and suffering.

Selected verses in Genesis LXX (See further discussions in Chapters 5 and 6)
ᾗ δ᾽ ἂν ἡμέρᾳ φάγητε ἀπ᾽ αὐτοῦ [from the tree], θανάτῳ ἀποθανεῖσθε. (2:17b)
[The woman tells the snake that God said:] εἶπεν ὁ θεός Οὐ φάγεσθε ἀπ᾽ αὐτοῦ οὐδὲ μὴ ἅψησθε αὐτοῦ, ἵνα μὴ ἀποθάνητε. 4 καὶ εἶπεν ὁ ὄφις τῇ γυναικί Οὐ θανάτῳ ἀποθανεῖσθε· (3:3b–4)

---

89. In Gen 3:16, 17, λύπη appears three times and στεναγμός once.

90. See Appendix A for a list of affliction-related words in Rom 8:17–35.

91. See the use of κυριεύω in Gen 3:16.

92. In Gen 2:17; 3:3, 4, ἀποθνήσκω and θάνατος occur five times.

93. See Appendix A for statistics of the use of "death" in Romans.

15 καὶ ἔχθραν θήσω ἀνὰ μέσον σου καὶ ἀνὰ μέσον τῆς γυναικὸς καὶ ἀνὰ μέσον τοῦ σπέρματός σου καὶ ἀνὰ μέσον τοῦ σπέρματος αὐτῆς· αὐτός σου τηρήσει κεφαλήν, καὶ σὺ τηρήσεις αὐτοῦ πτέρναν. (3:15)

16 καὶ τῇ γυναικὶ εἶπεν Πληθύνων πληθυνῶ τὰς λύπας σου καὶ τὸν στεναγμόν σου, ἐν λύπαις τέξῃ τέκνα· καὶ πρὸς τὸν ἄνδρα σου ἡ ἀποστροφή σου, καὶ αὐτός σου κυριεύσει. 17 τῷ δὲ Αδαμ εἶπεν Ὅτι ἤκουσας τῆς φωνῆς τῆς γυναικός σου καὶ ἔφαγες ἀπὸ τοῦ ξύλου, οὗ ἐνετειλάμην σοι τούτου μόνου μὴ φαγεῖν ἀπ' αὐτοῦ, ἐπικατάρατος ἡ γῆ ἐν τοῖς ἔργοις σου· ἐν λύπαις φάγῃ αὐτὴν πάσας τὰς ἡμέρας τῆς ζωῆς σου· (3:16–17)

The second reason why Gen 1–3 may be evoked when reading Romans is the similarities between the underlying narrative of Adamic humanity in the letter and that of Adam in Genesis. In Genesis, God warned Adam that disobedience would lead to "death," but Adam disobeyed nonetheless. The "death" took place in terms of several curses, with the result that humans would suffer from pain and toil. In Romans, Adam disobeyed and indeed all sinned. Therefore, sin and death reign in the cosmos, with the result that Adamic humanity will suffer from pain and hardship—for sin and death are the ultimate powers behind the suffering of Adamic humanity. The story of Adam and his descendants in Genesis is similar to that of Adamic humanity in Romans in two aspects. First, in both cases Adam/humanity is the main character. Second, both storylines start with disobedience, which then leads to "death" and suffering.

Paul has, however, reworked the Genesis narrative in his letter. The curses in Genesis have been reworked in terms of the dominion of the cosmic forces of sin and death. The enmity between humanity and the serpent's offspring has been reworked as enmity between God and Adamic humanity (although arguably that is implicit in the Genesis account). But the basic structures of the narrative in Genesis and Romans are similar enough for the former to be evoked within the symbolic universe of the audience.

The evocation of Genesis has immense implications for our understanding of Rom 8:18–23, which will be discussed in detail in Chapter 6. For now, two matters need to be mentioned in relation to 5:1–21. First, Gen 1–3 affirms the all-encompassing effects of Adam's disobedience on the suffering of humanity, which in turn resonates with the daily experience of an audience suffering from socioeconomic injustice. Our discussion of Rom 5:12–21 has suggested that the introduction of evil into the cosmos at Adam's trespass is the ultimate reason why Adamic humanity suffers. Genesis affirms this. "Death" is the result of Adam's trespass. The resulting curses are often considered by scholars to cause far-reaching social and physical pain and suffering. This is especially the case when Gen 1–3 is read from the perspective of an agrarian society, where close-knit family units form the basis of society.[94] The "shame" of nakedness shows a breakdown of relationships among humans and between humans and God (3:7, 11). The thorns and thistles point to a sense of futility in life and work. There is physical pain in childbirth and toil in working in the fields. The husband's domination over his wife is symbolic of systemic human oppression, and Gen 3:19 speaks of the physical death that humanity would experience. In Fretheim's words,

> [O]ne could speak of humiliation, domination and subordination, conflict, suffering, and struggle. The sentences touch every aspect of human life: marriage and sexuality; birth and death; work and food; human and non-human. In all these areas, one could speak of death encroaching on life.[95]

In light of all this, Genesis provides Paul's audience with valuable additional resources to explain the ultimate reason for their affliction.

Second, Gen 1–3 affirms the cosmic nature of humanity's struggles, which can only be overcome by God's power. The deceit of the serpent in Gen 3 symbolizes an anti-God power that seeks to destroy humanity, even before Adam rebelled.[96] The enmity between the offspring of the serpent and that of the woman is symbolic of ongoing evils in the cosmos.[97] It should be noted that these pictures of cosmic struggles would not be new to the ancients, for the fact that human suffering and cosmic battles are interconnected can be found in ancient documents and artifacts. For example, in ancient Near Eastern art and literature, labor pains are considered as the worst possible experience for both humans and gods. Sometimes demons

---

94. Here I am indebted to the insights of Pahl, *Beginning*, 38–39.

95. Fretheim, *Genesis*, 362–63. Cf. Wenham, *Genesis 1–15*, 90; Brueggemann, *Genesis*, 49–50. Fretheim also says, "Every conceivable relationship has been disrupted: among the animals; between an animal and humans; between the ground and humans; between human beings and God; between an animal and God; within the individual self (e.g., shame) . . . Disharmony reigns supreme."

96. Cf. Gow, "Fall," 289; McKeown, *Genesis*, 34–35; Gunkel, *Genesis*, 15–16. Fretheim, *Genesis*, 359–60, rightly points out that the association of the serpent with the "devil" is not found in Genesis but in later Jewish literature (e.g., Wis 2:24). But of course the audience of Romans reads Genesis with a worldview during or after that later period. See also Isa 27:1, where Leviathan is depicted as a serpent and an anti-God power.

97. Cf. Gow, "Fall," 289; Wenham, *Genesis 1–15*, 80. Brueggemann, *Genesis*, 43–44, rightly says that the purpose of Gen 2–3 is not about the *origin* of evil (e.g., did evil originate from God or the devil?). My point here is that the primordial account in Genesis assists the audience to make greater sense of Rom 5:12–21, in that Adam opened the door for evil (the personified sin and death) to reign in the cosmos.

are associated with the pain of childbirth,[98] and in *Enuma Elish* "the entire purpose for creating people was to relieve the gods of their toil."[99] Also the serpent is associated with the gods and symbolizes death, chaos, infertility, and struggles in life.[100] With this in mind, Rom 5:12–21 implies that God has overcome the powers of sin and death through the death and resurrection of Christ. The cosmic battle has been won,[101] and humanity's enmity with God has ceased because of the reconciliation that has been accomplished through Christ.

In short, the primordial stories in Genesis help to explain how the dominion of sin and death leads to affliction and pain in the world. At the same time, Romans declares through Christ's death the powers of sin and death have been overcome, and hence God has defeated evil and a new humanity has been created. In other words, through Christ's obedience God has restored humanity so that they may have peace with him. Indeed, since the formation of a new humanity is based on the surpassing grace of God in Christ (5:15–21), this new humanity enjoys a newness of life that surpasses that of Adam. What we find here is God's project of reconciling humankind to him, and it gives hope to an audience living with suffering. In view of this, God's purpose includes not only the restoration of humanity, but also, as the forthcoming chapters will show, the *transformation* of this new humanity so that they may display God's glory through Christ and the Spirit. In other words, what we see in Rom 5–8 is God's program of restoring and transforming humanity.

98. For example, Lamashtu is a fearsome Babylonian/Assyrian divinity known for trying to touch a pregnant woman's stomach to kill her unborn baby. See the amulet shown and described in Saggs, *Babylonians*, 150. See also Burkert, *Orientalizing Revolution*, 82–84; Walton, et al., *Bible Background*, 32–33.

99. Walton, et al., *Bible Background*, 33. See, for instance, in Book 6 of *Enuma Elish*, it is said that when Ea the wise created humankind, the toils of the gods are imposed on humanity so that the gods may be released from them.

100. Walton, et al., *Bible Background*, 31–32. In Greco-Roman literature, Virgil's *Georgics* talks about Jupiter causing humans to cultivate the land, and adding venom to the black snakes (1.118–149).

101. In Israel's Scripture, Israelites look to their God for his triumph over evil forces. In Ps 89:9–13, for example, YHWH is portrayed as the Creator God who crushes Rahab, the sea monster of chaos. See also, Broyles, *Psalms*, 356; Goldingay, *Psalms 42–89*, 672–4. In addition, Ps 93:3–4 probably points to YHWH's "tamping the primordial waters into submission." Enns, *Evolution*, 63.

THE PAX ROMANA AND PEACE IN ROMANS

Scholars often note the possible relationship between the εἰρήνη in Rom 5:1 and the *pax Romana* within the Roman Empire.[102] "*Pax Romana*" was a term used to designate Roman political rule in the two and a half centuries from the time of Caesar Augustus, in which the Empire enjoyed comparative peace, freedom from civil wars, material prosperity, and political stability. In his *Res Gestae*, Augustus made clear his desire to be known as the creator and architect of sustained peace.[103] According to Georgi, the "*Pax Romana* was based on the theory of an eternal Rome, whose foremost representatives are divine and immortal . . . "[104] In the well-known *Ara Pacis Augustae*, we find images of goddesses who served as guarantors of the Golden Age that Augustus was seen to have restored.[105] Roman coins showed the goddess of peace, *Pax*, trampling on the weapons of subdued enemies, and the goddess of conquest, *Victoria*, treading upon the globe itself.[106] These served as Roman propaganda to demonstrate the favor of the gods to the Empire. As is often pointed out, Augustan "peace" was amply developed by the poets Ovid, Virgil, and Tibullus.[107] In the early years of his reign, Nero was also portrayed as a ruler of peace. The poet Calpurnius Siculus ascribed the accomplishment of peace to Nero, and said that he was one of the gods.[108] Similarly, Lucanus, a nephew of Seneca, spoke of the deification of Nero and the associated end of all wars.[109] In short, most likely Paul's audience in Rome would be familiar with the notion of the *pax Romana*, where Caesar achieved peace and prosperity in the Empire with the blessings of the gods.

---

102. See Matera, *Romans*, 131; Wright, *Romans*, 515–16.

103. According to *Res Gesta* 25, 26, Augustus restored peace from pirates and that all Italy swore allegiance to him voluntarily. He won the battle at Atium and the provinces of Gaul, Spain, Africa, Sicily and Sardinia swore allegiance to him. It also says that Augustus brought peace to Gaul, Spain, Germany and the Alps, and that he sailed ships on the ocean from the mouth of the Rhine to the borders of the Cimbri, as well as Ethiopia and parts of Arabia. Cf. Bowley, "Pax Romana," 772; Horsley, *Paul and Empire*, 18.

104. Georgi, "God Turned Upside Down," 154n171.

105. Jewett, "Corruption," 28–29.

106. Elliott, "Anti-Imperial Message," 169.

107. See Haacker, *Theology*, 117; Virgil's 4th *Eclogue*, and Ovid's *Fast.* 1.709–22. Virgil's 4th *Eclogue* speaks of what happened at the birth of the boy, Octavian, namely, the return of Saturn's reign and the rise of a golden race. It also says that this boy is a child of the gods, an offspring of Jove (Jupiter) and with his father's virtues he will reign over a world of peace. *Fasti* 1.709–22 is about the dedication of the *Ara Pacis Augustae*.

108. Haacker, *Theology*, 118. See especially Calpurnius Siculus, *Eclogues* 4.142–6.

109. Haacker, *Theology*, 118. See Marcus Annaeus Lucanus, *Pharsalia* 1.44–62, which talks about the close of the temple of the "god of war" at Caesar's coming.

The message of the *pax Romana* was reinforced by the prevailing cosmology. As mentioned, this cosmology provided the microcosmic-macrocosmic scheme that validated the entire institutional order of a society and its associated kinship and family relations, and hence it provided the ultimate sanction for the political and power structure of the day.[110] Thus, Rome legitimized its rule and the entire hierarchical social system by claiming that the gods were on Caesar's side.

But for the prisoners-of-war and their descendants in Rome, and for the slaves who suffered from exploitation and abuse, the alleged favor of the gods would evoke a sense of biting irony. Their recent experience of the brutality of the Julio-Claudian dynasty would very likely make them suspicious of Nero's propaganda of peace in his early reign.[111] For the believing Jews expelled from Rome at Claudius's Edict, the *pax Romana* would not make sense in terms of their personal experience and in light of their Scripture, where *shalom* comes from YHWH. In more general terms, since the *pax Romana* promised prosperity, safety, and security, many in Paul's audience would feel alienated, given their socioeconomic hardship.

Here, Rom 5:1–21 provides an alternative narrative of peace for the audience. The reality is that chaos exists in the cosmos. The cause of the chaos is sin and death, which works through human sin in general, and Caesar's brutality and socio-political institutions in particular, to harm human beings.[112] But through Christ evil has been defeated and the audience

110. Adams, *Constructing*, 70–71.

111. See Elliott and Reasoner, *Documents*, 146–62, for a helpful discussion of Nero in the so-called "good years" of his early reign.

112. In recent scholarship there are those who read Paul's letters as anti-imperial texts. These scholars have helped us to see the subversive elements of Pauline texts in the context of the Roman Empire. But the caution of Barclay, *Pauline Churches*, 363–87, is important. Barclay says that "Paul's gospel is subversive of Roman imperial claims precisely by not opposing them within their own terms, but by reducing Rome's agency and historical significance to just one more entity in a much greater drama . . . Paul, more radically, reframes reality, including political reality, mapping the world in ways that reduce the claims of the imperial cult and of the Roman empire to comparative insignificance" (386). Barclay's conclusion, especially his view of the power of sin and anti-God power, is noteworthy for our purposes:

> We thus reach the paradoxical conclusion that Paul's theology is political precisely in rendering the Roman empire theologically insignificant . . . [Paul's remapping of the cosmos] includes the "political," but so fuses and enmeshes it with other realities within a broader frame of analysis that it refuses to interpret Rome (or any other empire) on its own terms. Since the Lordship of Christ is destined to operate in every sphere of existence (Phil 2.11), the Pauline gospel penetrates every dimension of life, including what we label "political," but it declines to separate the political from the personal, the state-power of Sin from the interpersonal-power of Sin. In

can enjoy true peace and reconciliation with God, so that they may have hope in their suffering.

SUMMARY

In sum, Rom 5–8 is a distinct section in the letter, which is most important to our inquiry because of its explicit references to suffering. The section speaks of the formation of a new humanity out of Adamic humanity. There seem to be three underlying narratives at play, all with life and/or death in their trajectory. They are: the Adamic narrative, the story of God's Son, and the story of the new humanity in Christ. Romans 5:1–21 speaks of the educative value of suffering, but goes beyond that and asserts the hope of glory in affliction. This hope is like the eschatological hope found in the apocalyptic literature and the martyrdom theology in Jewish writings, where God's people are to persevere faithfully in their present suffering under the oppression of the socio-political powers, in anticipation of God's deliverance in the age to come. The basis for this hope is that reconciliation with God has been accomplished through the death and resurrection of God's Son. For God's work of reconciliation to be accomplished, he has overturned the effects of Adam's trespass by defeating sin and death, which, in turn, is the ultimate cause lying behind human suffering. In other words, Rom 5 speaks of God's project of delivering humanity from the powers of sin and death through the death and life of Christ.

Genesis 1–3 is evoked through the vocabulary and themes of Rom 5–8. The wide-ranging effects of Adam's disobedience in Gen 1–3 resonate with the many forms of suffering that the audience experiences in Rome. The cosmic dimension of Adam's story in Genesis also affirms that the cosmic forces of sin and death are the ultimate powers behind the pain and systemic injustice in the world. These suggest to the audience that humanity needs God's gracious intervention to restore and transform the cosmos. The

---

an age when "politics-as-state-power" is proving increasingly inadequate as a framework in which to analyse the corruption, oppression and degradation of our world, it may in fact be a theological advantage that Paul does not oppose Rome *as Rome*, but opposes anti-God powers wherever and however they manifest themselves on the human stage (387; emphasis original).

In view of this, when I mention "alternative narrative," I do not mean an anti-imperial stance on Paul's part. Rather, the story embedded in Romans is, for the audience in Rome, an alternative narrative to that of the Roman Empire. The story found in the text of Romans can also be an alternative narrative to that of other empires, systems, or any specific manifestation of anti-God powers.

peace with God in Rom 5:1–11 is set in sharp contrast to the *pax Romana*. The reality of the audience's daily suffering can be explained by the presence of sin and death in the cosmos (and not by Roman propaganda of peace). Paul's message of reconciliation and God's triumph over evil powers provide an alternative narrative that offers true peace and hope in suffering.

LOOKING FORWARD

Before we move on to Rom 8, a short discussion of 6:1—7:25 is in order. There is no explicit mention of suffering at all in Rom 6 and 7, and hence there is no pointer for the audience to detect any material that is specifically relevant to their daily experience of suffering. What would be of interest to them, however, is how God's project of transforming a new humanity works. With the rhetorical questions in 6:1, 15, the pericope in Rom 6:1–23 deals with the issues regarding whether believers should live in sin. Paul argues that God's grace does not mean freedom to sin. Based on Christ's obedience (5:19), the Christ-community has been set free to live a life of obedience and right living (6:12, 16, 17).[113] They are exhorted to identify with Christ's death and resurrection, so that, by dying and living with Christ, they will not live under the dominion of sin (6:1–14). Instead of being slaves to sin, they should become slaves to δικαιοσύνη (6:15–23). Rather than presenting their "members" (μέλη in 6:13, 19) to sin, they are to present them to δικαιοσύνη. In doing so, they participate in God's restorative program and have life eternal (cf. 6:23).

Guided by the rhetorical questions in 7:1, 7, 14, Rom 7:1–25 exonerates the law and makes sin the culprit for human disobedience. Regardless of the identity of the "I," the ultimate reason for the predicament of the "I" is the enslaving power of sin over humanity. It seems that the rhetorical effect of the pericope serves to invite the audience to identify with the struggles of the "I." Life under the cosmic power of sin means that the "members" are caught up in the battle between wanting to obey God's law and being captive to sin (7:22, 23). The result is the cry: Who will rescue the wretched "I" from the body of death (7:24)? Given our discussion of Rom 5, the underlying issue here is how God's program of transforming humanity works. That is, how can the dominion of sin and death be overcome in believers' daily lives? What are the resources available to them to be free from sin's mastery? Romans 8:1–13 will deal with these issues with its elaboration on the role

---

113. See the language of ὑπακούω/ὑπακοή in Rom 6:12, 16, 17. Also, as is often noted, the δικαιοσύνη in Rom 6:13, 16, 18, 19, 20 carries ethical overtones (which include not only personal morality but also relational righteousness-justice).

of the eschatological Spirit, and at the same time introduce the subsequent pericopes concerning suffering (8:14–17, 18–30, 31–39). The task of the next chapter is to study this pericope.

4

The Work of Christ and the Eschatological Spirit

INTRODUCTION

Paul says in Rom 5:5 that the believers' hope in their suffering does not shame them, for God's love is poured out through the Spirit. Paul does not elaborate on the details of the role of the Spirit until Rom 8, where the Spirit undoubtedly plays a major part.[1] Our primary goal here is to determine how 8:1–13 prepares the way for the audience to read 8:14–17 and 8:18–30. These latter passages are obviously important to our inquiry, because 8:14–17 contains the first reference to suffering since 5:2–5, and 8:18–30 consists of an extended discussion of hope and suffering.

We will first outline the argument in 8:1–13 and suggest that several elements of the text may draw the audience's attention because of their links to Rom 5. Then we will take a close look at 8:1–4, which contains important information for our analysis of 8:14–39. A brief examination of 8:5–13 will follow. After that we will investigate the possible references to Israel's Scripture in Rom 8:1–13, and how it might have enriched the audience's understanding of suffering.

We will find that Rom 8:1–13 is a continuation of the argument in 5:1–21 regarding the formation of a new humanity that has been reconciled to God. Our analysis will show that God has accomplished this work by

---

1. The Spirit is mentioned in Rom 7:6, but 7:7–23 does not elaborate on that at all.

sending his own Son to identify with humanity, suffer and die for them. We will find that the Spirit plays an important role in defeating the powers of sin and death, and hence effects the reversal of the consequences of Adam's disobedience. The Spirit also engages in God's project of transforming humanity by empowering believers to live a life that pleases God.

This work of the Spirit has been foretold in Jer 30–33 and Ezek 34–37, which speak of God's upcoming outpouring of the Spirit and the restoration of Israel from exile. But the audience will find that the message of these Scriptures has to be reinterpreted. For a start, God's eschatological blessings have now been universalized for the entire humanity, not only ethnic Israel. Then, unlike the peace and prosperity that the prophets anticipated, the audience still experiences affliction and pain, despite the coming of Christ and the bestowal of the Spirit. This is the matter that 8:14–39 will deal with.

OVERVIEW OF ROMANS 8:1-13

Our exegesis will begin with a brief overview of Rom 8:1–13, before embarking on a verse-by-verse analysis. With the emphatic ἄρα νῦν, 8:1 signals that it is bringing the section 5:1—8:39 to a conclusion.[2] There are several verbal and thematic links between 8:1–13 and 5:1–21 that take the audience back to the argument started in Rom 5. The Spirit is mentioned in 5:5, and the term πνεῦμα appears in 8:1–13 frequently.[3] The language of "condemnation" (κατάκριμα, κατακρίνω) appears in 5:16, 18 and prominently in 8:1, 3 (but nowhere else in the letter). Christ as God's Son was mentioned in 5:9 for the first time since 1:3, 4, 9.[4] Now it is mentioned again in 8:3, and with significant theological implications (see below). Sin and death are the cosmic powers that dominate Adamic humanity according to 5:12–21, and in 8:1–2 the Spirit is said to have set people free from the law of sin and death.[5] These verbal and thematic links between 5:1–21 and 8:1–13 serve to prompt the audience to realize that the latter is a continuation of the argument from Rom 5.

At the same time, Rom 8:1–13 is closely connected with 7:7–25. The term νόμος occurs frequently from 7:7 to 8:7. Indeed, 8:1–13 answers the cry

2. See, for example, Moo, *Romans*, 472. Paul commonly uses the "ἄρα οὖν" in Romans, but the combination ἄρα νῦν only appears once in the NT. It is likely that Paul intends the orator to pause between chapters 7 and 8. See also the discussion by Dunn, *Romans 1–8*, 415.

3. As mentioned, between Rom 5:5 and 8:2, πνεῦμα only appears once (in 7:6).

4. See Appendix A for the places where υἱός and τέκνον appear in Romans.

5. The term ζωή appears in Rom 5 and 8. But I note that it also occurs throughout Rom 6–7, and so it does not constitute a special link between Rom 5 and 8.

of the "I" in 7:24, "Who will rescue me from this body of death?" The "I" is not able to do what the law requires because of its inability to overcome the sin in the flesh (7:7–23). But 8:1–13 says that the Spirit of life empowers believers to fulfill the law's requirement (see especially 8:3–4). Romans 8:1–13 also harks back to 7:1–6, where Paul speaks of the enslaving work of sin, the flesh, and the law. But 7:6 hints that the Spirit would come to the rescue, and 8:1, 2 speak of the Spirit's work to deliver believers from sin and death. Verses 3–4 elaborate on that by referring to the atoning death of God's Son. The flow of the argument from 8:3–4 to 5–11, as it will be argued, is clearly heading from Christ's work towards the ongoing work of the Spirit in empowering the Christ-community to live a life that fulfills the just decree of the law. Then vv. 12–13 exhort believers to live by the Spirit, which in turn prepares the way for the statement in 8:14—that those who are led by the Spirit are children of God.

ROMANS 8:1-4

Romans 8:1–2

The term κατάκριμα and the notion of freedom from sin and death in 8:1–2 recall the key message of 5:12–21, that is, God has created a new humanity out of Adamic humanity. Romans 5:12–21 speaks of the condemnation of humanity and the release from the dominion of sin and death through Christ. In 8:1–2 Paul says that there is no condemnation for those who are in Christ and that the Spirit has effected freedom from the reign of sin and death.[6] Given the ancient cosmological worldview of the audience, the intervention of the Spirit might well be viewed as God's cosmic power over sin

---

6. There is a debate about the meaning of the two uses of the νόμος in Rom 8:2. For example, Dunn, *Romans 1–8*, 416–19, insists that the Torah is denoted in both instances. Cf. Dunn, *Theology of Paul*, 576–77; Wright, *Romans*, 576–77. Others, such as, Fee, *Empowering*, 522–23; Matera, *Romans*, 190–91; Heil, *Romans*, 80; Kruse, *Romans*, 324; Hultgren, *Romans*, 297, think that the term is used as a rhetorical device to mean "principle," "rule," or "norm." If it is the latter (my preferred view), then the Spirit's work is clearly about setting free people from the powers of sin and death. In the case of the former, I take that sin and death are cosmic forces that work through God's good law (7:16) to enslave humans. But through the Spirit the eschatological people can now fulfill the just requirement of the Torah, and hence the Spirit sets them free from the reign of sin and death (8:3–4). Cf. Dunn's argument. Interestingly, Bertone, *Law of the Spirit*, 216–25, suggests that "Paul intended νόμος to take on a double sense and function as *polysemy*," which, according to Bertone, means that some hearers would have understood that the Spirit has replaced the Mosaic Law and others would think that the role of the Spirit is continuous with that of the Law (225). At any rate, the Spirit has freed believers from the powers of sin and death.

and death. The fact that the Spirit is a cosmic power can be found in both Greco-Roman and Jewish thought. In Stoicism the spirit not only dwells within human beings,[7] but also pervades the whole cosmos and holds it together.[8] In Israel's Scripture the רוח is understood to be the power of God.[9] Indeed, the Spirit has the power to create and overcome (human and cosmic) adversities.[10] So, for example, Job 26:12–13 says that by God's power and understanding he stilled the sea and struck down Rahab (the sea-monster); and by his רוח the heavens are made fair and his hand pierced the fleeing serpent.[11] In view of these, it seems that the Spirit in Rom 8:1–2 may be understood as God's power to overcome the cosmic forces against him and to restore the disorderly cosmos to wholeness. Just as sin and death can be seen as anti-God powers, the Spirit's work can be understood to be God's triumph over evil forces by exercising his (cosmic) power.[12] As we noted previously, 5:12–21 is the ground for the reconciliation of believers in 5:1–11, which is the basis for the audience's hope. This means that the work of the Spirit and the audience's hope are interconnected. Interestingly, in 8:1 it is the Spirit "of life" (τῆς ζωῆς) that has set people free, and 5:10, 17, 18, 21 speak of the eternal ζωή and reconciliation of believer through the ζωή of Christ.[13] In light of these, the Spirit's work is an integral part of God's reconciliation with humanity and his program of rescuing Adamic humanity from death to life.

7. Levison, "Holy Spirit," 509. According to Konsmo, *Metaphors*, 4, in Hellenistic mysteries the spirit can also "come upon a special person." The spirit is also perceived to be a force that responds to incantations.

8. Alexander of Aphrodisias summarizes the view of Chrysippus and says, "he assumes that the whole material world is unified by a pneuma which wholly pervades it and by which the universe is made coherent and kept together" (*Mixt.* 216.14–17; cited by Levison, *Spirit*, 135). Cf. Konsmo, *Metaphors*, 6.

9. See Exod 15:8; 2 Sam 22:16; Isa 28:6; 30:28; 34:16. The Spirit in the OT is not only a power from God, but also power *of* God, as noted by Dunn, *Christology*, 133. See Fatehi, *Spirit's Relation*, 50, 51, 53, 54, for a detailed discussion on the Spirit being the power of God in the OT.

10. See, e.g., Pss 33:6; 104:30; Isa 30:28; 32:15. Cf. Fatehi, *Spirit's Relation*, 52.

11. And the Spirit of God has made humans and given them life (Job 33:4).

12. The Spirit, however, is not a "force" *per se*. There seems to be a trinitarian theology in Rom 8, as scholars point out. See, e.g., Fee, "Christology and Pneumatology," 230–34.

13. Cf. Johnson, *Reading*, 128.

Romans 8:3

The γάρ in Rom 8:3 indicates that it elaborates on the previous verses. Here we have the first appearance of the "Son" since 5:10.[14] In 5:10, it is said that the Son's death effected reconciliation and through his life believers will be saved. Indeed, Paul opens his letter by stating that the gospel is concerning the Son and his death and resurrection (1:3, 4, 9). Now in Rom 8:3 the πέμπω expressly informs the audience that the Son's work was a deliberate initiative on God's part.[15] The term "Son" will appear again in 8:29, 32, and, as we will see, it will play an important role in the life and identity of God's children (8:14, 16, 17, 19, 21). But what exactly did God send his own Son to do? The following two matters are particularly important for our inquiry.[16]

First, the Son participated in humanity. God sent his own Son ἐν ὁμοιώματι σαρκὸς ἁμαρτίας. The ὁμοίωμα implies that there are similarities and distinctions between Christ and the "flesh of sin."[17] Along with many scholars, I think 8:3 speaks of Christ's sharing of humanity in that he was truly human, but without sinning.[18] The cosmic power of sin would try to reign over him just as it would over Adamic humanity.[19] By implication, he was subject to suffering just as much as other humans, and indeed cosmic forces could work against him to cause harm and pain, just as much as the rest of humanity. In fact, his suffering and death would not have happened if evil powers were not at play.

Second, the Son died as an atoning sacrifice. There is much debate about the expression περὶ ἁμαρτίαν in Rom 8:3. It seems to me that the

14. We use the "Son" (capital "S") to refer to υἱός when the term is used to denote Christ being God's Son.

15. For a concise study of Jesus' divine sonship in Romans, see Hurtado, "Divine Sonship," 223–33. Hurtado concludes, "[Jesus] is 'the Son' in relation to God, as uniquely honored by God and unique agent of God."

16. It is beyond our scope to engage in a detailed discussion on the compact content of Rom 8:3–4.

17. Cf. Jewett, *Romans*, 484.

18. See, e.g., Fee, *Empowering*, 532–33; Wright, *Romans*, 578; Byrne, *Romans*, 236; Kruse, *Romans*, 326. Matera, *Romans*, 192, puts it quite well, "the Son entered the realm of sinful flesh—a realm determined by the cosmic powers of sin and death—as one totally human, but not as a sinner." For fuller discussions, see Gillman, "Another Look at Romans 8:3," 597–604 and Branick, "Sinful Flesh," 246–62. Branick argues that there is no distinction between Christ and sinful flesh. Wilckens, *Röm 6–11*, 125–26, comes close to this view, but maintains that Christ did not sin.

19. Incidentally, there is plenty of evidence in the Gospels that cosmic forces tried to work against Christ. Jesus' triumph over the devil/Satan in the wilderness (Matt 4:1–11; Mark 1:12–13; Luke 4:1–13) is a good demonstration of the early Christian belief that he was tested by cosmic power but overcame. See Boring, *Mark*, 47–48.

phrase carries the motif of the atoning sacrifice in Israel's Scripture.[20] The LXX frequently uses περὶ ἁμαρτίας as the translation for לחטאת or simply חטאת ("sin" or "sin-offering") in the MT (cf. Lev 5:6–10; Num 6:11, 16; 7:16–82; Ezek 42:13; 43:19, 21).[21] As Campbell says, the phrase is a "standard septuagintal locution for the sin offering."[22] The sin-offering motif recalls the imagery of the death of an animal without blemish sacrificed to God on behalf of the sinner/community so as to atone for their sin. This implies that God sent his own Son to die for sinners to atone for their sins.[23] In this act God κατέκρινεν τὴν ἁμαρτίαν ἐν τῇ σαρκί (8:3), which probably means passing judgment on "sin"—the real culprit of human predicament (7:7–13)—and breaking its grip on human life.[24] Thus, by virtue of the Son's atoning death, there is now no condemnation for those who are in Christ (8:1), and the condemnation on Adamic humanity has been dealt with (5:16, 18). This, in turn, is the basis for reconciliation in 5:1–11, and is the

---

20. Campbell, "Story of Jesus," 104, rightly says that the περὶ ἁμαρτίας carries a general sacrificial connotation (because of the usage in the LXX), but one must be careful in applying the sin-offering motif to Christ's death and the life of believers. In my view, we must be careful not read the later theories of atonement into the περὶ ἁμαρτίας here. We have to be guided by the text in Rom 8:1–13, which is about the defeat of sin and death (8:2) and the Spirit-empowered life pattern of believers (8:5–13). See Wright, *Paul*, 897–9, for a summary of the major theologies of atonement in relation to Rom 8:3. See also the discussion below.

21. Interestingly, one rare exception is found in Isa 53:10, where περὶ ἁμαρτίας translates אשם ("guilt-offering"). But nonetheless the cultic sense of sacrifice is present. And for those hearers of Paul's letter who are not so familiar with the Hebrew texts, περὶ ἁμαρτίας will likely be understood as sin-offering due to its frequent usage in Leviticus and Numbers. Περὶ ἁμαρτίας in Rom 8:3, then, probably carries a meaning that goes beyond a narrow sense of "deal with sin." Cf. Dunn, *Romans 1–8*, 422; Byrne, *Romans*, 243; Wright, *Climax*, 222; Witherington, *Romans*, 213–4; Wilckens, *Röm 6–11*, 126–28; Michel, *Römer*, 251. All of these scholars see that "sin offering" is in the background of Rom 8:3. For less sympathetic voices, see Cranfield, *Romans I-VIII*, 382; Giesen, "Befreiung des Gesetzes," 201–2. For Giesen, the best translation of περὶ is "because of," since the context of Rom 8:3 does not unequivocally refer to Christ as the sacrifice of atonement for sins.

22. Campbell, "Story of Jesus," 104.

23. Again, here the audience's concern would not be the same as those of the later doctrines of atonement. The death of Christ on the Roman cross was a historical event, and the sacrificial system in Israel was well known. It seems to me that the ancients would have no problems in accepting the metaphor, for it fittingly represents the effectiveness of Christ's death in breaking the powers of sin and death. See Marshall, *Beyond Retribution*, 59–69, who understands that Rom 3:25; 4:25 and 8:3 refer to "a sin offering" (63), but cautions that the sacrifices in ancient Israel "were made for a variety of purposes."

24. Cf. Byrne, *Romans*, 243; Wright, *Romans*, 578–79.

point made in 5:10. That is, believers were reconciled to God through the death of his Son.[25]

What God sent his own Son to do, then, is to participate in humanity and deal with sin as a sin-offering, so that the power of sin may be broken and reconciliation with God effected. Since believers' hope in their suffering is based on their reconciled relationship with God, the Son's identification with humanity and his atoning death is the ultimate reason for their hope. It should be noted that the Son's participation in humanity is crucial, for otherwise there would not be an atoning death or the breaking of the power of death. Also, as mentioned above, the return of the language of the "Son" may have drawn the attention of the audience. This will become even more significant as the Son/children/heir language continues in Rom 8:14–17, 23, 29, 32.

What the Son has done seems to be what the law is incapable of (ἀδύνατος)—dealing with sin, reconciliation, giving life and hope. But it appears that the law is also unable to enable right living—hence the experience of the wretched "I" in Rom 7. In Israel's Scripture, the sin-offering motif also implies that sinners (or the sinful community) have to participate in the cultic event by committing themselves to a total self-renewal and turning-away from sin, because they are the beneficiaries of the victim's death (that is, the sacrificial animal's death).[26] This fits into the demand for right living (by participating in Christ's death and resurrection) that was delineated in Rom 6:1–23.[27] It also seems to be the point of the rest of Paul's sentence in v. 4, which we will discuss in detail now.

Romans 8:4

Romans 8:4 provides a crucial link between the work of Christ in v. 3 and the work of the Spirit in the rest of chapter 8. It will be argued that the purpose (and result) of Christ's participation in humanity and his atoning sacrifice is that his followers may be able to live a Spirit-empowered life to fulfill the law.

---

25. The sin-offering motif also fits in well with the reference to Christ's blood in Rom 5:9, although the focus there is justification. Also, we need to note that the purpose of Christ's death is that believers may be able to live a Spirit-empowered life to fulfill the law. We will discuss this in our analysis of Rom 8:4.

26. Cf. Tannehill, *Shape of the Gospel*, 226.

27. This is an aspect of the cultic metaphor that fits into the context of Rom 8 quite well.

The audience hears that it is the δικαίωμα of the law that is fulfilled. The word δικαίωμα most likely refers to the just or righteous requirement demanded by the law (2:26), which is the usual LXX meaning of the word.[28] The ἵνα-clause signals that the purpose (and result) of Christ's atoning death is that the just requirement of the law may be fulfilled.[29] But in what sense is it fulfilled? At issue is whether the law's requirement is fulfilled through the work of Christ, or in terms of the life of believers through the work of the Spirit. That is, either (a) Rom 8:4 points backward to the work of Christ outlined in 8:3, which has satisfied the law's just requirement and consequently the followers of Christ are under no condemnation (8:1);[30] or (b) Rom 8:3 points forward to the Spirit-oriented righteous living on the part of believers described in 8:5–13, which meets the just demand of the law.[31] In my view, option (b) is preferred for the reasons below.

First, there has been a shift from the work of Christ to the work of the Spirit in the flow of argument in 5:1—8:39. Christ is mentioned frequently throughout the section, and the Spirit is only mentioned twice before Rom 8 (in 5:5; 7:6). Romans 8:2 picks up from 7:6 and speaks of the Spirit's role in setting the Christ-followers free from sin and death. The emphasis on the Spirit continues throughout the rest of the chapter.[32] Second, there seems to be a shift in emphasis from the work of Christ to that of the Spirit in the

28. Cf. Jewett, *Romans*, 485, Moo, *Romans*, 482, Morris, *Romans*, 303n19; Kruse, *Romans*, 328. The singular δικαίωμα probably refers to the Law of Moses as a unity. Both Byrne, *Romans*, 244, and Kruse, *Romans*, 328, reject the proposal by Ziesler, "Just Requirement," 79, that it refers to the tenth commandment. The term δικαίωμα occurs in a few places in the letter. The δικαίωμα in 1:32 is qualified with τοῦ θεοῦ, while in 8:4 it has τοῦ νόμου. I think in the latter case it is clear that the term refers to the just decree of the Torah, while the meaning of the term in the former is harder to determine. The term is also used in 5:16, and its usage there is also hard to determine. See the discussion by Kirk, "Dikaiōma," 787–92. In 5:18 the term most likely refers to the one righteous-just act of Jesus at his obedient death.

29. Sometimes in a ἵνα-clause it is hard to differentiate purpose and result, especially when the clause is used in relation to God's work. (Moo, *Romans*, 481 and Dunn, *Romans 1–8*, 423, seem to take it as a purpose clause. Matera, *Romans*, 192, and Jewett, *Romans*, 485, however, translate it as "so that.") As Wallace, *Greek Grammar*, 473–4, says, "the NT writers employ the language to reflect their theology: what God purposes is what happens and, consequently, ἵνα is used to express both the divine purpose and the result." Cf. John 3:16; Phil 2:9–11. Here in 8:4 the ἵνα-clause probably indicates both purpose and result. Cf. Wright, *Romans*, 580.

30. For example, Moo, *Romans*, 481–85, and Hultgren, *Romans*, 300, seem to hold this view.

31. See, for instance, Kruse, *Romans*, 329; Fee, *Empowering*, 534–36; cf. Bertone, *Spirit*, 241. Fee provides a good description of the issue and a good summary of the evidence supporting the two sides of the argument.

32. Fee, *Empowering*, 535–36.

immediate context of 8:4. The use of the ἵνα-clause in v. 4 indicates that shift.[33] God not only sent his Son to accomplish what the law could not do (8:3), he will also carry out the fulfillment of the law through his Spirit (8:4). Third, the language of "*walking* not according to the flesh but the Spirit" in 8:4 points to the fulfillment of the law in terms of the life pattern initiated by the Spirit, rather than a "forensic" fulfillment of the law as implied by option (a).[34] The verb "walk" (περιπατέω) is used in Rom to denote how the community should conduct themselves (e.g., 6:4; 13:13).[35] Fourth, the use of the word "fulfilled" (πληρωθῇ) rather than "kept," "obeyed," or "performed," suggests that the work of the Spirit in enabling right living is in view, rather than lifestyle lived out by human beings unaided by the divine Spirit.[36] This is another indication to the audience that the argument is moving forward to the Spirit-empowered life in 8:5–8. Fifth, the passive "fulfilled" does not necessarily mean that it is about what is done by Christ for his followers.[37] Instead, the passive verb probably refers to God's initiative—through his Spirit—to enable a righteous life pattern on the part of the Christ-community.[38]

What fulfills the just requirement of the law is, therefore, the Spirit-led life pattern of the Christ-community—those who walk not according to the flesh but the Spirit.[39] With this in mind, I will summarize our findings in 8:1–4 and suggest what their implications for the audience might be.

33. Fee, *Empowering*, 536.

34. See the discussion of Schreiner, *Romans*, 405.

35. See, e.g., Hultgren, *Romans*, 300; Kruse, *Romans*, 329. Note that the term περιπατέω and the notion of "walking by the Spirit" would echo words like πορεύομαι ("walk/go/travel") and הלך in Israel's Scripture (LXX and MT) and hence the notion of walking in the way of God/YHWH (e.g., Gen 5:24; 17:1; Isa 2:5; 33:15; Ezek 37:24; Mic 6:8).

36. Fee, *Empowering*, 536.

37. Those who prefer option (a) would probably argue that the passive voice indicates that the work of Christ and his perfect obedience is in view—hence Paul is not referring to what the believers do, but what has been done for them.

38. Note that the ἡμῖν is unlikely to be instrumental. If Paul had meant the instrumental use, he would have followed the passive verb with ὑπό with the genitive. See Fee, *Empowering*, 536n191. Note that those who reject (b) in favor of (a) above would likely argue that the imperfect obedience of the law by the followers of Christ does not satisfy the just requirement demanded by the law. Instead, it is the perfect obedience of Christ that has met the law's just requirement. See Moo, *Romans*, 483. However, Paul is probably referring to the godly behavior that the Spirit can lead the Christ-community to achieve rather than perfect obedience. It is the Spirit-led conduct that fulfills the law's requirement.

39. The Spirit-empowered life pattern is not automatic, as our discussion of Rom 8:12–13 will show.

Summary and Implications

In sum, the ἄρα νῦν in Rom 8:1 signals that the chapter concludes the whole section in 5:1—8:39. Verses 1-2 say that those who are in Christ are not under condemnation, and the Spirit of life has set them free from the law of sin and death. The intertextual links to 5:12-21 suggest that the work of the Spirit in Christ is an integral part of God's work in overturning the effects of Adam's disobedience. Rom 8:3-4 elaborates on this and says that God sent his own Son to participate in humanity and become a sin-offering, with the purpose that those who are in Christ may live a Spirit-empowered life that fulfills the just requirement of the law. This answers the question posed by the "I" in 7:24. That is, it is the work of Christ and the Spirit that can rescue people from the body of death. Romans 8:1-4 also picks up the argument from 7:1-6, where it says that believers have died to the law and now live in the newness of the Spirit. Those who are in Christ are empowered by the Spirit to fulfill the law, not be enslaved by it.

Recalling the letter's argument that started at the beginning of 5:1—8:39, God's work of reconciliation is the basis for the believers' hope in their affliction. This is in turn dependent upon God's purpose of restoring and transforming Adamic humanity through Christ. Hence, Rom 8:1-4, with its opening ἄρα νῦν and intertextual links to 5:1-21, is the letter's continuing exposition of God's work of reconciliation and his ongoing work of transforming a new humanity. All of these are based on Christ's participation in humanity, his death and resurrection, as well as the work of the Spirit.

We should also note that the suffering and death of Christ on the Roman cross is no abstract theology for the audience. People in the Empire were familiar with the socio-political overtones that the Roman cross carried. The cross was a symbol of Roman oppression and domination of Rome's subjects, including the conquered peoples. Thus, for the audience in Rome, there would have been a sense in which Christ's identification with humanity had something to do with sharing in their present hardship and injustice in imperial Rome, and, strikingly, it was through his participation in an unjust death that deliverance from sin was accomplished.

ROMANS 8:5-13

Connected to 8:1-4 by the repeated use of γάρ and the theme of the Spirit, Rom 8:5-13 should be considered as part of the argument that started from 8:1-2. There are three subunits in 8:5-13, namely, 8:5-8, 8:9-11, and 8:12-13. Romans 8:5-8 sets two patterns of life in sharp contrast. On the one hand a life pattern according to the flesh cannot please God (8:8). Such existence is enmity (ἔχθρα) against God and cannot submit to God's law (8:7). Living with a flesh-oriented mindset is death (8:6), because such a life is characteristic of Adamic humanity, which is under death's bondage. On the other hand, there is ζωή and εἰρήνη for those whose mindset is Spirit-oriented (8:6). Notably, in Rom 5–8 the term εἰρήνη only appears in 5:1 and 8:6, and the language of enmity (ἔχθρα, ἐχθρός) only in 5:10 and 8:7. The shared vocabulary makes sense if we examine the messages of 5:1–11 and 8:5–8 together. The fleshly existence of Adamic humanity is enmity against God, but a life that is oriented towards the Spirit enjoys peace with God. The ongoing work of the Spirit is very much an integral part of God's program of reconciling humanity.

Paul starts 8:9–11 by stating clearly that his audience is not in the flesh but in the Spirit. It is because the Spirit dwells (οἰκέω) in them (8:9). The focus of 8:10–11 seems to be life *in the body* (σῶμα).[40] The body is dead because of sin, presumably due to the power of sin that is in the cosmos. It seems, then, that despite having been set free from the reign of sin and death, bodily existence is still in some way characterized by death and mortality.[41] Yet the Spirit is life διὰ δικαιοσύνην. The Spirit dwells in the audience and gives life to their mortal body (θνητὰ σώματα)—which most likely refers to the final bodily resurrection.[42] In other words, believers have an already-not-yet existence. On the one hand the life-giving Spirit already dwells in them. On the other hand they have a body that is subject to death, and hence have to wait for their future bodily resurrection.[43] Implicit here is that the present bodily existence is not free from pain and affliction. In fact, as 8:23 will mention, bodily life involves groaning, and believers eagerly await the redemption of their bodies.

40. The εἰ δέ at the start of Rom 8:10 follows the εἰ δέ τις πνεῦμα Χριστοῦ οὐκ ἔχει, οὗτος οὐκ ἔστιν αὐτοῦ in v. 9. It indicates that Paul is affirming that Christ is indeed in/among his audience. That is, they do belong to Christ.

41. See the adjectives νεκρός, θνητός in Rom 8:10, 11.

42. The reference to believers' final bodily resurrection in Rom 8:11 is indicated by the future ζωοποιήσει, and the references of ἐγείρω (two times) to Christ's resurrection. Cf. Dunn, *Romans 1–8*, 432; Moo, *Romans*, 492–93; Kirk, *Unlocking*, 127–28; Wright, *Resurrection*, 255–57.

43. Incidentally, the notion that the Spirit infuses life is found in Ezek 36–37. I agree with Yates, *Spirit and Creation*, 151, that we cannot say that Paul borrows from Ezekiel in Rom 8:11, but it is likely that the prophet contributes to the thinking there. Yates also says, "When the early Christians experienced what they believed to be the indwelling of the spirit after Christ's resurrection it would have been natural for them to associate the giving of the spirit of Christ with his resurrection, believing that in Christ the eschatological resurrection of the dead had begun."

The ἄρα οὖν in Rom 8:12 indicates that vv. 12–13 introduce a new point in the argument in 8:1–13.[44] Quite clearly Paul is saying in 8:12–13 that right living is not automatic. Although believers are in the Spirit, they need to "put to death" (θανατόω) the deeds of the body so that they will live. In expectation of the future bodily resurrection, the community is to actively allow the Spirit to work in their lives. This paves the way for 8:14–17, which says that those led by the Spirit are children of God, and that they are to participate in the suffering and glory of Christ.[45]

THE SCRIPTURAL PROMISE OF THE SPIRIT AND ITS ALREADY-NOT-YET FULFILLMENT

Not uncommonly scholars mention the connections between the Spirit-empowered fulfillment of the law's requirement in 8:1–13 and God's promised restoration of exilic Israel in the prophets, especially in Jer 30–33 and Ezek 34–37.[46] It seems that there are contact points between Paul's argument and the scriptural expectation of God's eschatological salvation, in which his people will walk in his ways through a Spirit-led, circumcised heart. But at the same time the prophets' message has been reworked by the letter's emphasis on the creation of a new humanity. We will start our analysis of this connection by examining the thematic and verbal links between Romans and the Scriptures that speak of God's upcoming deliverance. We will then outline how the prophets' message has been reworked to fit into the letter's rhetorical strategy.

Links to Israel's Scripture

The first contact point is the language that signifies eschatological fulfillment of God's promises. The νῦν in Rom 8:1 (as well as the νυνί and the "old written code"/"newness of the Spirit" in 7:6) highlights the eschatological character of the pericope.[47] Those who are in Christ belong to the new era

---

44. Note that "ἄρα οὖν" appears in Rom 5:18; 7:3, 25; 8:12; 9:16, 18; 14:12, 19. While it can introduce a new point within a given pericope, it does not necessarily start a brand-new argument.

45. With this Spirit-led participation-in-Christ life explicated in 8:1–17, the letter will then turn to the extended treatment of hope of glory in suffering in 8:18–30. Cf. Matera, *Romans*, 197.

46. E.g., Dunn, *Romans 1–8*, 417; Moo, *Romans*, 475; Byrne, *Romans*, 239–40; Yates, *Spirit and Creation*, 143–51; Gorman, *Cruciformity*, 52–54.

47. See Dunn, *Romans 1–8*, 415; Moo, *Romans*, 472.

that God has ushered in. The equivalent eschatological language in Israel's Scripture would be the day of YHWH, new spirit, and new covenant, which are often found in prophetic writings.[48] This language is prominently found in the message of consolation in Jer 30–33, and Ezekiel's message of restoration in 36:16–37:14. The backdrop to these Scriptures is the prophets' expectation of a future restoration graciously given to exilic Israel by their God despite their previous unfaithfulness. This restoration involves the return to their homeland from the nations to which YHWH has scattered them.

There are several other thematic and verbal links between Rom 8:1–13 and Scriptures relating to the expected restoration. Obviously the work of the Spirit is a key theme in Rom 8. The same theme is found in Ezekiel. The notion that YHWH will pour out his Spirit when he restores Israel is stated in Ezek 36:27 and 37:14.[49] The language of ζάω/ζωή appears six times in Rom 8:1–13.[50] The same language is used frequently in the "valley of dry bones" in Ezek 37 (see 37:3, 6, 9, 10, 14 LXX), which speaks of the deliverance of Israel and the new life they will have after their exile. Significantly, 37:14 LXX says that the Lord (YHWH in the MT) will put his Spirit in them and they will live (ζάω),[51] and Ezek 37 is full of the metaphorical use of "breath/spirit," through which Israel is given new life. Indeed, 37:5 LXX says that the Lord will bring to the "bones" a "spirit of life" (πνεῦμα ζωῆς).

Romans 8:5–6 says that there will be εἰρήνη for those who walk by the Spirit. As mentioned in Chapter 3, at a basic level peace refers to a sense of safety and security for individuals and communities, especially in terms of their relationships with their neighbors. Significantly, in Jeremiah YHWH promises "peace" (*shalom* [שׁלום] in the MT and εἰρήνη in the LXX) when he restores Israel to their land. A picture of peace, security, and joy enjoyed by the community in their restored land is painted in 33:6–9 as well as 30:19; 31:4–5, 12–13.[52] In addition, Ezek 34:25 and 37:26 speak of a renewed

---

48. The references to the day of YHWH are numerous—e.g., Jer 4:9; 9:25; 16:14; 23:5, 7; Ezek 30:3; 39:8, 13; Joel 1:15; 2:1; 3:14; Amos 5:18; Obad 15. Examples of new spirit, new heart, and new covenant, can be found in Isa 42:9; 43:19; Jer 31:22, 31 (38:22, 31 LXX); Ezek 18:31; 36:26.

49. Cf. Joel 2:28–32.

50. It is, of course, also prominent in Rom 5–8. See the statistics in Appendix A. Not uncommonly commentators mention Ezek 37 as the background for the Spirit of life in Romans. See Yates, *Spirit and Creation*, 144–6; Dunn, *Romans 1–8*, 417; Schreiner, *Romans*, 400; Thielman, *Paul and the Law*, 202.

51. The same message is found in the MT.

52. Brueggemann, *Jeremiah*, 314–5.

covenant called "the covenant of *shalom*."[53] Again there is a picture of joy, peace, security, and economic well-being.[54]

A notable link between Rom 8:1–13 and Israel's Scripture is found in Rom 8:1–4, where Paul talks about believers' fulfilling the just requirement of the law through the Spirit's empowerment.[55] This resembles the notion of circumcision of the heart *in the Spirit* in 2:29, in that the Spirit-inspired heart and its associated life pattern in fact fulfills the law's requirement. This concept is found in several Scriptures that speak of YHWH's restoration of Israel. The circumcision of the heart is mentioned in Deut 10:16 and 30:6, where the context is the return of Israel from exile.[56] Significantly, in Jer 31:33; 32:39, 40, 41 (38:33; 39:39, 40, 41 LXX) the prophet speaks of the covenant that YHWH will make with Israel, and that he will put his law in their minds and write it on their hearts when he brings them back to the lands from which he has banished them.[57] In Ezek 11:14–21 (cf. 18:31), the prophet talks about the return of the exiles and states that YHWH will give them a new heart and spirit. More significantly, Ezek 36:26–27 says that YHWH will give Israel a new spirit, remove their heart of stone, and give them a heart of flesh, so that they may follow his statutes.[58]

---

53. In the LXX it is διαθήκην εἰρήωης. Cf. Bertone, *Spirit*, 260–64, who examines several passages in Ezekiel and Romans, and argues that the "Spirit ensures covenantal 'peace' with God."

54. Wright, *Ezekiel*, 281–2. Another thematic link between Romans and the prophets is the notion of knowing God. In Rom 8:5–6, those who live by the Spirit will set their mind (φρονέω) on the things of the Spirit. With a Spirit-led "mind"/"understanding" (φρόνημα) there will be life and peace. According to Jeremiah, the days are coming when God's people will no longer teach each other, "Know the Lord" (Γνῶθι τὸν κύριον; 31:34; 38:34 LXX)—for they will all know (οἶδα) him, from the small to the great.

55. Cf. Yates, *Spirit and Creation*, 143–46; Dunn, *Romans 1–8*, 417; Fee, *Paul*, 16.

56. See the observations by Fee, *Empowering*, 491–92, who sees Deut 10:16; 30:6 as the OT background for Rom 2:29, and that Rom 2:29 points forward to 8:4.

57. See Cranfield, *Romans I-VIII*, 384, who thinks that Rom 8:4 speaks of the fulfillment of the promises of Jer 31:33 and Ezek 36:26–27. Cf. Moo, *Romans*, 484n66.

58. See Bertone, *Spirit*, 48–55, 62, for a comprehensive survey of Ezek 11, 36–37 regarding the prophet's vision of an era of the Spirit under a new covenant. Bertone also mentions the relevant passages in Jeremiah.

Also, a close look at Ezek 36:27 (LXX) is most interesting, given its similar vocabulary to Rom 8:4.

> And I will give my Spirit in you and will act so that you may walk in my statutes and keep my judgments and do them.
>
> καὶ τὸ πνεῦμά μου δώσω ἐν ὑμῖν καὶ ποιήσω ἵνα ἐν τοῖς δικαιώμασίν μου πορεύησθε καὶ τὰ κρίματά μου φυλάξησθε καὶ ποιήσητε

Here YHWH says that he will give his *Spirit* (πνεῦμα) to his people *so that* (ἵνα) they may *walk* (περιπατέω) in his *statutes* (δικαιώμασίν). It seems that what Ezekiel said

The Prophets' Message being Fulfilled but Not Yet Fully Realized

In short, the Spirit-empowered life pattern in Rom 8:1–13 echoes the promised eschatological salvation in Israel's Scripture, where the restored exilic Israel will walk in God's way through the Spirit and enjoy peace and security under his protection. But it is clear that Paul has reworked this for his own rhetorical purposes.

We have already mentioned that the work of Christ and the Spirit in Rom 8:1–13 is an integral part of God's program of rescuing Adamic humanity from the stranglehold of sin and death. Thus, Rom 8:1–13 widens the prophets' expectation of eschatological blessings to all humanity, not only ethnic Israel.[59] This universalization of God's promise can in fact be traced back to the primordial accounts in Scripture. Given the background of Adam's story in Gen 1–3 in Rom 5–8, the πνεῦμα ζωῆς in Rom 8:2 sounds very similar to the πνοή ζωή in Gen 2:7 LXX.[60] Genesis 2:7 says that Adam was formed from the dust and God breathed into his face a "breath of life." Humans are not living beings unless God has given them life.[61] What the Spirit of life does in Rom 8:1–13 is to give the Christ-community life and peace by setting them free from the bondage of sin and death and enabling a life pattern that pleases God.[62]

Having said that, Jer 30–33 and Ezek 34–37 do provide extra resources for an audience that is familiar with affliction and oppression. These prophetic texts affirm that God has not abandoned his people, for the eschatological Spirit has been poured out, although believers need to reconfigure what that means in their own circumstances. The existential reality of exilic Israel would be similar to that of the audience in Rome in many ways. Exilic Israelites—like the slaves and war-captives (and their descendants) in

---

regarding YHWH's future act has now been fulfilled in the life of the Christ-community. See Yates, *Spirit and Creation*, 143–4, for a similar observation.

59. The rest of Romans seems to have incorporated the message of other Scriptures where YHWH's blessings will be extended to all peoples (e.g., Isa 42: 1, 4, 7; 49:1), not least Gen 12:1–3, where God promises to Abraham that he and his descendants will be a blessing to all peoples. For example, Rom 1–4 speaks of the inclusion of Gentiles in God's salvific purposes, and chapters 12–15 is about the life of a Jew-Gentile community.

60. The LXX translates the MT very closely in Gen 2:7. For a discussion on the linguistic link between Rom 8:2 and Gen 2:7, see Grappe, "Qui me délivrera," 476. According to Grappe, an obvious translation of the Hebrew word would be ἐμφυσάω. However, the LXX uses πνέω, which is linguistically related to Paul's πνεῦμα.

61. More will be said about the echo of Gen 2:7 in Chapter 5.

62. Cf. Dunn, *Romans 1–8*, 418; Kirk, *Unlocking*, 127. See Ps 104:29–30 (103:29–30 LXX) for a similar notion where all creatures die and return to dust but God sends his Spirit to renew them.

Rome—knew what it meant to live in bondage and captivity, which often involved forced relocation from their homeland. The economic deprivation and socio-political marginalization that many in the audience experienced would also be familiar to exilic Israelites. In fact, the Jewish audience in Rome would consider themselves in a form of exile because their homeland was occupied and their ruler was not Jewish. These shared experiences of hardship meant that the audience could identify with the pain and hope of exilic Israel. Thus, the Spirit they had received was a sure sign of God's restorative purposes being fulfilled.

But the fact that believers are still suffering means that God's deliverance and *shalom* are not yet full realized, although through the Spirit they do experience a measure of it. Romans 8:1–13 only says that the Spirit has been poured out for right living and that the reign of sin and death has been broken. In other words, the audience still needs to hope, because their suffering continues to be a reality.

In sum, there are considerable thematic and intertextual links between Rom 8:1–13 and the prophetic message in Jer 30–33 and Ezek 34–37. This, together with the shared experiences of suffering between exilic Israel and the audience of Romans, suggests that the prophetic writings might be evoked in the mind of the audience. But the prophets' message of God's restoration and the outpouring of the Spirit have been reworked in the letter. Firstly, God's blessings are now universalized so that the entire humanity—not merely ethnic Israel—can benefit from God's mercy. Secondly, despite the bestowal of the Spirit, the people of God are still suffering and the full realization of God's *shalom* is still to come. The prophetic writings provide extra resources for the letter's audience to know that God's visitation has indeed taken place, and that the Spirit's empowerment is available. This not only gives them hope in the midst of suffering. It also provides the basis for the letter's forthcoming exposition of the Spirit's role in leading believers into a familial relationship with God (Rom 8:14–17), which will, in turn, pave the way for the extended discussion on suffering in Rom 8:18–30.

CONCLUSION

Our findings have suggested that Rom 8:1–13 is a continuation of the argument in 5:1–21 regarding the formation of a new humanity that has been reconciled to God. God has accomplished this work by sending his own Son to identify with humanity and become a sin-offering for them. The Spirit has set free the believers by breaking the powers of sin and death, and the Spirit continues to empower them to live a life that pleases God. Given the cosmological framework of the audience, the work of the Spirit would be understood as God's cosmic power over the forces of evil. The work of Christ and the Spirit is informed by Israel's Scripture, which speaks of God's restorative purpose for exilic Israel, although the letter has reworked that to include the transformation of humanity.

A few corollaries can be drawn from the above discussion. By implication, the suffering of the audience cannot be punitive, in the sense that they do not need to take any specific actions to avert God's wrath (such as offering sacrifices). That is, their suffering is not the result of God's punishment according to the principle of retributive justice. This is because they are under no condemnation and right living is possible through the Spirit. In other words, they are in fact "righteous sufferers." In addition, the scriptural allusions point to God's eschatological restorative act, rather than his judgment on Israel for its unfaithfulness. Recalling Rom 5:2–5, suffering has educative value. But most of all, the audience can boast in the hope of glory despite their affliction and apply the eschatological hope found in the prophets to their own lives. How do they do that? The answer can be found in 8:14–17 and 8:18–30. Our next chapter will focus on 8:14–17.

5

The Vocation to Participate
in Christ's Suffering

INTRODUCTION

For an audience living with socioeconomic hardship and religio-political injustice, Rom 8:14–17 would be an important passage. It contains the first explicit mention of suffering since 5:1–11. Verse 17 says that believers are co-heirs with Christ. They are to suffer with him so that they may be glorified with him. Indeed, 8:17 harks back to the themes of hope of glory and suffering in 5:2–5, and at the same time it serves as a transition to the extended exposition of the same themes in 8:18–30. As will be argued, participation in Christ's suffering is the vocation of believers, and the purpose of that vocation is that they may participate in his glory.[1] Verse 17 also says that the believers' suffering and glorification are based on the fact that they are heirs of God and joint-heirs with Christ, which, in turn, are based on their identity as God's children. I will argue that there is a merge of identities

---

1. The language of participation here may suggest to some readers that I have in mind the notion of deification or "union with Christ" in Paul. But of course my focus is the exegetical analysis of the text and what it means to the audience's understanding of suffering, rather than the theological implications to the notion of "union with Christ." For a recent comprehensive survey of "union with Christ" in Paul since the late nineteenth century, see Campbell, *Union*, 31–66. Campbell thinks that, to "do justice to the full spectrum of Paul's thought and language, the terms *union, participation, identification, incorporation*" should be adopted (29; emphasis original).

and vocations of believers and Christ, in that they share the identity of being God's children/Son as well as God's call to suffer.

Paving the way for v. 17, the letter speaks of believers' status as υἱοί/ τέκνα of God, their privileges in their υἱοθεσία, and the *Abba*-cry (8:14–16). These signify different aspects of believers' filial relationship with God, and are set in contrast to the characterization of Adamic humanity. Paul also delineates the roles of the eschatological Spirit in confirming and bringing about the identity of believers as God's children. We will discuss how a Spirit-inspired familial relationship with God provides the audience with an affirmation that they belong to God, which, in turn, lays the foundation for the statement in 8:17 regarding their vocation of suffering with Christ. We will show that participating in Christ's suffering and glory is an essential part of God's intention to restore and transform humanity. As we shall see in Chapter 6, this restoration of humanity is indeed an integral part of God's plan of renewing the entire creation, and the believers' vocation of suffering is an essential component of that plan. Finally, we will take a look at the primordial accounts in Genesis and see how they provide further resources for the audience to understand their vocation of suffering with Christ and their place in God's creation.

THE PIVOTAL ROLE OF ROM 8:14–17

Our discussion begins with a good look at the function of 8:14–17 within Rom 5–8. The γάρ in 8:14 indicates that the verse explains Paul's exhortation in the preceding verses. Verse 12 implies that it is possible for believers to live by the flesh, despite the fact that they are "in the Spirit" (8:9). In order to "live" (ζάω) they must put to death the deeds of the body "by the Spirit" (πνεύματι) (8:13). As discussed previously, 8:12–13 is part of Paul's exposition on the work of the Spirit from 8:1–4. The exhortation in 8:12–13, therefore, is a practical instruction about how believers should conduct themselves, so that their Spirit-empowered life pattern can truly fulfill the just requirement of the law (8:4)—given the fact that the Spirit has set them free from sin and death (8:2). Thus, by making a connection between the eschatological Spirit and the believers' identity as children of God, 8:14 serves as a continuation of the argument concerning the work of the Spirit in 8:1–13.

The γάρ in 8:15 indicates that 8:15–17 elaborates on 8:14. This, together with the dominant theme of the Spirit in 8:14–17, suggests that the passage is in fact an integral part of the argument in 8:1–17. Since, as discussed in Chapter 4, 8:1–13 is an extension of the argument in 5:1–21 regarding the formation of a new humanity that has been reconciled to God, it follows that 8:14–17 should be read with Rom 5 in mind. In other words, the work of the Spirit in 8:14–17 is very much part of God's project of transforming humanity (5:12–21). Indeed, the verbs συμπάσχω and συνδοξάζω in 8:17 echo the terms θλῖψις and δόξα in 5:2, 3. Also, the Spirit-inspired intimate *Abba*-cry in 8:15 recalls the Spirit-led love relationship between believers and God in 5:5.[2] Thus, Rom 8:14–17 essentially returns to what was said briefly about the place of affliction and glory within God's reconciling act in 5:1–11, and this would alert an audience familiar with suffering to pay attention to what the letter is about to say. Indeed, 8:14–17 paves the way for the argument in 8:18–39. In v. 18 Paul says that he considers that the present sufferings are not worth comparing with the glory to be revealed.[3] This is often considered to be the thesis statement for the pericope in 8:18–30.[4] Also, the theme and language of "Son"/"children" and "glory" is found throughout 8:18–39 (8:18, 19, 21, 29, 30, 32). This, together with the theme of suffering, means that vv. 14–17 play a preparatory role for the subsequent passage.[5]

In short, 8:14–17 is a pivotal passage.[6] It is an integral part of 8:1–17 and hence a continuation of the argument concerning the transformation of humanity since 5:1–21. It also introduces the extended treatment of hope, suffering, and glory in 8:18–39, which in turn concludes the argument started in 5:1—8:39. In the following we will investigate 8:14–17 in two steps. We will first examine the work of the Spirit and the identity of believers as children of God in 8:14–16. After this we will offer a detailed exegesis of 8:17.

ROMANS 8:14–16

Clearly believers' filial relationship with God is a major theme in Rom 8:14–16, and the Spirit plays an indispensable role in confirming and bringing

2. It seems that the compact statement in Rom 5:5 is unpacked by various elements of Rom 8, with the theme of the Spirit throughout the chapter but the theme of love only appearing in 8:28, 35–39.

3. The translation of οὐκ ἄξια πρός here follows the NRSV, but see discussion in Chapter 6 for an alternative translation.

4. See discussion in Chapter 6.

5. Some suggest that Rom 8:17 belongs to the pericope 8:17–30. But since 8:18 is a thesis statement for 8:18–30, it should be placed at the beginning of the pericope.

6. Not uncommonly commentators treat Rom 8:1–17 or 8:12–17 as a pericope, rather than discuss 8:14–17 separately. But I think 8:14–17 is significant enough to warrant special treatment. See Byrne, *Romans*, 247; Moo, *Romans*, 496; Fee, *Empowering*, 560; Kruse, *Romans*, 336.

about this relationship. The terms υἱός, τέκνον, υἱοθεσία, and the expression αββα πατήρ serve to inform the audience of the different aspects of the relationship. In turn, the believers' identity as God's children lays the foundation for the statement in 8:17 concerning the call for believers to suffer with Christ.

I will argue that their identity and status as the children of God means that they belong to God's domain and do not live under the cosmic powers of sin and death, which are, in turn, the ultimate forces behind their suffering. This is affirmed by the fact that they have not received the Spirit of slavery that leads them to fear—the fear that is associated with a life bound by sin's power. Instead, believers have received the Spirit of υἱοθεσία, which implies that they enjoy the full privileges of being God's eschatological people. As will be seen, the *Abba*-cry in 8:15 invites the audience to share in Christ's intimate relationship with God as well as his suffering. Finally, the Spirit bears witness in their spirit that they are indeed God's children, assuring them that their relationship with God is firm and secure.

Spirit-Led Identity as God's Children

Romans 8:14 says that all who are led (ἄγονται) by the Spirit of God are the υἱοὶ θεοῦ.[7] Fee rightly says that the verb ἄγω does not refer to "ecstasy" or "guidance" in the narrow sense.[8] The term itself probably carries some connotation of God's leading. This notion is found in Exod 13:17; 32:34; Pss 77:14, 53; 104:37, 38, 42, 43 LXX;[9] and Isa 63:13, 14,[10] where YHWH's/God's guidance and protection in the Exodus story is recalled.[11] But else-

7. Throughout our discussion I will use the gender-inclusive "children of God" for υἱοὶ θεοῦ, unless otherwise stated. Modern commentators often use the inclusive "children" for the υἱοί in Rom 8:14. See Hultgren, *Romans*, 313; Wright, *Romans*, 593; Matera, *Romans*, 197–98.

8. Fee, *Empowering*, 563. See also Moo, *Romans*, 499. Jewett, *Romans*, 496, notes the usage of the term in magical texts in Paul's days—where it is used as a "technical term for gods, spirits, or ghosts of the dead, who are commanded to supernaturally 'lead' a targeted person to act in a way that the practitioner desires." This suggests that the Spirit's leading has an element of divine intervention in the decision making process of believers. This, however, is not the same as ecstasy.

9. Note that the verb ὁδηγέω is used in these LXX texts.

10. The verbs ἄγω and ὁδηγέω are used in Isa 63:13, 14 LXX.

11. Kruse, *Romans*, 336. Dunn, *Romans 1–8*, 450, briefly notes the use of "leading" vocabulary in the Exodus tradition in the LXX. Also, the leading of the pillars of cloud and fire is similar to the leading of the Spirit in Rom 8:14. See Wright, "New Exodus," 29. Also, I note that the terms κύριος and θεός in the LXX—and the corresponding "YHWH" (יהוה) and "God" (אלהים) in the MT—are used in the different texts I have

where the leading of YHWH has much to do with his people walking in his ways—that is, living out his righteousness and justice (Pss 5:9; 22:3; 24:5, 9; 26:11; 85:11 LXX; cf. Exod 15:13).[12] Given Paul's exhortation in 8:12–13 and the Spirit's role in empowering right living in 8:3–11, it is highly likely that "lead" primarily refers to the Spirit's work in leading believers to walk in God's ways.[13] That is, all who allow the eschatological Spirit to lead them to walk in righteousness are children of God.[14]

The appellation υἱοὶ θεοῦ carries various connotations in the ancient world. The Stoic idea of Zeus as the father of all humans is well known (cf. Acts 17:28),[15] and heroes (and some other individuals) in the ancient world are celebrated as sons of (the) god(s).[16] Successive emperors since Augustus were called the "son of the deified" in the civic cult and on Roman coins.[17] But the deities within this Greco-Roman worldview are not the Creator God that Romans refers to (see 1:18–23).[18] In Jewish literature Israel is said to be YHWH's "son," notably in Exod 4:22–23 and Hos 1:10 (cf. Deut 14:1; Isa 1:2–4; 30:9; 63:8; Wis 12:7, 21; 16:10, 21, 26; Sir 36:17).[19] However, we note that in Rom 5–8 the letter's focus is the entire humanity rather than specifically Israel, although Paul will explicitly refer to Israel's filial relationship with God later (9:4, 7, 8, 9, 26, 27). In light of this, it seems better to view the believers' identity in terms of a reworking of Israel's sonship at the

---

listed regarding YHWH's/God's leading. For instance, in Exod 13:17 it is God who led Israel, but in Isa 63:13, 14 it is YHWH. This probably reflects the different traditions behind the final canonical documents.

12. Fee, *Empowering*, 563.

13. Cf. Byrne, *Romans*, 252; Cranfield, *Romans I-VIII*, 395; Fee, *Empowering*, 563. Fee cites YHWH's leading in Ps 23:3 as an example.

14. The notion that those who walk in righteousness are children of God can be found in Jewish literature. For instance, *Ps Sol* 17:26–27 says, "He will gather a holy people whom he will lead in righteousness . . . For he shall know them that they are all children of their God." Cf. Sir 4:10. See Jewett, *Romans*, 497. As Jewett points out, the innovation of Romans is that righteous living is the product of the Spirit's leading.

15. Dunn, *Romans 1–8*, 450–51.

16. See Jewett, *Romans*, 496; Dunn, *Romans 1–8*, 451.

17. For example, the inscription on Porta Tiburtina (a gate in the Aurelian Walls of Rome) says, "*Imp(erator) caesar divi Iuli f(ilius) Augustus / pontifex maximus cos(n) s(ul) XII . . . rivos aquarum omnium refecit*," which can be translated as, "The Emperor Augustus, son of the deified Julius, Pontifex Maximus, consul for the 12th time . . . rebuilt the channels of all aqueducts." Source: Gordon, *Latin Epigraphy*, 104.

18. In fact, Rom 1:18–23 implies that the worship of the Greco-Roman deities is idolatry.

19. Byrne, *Romans*, 249, lists many other references to Israel's being YHWH's "son" or "firstborn"—e.g., Wis 12:7, 21; 16:10, 21, 26; 18:13; 19:6; Sir 36:17; *1 Enoch* 62:11; *Ps Sol* 17:30; 3 Macc 6:28. See also Moo, *Romans*, 499nn15–16.

coming of the eschatological Spirit. That is, believers are members of an eschatological people promised in the Scripture, and, like Israel, they share the privileges of being God's children.[20] But unlike much Jewish expectation, this eschatological people consists of both Jews and Gentiles.

So, all who are led by the Spirit to walk in God's ways belong to the eschatological people foretold by the prophets. But, given its opening γάρ, what is the connection between 8:14 and the preceding argument of the letter? Indeed, what is the significance of the notion of "children of God" within the argument of Rom 5–8, and how is this notion relevant to the circumstances of an audience dealing with daily hardships? We may answer this by tracing the letter's argument backwards. The audience has just been exhorted not to live according to the flesh (8:12–13). They are to put to death the deeds of the body by the Spirit so that they may live (ζάω) (8:13). Thus, believers will live if they allow the Spirit to empower right living, and the *reason* for taking heed of this exhortation is that they can truly be children of God. Also, the audience has just heard the contrast between the Spirit-empowered life pattern and the flesh-oriented pattern, where the former is characterized by life and peace (ζωή καί εἰρήνη), and the latter is hostile to God (8:5–8). Believers are of course in the Spirit, not the flesh (8:9), and that is because the Spirit of life (ζωή) has set them free from sin and death and there is no condemnation against them through the atoning death of Christ (8:1–4). As argued in Chapter 4, these notions of life, peace and condemnation, among other things, show that Rom 8:1–13 is a continuation of the argument in 5:1–21, where God's plan of restoring and reconciling humanity was explicated. Spirit-filled people, and hence *Spirit-led children*, belong to a transformed humanity. They have been reconciled to God and have peace with him. In light of this, it seems that God's program of restoration and transformation provides the framework and basis for the audience to understand their Spirit-led identity as God's children.

We can understand this further by tracing the train of thought since the first mention of affliction in 5:1–11. In Rom 5 the audience has heard that believers can boast in the hope of glory in suffering because they have been reconciled to God and have peace with him (5:1–11). The ground for that is God's gracious act of defeating sin and death through Christ

---

20. Cf. Hodge, *Sons*, 77, who argues that Paul "establishes a kinship for gentiles which is based not on shared blood, but on shared spirit." And in doing so, "Paul weaves his own definitions of kinship into traditional patrilineal notions." Hodge presents an interesting discussion of kinship and ethnicity in Paul's letters. But our focus on Rom 5–8 alone means that we will not interact with Hodge in detail, for much of her work concentrates on other passages in Paul, especially those concerning Abraham and Israel.

(5:12–21). Now Paul says that the Spirit has set them free from sin and death (8:2), and if they allow the Spirit to lead them in right living, they are God's children (8:14). This means that their identity as God's children is ultimately based on the fact that they belong to the domain of God, and not under the reign of sin and death—which are anti-God evil powers and are the ultimate reason behind human suffering.

The implication of this Spirit-led identity of being God's children is significant to an audience living with hardship and injustice. Their freedom from sin and death (5:12–21; 8:1–2) means that the ultimate forces behind suffering have been dealt with. Their suffering is not the result of God's retributive justice against their sins, because the Spirit enables them to live right and please him. Indeed, the bestowal of the Spirit is the sure sign of the restorative and gracious act of God anticipated by the prophets. Their status as God's children affirms that they do belong to God's family, not Adamic humanity. Despite their affliction and trials, they have peace with God.

The Spirit of υἱοθεσία, Not Slavery

Romans 8:15 has three components. The first is that believers did not receive the Spirit of slavery again to fear, and the second is that they have received the Spirit of υἱοθεσία. As we will see, these two connections imply that believers are not subject to the powers of sin and death, and hence they do not have to fear those destructive forces. In contrast, they can enjoy the full privileges of being God's eschatological people, and they are no longer a people under Adam. The third component of 8:15 is the *Abba*-cry, which we will examine separately.

Romans 8:15a says that believers did not receive the Spirit of slavery that brings fear. The slavery-freedom motif is frequently found in Rom 6 and 7, and it appears three times in the current chapter (8:2, 15, 21).[21] It is most likely that the δουλεία refers to the bondage of sin and death in 8:2, because 8:2 has the most recent reference to the motif.[22] That is, the Spirit does not lead to slavery because the Spirit has set believers free from the dominion of sin and death (8:2).[23] In light of this, the φόβος in 8:15a would

21. See Rom 6:6, 16, 17, 18, 19, 20, 22; 7:3, 6, 25, where the language of freedom and slavery appears. Note also the language of dominion in Rom 5.

22. The motif is indicated by the term ἐλευθερόω in Rom 8:2. Apart from 8:15, 8:2 is one of the only three places in the letter where the Spirit and the slavery-freedom motif are placed together. The third is 7:6, where the Spirit is contrasted with slavery under the law.

23. Cf. Dunn, *Romans 1–8*, 451–52; Heil, *Romans*, 84. Like Jewett, *Romans*, 497, I think the genitive in πνεῦμα δουλείας in Rom 8:15 is most likely "genitive of direction"

be the fear of living under the reign of sin and death as members of Adamic humanity.[24] The destructive effects of sin and death are, as argued before, multifaceted and far-reaching, and would include the hardship and system-ic injustice that the audience experiences in imperial Rome. The audience would be familiar with the general Greco-Roman usage of the φόβος–φοβέω word group, which refers to the terror and anxiety when humans react to a hostile or adversarial force—which, in turn, includes the dread of death, the unknown future or awfulness of fate, as well as the fear of the authority of the state or the power of deities.[25] These types of dread and anxiety would be exactly what the audience in Rome experienced in their daily suffering because of the anti-God powers in the cosmos. In fact, those outside Christ would live in the fear of the (pagan) gods, as Cranfield suggests.[26] If believ-ers still belong to Adamic humanity, then there is much to fear, because the effects of sin and death are evil and hence fearful.

But as it is, the Spirit they have received means that they do not have to fear because God has defeated sin and death, which are the ultimate forces behind their affliction. It does not mean that there is no suffering, but that evil powers do not have a stranglehold over them. In light of this, 8:15a affirms our findings in v. 14, where we discovered that the believers' Spirit-led identity as God's children is about their life in the domain of God, with the implication that they are free from sin's power, and hence, they can enjoy peace with God.

Romans 8:15b says that believers have received the Spirit of υἱοθεσία. The term υἱοθεσία is not found in the LXX, and in the New Testament it is only used in Rom 8:15, 23; 9:4; Gal 4:5; Eph 1:5. The usage of the term in Greco-Roman literature is comprehensively summarized by James Scott. It can refer to a practice in Hellenistic law, where adoption is an institution especially connected with inheritance. Or else it may be understood "in light of the elaborate Roman ceremony of *adoptio*, in which the minor to be adopted was emancipated from the authority of his natural father and placed under the new authority of his adoptive father, often for the purpose

---

or "purpose," indicating that the Spirit does not *produce* the result of slavery. Cf. Kruse, *Romans*, 337.

24. The language of φόβος/φοβέω occurs only in 8:15 in Rom 5:1—8:39. Elsewhere in the letter it appears in 3:18; 11:20; 13:3 (x2), 4, 7. Twice it refers to the fear of God (3:18; 11:20), and in 13:3 it refers to the fear of rulers and authorities (cf. Matt 2:22). In 8:15, the term is unlikely to refer to the fear of God when people sin against him, for the work of the Spirit in 8:3–14 has been about right living. See Balz, "φοβέω, φοβέομαι, φόβος, δέος," 4:189–219, for a comprehensive analysis of the word group.

25. See Balz, 4:189–97.

26. Cranfield, *Romans I-VIII*, 396–7.

of social and/or political maneuvering."[27] But Scott argues that Paul borrows from the notion of divine adoption in 2 Sam 7:14 to say that the followers of Jesus "participate with him in the Davidic promise of divine adoption and in the Abrahamic promise of universal sovereignty."[28] Byrne, however, disagrees with Scott. He says, rightly, that it is not possible to account for the full range of the Pauline divine filial motif primarily on the basis of 2 Sam 7:14.[29] Having said that, Byrne thinks that "behind his [Paul's] use of this term stands that broad Jewish tradition of Israel, especially eschatological Israel, as 'son/child (sons/children) of God.'"[30]

Given the range of motifs available to the audience, it seems better to think that the υἱοθεσία could carry the general notion of adoption in the Greco-Roman world as well as the Jewish view of "sonship."[31] In other words, υἱοθεσία refers to an "adoption to sonship" through which believers inherit the full privileges of being God's adoptive children. On the one hand, as God's children led by the Spirit, believers belong to the eschatological people promised in Israel's Scripture and hence are entitled to inherit all the blessings from Israel's God because they have been adopted into his family. But the promise to Israel has been universalized to include both Jews and Gentiles through the Spirit. Unlike Adamic humanity, which lives in fear because of the dominion of sin and death, a Spirit-led humanity has been set free to enjoy God's abundant blessings.

On the other hand, the audience in Rome would be familiar with the important practice of adoption in Greco-Roman culture. Adoption ensured that the lifeline of the *familia* would not die out when a family's biological children failed to live to adulthood (which was not uncommon in the ancient world).[32] It also made sure that the family's household gods could continue to be venerated should one's heirs die at a young age.[33] Successive emperors' reigns and powers were legitimized by imperial adoptions, with Nero being Claudius' adopted son as the most recent example. The audience's familiarity with the practice means that we cannot ignore the Greco-

27. Scott, "Adoption, Sonship," 16. See Scott, *Adoption as Sons of God*, 3–13, for a fuller discussion.

28. Scott, "Adoption, Sonship" 17. See Scott, *Adoption as Sons of God*, 259–66, for a detailed discussion.

29. Byrne, *Romans*, 252. See Byrne, *Sons of God*, 97–103, for a fuller discussion.

30. Byrne, *Romans*, 250.

31. "Sonship"/"adoption" will be directly applied to Israel when υἱοθεσία appears in Rom 9:4.

32. Walters, "Paul, Adoption," 52–54. It also ensured that the family did not lose their property or estate.

33. See the concise discussion by Burke, *Adopted*, 65–66.

Roman notion of adoption. Importantly, in the Roman system, adopted sons held the same legal positions as real sons,[34] and the natural father of the adoptees severed his legal authority over them.[35] This well-known practice in the Roman world means that adoption would provide the audience with a highly relevant metaphor regarding their relationship with God.[36] Romans 5:12–21 has made it clear that believers have been delivered from the cosmic powers of sin and death, and hence they no longer belong to Adamic humanity. Likewise, the Spirit has set them free from their bondage (8:2). The same Spirit leads them so that they may be children of God (8:14). As a result, just like the natural father has no authority over children who have been adopted by another family, sin and death can no longer claim ownership or power over believers, for the work of Christ and the Spirit has severed the rule of sin and death over believers. Since these cosmic powers are the ultimate cause of suffering, the implication is that believers no longer have to fear. Thus, υἱοθεσία refers to the sonship of adoption that speaks of believers' liberation from the slavery of Adamic humanity, and, by implication, the deliverance from anti-God powers.

But what is the role of the Spirit in this divine "sonship"? Scholars disagree here, especially in terms of the interpretation of the genitival expression πνεῦμα υἱοθεσίας.[37] Burke and Byrne both take the genitive as qualitative, and think that the Spirit "goes with" υἱοθεσία.[38] Burke goes on to say that adoption and the Spirit are "mutually dependent and interrelated

34. Burke, *Adopted*, 63; Walters, "Paul," 53. Gaius (the jurist) says that adopted children occupy the place of natural children (*Inst.* 2.136). Although Gaius probably wrote this in the second century CE, the practice had been around for a long time. In fact, Book 2 of *Institutes* is about the laws around family and adoption, and 2.62 speaks of the marriage between Claudius and Agrippina, which took place before Paul wrote Romans.

35. For example, Gaius says that the natural father should consider the adoptive children (of the adoptive family) as strangers (*Inst.* 2.137). Burke, *Adopted*, 59, helpfully points out that a clear difference between Greek and Roman legal procedures is that the latter's "absolute nature of adoption" is absent in Hellenistic law. In Greek laws, the adoptees do not sever completely their relationships with the old family.

36. Burke, "Pauline Adoption," 128–31, talks about how sociologically the metaphor of adoption refers to "the radical separation from one group and incorporation into another group." In this way, God functions as the "Divine Parent," and now believers constitute a "family." This, according to Burke, allows Paul to develop a "pattern of ecclesiology based on the family," which, I think, will have implications for the interpretation of Rom 12–15.

37. Burke, *Adopted*, 141–3, provides a comprehensive discussion on the different views here. Burke rightly rejects the view that the Spirit only assists us in testifying to the filial relationship (cf. Rom 8:16).

38. Ibid., 142–3; Byrne, *Romans*, 252.

aspects of the Christian's experience of salvation rather than separate developments in the believer's life."[39] Burke is right in that the Spirit has an ongoing role in affirming our relationship with God. But given the active role of the Spirit throughout 8:1–16 and that v. 11 specifically speaks of the life-giving role of the Spirit, I prefer to take the υἰοθεσίας as a genitive of product. That is, the Spirit *brings about* (or produces) υἰοθεσία.[40]

Hence, the Spirit's role is all-encompassing. It goes beyond empowering right living. The Spirit is the agent that not only affirms but also brings about the υἰοθεσία of believers.[41] Significantly, the Spirit who plays such a crucial role in believers' υἰοθεσία is the same Spirit who has set them free from sin and death. That is, through the Spirit they are members of God's restored humanity, and by the Spirit they enjoy the full privileges of being God's children. They have no fear of the cosmic powers that cause harm and affliction, because they have not received the Spirit of slavery.

The Spirit-Inspired Cry

The third component of Rom 8:15 is the *Abba*-cry. I will argue that the cry to *Abba* Father in 8:15c invites the audience to recall Jesus' intimate relationship with God in his prayer to his Father, in his time of intense emotional need at Gethsemane (Mark 14:36). Understood this way, the mention of the *Abba*-cry invites the audience to identify with Christ's suffering as they themselves face hardship and injustice in Rome.[42]

Along with not a few commentators, I take the ἐν ᾧ in Rom 8:15c as "by whom."[43] That is, it is by the enablement of the Spirit of υἰοθεσία that we "cry out" (κράζω) "*Abba* Father" (αββα πατήρ). The verb κράζω depicts a (possibly) loud cry and passionate call.[44] In Matt 27:50 it refers to Jesus' cry when he breathed his last. Indeed, κράζω is frequently found in the Psalms

39. Burke, *Adopted*, 143.

40. Scholars who take a similar view include Fee, *Empowering*, 566; Cranfield, *Romans I-VIII*, 397. An example of genitive of product can be found in the "God of hope" in Rom 15:3 and "God of peace" in 15:33. See Wallace, *Greek Grammar*, 106.

41. In the words of Moo, *Romans*, 502, the Spirit may be thought of "as the agent through whom the believer's sonship is both bestowed and confirmed."

42. Perhaps it is because of the necessary focus on the intimate filial relationship in Rom 8:15 and the need to determine the origin of the term *Abba*, commentators seldom spend time making a strong connection between suffering and the emotional *Abba*-cry, at least not with the emphasis I have here.

43. Cranfield, *Romans I-VIII*, 399; Fee, *Empowering*, 567n280; Jewett, *Romans*, 474; Dunn, *Romans 1-8*, 447.

44. See Jewett, *Romans*, 498–99, for a survey of the use of the term.

to refer to fervent and passionate prayer in the face of suffering (e.g., 21:3, 6, 25; 106:6, 13, 19, 28 LXX).[45] Psalm 33:18 LXX is a case in point, where it says that the righteous cried out (ἐκέκραξαν οἱ δίκαιοι), and the Lord listened to them and delivered them from all their afflictions (θλίψεων).[46] It seems, then, that 8:15c speaks of a Spirit-inspired cry that can express the emotional plea and petition of a sufferer.[47]

We note that starting from the use of the κράζομεν here, most of the verbs in the rest of Rom 8 are in the first person plural, which is a prominent change from the second person plural up to this point. Here Paul is not so much exhorting his audiences, as in 8:12–13, or describing certain life patterns as in 8:5–8. Instead, he is speaking of the shared experience between himself and his fellow siblings in Christ, who cry out to God in their afflictions. From the perspective of the audience, they may sense Paul's intention to identify with their affliction. Since suffering is an experienced reality, this identification is significant, for it implies that Paul is personally involved in suffering and that the audience is not alone in their daily troubles.[48] It also shows that suffering is a communal experience for all members of God's family, as the use of first person plural in 8:18–39 shows.

Most likely the prayer to αββα borrows from the early Christians' understanding of Jesus' own prayer life, regardless of whether it specifically came from the Lord's Prayer itself.[49] Witherington notes that there is no evidence for God being prayed to as *Abba* outside the Jesus and Christian tradition.[50] In addition, Witherington is probably right to argue that the *Abba*-prayer is "indeed a form of praying Jesus used and taught his disciples to use and that it is characteristic and perhaps even distinctive of the Jesus

45. Other examples include Pss 3:5; 4:4; 16:6; 17:7, 42; 27:1; 31:3; 33:7, 18; 54:17; 60:3; 68:4; 76:2; 85:3, 7; 87:2, 10, 14; 118:145, 146, 147; 119:1; 129:1; 141:2, 6 LXX.

46. This is remarkably similar to the audience's situation. Like the suffering righteous in the Psalm, the audience is suffering even though they are under no condemnation.

47. Obeng, "Abba, Father," 363–64, argues that the "Abba, Father" in Rom 8:15 *is* a prayer.

48. In fact, Rom 16 indicates that Paul has many friends in Rome, which means that the apostle's trials and hardships are probably not unknown to the audience. If that is the case, then the audience is invited to share in Paul's apostolic sufferings. Of course, this is an "invitation" (an encouragement to participate), and does not mean that the audience does have a "shared" experience of suffering with Paul, since he has not been to Rome himself.

49. See, e.g., Dunn, *Romans 1–8*, 453–54; Byrne, *Romans*, 252–3; Moo, *Romans*, 502–3; Johnson, *Reading*, 134; Obeng, "Abba, Father," 364. See Burke, *Adopted*, 90–98, for a recent succinct discussion on the use of ἀββά in Romans and Galatians. See also Paulsen, *Überlieferung*, 92–93, who argues that the *Abba*-Father comes from Hellenistic Jewish Christianity.

50. Witherington, *Romans*, 218n37.

movement."[51] Importantly, it is in Jesus' anxious prayer in Gethsemane that he cried *Abba* (Mark 14:36).[52] This suggests that the audience—and Paul himself included—are called to share in Jesus' suffering, a point that the letter will make explicit very soon in 8:17.[53] As Burke says, "Just as Jesus, God's Son, suffered, so the adopted son is called upon to share in Jesus' sufferings."[54] The term αββα itself probably denotes the intimacy that Jesus has with his Father, given its general Aramaic usage, and given the fact that Jesus used it in his time of deep emotional need before the cross.[55] Noting that Gethsemane functions as a crisis point in the passion narrative, Joel Green suggests that "Gethsemane, then, does not so much demonstrate Jesus' anguish in the face of death as his fear of being abandoned by God."[56] This is possible, I think, because those experiencing severe hardship yearn for assurance that God will not leave them. In light of these, the *Abba*-cry in Rom 8:15c implies that believers can share the same intimacy with God that Jesus had, and they can call upon the Father in their trials and pain, no matter how intense their afflictions are. This *Abba*-cry is of course Spirit-inspired. If we recall that the Spirit is the "Spirit of Christ" (8:9), then it makes sense to think that the Spirit's role is to inspire believers to share in Christ's suffering and intimacy with the Father.

In sum, 8:15c speaks of an emotional cry to the Father God that is enabled by the Spirit of υἱοθεσία. This Spirit-inspired passionate cry expresses

51. Ibid., 218.

52. Mark 14:36, Rom 8:15 and Gal 4:6 are the only three places in the NT where the term ἀββά is used. Jesus' prayer of course expresses his anxiety, but Boring, *Mark*, 399, is right to note that Jesus is not the tragic hero of Greek drama. Boring also mentions briefly the possibility of Greek-speaking Hellenistic Christianity using Jesus' usage of *Abba*.

53. Wenham, *Paul*, 278–79, argues for a connection between the *Abba*-cry in Rom 8 and the Gethsemane story in the Gospels. In addition, Wenham says, "The Christian is called to face suffering and physical death with Jesus . . . the way to face it is, as Jesus did, by prayer through the Spirit to the Abba, Father; the present longing, but also confident expectation, is to share in Jesus' resurrection and the redemption of the body."

54. Burke, *Adopted*, 95–96.

55. See Burke, *Adopted*, 94, for a concise discussion on the Aramaic use of *Abba*. Responding to the argument that the Aramaic term is not only used by infants but also adult children (and hence stripping its sense of intimacy), Fee, *Empowering*, 411, says that "but its use by adult children in an Aramaic home does not thereby make it a more adult word." Fee goes on to say, "Most likely the word was in fact an expression of intimacy, used by children first as infants and later as adults, reflecting what is true in many such cultures where the terms of endearment for one's parents are used lifelong." Cf. Dunn, *Romans 1–8*, 454–55. The suggestion by Jeremias, *Abba*, 15–67, that αββα refers to something like "Daddy" is not widely accepted today. But that does not mean a lack of intimacy. See discussion by Jewett, *Romans*, 499.

56. Green, "Gethsemane," 266.

believers' intimate filial relationship with God, which is a relationship that they share with Christ. Through the Jesus-tradition, they would be familiar with the intensely relational word *Abba* used by Jesus in his prayers, especially the prayer at Gethsemane in Mark 14:36. It is likely, then, that they find themselves identifying with Jesus. That is, they share the same yearning for intimacy with the Father God during their times of great needs. The mention of this kind of intimate emotional prayer invites the audience to pray in the same manner as they face their daily hardship and injustice. Just as Jesus cried to the Father, they can do likewise.

The Co-Witness of the Spirit

The somewhat surprising lack of a conjunction or particle at the beginning of Rom 8:16 suggests that Paul is unpacking the preceding verse and clarifying the *Abba*-cry.[57] The point of v. 16 seems to be that, by means of inspiring believers to cry "*Abba* Father," the Spirit bears witness with their spirit that they are God's children. I will argue that this affirmation by the Spirit is significant for an audience facing hardship because it implies that God has not abandoned them despite their suffering.

Romans 8:16 uses τέκνα rather than υἱοί. This is the first use of the term τέκνον in Romans,[58] and it is never used to refer to Christ's Sonship. Given the ease with which Paul switches between τέκνον and υἱός in 8:14, 16, 17, 19 and 21, it is likely they are interchangeable (when applied to believers).[59] The verb συμμαρτυρέω is worth noting. In 6:1–11 there was a string of συ-compounds and a σύν preposition (five in total), which were used to denote the participation of believers in Christ's death and resurrection.[60] Here in 8:16 we see the first of the frequent use of συ-compounds in Rom 8 (ten in total).[61] The work of the divine Spirit takes place in the form of co-witnessing (συμμαρτυρέω) with the human spirit.[62] Given the

57. See Jewett, *Romans*, 500; Dunn, *Romans 1–8*, 454; Fee, *Empowering*, 567.

58. The term υἱός appears twelve times in Romans, six of which refers to Christ as God's Son. The term τέκνον appears seven times in Romans.

59. See Dunn, *Romans 1–8*, 454–55. But, as suggested by Jewett, *Romans*, 500–501 and Byrne, *Romans*, 253, τέκνον may carry some "inclusive" connotations, including gender and social status inclusivity.

60. Here is the list: συνθάπτω ("bury with"; 6:4); σύμφυτος ("united with"; 6:5; note that this applies to both death and resurrection); συσταυρόω ("crucify with"; 6:6); [ἀποθνῄσκω] σὺν Χριστῷ ("[die] with Christ"; 6:8) and συζάω ("live with"; 6:8).

61. They appear in 8:16, 17(x3), 22(x2), 26, 28, 29, and 32.

62. Most likely in Rom 8:16 the first πνεῦμα refers to the divine Spirit and the second to the human spirit. See the discussions in Fee, *Empowering*, 567–69; Jewett, *Romans*,

notion of participation that is found in the συ-words in 6:1–11 and soon in 8:17, I suggest that there is an element of the believers' participation in the witnessing in 8:16. That is, the Spirit of God (who is also the Spirit of Christ; 8:9) works alongside the spirit of believers (corporately), leading them and affirming them as they simultaneously participate in the Spirit-inspired *Abba*-cry. This, in turn, means that the Spirit affirms their relationship with God as their Father.[63] This Spirit-human working-together will appear again in 8:24–27.

It was suggested in the discussion above that an audience living with daily trials would identify with Jesus' prayer at Gethsemane, and an aspect of this prayer would be a plea that the Father would not abandon them in their times of need. In light of this, the co-witness in v. 16 is the Spirit-empowered testimony of God's abiding presence when believers take part in the *Abba*-cry, and the content of this testimony may be that God will not leave them in their pain and sorrow. Recalling the point we made earlier about the Spirit of slavery in 8:15a, v. 16 affirms the fact that believers should have no fear of the evil that stems from the cosmic powers of sin and death, for the co-testimony is that they are indeed God's children, having been liberated from Adamic humanity.

Concluding Remarks on Rom 8:14, 15, 16

In conclusion, believers' Spirit-led filial relationship with God is at the center of 8:14–17. The Spirit brings about the υἱοθεσία of believers. That is, through the Spirit they have received the "adoption to sonship," and as a result they inherit the full privileges of being God's eschatological people. Their Spirit-led identity as the children of God is an integral part of God's program of transforming humanity. They do not need to fear (as Adamic humanity would), because they no longer live under the dominion of sin and death but the domain of God, having been set free by the Spirit. As they live out this Spirit-led life, they are inspired by the Spirit to identify with Christ in his intimate *Abba*-prayer to the Father in his time of need.

500; Kruse, *Romans*, 339. Also, Jewett rightly says that Paul is not concerned with a doctrine of the Spirit or anthropology in Rom 8:16. It is best not to be over-concerned with the mechanism of how the co-witnessing works between the divine Spirit and the (corporate) human spirit.

63. Fee, *Empowering*, 567, puts it this way, "In saying this, Paul picks up the language of his heritage ('out of the mouth of two witnesses') and indicates that our *awareness* and *assurance* of this new relationship with God has the twofold witness of God's Spirit together with our own spirits." (Emphasis original)

All of these are of course valuable to an audience experiencing socio-economic hardship and religio-political injustice in Rome. Their identity as God's children means that God will not abandon them despite their suffering, and indeed the Spirit bears witness to their relationship with him. In the verse that immediately follows 8:14–16, the audience will hear the first explicit mention of suffering since 5:2–5, and to this important verse we now turn.

ROMANS 8:17

As it will be argued, 8:17 hinges on the fact that believers are children of God, which has been the dominant theme in vv. 14–16. Since believers are children of God, they are heirs of God and co-heirs with Christ. We will find that the inheritance spoken of in 8:17 points to the hope of believers inheriting the cosmos, which paves the way for the themes of hope and creation in the subsequent pericope in 8:18–30. Indeed, 8:17 is crucial for the argument in 8:18–30. This is because much of the subject matter in 8:18–30 depends on the believers' vocation of participating in Christ's suffering and glory, which, I will argue, is an important point stated in 8:17.[64]

Jewett rightly calls Rom 8:17 a "rhetorical climax."[65] It brings believers' identity as God's children to a new height by referring to their heirship. Verse 16 finishes with "τέκνα θεοῦ" and 8:17 begins with the words "εἰ δὲ τέκνα." This means that 8:17 is linked to the theme of God's children in 8:14–16 and hence the work of Christ and the Spirit throughout 8:1–16. At the same time, v. 17 reintroduces the themes of suffering and glory that have been in the background since 5:2–5. It speaks of believers' co-suffering and co-glorification with Christ, which will be elaborated in detail in 8:18–30. The συμπάσχομεν and συνδοξασθῶμεν in 8:17 correspond to the παθήματα/δόξαν in 8:18 and the ἐδόξασεν in 8:30, which in turn bookend the next pericope (8:18–30) and highlight the theme of the anticipated glory in the midst of suffering (as stated in 8:18).[66] Lastly, 8:17 is the first of only four references to "glory" in the letter where glory is directly attributed to believers.[67] Since

---

64. Wright, *Paul*, 440, rightly says that Rom 8:17 speaks of the vocation of believers to suffer.

65. Jewett, *Romans*, 501.

66. Thus, Rom 8:17 has a transitional role between 8:1–17 and 8:18–30. Cf. Moo, *Romans*, 504; Kruse, *Romans*, 341. But of course the subject matter of 8:17 has much to do with the believers being God's children, and hence it belongs to the unit 8:14–17.

67. The term συνδοξάζω only occurs in Rom 8:17. The terms δόξα and δοξάζω appear twenty times throughout Romans. (See Appendix A.) Apart from the usage in 8:18, 21, 30, and perhaps 5:2, nearly all of the others are used in reference to God. That is, they

the other three references are in 8:18–30 (8:18, 21, 30), v. 17 introduces an important notion in the next pericope, which, as I will argue, is about God's purpose of glorifying the new humanity through their vocation of suffering with Christ.[68]

Linguistically, 8:17 contains three συ-compounds, namely, συγκληρονόμος, συμπάσχω, and συνδοξάζω. The concentration of occurrences (three in one verse) is a rare phenomenon, and it must have a rhetorical effect on the hearers.[69] All three words are about participation in Christ.[70] Here we must note that the notion of identification with Christ is not new to the audience. In 6:4, 5, 6, 8 there are four συ-compounds and a preposition σύν, namely, συνθάπτω (6:4); σύμφυτος (6:5);[71] συσταυρόω (6:6); [ἀποθνῄσκω] σὺν Χριστῷ (6:8) and συζάω (6:8).[72] All of these concern participation in Christ's death and resurrection.[73] The concern of 6:1–11 is about the fact that believers should not continue in sin because they have been baptized into Christ (6:1–3). Having been baptized into Christ, they are to share in Christ's death and resurrection, and in doing so they are to consider that

---

either refer to the glory of God or glory given to him by humans. The terms are used in 8:18, 21, 30 (and possibly in 5:2) to *directly* refer to the glory of believers (in that they reflect/display God's glory). In the case of 2:8, 10, δόξα refers to anyone who does good, and one may say that it indirectly refers to believers. In 9:4, it refers to Israel's privilege. In 11:13 δοξάζω refers to Paul's ministry. Finally, I note the study by Gaventa, "Glory of God," 34–36. For Gaventa, the glory of God in Romans is about God's presence, and it also signals "God's presence as it triumphs over God's own enemies, most especially the enemies named Sin and Death" (36).

68. Still, "Placing Pain," 83, arrives at a similar view that suffering is "constitutive of the Christian vocation in the time between times; and anything but a sign of God-forsakenness." (I am grateful to Professor Still for sending me a draft version of his paper, so that I could work on it before its publication.)

69. Cf. Hultgren, *Romans*, 317.

70. The συγκληρονόμοι Χριστοῦ indicates that all three συ-compounds refer to a quality that one shares with Christ or an action that one performs with him. See, for example, Hultgren, *Romans*, 317. Gorman, *Apostle*, 374, is another scholar who notes the frequent use of the συ-compounds in Rom 8 and its relevance to believers' identification with Christ. Campbell, *Union*, 231, helpfully suggests that συμπάσχω and συνδοξάζω refer to "a dynamic participation in the events of Christ's experience." He, however, thinks that συγκληρονόμοι "must be understood as indicating a positional state." But he notes that "the two notions are closely connected—in fact, they may be understood as referring to the same ultimate spiritual reality."

71. Note that this applies to both death and resurrection.

72. Likewise, Hooker, *From Adam*, 45, finds an echo of Rom 6:4, 5, 8 in 8:17.

73. I am in substantial agreement with the study of Rom 6:1–7:6 by Gorman, *Inhabiting*, 73–85, where he argues that Christ's crucifixion and the believers' participation in the crucifixion are both important in the letter's soteriology. (Gorman's focus is, however, on Paul's view of justification.) See also Powers, *Salvation*, 109–10.

they are dead to sin and alive to God in Christ (6:11). In Chapter 3 we high-lighted the narrative structure of the Christ-story, as well as that of the new humanity in Christ. The συ-compounds in 6:1–11 underscore the interface between the two stories. In Christ a new humanity has been formed, who shares the crucifixion and resurrection of Christ. Romans 8:17 speaks of a pattern of identification with Christ that is not dissimilar to 6:1–11, but the focus here is on being heirs, suffering, and glorification. Thus, the interface between the stories of Christ and believers is extended.[74] With this in mind, we will examine the different components of 8:17 in detail.

Joint-Heirs of God with Christ to Inherit the Cosmos

Romans 8:17 says that we are heirs of God and co-heirs with Christ. The term κληρονόμος has already appeared in 4:13, 14, which indicates that believers are heirs of the age-old promise to Abraham and hence heirs of the κόσμος.[75] Also, in Exodus Israel is led by YHWH to enter and inherit (κληρονομέω) the promised land (Exod 15:17; 23:30; 32:13).[76] But in 8:17 the emphasis of believers' heirship is not so much about them being Abraham's descendants or that they will inherit a land, but that they are children of God, as indicated by the opening εἰ τέκνα. That is, they are heirs of God because they are members of a Spirit-led people who have an intimate filial relationship with the Father.[77] In other words, we may speak of the universalization of God's promised inheritance for an eschatological people that consists of both Jews and Gentiles, and this inheritance involves the future possession of the entire cosmos.[78]

74. As mentioned, more συ-compounds will appear in Rom 8 (8:16, 17(x3), 22(x2), 26, 28, 29, 32). One of them is about identification with Christ (8:29), and it is of great significance (see later discussion).

75. The promise to Abraham was originally primarily about the inheritance of the land for him and his descendants (Gen 15:7). But in later Judaism this was broadened to include the whole world (cf. Sir 44:21) and (eschatologically) the "world to come" (cf. Sir 44:21; 4 Ezra 6:59). See Byrne, *Romans*, 157, 253.

76. See also Deut 1:8, 21, 39; 28:21, 63; 30:5, 16, 18. Cf. Keesmaat, *Paul and His Story*, 81–84.

77. Like the terms υἱός, τέκνον, and υἱοθεσία in 8:14–16, the notion of "inheritance" is also found in the Scripture to refer to Israel's privileges as their God's chosen people, especially in terms of their possession of the promised land (e.g., Exod 23:30; 32:13; Deut 28:63; 30:5). But just as the notion of "sonship" has been universalized, what we see in Rom 8:17 is that believers share the privileges of being God's worldwide eschatological people.

78. Cf. Walters, "Paul," 56, 65, who thinks that Paul refers to "Jewish and Gentile Christians without ethnic distinctions" in Romans. Walters also points out that Rom

The rhetorical effect of believers being heirs is magnified by the three-fold use of κληρονόμος/συγκληρονόμος. They are "heirs," "heirs of God," and "joint-heirs" with Christ.[79] The term συγκληρονόμος is used in both the New Testament and extra-biblical literatures to refer to fellow sharers (or fellow partakers) of someone's property or God's promises.[80] Since Christ's identity as God's Son was recently mentioned in 8:3, it is highly likely that Christ is an heir by virtue of the fact that he is the Son of God.[81] Being children of God, believers are joint-heirs with Christ, sharing the inheritance that is rightfully ascribed to God's children. Note that in 8:17 we have the first mention of Christ since v. 11. Verses 12–16 have shown that the Spirit is instrumental to the identity of believers being God's children. But here in 8:17 Christ comes into the picture, with a clear focus on the participation of believers in him.

Recalling the argument from 8:1, the Spirit-led new humanity enjoys the privileges of being God's children. The Spirit-empowered life pattern is possible because of Christ's atoning death (8:3–4). The Spirit-inspired identity of believers being God's children lays the foundation for their heirship (8:14–17a). In 8:17 the christological focus of the letter returns in earnest. The children of God *are* co-heirs *with Christ*. This then leads to their call to co-suffering and co-glorification with Christ. We will discuss this matter shortly, but before that some grammatical considerations are in order.

The Usage of εἴπερ and ἵνα in Romans 8:17

In the following we will take a close look at the εἴπερ and ἵνα in the final part of 8:17 (εἴπερ συμπάσχομεν ἵνα καὶ συνδοξασθῶμεν). The εἴπερ can be translated as "seeing that" (or "since, as it is the case"),[82] or "provided that." The former means that suffering with Christ is the evident fact of being heirs with him. It is not really a condition, but an integral part of being his followers.[83] The latter means that suffering with Christ should be accepted

8:17 reflects the Greco-Roman notion of adoption.

79. The Χριστοῦ in Rom 8:17 here seems to be a genitive of association.

80. The term συγκληρονόμος appears in the NT four times (Rom 8:17; Eph 3:6; Heb 11:9; 1 Pet 3:7). See Jewett, *Romans*, 502nn308–309, for a comprehensive list of extra-biblical use of the term.

81. Elsewhere in Paul the idea of Christ inheriting God's kingdom can be found in Phil 2:9–11 and 1 Cor 15:22–28. (But note that in the Philippians passage Christ is not referred as God's Son, although in 1 Cor 15:28 he is.)

82. This seems to be the usage in Rom 8:9.

83. See, e.g., Cranfield, *Romans I-VIII*, 407, Jewett, *Romans*, 502, Smith, *Seven Explanations*, 178.

as something reasonable. That is, the conjunction carries a hortatory and conditional sense. I agree with Dunn, along with not a few other scholars, that "provided that" seems to be a better translation.[84] Taking this sense of εἴπερ means that the ἵνα (which is after the συμπάσχομεν and before the συνδοξασθῶμεν) is not weakened.[85] The purpose of God glorifying his people will stand, and suffering with Christ is an important part of that purpose. It seems, however, that the call to suffer with Christ is not a warning, as if the audience exhibits strong reluctance to do so. Instead, Paul is simply urging his audience to join him in following Christ's pattern of life.[86]

Thus, believers are joint-heirs with Christ provided that they suffer with him. Paul goes on to say that the purpose of their suffering with Christ is that they might be glorified with him. The ἵνα here in Rom 8:17 is most probably used to indicate both purpose and result.[87] That is, it signifies both God's intention and the certainty that he will accomplish the shared glorification of Christ and believers. Dunn puts it well,

> The final force of the ἵνα should not be weakened. The implication is again clear: suffering with Christ is not an optional extra or a decline or lapse from the saving purpose of God. On the contrary, it is a necessary and indispensable part of that purpose. Without it future glory would not be attained.[88]

84. Dunn, *Romans 1–8*, 456. Scholars who hold this view are not hard to find. See, e.g., Byrne, *Romans*, 253–54; Schreiner, *Romans*, 428, Moo, *Romans*, 506, Kasemann, *Romans*, 229, Beker, *Paul*, 364–65, Gorman, *Cruciformity*, 305, 326; Hultgren, *Romans*, 317; Forman, *Politics*, 109.

85. Dunn, *Romans 1–8*, 456. See also Gorman, *Cruciformity*, 326n36.

86. And, as they do so, they too (like Paul) can look forward to the glory that God has in store for them (cf. 8:18).

87. See Wallace, *Greek Grammar*, 474.

88. Dunn, *Romans 1–8*, 456. Note that Dunn translates ἵνα as "in order that." So do NIV and ESV, as well as Schreiner, *Romans*, 419, 428; Byrne, *Romans*, 248, 253; Jewett, *Romans*, 474; Hultgren, *Romans*, 310. But note the comments by Moo, *Romans*, 506n51, "The ἵνα ('in order that') that Paul uses to connect our suffering with Christ and our being glorified with him does not indicate the purpose *we* have in suffering with Christ but the objective goal, or outcome, of the sufferings as set forth by God" (Moo's emphasis). My view is that we need to come to terms with the tension that, on the one hand, without suffering with Christ there is no glorification with him. But on the other hand, glorification is God's initiative and he will accomplish his purpose. Suffering with Christ is about believers' willingness to participate in Christ's death rather than a virtue or a means to attain glorification.

The Vocation to Suffer with Christ

With the above interpretation of εἴπερ and ἵνα, a literal translation of 8:17 can be provided as follows:

> and if children, then heirs, heirs of God and co-heirs with Christ, provided that we co-suffer, in order (and with the result) that we might also be co-glorified.[89]

Although in classical Greek συμπάσχω can mean "suffer with" or "sympathize with," there is no doubt that the former is the case here.[90] Most likely the term refers to sharing in Christ's suffering.[91] The first person plural (συμπάσχομεν), again, indicates that both Paul and the audience partake in suffering as siblings in Christ, and they do so because they are all joint-heirs with Christ in God's family. As mentioned, this resembles the notion of identification with Christ's death and resurrection expressed through the συ-compounds in 6:1–11, which indicates that the life pattern of the new humanity is shaped by Christ's life pattern. That is, to suffer with Christ means that believers understand their suffering as a necessary component of identifying with Christ's death. In other words, there is a merging of identities and patterns of existence between Christ and his followers.[92]

Significantly, the εἴπερ (as discussed above) indicates that suffering with Christ should be accepted as essential for the believers' co-heirship with Christ. That is, they are joint-heirs with Christ provided that they share in his suffering. Since being heirs of God is the product of the Spirit's leading and the associated Spirit-inspired intimate relationship with God, and since the Spirit's work is an integral part of God's project of transforming humanity, it seems that the call to suffer with Christ is also part of God's purpose of reconciling humanity to himself.

What types of suffering does the letter refer to? We have to wait for the affliction-list in 8:35 for detailed information. But two comments are needed here. First, given the lack of emphasis on any particular type of hardship from 8:35 (e.g., persecution), Moo is right to say that the sufferings in

89. The καί in Rom 8:17 is omitted by P46. This is likely to be a copying accident. See Jewett, *Romans*, 476; Fee, *Empowering*, 560n259.

90. See Jewett, *Romans*, 503, and the translation of most commentaries and English Bibles.

91. Hultgren, *Romans*, 317; Dunn, *Romans 1–8*, 456; Byrne, *Romans*, 253; Jewett, *Romans*, 503; Kruse, *Romans*, 340; Heil, *Romans*, 84; Kasemann, *Romans*, 229. See most English translations (e.g., NET, NIV, NRSV).

92. I have borrowed this language from Smith, *Seven Explanations*, 176, who says, "[T]here is a merging of identities between the believer and Christ, so that the believer is said to participate in the death and resurrection of Christ."

view here "encompass the whole gamut of suffering, including things such as illness, bereavement, hunger, financial reverses, and death itself."[93] This means that we can include the socioeconomic hardship and religio-political injustice that are commonly experienced by the audience in imperial Rome. As Jewett says,

> [Commentators] tend to overlook the contextual implications of this formulation [ie., the sufferings of the νῦν καιρός in Rom 8:18] would have had for the Roman believers who had already experienced harassment and deportation and whose everyday life as members of the Roman underclass was anything but idyllic.[94]

Second, not only is there little evidence that specific types of suffering are in view, there is also little information about the manner in which suffering takes place. For example, it does not specify that one has to suffer *for following Christ*, as in being persecuted because of the proclamation of his name. What the text does say is that believers are to suffer *with* Christ. This, at the very least (but not exclusively), points to the death of Christ, and hence the suffering associated with it. But in the context of imperial Rome, the audience might be drawn to associate the suffering of Christ with the injustice and affliction of his death on the Roman cross, which was a symbol of shame and humiliation.[95] The cross, as is often pointed out, was the Empire's means to execute its subjects when they rebelled against them.[96] From the perspective of Rome's conquered peoples, the cross represented Caesar's unjust socio-political oppression. Given this context, the audience would find that their present socioeconomic hardship and religio-political injustice were part and parcel of the call to suffer with Christ.[97]

93. Moo, *Romans*, 511. Scholars tend to relate the affliction-list in Rom 8:35 (and other references to suffering in Rom 8) to Paul's own suffering. (Cf. e.g., Dunn, *Romans 1–8*, 504–5.) But the audience in Rome probably did not have exactly the same type of suffering as Paul had. Nor was the cause of their suffering necessarily be the same as that of Paul's. In addition, the text in Rom 8 does not indicate that Paul (the implied author) himself expects his Roman audience to experience the exact types of suffering he has.

94. Jewett, *Romans*, 509. See my forthcoming exegesis on Rom 8:18.

95. Elliott and Reasoner, *Documents*, 102.

96. See the well documented discussion by Elliott and Reasoner, *Documents*, 102–7.

97. We should note that the very notion of suffering with Christ is unique. In his detailed study of Paul's explanations of suffering of the righteous, Smith, *Seven Explanations*, 174–83, is able to find (at least partial) references in Israel's Scripture and/or Jewish literatures to different types of explanations *except* for the "participation in the suffering of Christ." Smith finds only the following examples of "participation in the

In short, Christ-followers, as members of God's new humanity, are called to suffer with Christ. It is an integral part of being Spirit-led children of God. This fits in well with our discussion on the *Abba*-cry in 8:15. There the audience is invited to participate in Jesus' prayer at Gethsemane at a time of intense trial before the cross. Now in 8:17 the audience is emphatically asked to participate in his suffering, including the type of suffering Jesus endured on the cross. Being children means that they are joint-heirs with Christ, with the hope of inheriting the cosmos. But they enjoy this privilege provided that they identify with Christ's suffering. The audience is invited to understand their present sufferings as an essential part of their vocation of participating in Christ's life pattern.[98] With this we are ready to look at the meaning of being glorified with Christ.

Be Glorified with Christ to Display God's Glory

The purpose of suffering with Christ is that believers may be glorified with him. Συνδοξάζω is a rare verb, and only appears in classical sources in the active voice.[99] Only Paul uses it in the passive, and it is used only in Rom 8:17. The passive συνδοξασθῶμεν suggests that it is the work of God and his Spirit that will accomplish glorification. The terms δόξα and δοξάζω occur frequently in the letter,[100] and they almost always have something to do with God. Glory is an attribute of God (1:23; 3:7, 23; 6:4; 11:36; 15:7; 16:27), and he acts according to his glory (9:23). Human beings are to glorify him (15:6) and give him glory (4:20; cf. 1:23; 11:36; 15:7; 16:27). Since glory is about the honor that is due to God, it seems that the usage in 3:23 is highly significant for our discussion here. Romans 3:23 says that all have sinned and fall short of the glory of God. Commentators often refer the "glory" here to the trespass of Adam and the motif of the primeval loss of glory that is found in

---

suffering of Christ": Rom 8:16–18; 2 Cor 1:4–6; 2 Cor 4:10–12, 17; Phil 3:7–11; Col 1:24 (177–82). These are all in the Pauline tradition, not elsewhere.

98. As Gorman, *Cruciformity*, 305, says, "In this text [8:15b–17] Paul infers the absolute necessity of suffering on the part of those who live in Christ . . . " For observations regarding Paul's theology of suffering outside Romans, see Wolter, "Der Apostel," 556–57. Wolter finds that identification with Christ's suffering is inseparable from the apostle's mission to proclaim the gospel, and that just as Paul's suffering signifies that he belongs to Christ, so does the suffering of the eschatological community signify that they belong to Paul. But, again, as far as Romans goes, the text does not specify that the audience has to share in the apostle's suffering.

99. Jewett, *Romans*, 503.

100. See Appendix A for the distribution of the use of the terms δόξα and δοξάζω in Romans. See Blackwell, "Immortal Glory," 298–99, for a helpful summary of the usage of δόξα/δοξάζω in Romans.

Jewish apocalyptic literature.[101] For example, in *Life of Adam and Eve* 21:6 Adam says to Eve, "You have estranged me from the glory of God."[102] Also, *3 Bar.* (Greek) 4:16 says, "Then know, Baruch, that just as Adam through this tree was condemned and was stripped of the glory of God, thus men now . . . become distant from the glory of God . . . "[103] In view of this, before his trespass Adam's life reflected God's glory.[104] But afterwards, the glory was lost, or tinted. Adamic humanity is "dead" because it is under the reign of sin and hence cannot reflect/display God's glory. But according to 5:12–21, through Christ's death sin's power has been defeated, and a new humanity has been created. This suggests that the glorification in 8:17 refers to how the new humanity in Christ may display God's glory.[105]

The other usage of "glory" relevant to our discussion is found in 1:23–25,[106] which says that human beings exchanged the glory of the immortal God for an image (εἰκών) resembling a mortal human being or animals, and that they worshipped the creature rather than the Creator. This apparent reference to idolatry reflects the notion that the images of idols display the attributes of the associated deities.[107] Likewise, having been made in the Creator God's image, Adamic humanity is supposed to display his glory. Idolatrous behavior takes place when Adamic humanity fails to exhibit

101. For example, Dunn, *Romans 1–8*, 168; Kruse, *Romans*, 182. See also Witherington, *Romans*, 102.

102. Dunn, *Romans 1–8*, 168. See also Byrne, *Romans*, 131; Kruse, *Romans*, 182. Byrne also points us to an oft-quoted passage in *2 Bar* 51:3, which says, "Also, as for the glory of those who proved to be righteous . . . their splendor will then be glorified by transformations, and the shape of their face will be changed into the light of their beauty, so that they may acquire and receive the undying world which is promised to them."

103. Cf. Byrne, *Romans*, 131.

104. I note the caution issued by Gaventa, "Glory of God," 31, that Rom 3:23 does not explicitly refer to "humanity's original state of glory" in Genesis. Gaventa prefers to say that Paul refers to "the loss of its proper, worshipful relationship to God."

105. This does not mean that the glory of the new humanity is simply a restoration to Adam's glory. Rather, as our discussion of Rom 8:29 will show, it is about displaying God's glory by conforming to Christ's image. Blackwell, "Immortal Glory," 301–2, makes a similar point.

106. Cf. Ps 106:20.

107. For example, Jupiter was the god of sky and thunder, and was portrayed majestically with an eagle and thunderbolts. Minerva was the goddess of wisdom, and in the Capitoline triad she was seated on the right of Jupiter with an owl, which symbolized wisdom. The Egyptian sun god, Ra, is often depicted with the head of a hawk with a *solar* disk on top. See Rodgers, *Roman World*, 166–67, for a description of the Capitoline triad. See also Walton, *Ancient Near Eastern Thought*, 212. Incidentally, people in the non-Western world today (including myself) who are familiar with temples and idols would know well that the attributes of the deities are depicted in the images of idols.

God's glory and "exchanges" that calling with worshipping the images of idols.[108] If we understand the "glory" in 8:17 in light of this, then, again, the glorification of the believers would have something to do with how the children of God—who belong to a new and transformed humanity—may display God's glory.

What is surprising in 8:17 is that, instead of displaying God's glory primarily by means of a righteous life, glorification will take place when believers suffer with Christ. Of course, their identity as God's children depends on the atoning death of Christ and the consequent Spirit-empowered fulfilling of the law (8:1–4). But at the same time they are co-heirs provided that they share in Christ's suffering. It is in their participation in his suffering that they will be glorified with him.[109] This is the way to exhibit the glory of God. So, a righteous life pattern is presupposed, and indeed required from God's children. The emphasis in 8:17, however, is that God intends to glorify his children and they are to suffer with Christ in order that God's purpose may be fulfilled.[110]

It should be noted that glorification is *with* Christ, as highlighted by the συ-prefix. The heirship, suffering, and glorification of believers are all thoroughly christocentric. Just as they are to participate in Christ's death and resurrection (6:1–11), they are called to identify with Christ's suffering and glorification.[111] Indeed, 8:29 says that they are being conformed to the image of the Son (which is a matter we will discuss in detail). It should also

108. See the discussions in Byrne, *Romans*, 67–68, 75; Dunn, *Romans 1–8*, 61–64; Moo, *Romans*, 108–13; Jewett, *Romans*, 160–62.

109. This comment by Blackwell, "Immortal Glory," 304, resonates with certain aspects of our discussion: "Accordingly, Paul both subverts and fulfils Roman striving for *gloria* and redefines Jewish hopes for glory and immortality through the crucified and risen saviour . . . At the same time, the role of suffering shows that *gloria* is not achieved through 'success' but through the christoform life empowered by the Spirit."

110. The notion of God being glorified at the suffering of his people is not new. It can be found, for example, in Ps 50:15 (49:15 LXX). The LXX, which follows the MT closely, says, "And call on me in a day of affliction [θλῖψις], and I will deliver you, and you will glorify me." See Forman, *Politics*, 128, who looks at a number of Jewish texts, including Isa 52:13—53:12; Dan 7:21–22, and argues that "suffering-as-prelude-to-glory" is found in Paul as well as in Jewish writings.

111. After a detailed analysis of Paul's use of "with Christ," Campbell, *Union*, 236, helpfully concludes that "both σύν-compound and noncompound expressions share the fundamental tenor of participation: believers partake *with Christ* in his death, burial, resurrection, ascension, glorification, and session in heaven." I am, at first, a little surprised that "suffering" is not mentioned here. But later Campbell returns to the topic and affirms the value of participating in Christ's suffering. He concludes that "the issue of suffering and the Christian life is that suffering is to be viewed as a *participatio Christi* and not as an *imitatio Christi* only. Believers share in the ongoing force of Christ's death and the power of his resurrection" (381).

be noted that the glorification in 8:17 has a present dimension as well as a future one. As Jewett says, "Some commentators insist that this [sharing in Christ's glory] is purely a future promise . . . nothing in Paul's formulation demands this. The future passive is not employed here."[112] The evidence for the dual present and future dimensions of glorification can be found in the usage of the terms δόξα and δοξάζω in 8:18, 21, 30, and we will examine them in Chapter 6. Suffice it to mention now that vv. 20 and 21 focus on the future aspects of the glory of the children of God, and that 8:30 indicates that the glorification is a process that has already started. As it will be shown in 8:18–23, the entire creation will be renewed *in the future* together with the children of God at the redemption of their bodies. At the same time, Jewett is probably right to think that the ἐδόξασεν in 8:30 refers to the present process of transformation on the part of the suffering followers of Christ.[113]

Finally, in light of the socioeconomic hardships and religio-political injustices faced by Paul's audience, the full realization of their glorification at the resurrection would be a sure reason for hope. But at the same time their present sufferings would serve as visible signs of the glory of God in the Roman Empire. Jewett says it well,

> Although a measure of glorification is currently visible among the saints, in partial and vulnerable forms, those who persist in living according to the Spirit will participate in its fulfillment now and at the end of time. It comes only as a gift of grace, however, and only in the context of suffering with Christ.[114]

In sum, Rom 8:14–17 is a pivotal passage. It introduces the new notion that those who are in Christ are children of God. The theme of restoring and transforming humanity that started in Rom 5 now culminates in the fact that the new humanity consists of God's children. They are children because of the work of Christ and the Spirit. But the goal of creating a new humanity is their glorification. Yet glorification can only happen if they suffer with Christ. That is, sharing in Christ's glorification requires participation in his suffering. The notion of participation in Christ has already appeared in Rom 6:1–11. It is, we may say, in the audience's identification with Christ that they show the world what it means to be truly human. That is, their life pattern of right living, perseverance in afflictions, and faithfully sharing in

---

112. Jewett, *Romans*, 503. Jewett continues to cite 2 Cor 4:18, and says that "the gift of glory is both a present and a future bonus."

113. Jewett, *Romans*, 530. This probably explains why the aorist, rather than the future tense, is used. Cf. Cranfield, *Romans I-VIII*, 432; Fee, *Pauline Christology*, 251n33.

114. Jewett, *Romans*, 503.

Christ's suffering, is an exhibition of what it is like to be the true humanity that God desires. This is how they display the glory of God, as they eagerly await their full glorification at the final resurrection. The vocation of believers, then, is to participate in Christ's suffering and glorification (8:17). Hooker puts it well,

> It is only if we suffer with him that we shall be glorified with him. We may become children of God and heirs of glory through Christ's act of self-identification with us, but if we are indeed to share his glory, we must identify ourselves with his suffering. Once again, we find the paradox that though in identifying himself with us Christ made an act of self-abnegation, those who are "in Christ" must in turn identify themselves with *his* humiliation if they are to share his glory: the pattern of death–resurrection, suffering–glory must be worked out in them.[115]

As believers fulfill their vocation, they find hope in their present sufferings because of the glory to be revealed, which is a key message of 8:18–30.

THE SHARED IDENTITY AND VOCATION OF THE SON AND GOD'S CHILDREN

Now that we have finished the detailed exegesis of 8:14–17, it is time to take a closer look at a notion that we have already mentioned briefly, namely, the merging of identities and vocations of Christ and believers. This concept will prove to be a useful interpretive tool as we study the outworking of the believers' calling. Our discussion so far has focused on the text of 8:14–17 and its role within Rom 5–8, especially 8:1–39. One emerging matter that may be more readily detected by the audience (who heard, not read, the letter) is the intertextual and thematic links between Christ as God's *Son* and the believers as God's *children*. The terms υἱός and τέκνον occur nine times in Rom 5–8, with eight of them in chapter 8. So far, υἱός has referred to Christ's Sonship in 5:10; 8:3, and the believers' filial status in 8:14. Τέκνον has referred to the believers' relationship with God in 8:16, 17. As already noted, the letter mentions believers' filial status for the very first time in 8:14–17. Indeed, nothing in the letter so far prepares the audience for the notion that they are God's children and that they have been adopted into "sonship."[116] The concentrated use of the υἱός/τέκνον language in 8:14–17, and the new notion of believers' filial relationship, serve to draw the audience's attention.

---

115. Hooker, *From Adam*, 45–46.

116. An observation noted by Fee, *Empowering*, 560.

As discussed in Chapter 4, Rom 8:3 refers to the Son's identification with humanity. We suggested that the ὁμοίωμα in 8:3 implies that the "Son" (υἱός) was truly human and was not exempt from the destructive powers of sin and death, although he did not sin. We also suggested that as a human he endured the suffering caused by the cosmic forces of sin and death, which included death on the Roman cross. Romans 8:14–17 says that the Spirit-led believers are "children" (υἱοί) of God, and that they identify with Christ's heirship, suffering, and glorification. Indeed, the *Abba*-cry in 8:15c invites the audience to share Christ's intimate filial relationship with God and participate in his passionate plea at a time of great trial. Thus, both Christ and believers share the identity of being God's Son/children, and both have the vocation of participation—that is, the Son participated in humanity and believers participate in Christ.

This shared identity and vocation between the Son and God's children can be expressed in terms of the merging of the Christ-story and the story of humanity. God sent his Son to become a human. He suffered and died, and was raised and exalted. The story of the new people of God is about participating in the Christ-story.[117] They were baptized into Christ. They were crucified with him and now live with him (6:1–11). Additionally, they suffer with him and will be glorified with him (8:17). Their shared stories are similar to the Adamic story, except that the events take place in different orders. Adamic humanity disobeyed God and died. Suffering is inevitable for humanity because of the entry of the cosmic powers of sin and death. But the eschatological people of God (God's new humanity) have been set free from those powers and are empowered by the Spirit to live right. Yes, they do suffer. But they do so because they identify with Christ's suffering, with the purpose (and result) of being glorified with him. As we will see in the next chapter, these narratives assist the audience in finding their place in God's plan of renewing the entire creation.

OVERTURNING THE EFFECTS OF ADAM'S DISOBEDIENCE IN GENESIS

As argued in Chapter 3, Genesis is most likely evoked in Rom 5–8. In fact, the creation will be explicitly mentioned in 8:19–23. Here we must ask whether the audience would detect the Genesis narratives in Rom 8:14–17.

---

117. Although Jervis, *At the Heart of the Gospel*, 108, approaches this notion from a different angle, she aptly says, "The *drama* of Christ's life is the drama of our own, and we know that we are in the period before resurrection and so will suffer." (Emphasis added)

I will argue that the language and themes of filial relationship and Spirit-led life in Rom 8 would point the audience to the fact that Adam was God's son and that he became a human being through the Spirit's activity. This evocation of Genesis, in turn, provides valuable resources for the audience to understand God's project of reversing the effects of Adam's disobedience through the faithful co-suffering of the children of God.

Throughout our study on the meaning of "children" and heirship in Rom 8:14–17, we have noted the fact that Israel is understood as YHWH's "son" and that they are to inherit the promised land. But we also noted that, as an eschatological Spirit-led people of God, believers' "sonship" has been *universalized* to all members of God's new humanity.[118] It should also be pointed out that the language of Jew-Gentile is absent in Rom 5–8. Instead, this distinct section of the letter begins with repeated references to Adam in 5:12–21. It is, then, fitting for us to investigate whether the Genesis accounts of Adam shed any light on the believers' filial relationship with God and their vocation to suffer with Christ. In other words, are there any thematic and verbal links between Genesis and Rom 8:14–17, and do they assist the audience to gain further insights into the letter?

The first contact point between the two texts can be found in Gen 5:1, 3. Gen 5 begins by stating that the chapter consists of a list of descendants of Adam. More specifically, 5:1 LXX says that this is the book (βίβλος) of the "origin"/"lineage" (γένεσις) of humankind (ἄνθρωπος). It then proceeds to say that God made Adam in his image (5:1), and that Adam became the father of (γεννάω) Seth according to his image (5:3). Here, the genealogy and the terms γένεσις, γεννάω, εἰκών suggest strongly that "sonship" and

---

118. Scholars have suggested that Romans echoes the Exodus tradition. This is notably found in the essay by Wright, "New Exodus," 26–35, and the monograph by Keesmaat, *Paul and His Story*, 54–154. I find that the best intertextual links they suggest are Paul's use of the terms of υἱός, κληρονόμος, δουλεία, and ἄγω, for they do appear in the Exodus tradition. I have mentioned these terms and their use in Exodus in my exegesis. It seems to me that the letter's use of these terms cannot be restricted to how they are used in the Exodus tradition. Most likely the audience would have understood these terms using a range of materials available to them, including those *outside* the Exodus tradition. (For example, the notion that the righteous will inherit the land is strongly present in Ps 36 LXX, with κληρονομέω/κληρονομία appearing five times. Yet the Exodus tradition seems to be absent in the Psalm.) The strength of Keesmaat's work is her argument concerning the retelling of the Exodus story in Israel's Scripture and in intertestamental Jewish literature. Thus, Keesmaat's thesis very much depends on the reinterpretations of the tradition in Israel's history, including the Second Temple period. The interest of our study, however, lies elsewhere. Our concern is primarily how the Scripture provides resources for the *audience* to understand Romans, rather than how the retelling of a certain tradition influences *Paul's* thinking.

image-bearing are intertwined. That is, the "son" bears the image of the father.[119] In other words, 5:1 and 3 indicate that just as Seth is Adam's son, so is Adam God's son.[120] Given the Adamic theme in Rom 5–8, the notion that "Adam is God's son" would be a pointer to Genesis when the audience hears Rom 8:14–17, where the text says that they are God's children.

The second contact point is the language of πνεῦμα/πνοή and the notions of life and death. Genesis 2:4–7 begins by stating that what follows is the book (βίβλος) of the "origin" (γένεσις) of heaven and earth (2:4).[121] Then in 2:7 it says that the God breathed into the face of the human the "breath"/"wind" (πνοή) of life (ζωή).[122] Thus, it is the divine inbreathing that gives life.[123] Metaphorically speaking, one may say that it is God's Spirit that has given Adam the breath of life.[124] Subsequently, the person became a living (ζῶσαν) being. Human beings, therefore, have "life" because God has given them his breath (or, spirit) of life. Without that they only have a lifeless form made of dust from the earth (2:7). Then in 2:17 God warns Adam that he will die if he disobeys him (cf. 3:3, 4). Unfortunately Adam did disobey, and both humans and the earth were cursed in Gen 3. As we said, Gen 3 is evoked in Rom 5:12–21, for both texts speak of Adam's disobedience and the "death" of Adamic humanity. With Rom 5:12–21 and Gen 3 in the background, it seems that 8:2, 6, 10, 12–13, will also alert the audience to Gen 2:7, 17. In Romans the noun ζωή is used in association with πνεῦμα in 8:2, 6, 10, and each time it refers to the life-giving work of the Spirit. The verb ζάω appears three times in 8:12–13. Twice it refers to the warning that they should not "live" (ζάω) according to the flesh, or else they will "die" (ἀποθνήσκω). The exhortation is that they should put to death the deeds of

119. Cf. Hodge, Sons, 111, who helpfully refers to the ancient worldview of "patrilineal descent," where "the image of the father is passed down to the next generation, whether the progenitor is divine or human."

120. Not surprisingly, then, the genealogy of Jesus in Luke says that Adam is God's son (Luke 3:23, 38). Interestingly, the genealogy follows immediately after the voice from heaven declaring that Jesus is God's Son at his baptism (3:22).

121. Note the intertextual link between Gen 2:4 and 5:1.

122. Note that in the MT it is the "LORD God" (יהוה אלהים)—not "God"—who breathed into the nostrils of the man in Gen 2:7. In the LXX it is θεός who did that. But note that in Gen 2:8 LXX the author switches to κύριος ὁ θεός.

123. This echoes the picture in Ezek 37, as mentioned in Chapter 4. See Wenham, Genesis 1–15, 60. Fretheim, Genesis, 350, says that Gen 2:7 speaks of "God's own living breath." Waltke, Genesis, 85, goes as far as saying that "it is the narrator's intention to stress that human beings have the very breath of God sustaining them."

124. I also find this picture of God's breath becoming human breath of life somewhat similar to the co-witnessing of divine Spirit and human spirit in Rom 8:16. Even though the type of the activities of the S/spirit are different, in both Gen 2:7 and Rom 8:16 God's Spirit and the human spirit are interconnected.

the body "by the Spirit" (πνεύματι) so that they will "live" (ζάω). The point is clear, the Spirit gives life, but the warning is that fleshly living will lead to death. This is precisely what we find in Gen 2:7, 17. God's breath (Spirit) gave life to Adam, but the warning is that disobedience will lead to death.[125]

If we put the above two contact points together, then the likelihood of detecting the primordial accounts of Genesis in Rom 8:14–17 seems to increase considerably. The two can be put together because there is a close connection between Rom 8:1–13 and 8:14. The γάρ in the beginning of 8:14 indicates that 8:14–17 explains the preceding verses. The exhortation in 8:12–13 is that believers are to walk by the Spirit so that they will live (ζάω). The reason for the exhortation is that they may enjoy all the privileges associated with their "sonship" and being God's children. In other words, life in the Spirit brings about the blessings of being God's daughters and sons, but one is warned that disobedience will lead to death. This resonates with the accounts in Genesis. Adam is God's "son," and he is a living being because he has been given the breath of life. Subsequently, he enjoys all the blessings of God's creation. But disobedience will lead to death.

If we recall the fact that 8:1–17 is a continuation of the argument from 5:1–21 (where Adam was explicitly mentioned), then it is highly likely that Genesis is evoked in 8:14–17. How does it, then, assist the audience to understand the letter? Here I want to make three suggestions. First, as argued above, as God's children the audience belongs to a new humanity. It seems that Genesis affirms that they are indeed part of this new people of God, because just like Adam was the son of God, so are they God's children. Yet where Adam failed, they will succeed, for their identity is based on and indeed merged with Christ's Sonship. Second, just as 8:14–17 prepares for the pericope in 8:18–30, so does its evocation of Genesis paves the way for the renewal of creation that will be central to 8:19–23. Our forthcoming discussion will show that, while Genesis speaks of the curse on creation, Romans talks about the hope of creation being renewed. The destinies of the children of God and creation are interdependent.

Finally, the Genesis account provides extra resource for the audience to understand their vocation of suffering. The story of Adam in Genesis is a tragic one. Our analysis in Chapter 3 has shown that the narrative in Gen 3 affirms the cosmic dimension of the powers of sin and death, and helps to explain why systemic injustice and socioeconomic hardship exist in this world. Our study of Rom 8:14–17 indicates that believers' suffering is an integral part of God's purpose of reversing the effects of Adam's disobedience.

---

125. See also *4 Ezra* 3:4–5, which also says that God breathed into Adam the breath of life. Cf. Grappe, "Qui me délivrera," 476, who sees a link between Rom 8:2 and Gen 2:7.

While the primordial history in Gen 3 explains why evil exists because of the trespass of the first "son of God" (Adam), Rom 8:14–17 tells us how the suffering of the "children of God" will be instrumental in transforming humanity despite the present sufferings. While Adam's glory was lost in Genesis, the children of God in Christ will be glorified as they participate in Christ's glory.

CONCLUSION

Romans 8:14–17 returns to the theme of suffering that commenced in 5:1–11, and is highly significant for an audience experiencing pain and affliction. Within the argument of Romans, 8:14–17 is a pivotal passage that finishes off 8:1–17 and introduces the theme of suffering and hope of glory in 8:18–39. It ultimately harks back to God's purpose to reconcile and transform humanity in 5:1–21. The passage speaks of believers' Spirit-led identity as the children of God (8:14). The Spirit brings about and affirms their full privileges as God's eschatological people (8:15b). The Spirit does not bring the fear that Adamic humanity has to endure (8:15a). It is because the Spirit has set believers free from sin and death, which are the cosmic powers that rule over Adamic humanity and the ultimate forces behind human suffering. In 8:15c Paul starts using the first person plural, which indicates to the audience that they and the apostle are enduring suffering together. The Spirit-inspired *Abba*-cry in 8:15c invites the audience to participate in Christ's intimate relationship with the Father and realize that they can call to God in our times of need, just as Jesus did at Gethsemane.

Most of all, 8:14–17 underlines the audience's vocation to participate in Christ's suffering. The purpose (and result) of this vocation is that they may display the glory of God. As they do so, they live in the hope of inheriting the cosmos as co-heirs with Christ. There is a merging of identities and life patterns between the Son and the children of God. Just as the Son identified with humanity, suffered, died, and was glorified, so do the children of God identify with Christ, suffer with him, and will be glorified with him. Their stories intertwine—and we may say that they effectively reverse the story of Adamic humanity. For the tragic story in the primordial accounts of Adam in Genesis is in the process of being rewritten as God's children carry out their vocation. With this in mind, we are well placed to study Rom 8:18–30, which speaks of the interdependent destinies of the children of God and creation.

6

Cosmic Renewal and the Purpose of Suffering

INTRODUCTION

Romans 8:18–30 is the first part of the letter's climactic conclusion to its argument since 5:1. The audience will find the frequent references to suffering and hope in this section highly relevant because of their experience in hardship and injustice. The terms πάθημα and δόξα in the opening verse of the pericope echo resoundingly the terms συμπάσχω and συνδοξάζω in the last verse of the pivotal passage 8:14–17. This, together with the γάρ in 8:18, indicates that the pericope explains how the audience may fulfill their vocation to suffer with Christ in order to be glorified with him. As it will be shown, the pericope shares the key vocabulary and themes concerning suffering, hope, and glory with 5:1–11, and it is part of the extended argument that started there. Also, the language of Ἀδάμ/κτίσις in 5:12–21 and 8:19–22 suggests that the latter harks back to the theme of restoring humanity found in the former passage. I will argue that 8:18–30 explicates how the vocation of believers to suffer with Christ is an integral part of God's purpose in bringing about the renewal of creation. Indeed, God's project of reversing the effects of Adam's disobedience is dependent on their identification with Christ.

More specifically, I will argue that 8:18 declares that the present sufferings of believers cannot thwart the glory that they will display. In line with the ancient worldview that the fortunes and destinies of humankind and creation are interlocked, we will find that the groaning and renewal of creation are connected with the groaning and glorification of the children of God (8:19–23). I will suggest that the renewal of creation is contingent on believers' faithful participation in Christ's suffering.

Two resources are available for the audience as they suffer. First, their hope of glory itself functions as a source of assurance and comfort as they endure hardship (8:24–25). Second, the Spirit assists them in their groaning (8:26–27), a notion that recalls the Spirit-inspired *Abba*-cry in 8:15. The hope of glory and the Spirit's assistance function as constant reminders and encouragement that the audience's present sufferings cannot thwart their eschatological glory. The pericope concludes by saying that the call for believers to conform to the image of the Son is an essential part of God's program of restoring humanity and renewing creation (8:28–30). I will argue that God's predetermined purpose is to gather a new people of God who will bear his image through suffering, with the purpose that they may display his glory in a process of transformation.[1]

As is often suggested, 8:19–23 alludes to Genesis, especially the curse on the earth in the account of Adam's trespass. We will investigate the various thematic and linguistic links between Genesis and Rom 8:18–30, and determine how the scriptural primordial history provides further resources for the audience to understand the place of suffering in God's redemptive purpose. I will argue that Genesis helps the audience to understand their role of being the vice-regents of God in the cosmos and the importance of their vocation to suffer with Christ.[2] After this, we will briefly outline Rome's promises of the Golden Age, and how Romans provides the audience with an alternative narrative to the Empire's propaganda.

THE HOPE OF GLORY AS BELIEVERS FULFILL THEIR VOCATION

Before our verse-by-verse analysis, several observations concerning the content of Rom 8:18–30 and its place in the argument of 5:1—8:39 need to be mentioned. The audience can hardly miss the fact that the present pericope echoes the themes of suffering, hope, perseverance, and glory in

---

1. Cf. Dunn, *Romans 1–8*, 467, who says, "Paul presents this cosmic outworking of salvation in strong Adam terms as the final reversal of man's failure and climax of his restoration." My emphasis, however, is that believers' vocation to suffer with Christ is an important integral part of this reversal.

2. Being vice-regents and at the same time having to suffer are of course paradoxical.

5:1–11. This is highlighted by the shared vocabulary of θλῖψις, ἐλπίς/ἐλπίζω, δόξα/δοξάζω, and ὑπομονή in 5:2–5, 9, 10 and 8:18, 20, 21, 22, 24–25, 30. While 5:1–11 mentions briefly how believers can boast in the hope of glory and in their affliction, 8:18–30 explains in detail how they can find hope and display God's glory as they persevere in their present sufferings. The pericope also echoes the themes in 5:12–21. This is indicated by the verbal and thematic links signified by the κόσμος/κτίσις, βασιλεύω/δουλεία, ἐλευθερόω/ἐλευθερία in 5:12, 13, 14, 17, 21 and 8:19, 20, 21, 22. While 5:12–21 speaks of the reign of sin and death that entered the cosmos, 8:18–30 talks about the freedom of believers and the associated liberation of creation from bondage (8:19–23). As discussed in Chapter 3, Rom 5:12–21 concerns God's work of delivering Adamic humanity from the dominion of sin and death, as well as his project of restoring and transforming Adamic humanity. This is, in turn, the ground for God's reconciling of humanity as they suffer and boast in the hope of glory (5:1–11). Thus, Rom 8:18–30 expands the argument in 5:1–11 and 5:12–21.[3]

Not only does 8:18–30 hark back to 5:1–21, it also specifically explains what has just been stated in 8:14–17. The repeated use of γάρ in 8:18, 19, 20, 22, 24 and 26 guides the audience to see the connection between 8:18–30 and the previous passage, and that the pericope is an elaboration on the vocation of believers to participate in Christ. The link to 8:14–17 is also affirmed by the use of τέκνον, υἱός, and υἱοθεσία in reference to believers in 8:19, 21, and 23, as well as the role of the Spirit in 8:26–27. The Spirit-led filial relationship with God is of course a prominent theme in 8:14–17. Rom 8:18–30 expands that and speaks of the inseparable link between the freedom of creation and that of the children of God (8:21). The pericope also talks about the role of the Spirit in sustaining believers in their trials (8:26–27), which is an extension of the vital role of the Spirit in 8:14–17.

But it is the theme of suffering and glory that provides the most important connection between 8:14–17 and 8:18–30. As mentioned above, the παθήματα and δόξαν in 8:18 unmistakably echo the συμπάσχομεν and συνδοξασθῶμεν in 8:17. Not only that, 8:18–30 also exhibits *a pattern of suffering and glory*, which clearly resonates with the co-suffering and co-glorification in 8:17. Verse 18 speaks of believers' eager anticipation of their glorification in the present sufferings. A picture of the "suffering" of creation can be found in 8:20–22. It was subjected to futility and "the bondage of decay" (τῆς δουλεία τῆς φθορᾶς) (8:21). The whole creation groans together and travails together (8:22). But it awaits the freedom of the glory of the

---

3. I note the terms δικαίωμα, δικαίωσις, δίκαιος, δικαιόω, δικαιοσύνη, and σῴζω in Rom 5: 1, 7, 9, 10, 16, 17, 18, 19, 21; 8:24, 30, and will discuss them when we study 8:24, 30.

children of God (8:21). Believers themselves groan in their suffering, but they await the redemption of their bodies (8:23). Verse 26 speaks of the weakness and groaning of believers, but 8:30 affirms the fact that they have been glorified. Thus, there is a pattern of suffering-to-glory throughout 8:18–30, by means of which the pericope guides the audience to understand their vocation of participating in Christ's suffering and glory (8:17).

Romans 8:18–30 functions as the *first part* of the conclusion of the argument in 5:1—8:39, which can be detected by its simultaneous connections with *both* 5:1–21 and 8:31–39. The δικ-words appear throughout 5:1–21 and the δικαιόω is found in 8:30 and 33.[4] The love language appeared briefly in 5:5 in reference to the believers' hope in their affliction. It will appear in 8:28 and then extensively in 8:35–39, again in the context of suffering. The Son was mentioned in 5:10, and will be mentioned again in 8:29 and 8:32. The intercession of the Son in 8:34 echoes the Spirit-prayer in 8:26–27, both of which are there to assist believers in their times of need. The cosmic powers of sin and death were mentioned in 5:12–21. They reign in the cosmos and are the ultimate reasons behind human suffering. In 8:19–23 the renewal of the entire cosmos constitutes the eschatological hope of believers. This cosmic renewal effectively completes the final defeat of sin's power. But, in the meantime, believers are assured that no cosmic forces can separate them from God's love (8:38–39). Finally, whereas 5:2–5 briefly mentions believers' affliction, their present sufferings (8:18) are spoken of regularly in 8:19–30. And then in 8:31–39 they are listed in detail in an affliction-list (8:35) and reiterated by the scriptural citation in 8:36. These interconnections between 5:1–21, 8:18–30 and 8:31–39 show a general escalation of the various suffering-related themes from 5:1–21 to 8:18–30 and 8:31–39, with *8:18–39 as a whole* constituting the conclusion of the argument that started in 5:1, culminating with the assurance of God's love in the midst of affliction and dangerous evil powers in 8:35–39.

Romans 8:18–30 consists of four subunits, namely, 8:18, 8:19–23, 8:24–27, and 8:28–30.[5] The argument of the pericope can be traced through the main messages of the subunits. The first subunit (8:18) states that the sufferings of the present time do not thwart the glory that is to be revealed. The next subunit (8:19–23) elaborates on v. 18. It speaks of the present groaning of creation and the children of God, as well as their eager expectation of the future glory of God's children. Verse 23 concludes 8:19–23 by mentioning

4. The δικ-words appear in Rom 5:1, 7, 9, 16, 17, 18, 19, 21.

5. Commentators differ in terms of how the pericope in Rom 8:18–30 should be subdivided. Having said that, most often 8:18 and 8:28–30 are considered to be distinguishable subunits by scholars. My way of subdividing the pericope resembles that of Jewett, *Romans*, 507–8.

the redemption of the body, and at the same time functions as a transition to the following subunit by introducing the Spirit's abiding presence. The third subunit (8:24–27) continues to elaborate on the statement in v. 18. Two resources, namely, hope and the Spirit, are available for the audience as they wait in anticipation of the future. The fourth subunit (8:28–30) concludes the pericope by stating God's predetermined purpose for believers is to be conformed to the image of the Son and display God's glory.

ROMANS 8:18

The γάρ in 8:18 indicates that 8:18–30 elaborates on the vocation of believers stated in 8:17. Byrne rightly says that v. 18 functions as a thesis statement for the pericope.[6] Here Paul expresses his conviction concerning the eschatological disclosure of the glory of God's children, and what it means to their lives in the face of the present sufferings.[7] Rhetorically, such a statement would serve to urge an audience familiar with hardship to live with a strong sense of expectation.

As commentators often recognize, there are eschatological overtones in the expression τοῦ νῦν καιροῦ and the verb ἀποκαλύπτω.[8] Indeed, Jewett thinks that the passive infinitive ἀποκαλυφθῆναι may convey "an apocalyptic disclosure of the triumph of God over adversity and the corruption of the cosmic order."[9] What is harder to determine, however, is whether the eschatological nature of the expression παθήματα τοῦ νῦν καιροῦ suggests that it refers to the "messianic woes" found in Jewish apocalyptic texts, which denote the intensifying evil and heightened level of trials and distress experienced by God's people before the appearance of the Messiah.[10] It should be noted that throughout the letter the νῦν often represents the fact that the time of the Messiah has already arrived, notably in 5:9, 11, and most recently in 8:1.[11] Also, in 3:26 the expression τῷ νῦν καιρῷ is used to indicate the time

---

6. Byrne, *Romans*, 255, 257. See also Matera, *Romans*, 199; cf. Dunn, *Romans 1–8*, 486.

7. The verb λογίζομαι means that the statement in Rom 8:18 is an opinion that the author has thought through carefully. Cf. Dunn, *Romans 1–8*, 468; Cranfield, *Romans I-VIII*, 408.

8. See Dunn, *Romans 1–8*, 468–69; Moo, *Romans*, 512n18.

9. Jewett, *Romans*, 510.

10. For example, *4 Ezra* 13:16–19.

11. The comments by Moo, "Romans 8.18–22," 83, are useful here. "There is not here, as the 'messianic woes' tradition, any indication that creation's groaning is intensifying because of the approach of the end."

since Christ's coming (cf. the νυνί in 3:21).[12] Hence, the present sufferings in 8:18 are likely to refer to the affliction and trials that Christ-followers experience as they live in the overlap of the ages—that is, the time when the old evil age is still present but the new age of Christ has already arrived.[13]

In light of our discussion of 8:17, the δόξα in 8:18 is best understood in terms of the new humanity's participation in the glory of Christ.[14] The εἰς ἡμᾶς probably implies that the glory is to be bestowed upon believers, in the sense that they are partakers of it.[15] That is, as they seek to fulfill their vocation to share in Christ's suffering, they partake in and subsequently display God's glory. On the one hand, this glory is still to be revealed, because the consummation of the new age has not taken place. The reference to the future bodily resurrection in 8:23 suggests that the δόξα in 8:21 refers to the final and full glorification of believers, which implies that the δόξα in 8:18 carries this same nuance. On the other hand, there seems to be a present dimension of "glory" in 8:18–30. The aorist ἐδόξασεν in 8:30 suggests that the glorification of believers has already taken place in some measure. We will discuss this in detail later. Suffice it to say now that the eschatological expectation of glorification in 8:18 is best understood in terms of believers' already-not-yet existence.

The meaning of the expression οὐκ ἄξια . . . πρός has a significant impact on how the audience understands 8:18. Although the common translation "not worth comparing with" is not technically wrong,[16] it conveys the sense that the present sufferings are worthless, which does not do justice to the fact that believers are sharing in *Christ's* suffering (8:17). Their sufferings *are* worthwhile because they are an integral part of being "with Christ." Here Gieniusz's careful study is useful.[17] Gieniusz has identified two categories

12. Cf. Jewett, *Romans*, 291; Moo, *Romans*, 241n110. Dunn, *Romans 1–8*, 175 rightly says that the ὁ νῦν καιρός in Rom 3:26 has eschatological overtones and denotes "the time between the death and resurrection of Christ and the consummation—the time when the eschatological promises are being realized but not yet completely."

13. Cf. Gieniusz, *Suffering*, 120–21.

14. The μέλλουσαν . . . ἀποκαλυφθῆναι is also used in Gal 3:23 (with the aorist passive infinity ἀποκαλυφθῆναι following the present active participle μέλλουσαν). Moo, *Romans*, 512n19, provides a concise summary of various views on the meaning of the μέλλω in Rom 8:18. There seems to be three alternatives. (1) It is part of a periphrasis for a future tense (cf. the usage in Gal 3:23). (2) It refers to the imminence of the revelation of the glory. (3) It conveys a nuance of certainty. Moo prefers (3), but says that there is no conclusive evidence from his survey on Paul's usage. In our discussion we will bear in mind the fact that there is no scholarly consensus on this matter.

15. Jewett, *Romans*, 510.

16. As in the NIV and NRSV.

17. Gieniusz, *Suffering*, 90–100.

of the usages of the expression. One is the case of simple comparison, in which "two juxtaposed things are not contrasted but simply compared in order to underline the *quantitative/qualitative* difference between them."[18] In this case the expression can be translated as "not worthy in comparison" or "worthless with respect to." The other is the case of contraposition, in which "the juxtaposed things are mutually opposing, antagonistic."[19] Here the translation can be "not to have weight against" or "not be able to oppose." In the case of Rom 8:18, the juxtaposed items are the present sufferings and the future glory, and so the usage of expression seems to fit into the second category because the two items represent opposing experiences and ideas. Importantly, since the audience's sufferings are a result of their participation in Christ, there must be value in the experience. Gieniusz's paraphrase, "not to have weight *to oppose*,"[20] therefore, is helpful. The present pains and trials are worthwhile, and regardless of their severity, present sufferings do not thwart the glory that the believers share with Christ.[21]

This understanding of οὐκ ἄξια . . . πρός would be helpful to the audience, in that their affliction would not be an obstacle against their future glorification. According to the prevailing social convention, suffering was a sign of the displeasure of the gods or YHWH.[22] Also, given the audience's social location in an intensely hierarchical society, their social and economic hardships would be a mark of dishonor. By all accounts their suffering was the opposite of glory and honor. Yet Paul's thesis statement would serve to assure them that it was no hindrance to the anticipated disclosure of the surpassing glory.

In sum, the thesis statement in 8:18 sets the stage for the audience to hear the letter's extended exposition of the believers' vocation to suffer with Christ. In 8:18 Paul expresses his conviction that the sufferings in the overlap of the ages do not thwart the glory to be revealed in believers.[23] This glory is concealed in the eyes of the world, because suffering people are not

18. Ibid., 93.

19. Ibid., 94.

20. Ibid., 100. Emphasis original.

21. I have borrowed the word "thwart" from the title of Gieniusz's monograph. The paraphrase by Byrne, *Romans*, 259–60, "a small price to pay" conveys the fact that the future glory is so desirable that the present affliction is a relatively minor matter in the grand scheme of things. But Gieniusz's paraphrase seems better.

22. See our discussion in Chapter 2 regarding the ancient worldviews of understanding suffering according to the principle of retributive justice.

23. See Appendix D for further discussion on the notion of eschatological hope found in Jewish martyrdom theology and apocalyptic literature.

considered to be glorious. Yet, as we will see below, the patient endurance of God's people is in fact a sign of their glory.

ROMANS 8:19-23

As mentioned, the γάρ in 8:19, 20, 22 indicates that the subunit 8:19–23 elaborates on the thesis statement in 8:18 and is part of the letter's explanation of how the vocation of believers will work. There are three components in this subunit, each of which refers to the solidarity between creation and the children of God. Verse 19 speaks of the longing of creation for the revelation of God's children. Verses 20–21 talk about the futility and corruption of creation and its relationship with the freedom of the glory of God's people. Verses 22–23 speak of the groaning of creation and that of believers, as well as their resurrection. I will argue that, by saying that the destinies of humanity and creation are interlocked, 8:19–23 guides the audience to realize that their suffering will ultimately lead to the liberation of creation from futility and decay, which, in turn, means that their vocation to suffer with Christ is an integral part of God's plan of transforming the cosmos.[24]

Verse 19

In 8:19 Paul says that the eager longing of creation awaits the revelation of the children of God. The opening γάρ indicates to the audience that Paul is unpacking his thesis statement in 8:18. What is new in v. 19 is the mention of κτίσις, which will continue to appear throughout the current subunit. What does κτίσις refer to?[25] The most common options identified by scholars are: (a) human and non-human creation together; (b) non-human creation plus humans who are not in Christ; (c) non-human creation only.[26]

---

24. Because of the modern concern for creation care, there has been a spike of scholarly publications on Rom 8:19–23. Although they may not be directly relevant to our inquiry, sometimes they provide exegetical insights for us. Publications helpful for our studies include: Horrell, "New Perspective," 3–30; Hahne, *Corruption*, 74–89; Adams, *Constructing*, 151–94; Moo, "Cosmic," 74–89; White, "Paul's Cosmology," 90–106; Gowan, "Fall and Redemption," 83–103; Horrell, *Greening Paul*, 63–86.

25. See, Adams, *Constructing*, 77–80, for the linguistic background of κτίσις. See also, e.g., Hahne, *Corruption*, 177–81; Byrne, *Romans*, 255–6, for more discussions of κτίσις in Rom 8:19–23.

26. The other options are (i) the human world and (ii) the angelic world. Combinations of the above mentioned three options and these two have also been suggested. (See, e.g., Cranfield, *Romans I-VIII*, 411; Byrne, *Romans*, 255.) These are less popular among recent scholarship. It is because the κτίσις hardly refers to angels in the NT, and

Option (c) is the near consensus among recent scholarship and is the view taken here.[27] In the following I will outline the main reasons for that choice. (See Appendix C for a more detailed discussion.)

Commentators often reject option (a) because the verb στενάζομεν in 8:23 makes a distinction between "creation" and human beings.[28] The οὐ μόνον . . . ἀλλὰ καί construction also indicates a distinction. Option (b) is also unlikely in that κτίσις is rarely used to denote non-human creation and those who are not in Christ.[29] The term can denote an "act of creation" (*Ps Sol* 8:7), a "creature/created thing" (Tob 8:5, 15), "non-human creation" (Wis 2:6; 5:17; 16:24; 19:6), or "created universe" (Sir 49:16).[30] The first of these usages does not apply to Rom 8:19–22. The rest refer to either "human-and-non-human creation *together*" or "non-human creation *alone*," but not "non-human creation plus some humans."[31] This means that option (b) should be rejected.

As a result, (c) is the best option, and hence κτίσις in 8:19–22 is used anthropomorphically to refer to non-human creation.[32] Having said that, several qualifications of this rendering of κτίσις need to be mentioned. It is important to remember that the ancients did not partition the components of the cosmos in clearly identifiable terms like moderns do. As our

the term almost always includes non-human creation in the NT.

27. For good discussions in favor of option (c), see Adams, *Constructing*, 176; Hahne, *Corruption*, 180. Both Adams and Hahne provide details of alternative views. Apart from Adams and Hahne, those who prefer option (c) include Byrne, *Romans*, 255–56; Dunn, *Romans 1–8*, 469; Witherington, *Romans*, 223; Cranfield, *Romans I-VIII*, 411–12; Kruse, *Romans*, 347; Forman, *Politics*, 110–11, although there are minor variations in their definitions of the term κτίσις. That option (c) is a near consensus is also observed by Gaventa, "Neither," 276, although Gaventa prefers option (a).

28. See Witherington, *Romans*, 222–3; Byrne, *Romans*, 255; Cranfield, *Romans I-VIII*, 411.

29. Adams, *Constructing*, 176.

30. See Adams, *Constructing*, 77–81, for a detailed discussion. See Appendix C for more examples of these usages.

31. Another reason why option (b) is rejected is that the phrase οὐχ ἑκοῦσα in 8:20 seems to stand in contrast to the autonomous human idolatrous actions in 1:20–25. See Byrne, *Romans*, 255–6; Moo, *Romans*, 514.

32. See Appendix C for a discussion of the possible objections to option (c) and why it is nonetheless preferred. By the way, an additional factor we might consider is how an audience familiar with suffering would understand the term κτίσις. The audience would hear in 8:22 that creation συστενάζει and συνωδίνει, which, as we will see, paints a very gloomy picture of suffering. It would be hard for them, at least existentially, to think that, for example, the perpetrators of injustice suffer that way. For the former war-captives, the Roman centurions did not suffer. The socioeconomic poor would find it hard to think that the elite suffer as severely as they do. In light of this, κτίσις is unlikely to include all human beings from the perspective of the audience.

discussion of the term κόσμος in 5:12, 13 has shown, the individual parts of the cosmos are inseparable from each other. For sure, the human and non-human components are distinguishable, but they are considered to be integral parts of the whole. Also, given our discussion in Chapter 3 regarding the entry of sin and death into the cosmos, we must recognize that the non-human creation can cause human suffering. Sickness and natural disasters such as famine, storms, and earthquakes bring immense suffering to humanity (especially in the ancient world with its inadequate medical healthcare and infrastructures), and the audience is not exempt from them. In our discussion below I will suggest that the letter's mention of the decay of creation would probably remind the audience of the fact that creation does not sustain life as it should.

The creation waits with eager longing for τὴν ἀποκάλυψιν τῶν υἱῶν τοῦ θεοῦ.[33] It seems that the phrase refers primarily to the glory that believers will share with Christ at the final renewal of all things. Like the ἀποκαλυφθῆναι in 8:18, the ἀποκάλυψιν here reflects the eschatological nature of the current pericope.[34] Given the fact that believers will participate in the glory of Christ (according to 8:17), it is likely that here the ἀποκάλυψις of God's children refers to the glory that they will share with Christ at his appearing.[35] Also, the term ἀποκάλυψις suggests that what is going to be revealed is hidden at the moment. As mentioned, their glory is masked in the eyes of the world. The slaves and the poorest among the audience would not appear to be glorious to most of the population. Nor would anyone living at or below subsistence level be considered as particularly honorable by those in the

33. The term ἀποκαραδοκία has been translated as "eager expectation," "earnest expectation," or "eager longing," as in the TNIV, NKJV, and NRSV respectively. The term is found only in Christian literature. "On tiptoe" is a helpful paraphrase—see Moo, *Romans*, 513n29; Wright, *Romans*, 596. But it should be noted that the term does not necessarily convey any sense of enthusiasm that stems from something exciting in the present situation of the person. Paul's personal circumstances in his usage in Phil 1:20 is an example. On the one hand, the apostle is determined to rejoice despite his imprisonment. On the other hand, life in jail in the ancient world was anything but pleasant. In Rom 8:20 it is said that the creation has been subjected to futility, and hence the "eager longing" stems from a position of weakness and frustration.

34. Cf. Dunn, *Romans 1–8*, 470.

35. While most commentators believe that the υἱοὶ θεοῦ in Rom 8:19 refers to believers (e.g. Dunn, *Romans 1–8*, 470; Kruse, *Romans*, 343n345), some think that it refers to the angels who will bring judgment. See the discussion by Hahne, *Corruption*, 184–85, who disputes such a view held by Christoffersson, *Earnest Expectation*, 120–21. Also, Susan Eastman, "Whose Apocalypse?" 264–72, suggests that υἱοὶ θεοῦ in Rom 8:21 include the Jewish people, since they too will share in the υἱοθεσία (9:4). I find Eastman's essay refreshing. But at this point of the letter (8:21), the audience would take the υἱοὶ θεοῦ to be those who are led by the Spirit to cry *Abba* Father (8:14, 15), for nothing in the text at this point prompts them to think otherwise.

upper segments of the social hierarchy. The glory of a suffering audience is invisible to the world.

Here we should recall that the identity of the children of God is a prominent theme in 8:14–17. Being children, believers are heirs of God and co-heirs with Christ. Our discussion of 8:17 has suggested that this heirship implies the inheriting of the cosmos. What 8:19 says, then, is that creation is waiting eagerly for them to fully receive the cosmos as their rightful inheritance. In light of this, 8:19 is anticipating what 8:20–23 is going to say concerning the fact that the renewal of creation is contingent on the unveiling of the glory of God's children (see discussion below).[36]

Putting the above together, 8:19 speaks of creation's eager longing for the glorification of God's children. In the eyes of the world, the audience in Rome was not particularly glorious. But as God's children, their glory will be revealed. Since the destinies of creation and God's people are interlocked, creation waits longingly for the revelation of God's children because it too suffers and groans (as the following verses will show).

Verses 20–21

The two occurrences of γάρ in v. 20 indicate to the audience that 8:20–21 elaborates on what the creation's longing in v. 19 is about. It serves to further explain and clarify Paul's thesis in v. 18, which has previously set the stage for the letter's extended treatment on the topic of suffering and the unveiling of believers' glory—a subject matter that is highly relevant to the audience's situation in Rome. Paul says that the reason for the creation's longing for the revelation of God's children is that it was subjected to futility and the bondage of decay. I will argue that, given their ancient worldview, the audience would see the decay of creation as the reason for some of the hardship and pain they experienced. The letter says that creation will be set free from the bondage to decay and brought into the freedom of the glory of the children of God. We will find that the destinies of God's people and creation are interlocked, and that their liberation will signal the consummation of God's project of reversing the effects of Adam's disobedience. In light of this, vv. 20–21 invite the audience to consider an important purpose

---

36. Thus, Jewett, *Romans*, 512, rightly says, "This idea of the natural world eagerly awaiting its own redemption reflects an ancient view of the world as a living organism. Paul implies that the entire creation waits with baited breath for the emergence and empowerment of those who will take responsibility for its restoration, small groups of the υἱοὶ τοῦ θεοῦ ("sons of God")."

of their suffering: their vocation to suffer with Christ is an integral part of God's program of renewing creation.

Creation is said to be subjected to ματαιότης in 8:20.[37] The term ματαιότης occurs in Ecclesiastes thirty-nine times, which is much more frequent than all the other books in the LXX.[38] This translates the Hebrew הבל, which means "absurdity."[39] Both the Greek and the Hebrew convey the fact that there are situations and realities in life that do not make sense and are contrary to reason.[40] This is of course in line with the teaching of Qohelet, who carefully makes observations about life and continually concludes that everything is absurd—despite the fact that there is goodness in life (Eccl 3:11–13; 9:7–10).[41] But perhaps the gloomiest reason for such an absurd life on earth is the fact that all came from dust (χοῦς) and all will return to dust (Eccl 3:20).[42] Human life on earth is indeed futile, whether one is righteous or not. Righteous living and impiety both lead to the same end: death (3:19; 9:1–6).[43] All humans toil under the sun, which is meaningless. The usage of ματαιότης in Ecclesiastes may resonate with the audience in that they have heard that "death" is a cosmic power that brings chaos in the cosmos (5:12–13). Having been subjected to futility, creation is under the domain of anti-God forces. Its toil and labor, figuratively speaking, are futile. It cannot sustain human life as well as it should. The earth is not always a safe place for its inhabitants.[44] Since creation and human existence are interconnected, life on earth is inevitably full of pain and turmoil. This is, of course, a reality

37. The audience has already heard the verb ματαιόω in 1:21, where it denotes the futility of humanity when they do not glorify God. This is set in contrast to the believers' vocation to share in Christ's glory in 8:17.

38. The term ματαιότης is found once in Proverbs and fourteen times in the Psalter, which is of course a much longer book than Ecclesiastes. Likewise, the Hebrew הבל is used thirty-eight times in Ecclesiastes and only twenty-nine times elsewhere. Commentators of Romans often find the usage of ματαιότης in Ecclesiastes informative. See, e.g., Jewett, *Romans*, 513; Byrne, *Romans*, 260. Hahne, *Corruption*, 190–91, provides a detailed discussion on the different views on ματαιότης in Rom 8:20.

39. The literal sense of הבל is "breath" or "vapor," and hence metaphorically it means "worthless" or "meaningless." Thus, Ps 144:4 says, "Human beings are like a breath (הבל); their days are like a passing shadow." See Enns, "Ecclesiastes 1," 129. See also Enns, *Ecclesiastes*, 31–33, for a fuller discussion.

40. Cf. Gieniusz, *Suffering*, 152.

41. That is, God has made everything good, and one can eat food with gladness and enjoy life with one's spouse (Eccl 3:11–13; 9:7–10).

42. There seems to be an echo of Gen 2:7 and 3:19 in Eccl 3:22, where Adam is said to have been made from the dust (χοῦς) of the earth, and that after his disobedience he will have to labor in pain until he returns to the earth. (See our later discussion.)

43. Gieniusz, *Suffering*, 153.

44. It should be noted that creation is not in and of itself evil.

that the audience can identify with, and indeed, in a moment, the audience will hear that both creation and believers groan in this life (8:22–23).

The expression οὐχ ἑκοῦσα is often translated as "not willingly" and "not of its own will."[45] But Gieniusz identifies four occurrences of the expression in Greek literature,[46] and concludes that "not through its own fault" is a better translation. I find the usage in Exod 11:13 LXX—where the expression is followed by ἀλλά, as is the case in Rom 8:20—a helpful indication for this translation. The law in the Exodus text says that if a person smites another, then the killer must be put to death. But if the person did that οὐχ ἑκοῦσα, then he/she can flee to a designated place for refuge. Here the translation "not through his/her own fault" seems to fit well in the context. In the case of Rom 8:20, at one level creation was subjected to futility "not willingly." But at another level it has done no wrong to deserve the subjection. This means that "not of its own fault" is a plausible translation, and indeed Cranfield thinks that this is a natural reading.[47] If the οὐχ ἑκοῦσα carries this sense, then creation is in fact, metaphorically speaking, an innocent sufferer that was subjected to futility by God without committing wrongdoing itself.[48]

Hope in suffering is a major theme in Rom 5–8.[49] The ἐλπίδι in 8:20 signals a return to the theme that appeared prominently in 5:2–5. The prepositional phrase ἐφ᾽ ἐλπίδι probably means "in view of hope" or "on account of hope," and it is connected with ὑπετάγη rather than ὑποτάξαντα.[50] As Byrne suggests, this "indicates the circumstances attending the subjection."[51] That is, God subjected creation to futility in view of the hope that the creation will be liberated from its bondage to decay into the glory of the freedom of the children of God (8:21). In other words, the hope of creation's

---

45. See NKJV, NRSV. In the NT, ἑκών is only found in Rom 8:20 and 1 Cor 9:17. In the LXX, it is found in Exod 21:13 and Job 36:19.

46. Gieniusz, *Suffering*, 155–56. The four texts are: Exod 11:13 LXX; Demosthenes, *Phaen.* 42.29; Polybius, *Hist.* 31.10; Philo, *Fug.* 65.

47. Cranfield, *Romans I-VIII*, 414.

48. For Hahne, *Corruption*, 212, creation is a "victim of human sin. . . . Creation is not itself fallen, in the sense of being disobedient to God." In my view, creation is not inherently evil. But I think the main culprit for creation's futility is sin, which is the cosmic power that brings chaos in the entire cosmos. At any rate, the concern of Rom 8:20 is not who/what causes creation's futility, but that creation itself is not at fault. Cf. Jackson, *New Creation*, 158.

49. The terms ἐλπίς and ἐλπίζω appear frequently in Rom 5–8. See Appendix A.

50. See Gieniusz, *Suffering*, 160–61; Cranfield, *Romans I-VIII*, 414; Moo, *Romans*, 516n43.

51. Byrne, *Romans*, 261.

future liberation is the basis on which God subjected it to futility.[52] Creation "suffers" as an innocent sufferer. But there is hope.

The ἐλευθερωθήσεται, δουλείας, and ἐλευθερίαν in 8:21 recall the motifs of dominion, slavery, and freedom in 8:15, and throughout Rom 5–6. More specifically, given the context of creation, they remind us of the dominion of sin and death in the cosmos (in 5:12, 13).[53] As argued previously, in 8:15 the δουλείας probably refers to the fear that humans experience under the threat of those cosmic forces. It seems, then, that the δουλείας in 8:21 speaks of creation's bondage under the domain of the same cosmic powers.

The term φθορά refers to the fact that creation is perishable.[54] Given the slavery-freedom motif and the dominion of sin and death in 5:12, 13, Adams rightly says that the phrase τῆς δουλείας τῆς φθορᾶς refers to the fact that the "created order has been made perishable, subject to dissolution and decay."[55] While the concern of modern readers is (rightly) about the degradation of the environment by human action, the ancient audience would likely relate the perishing of creation to destructive phenomena like famine, earthquakes, and plagues. An orderly creation would sustain life and ensure the wellbeing of human beings. But a creation in chaos does not. The use of φθορά and φθείρω in Isa 24:3–4,[56] and the theme of the earth's destruction in Isa 24, reflect a Jewish understanding of the connection between creation's decay and human rebellion.[57] According to Isaiah, the earth's ruin

---

52. Following many scholars, I take that it is God who subjected creation to futility. See Adams, *Constructing*, 178–9; Jewett, *Romans*, 513; Cranfield, *Romans I-VIII*, 414; Kruse, *Romans*, 343 (against Byrne, *Romans*, 260–61). See also Dunn, *Romans 1–8*, 470–71, who provides a helpful discussion on the grammatical considerations.

53. Likewise, Hahne, *Corruption*, 194, notes the possible reference to Rom 5:12–14.

54. See Hahne, *Corruption*, 194, for a comprehensive discussion on the term's usage in the NT.

55. Adams, *Constructing*, 179. Adams goes on to say, rightly, that "[a]gain the image of enslavement points to an imposed state rather than an inherent one."

56. The φθορά appears once in Isa 24:3 LXX and φθείρω twice in 24:3, 4.

57. Cf. Hahne, *Corruption*, 195; Kruse, *Romans*, 344. Note that the earth mourns (πενθέω) in Isa 24:7 LXX, which resembles the groaning of creation in Rom 8:22. Moo, "Cosmic," 83–88, argues for a strong correlation between Rom 8:18–22 and Isa 24–27. Moo concedes that the thematic and verbal parallels he notes between the two texts "cannot be said to provide anything like indisputable proof that" the former depends on the latter (86). But he goes on to use the links between Rom 8:18–22; 1 Cor 15:54; 2 Cor 5:4; and Isa 25:8 as extra evidence to support his proposal. Since our inquiry is about whether the audience can detect scriptural echoes, and since we cannot assume that they have access to Paul's other letters, we will not study Isa 24–27 in detail in our inquiry—except to say that Isaiah can potentially assist the audience to understand the term φθορά in a general sense. Cf. Wis 16:16–24, where the unrighteous are punished by storm and rain, which are in turn components of creation (16:24).

is caused by its inhabitants' sins (24:6), indicating that human sinfulness has cosmic implications.[58] Since Rom 5:12–21 speaks of the rebellion of Adamic humanity under the bondage of sin and death, it is possible to say that the disobedience of sin-bound Adamic humanity somehow causes cosmic devastation.[59] But the argument throughout Rom 5–8 suggests that ultimately it is the cosmic power of sin that is the culprit.[60] Of course, the point of 8:20–21 is not primarily about who/what causes the decay of creation.[61] Instead, as I will soon argue, it is about the new humanity's role in bringing about the freedom of creation, which, in turn, means that the world will once again be a safe place for humans to dwell.

The δόξα in 8:21, as mentioned above, most likely refers to the glory that believers will display at their resurrection as a result of their participation in Christ's suffering and glory. Given the creation motif in 8:19–23, Ps 8:5–6 (8:6–7 LXX) is useful for our analysis here. It says that human beings are crowned with glory. God has set them over the works of his hands, and subjected all under their feet. It is likely that the glory of God's children (8:21), as well as the co-heirship and co-glorification with Christ (8:17), imply the restoration of humanity's role to rule over creation.[62] In view of the future ἐλευθερωθήσεται here and the bodily resurrection in 8:23, the δόξα in 8:21 most likely focuses on the future dimension of believers' glory. Scholars are divided with regards to the use of the genitive δόξης here. It has been taken as a genitive of quality (hence "glorious liberty" in NKJ).[63] Others think that it refers to the "freedom which consists in sharing in God's glory."[64] Byrne, however, translates the phrase as "the freedom associated with the glory of the children of God."[65] Moo takes a slightly different nuance of the genitive, and speaks of "the freedom that belongs to, is associated with, the state of

---

58. Cf. Moo, "Cosmic," 85.

59. This does not mean that earthquakes and tsunamis are specifically caused by moral failure in, for example, personal holiness issues. What Isa 24 suggests is that the collective rebellion of the earth's inhabitants has caused devastation. Unfortunately there will be many innocent sufferers when the earth is ruined, which is of course a theodicy question that Jewish wisdom literature wrestles with. Again, Job, for instance, provides an alternative voice. Natural disasters can happen to innocent people, and the cause is not necessarily human sinfulness.

60. See Appendix D for a discussion on the relationship between creation and Adam's disobedience in *4 Ezra* and *2 Baruch*.

61. This is the case even though one may attempt to extract information from Rom 8:19–23 to answer that question.

62. Cf. Dunn, *Romans 1–8*, 472.

63. Wallace, *Greek Grammar*, 87–88.

64. Dunn, *Romans 1–8*, 472.

65. Byrne, *Romans*, 261.

glory."[66] Byrne and Moo seem to be on the right track. Since the glory of God's children has been the emphasis of the letter in 8:17, 18,[67] and since 8:21 is part of the continuous elaboration of 8:17, the mention of their glory in 8:21 suggests that creation's freedom is a result of believers' glorification. The ἀπὸ . . . εἰς construction is also informative. The εἰς seems to refer to the goal of creation's being set free.[68] That is, creation will be liberated from (ἀπὸ) the bondage of decay with the goal that it will partake in the freedom of the glory of God's children. Since the destinies of humans and creation are inseparable, creation's freedom is associated with, and indeed, resulted from the glory of God's children.[69] In short, 8:21 refers to the freedom that creation will possess, but it is one that is interlocked with and dependent on the glorification of the children of God at the final renewal.[70]

Implication of Verses 20–21

Putting the above together, Rom 8:20–21 speaks of God's subjection of creation to futility. This (figurative) suffering of creation is "innocent," for its subjection is through no fault of its own. But the subjection took place in the hope of the future eschatological unveiling of the glory of the children of God, at which point creation will be set free from its bondage to the power of sin and death. Simply put, the liberation of creation is contingent on the glorification of God's new humanity.[71] What is emerging from our

66. Moo, *Romans*, 517n48.

67. Following most commentators, I take the τῶν τέκνων in Rom 8:21 as possessive. That is, the glory belongs to God's children.

68. Cf. Moo, *Romans*, 517n49. The preposition εἰς in Rom 8:21 highlights the interdependence between the freedom of creation and the freedom of God's children. As Gieniusz, *Suffering*, 172, says in his analysis of the usage of the preposition here, "the future state of creation *somehow* depends on the future state of the children of God: so that one cannot happen without another and if one happens the second should be seen as assured." Also, the fact that the creation will be liberated from its bondage to decay means that it will not be subjected to annihilation. Instead, the final renewal will most likely undergo a transformation. See Gieniusz, *Suffering*, 165.

69. As Hahne, *Corruption*, 198, says, "The freedom is both an aspect of the eschatological glory (content) and the freedom will result from the glorification of believers (source). The non-rational creation will join with believers in this freedom that is part of eschatological glory."

70. It seems that both non-Westerners today and people in the ancient world hold a worldview that human and non-human creation share an interlocking destiny. See, for example, Yeo, "Christ and the Earth," 203, regarding the Native Americans' understanding.

71. Cf. Forman, *Politics*, 112.

analysis of 8:19, 20–21, is that the future freedom of creation will signal the completion of God's project of reversing the effects of Adam's disobedience.[72] While 5:12–21 and 8:1–4 spell out the entry of sin and death into the cosmos and the freedom that believers have through Christ and the Spirit, 8:19–21 speaks of the future liberation of believers and creation. Thus, the transformation of the whole cosmos has been set in motion, and will be consummated at the unveiling of God's children. For an audience living with socioeconomic hardship and religio-political injustice in Rome, this would be remarkable. The freedom of creation depended on their glorification, which, in turn, depended on their vocation of identifying with Christ's suffering. In fact, according to our analysis of 8:17, they were to inherit the cosmos. Romans 8:17 and 20–21 showed them how they would receive their inheritance, namely, by means of fulfilling their call to participate in Christ's suffering. In addition, the liberation of creation from decay would also mean the end of disease, famine, and other so-called "natural" disasters, because, according to the audience's worldview, these were part of a disorderly cosmos. This gave the audience further hope and comfort as they endured their suffering.

Romans 8:22–23

The γάρ in v. 22 indicates that 8:22–23 is part of the continuous elaboration of the thesis statement in 8:18. Paul's conviction in 8:18 is that the present sufferings do not thwart the glory that will be revealed. Verses 19–21 speak of the interdependent destinies of the children of God and creation. Now 8:22–23 brings the subunit 8:19–23 to a conclusion. The whole creation groans and travails together, and the children of God also groan. But creation will be set free, just as the redemption of the bodies of believers will happen.[73] I will argue that 8:22–23 delineates the shared experience of suffering between God's children and creation. It also speaks of the resurrection of believers, which signals the end of the final stronghold of sin and death, and hence the end of suffering.

The οἴδαμεν in 8:22 appeals to what is commonly accepted to be true.[74] What follows is assumed to be something that the audience knows accord-

---

72. Cf. Dunn, *Romans 1–8*, 472.

73. Concerning the connection between the new creation and resurrection, Kirk, *Unlocking*, 141, puts it this way, "New creation entails a glorification of God concomitant with a restoration of the glory of God's image in humanity. The restoration of the divine glory in new creation, however, is derivative from the resurrected Christ."

74. Dunn, *Romans 1–8*, 472; Byrne, *Romans*, 261.

ing to their worldview. The rhetorical effect of συστενάζει καὶ συνωδίνει, with their συ- prefix, should be noted.[75] As mentioned before, συ-compounds appear eight times in 8:16, 17, 22, 26, and 29. Only a few moments ago the συ-words in 8:17 have served to alert the audience of their call to identify with Christ. Here in v. 22 they hear that the whole creation groans together and travails together, suggesting that the different parts of the entire creation suffer agony together. This reflects a holistic worldview of creation, where there is co-dependency between all members of creation. Very soon in v. 23 the audience will hear that believers themselves groan, which implies a shared experience between them and creation.[76] Given the Christ-focused συ-compounds in 8:17, one may say that suffering is a common experience between Christ, humanity, and creation.

There is a strong sense of gloom and helplessness in the phrase συστενάζει καὶ συνωδίνει. While συστενάζω and συνωδίνω are not found in the LXX,[77] there are places where "groan" and "travail" appear together without the συ- prefix. When they appear, they often express a picture of dire hopelessness. For example, in Jer 4:31 the words are used to express the demise of Jerusalem: "I heard a sound of your groaning, as of one travailing in labor, as of one bringing forth her first child."[78] In Jer 22:23 they are used as part of a lament concerning the fate of Jehoiakim and Jerusalem: "You will groan as the pang of the one giving birth come upon you."[79] In both cases a picture of severe childbirth pain is painted without the joy of the birth of the child in view.[80] The sense of gloom and helplessness reflects the futility and enslavement that 8:20–21 mentions concerning creation. The audience in Rome might find that this figure of speech resonated with their experience of suffering. Food shortages caused by famine, the frequent sicknesses that caused high infant mortality rates, and short life expectancies, were all part and parcel of life in a creation that was groaning and travailing. The groaning of creation and their own experience were interconnected.

75. Cf. Jewett, *Romans*, 517.

76. Jewett, *Romans*, 517, puts it this way, "Paul views the creation as a holistic, interdependent system with a life and development of its own, yet anticipating appropriate human intervention to counter Adam's fall."

77. Nor do they appear anywhere else in the NT.

78. The verb ὠδίνω and the noun στεναγμός are used in Jer 4:31 LXX.

79. The noun ὠδίν and the verb καταστενάζω are used in Jer 22:23 LXX.

80. The language here may also allude to Gen 3:16, where the LORD God says to Eve that he will multiply her pains and groaning (στεναγμός), and in pains she will give birth to children (ἐν λύπαις τέξῃ τέκνα). (See also our later discussion.)

The use of πνεῦμα together with υἱοθεσία in 8:23 echoes the language in 8:14–16.[81] This suggests that the τὴν ἀπαρχὴν τοῦ πνεύματος in 8:23 most likely refers to the life-giving Spirit's presence in the community of believers, who is the guarantee of their inheritance and filial relationship with God.[82] The term πνεῦμα has been absent since 8:16, and its use in 8:23 reintroduces the place of the Spirit in the (communal) life of believers. The fact that believers have to await their υἱοθεσία is another example of the already-not-yet eschatological nature of the letter. Although believers already possess their "adoption to sonship" (8:15), the full realization of that privilege will not take place until the redemption of their bodies (8:23). Because the consummation of their redemption is yet to happen, they still groan (στενάζω). As Gieniusz argues, in the LXX the term στενάζω—whether it is used with or without ὠδίνω/ὠδίν—expresses a strong sense of human lament and powerless suffering, including the lament of a righteous person who is under oppression.[83] The act of groaning takes place ἐν ἑαυτοῖς, which probably means either "within ourselves"[84] or "among ourselves."[85] Both options are possible. But given the first person plural verbs since the κράζομεν in 8:15 (where the Spirit-inspired *Abba*-cry was mentioned), I prefer the latter. In that case, believers groan as a community (perhaps within a house church gathering) through the inspiration of the Spirit. As I will argue, the Spirit-intercession in 8:26–27 seems to echo the Spirit-inspired *Abba*-cry in 8:15. Given the υἱοθεσία in both 8:15 and 23, it is likely that the ἐν ἑαυτοῖς στενάζομεν in 8:23 refers to a Spirit-led communal expression (or corporate prayer) of frustration and lament over their present sufferings. Verse 23,

---

81. Along with Byrne, *Romans*, 265, Fee, *Empowering*, 572n295, Dunn, *Romans 1–8*, 465–6, I believe that the omission of υἱοθεσία by P46 (vid) D F G is most probably insignificant. As Fee says, "While it is easy to see why in light of 8:15 someone may have omitted it, it is not possible to imagine the circumstances in which some would have added this word at this point."

82. Cf. the Spirit being the down payment in 2 Cor 1:22; 5:5 and Christ being the first fruits in 1 Cor 15:20, 23.

83. Gieniusz, *Suffering*, 192n649, says,

> The LXX uses the verb (thirty occurrences) and the noun (twenty-seven occurrences) always as a strong expression for human lament and powerless suffering (pain and oppression) and sometimes also of entreaty to God for deliverance from oppression. As far as the latter is concerned, we have to do with cries to God of a (mainly righteous) person who is being oppressed, which express both pain and a plea for deliverance (Exod 2:24; 6:5; Judg 2:18; Ps 6:6; 12:5; 31:10; 38:9; 79:11; 102:20).

84. See Cranfield, *Romans I-VIII*, 418; Fee, *Empowering*, 574. But Fee thinks that "among ourselves" is also very possible.

85. See Matera, *Romans*, 202; Kasemann, *Romans*, 237.

therefore, invites the audience to consider their groaning as part and parcel of the shared experience of everything else in the cosmos. Despite the fact that they are children of God and are anticipating the full measure of their glorification, they groan in their present sufferings.

Most commentators think that the ἀπολύτρωσις τοῦ σώματος ἡμῶν refers to the future bodily resurrection of believers.[86] In Romans the only other place the term ἀπολύτρωσις appears is in 3:24. The δικαιοσύνη θεοῦ has been disclosed through the πίστις Χριστοῦ for all who put their faithful trust in him (3:21–22), because all have sinned and fall short of the glory of God (3:23). So, on the one hand, on the basis of Christ's atoning death, believers have a right standing with God (3:25; 8:3). On the other hand, their sharing in Christ's suffering and associated participation in his glory are also an integral part of God's saving purpose in dealing with sin's dominion over Adamic humanity (see our discussion of 8:17). Thus, while the redemption in 3:24 refers to the justification of believers through Christ's death, this redemption is not complete without the full realization of their glorification. This full transformation will take place when their bodies are redeemed— that is, when the bodily resurrection takes place. Romans 3:24 and 8:23, therefore, speak of two different (but connected) aspects of redemption. In 3:24 the audience hears that through Christ they are justified and redeemed from sin's power. In 8:23 they hear that the redemption of their bodies will take place, although in the meantime they groan. For redemption to be fully realized, participation in Christ's suffering is needed.

The redemption of the body is in fact a necessary component of God's restorative and transformative purpose for humanity. The "body" appears as the "body of death" (8:10), "mortal body" (6:12; 8:11), and "body of sin" (6:6). The body seems to be the ultimate stronghold of the dominion of sin and death, or the instrument through which those cosmic forces take control of humans. Participation in Christ is understood as crucial in dealing with the body of sin/death. The παλαιὸς ἄνθρωπος was crucified *with* (συνεσταυρώθη) Christ so that the body of sin might be destroyed (6:6). And those who have died *with* (σύν) Christ "will live *with*" (συζήσομεν) him.

Crucially, 8:11 says that the indwelling Spirit affirms believers that God will give life to their mortal body—which most probably refers to the final resurrection.[87] Thus, the Spirit enables believers to deal with the body of sin in the present age, and at the future resurrection the mortal body will be finally replaced. In this way, God's plan of transforming the human

86. Dunn, *Romans 1–8*, 491; Fee, *Empowering*, 574; Matera, *Romans*, 202; Cranfield, *Romans I-VIII*, 419; Byrne, *Romans*, 265.

87. Dunn, *Romans 1–8*, 432; Byrne, *Romans*, 246, Fee, *Empowering*, 546–47; Matera, *Romans*, 196. Against Jewett, *Romans*, 493.

body has been set in motion and will be consummated at the resurrection. What we see in 8:23, then, is a definitive statement about the sure future consummation of the transformation of the human person. Finally, the οὐ μόνον, δέ ἀλλὰ καί, and the αὐτοί at the beginning of 8:23 link the groaning of creation (8:22) and that of believers (8:23) together. Both the children of God and creation share a sense of gloom and lament as they await the consummation of God's restorative purpose. Hence, 8:23 serves as a climax at the midpoint of the pericope 8:18–30 by declaring the final renewal of the entire cosmos—human and non-human creation.[88]

Summary of Verses 22–23

In short, what we find in 8:22–23 is a succinct depiction of the final destiny of a humanity that participates in Christ's death and resurrection, which is the resurrection of their own bodies.[89] Before reaching this destiny, they suffer and groan, which is a shared experience with Christ as well as with creation. Just as Christ suffered, died, and was glorified, so his followers suffer and will be glorified. Creation shares a somewhat similar pattern of existence, it too groans and travails, and it will share the freedom of the children of God. For the audience, the resurrection ultimately represents the end of suffering, for it signifies the consummation of their transformation.

Conclusion of the Subunit Romans 8:19–23

To conclude, the subunit 8:19–23 elaborates on the thesis statement in 8:18 and speaks of the shared fortunes and destinies of creation and God's new humanity. Our study of 8:17 has shown that the purpose (and result) of the audience's participation in Christ's suffering is that they may be glorified with him. Verses 19–23 have served to invite the audience to consider how God will accomplish that purpose. The eschatological unveiling of glory in 8:19–23 primarily refers to the future resurrection of God's children, upon which they will inherit the cosmos and display God's glory just as Christ does. When that takes place, creation will be released from its bondage to decay (a bondage that it endures through no fault of its own), and be set

---

88. The role of this verse within its context is so significant that Fee, *Empowering*, 572, says that "[b]oth the larger context and the nature of the argument indicate that v. 23 is the main point of everything in vv. 18–27)."

89. See Appendix D for further discussion about resurrection and God's restoration in Jewish literature.

free from death's power.[90] All in all, 8:19–23 speaks of the anticipated conclusion of God's program of transformation and renewal, which includes both the consummation of believers' adoption to sonship and the renewal of creation. At the present time creation is not a safe place for the audience to dwell in. But their faithful participation in Christ's suffering will bring about a renewed creation that will sustain their wellbeing.[91]

ROMANS 8:24–27

The two occurrences of γάρ in 8:24 indicate that 8:24–27 continues to flesh out the thesis statement in 8:18. While the focus of 8:19–23 is the future disclosure of the glory of God's children and the associated cosmic renewal, 8:24–27 provides two important resources for the audience as they face suffering, namely, hope and the Spirit's empowerment. These were already briefly mentioned in the previous subunit (8:20, 23), but now they take center stage.

The first γάρ in 8:24 and the ὡσαύτως . . . καί in 8:26 suggest that the materials in vv. 24–25 and 26–27 have the same function, namely, to elaborate on what has been said in 8:19–23, although they deal with somewhat different topics.[92] That is, in light of the future renewal of the cosmos, how should God's children live now? While 8:24–25 describes hope and endurance in affliction, 8:26–27 speaks of the Spirit's help and intercession. Whereas 8:19–23 places hope in the *future* renewal, here in 8:24–27 there is a shift to the fact that believers *have already* been saved (8:24) and that the

---

90. Cf. Jackson, *New Creation*, 163–4.

91. Since resurrection is understood to be God's vindication and reward for the suffering righteous (Dan 12:1–3), what is emerging in Rom 8:19–23 is that the redemption of the body signifies the vindication of believers who seek to fulfill their vocation of suffering with Christ. Kirk, *Unlocking*, 152–3, helpfully says,

> Paul views the cosmic reversal as the completion of what has already been begun in Christ and as a consummation of humanity's and creation's participation in Christ. The suffering experienced by Christians is not, for Paul, the mere side effect of living in the world that fell with Adam; its quality has been redefined by the Christ event. Christian suffering is suffering with Christ. And Christian glory is being glorified with Christ . . . Christians suffer now, but glory is to come . . . God is just, God will reward the righteous, but now these rewards are reckoned through the resurrected Christ. Humanity will be wrapped up into the life of the new Adam. The suffering righteous will be vindicated. The groaning creation will be restored. God will triumph.

92. As Dunn, *Romans 1–8*, 476, says, Rom 8:26 refers back to v. 23. See also Byrne, *Romans*, 270.

Spirit assists them in their *present* weakness (8:26). The following discussion will look at vv. 24–25 and 26–27 in turn.

Verses 24–25

The vocabulary of ἐλπίς/ἐλπίζω (8:24–25), ὑπομονή (8:25), συνδοξάζω/ δοξάζω/δόξα (8:17, 18, 21, 30), and the theme of suffering throughout 8:17–39, recall the hope of glory in affliction in 5:2–5. But the emphasis here in 8:24–25 is specifically *"hope* in suffering," given the fivefold occurrences of ἐλπίς/ἐλπίζω. With the ἐλπίς in 8:20 and the opening γάρ in 8:24, the dative ἐλπίδι at the beginning of v. 24 seems to ultimately refer to the hope of resurrection and the full realization of υἱοθεσία in v. 23.[93] That is, it is in the hope of resurrection at the final renewal that believers were saved. The aorist passive ἐσώθημεν is somewhat surprising, in that almost all the other usages of the verb in the letter are future passive (5:9, 10; 9:27; 10:9, 13; 11:26).[94] The audience has heard previously that they *will* be saved from wrath (5:9, cf. 5:10), but here in 8:24 the text seems to take for granted that salvation has already taken place. There is a sense in which salvation is not fully complete, yet at the same time it has already happened.[95] The fact that they have already been saved is important in the context of 8:24–25. The hard evidence of their hope cannot be seen (8:24, 25), for their present sufferings are real. As Jewett says, there is a "lack of publicly visible evidence in altered political, economic, or ecological conditions" for the audience to see at the moment.[96] Yet the aorist ἐσώθημεν affirms that their salvation has already been set in motion in a decisive sense, and in that way they can and must hope for their resurrection without seeing.

The audience is asked to wait for the yet-to-be-fulfilled hope δι' ὑπομονῆς (8:25). Previously 5:4–5 said that believers boast in their affliction, knowing that affliction produces endurance (ὑπομονή), which in turn produces hope (via character). It seems that 8:24–25 has somewhat reworked 5:4–5. Previously the emphasis was that affliction would eventually bring

93. Jewett, *Romans*, 520. The simple dative τῇ . . . ἐλπίδι, however, means that its usage is open to a range of interpretations. See Moo, *Romans*, 521n72, for a list of options.

94. Rom 11:14 is the exception where the future *active* σώσω is used. But then in this case the verse is not referring to the salvation given by God, but that Paul tries to save people.

95. Recent scholars interpret the aorist ἐσώθημεν in 8:24 in terms of the already-not-yet eschatological tension in Paul's theology. See, e.g., Dunn, *Romans 1–8*, 475; Moo, *Romans*, 521–2; Kruse, *Romans*, 350; Hultgren, *Romans*, 325.

96. Jewett, *Romans*, 520.

hope. It provides the training ground for perseverance and hope. But here in 8:24–25 the point is that, in light of the fact that believers are already saved, and in view of the future hope of the final renewal, they wait patiently with perseverance. Surely, endurance still functions as a means of training in times of hardship, but it is the certain hope of future resurrection that forms the basis for endurance. In short, in 8:24–25 the audience is exhorted to resolutely put their hope in God's redemption through perseverance. This hope serves to invigorate the audience in situations that are sorrowful and depressing.

Verses 26–27

Apart from hope, the Spirit is the other resource the letter provides the audience as they face suffering. In 8:26–27 Paul says twice that the Spirit intercedes for his audience.[97] The Spirit helps them in their weakness (v. 26), and prays according to God's will (v. 27). By necessity, commentators have to spend time to interpret the manner and mechanism of the Spirit's prayer in these two verses.[98] But for our purposes we only have to focus on the following matters.

The Spirit intercedes with "groans" (στεναγμοῖς). The στεναγμοῖς in 8:26 recalls the συστενάζει and στενάζομεν in 8:22, 23. The whole creation groans and so do the children of God. Now in 8:26 the Spirit joins in this groaning. The use of στεναγμός functions as a wordplay to increase the rhetorical effect. It invites the audience to be aware of the Spirit's active involvement in their pain and struggle.

The Spirit helps believers in their ἀσθενείᾳ (8:26). The term ἀσθένεια, as Dunn says, "denotes the condition of man in this age, indeed in his creatureliness, as creature and not creator, with all that that implies for man's need of transcendent support."[99] But in light of the theme of suffering since 8:17, 18, and the language of groaning in the context, this creatureliness and dependency on the Creator must include the vulnerability of a new humanity in the face of their affliction.[100] It is because of this weakness that believers do not know how they ought to pray and require the Spirit's aid. Given the audience's daily reality of economic hardship and social oppression, they

97. See the verbs ὑπερεντυγχάνω and ἐντυγχάνω in 8:26, 27.

98. For instance, is the Spirit-empowered prayer a "silent groan," or does it imply speaking in tongues? See Fee, *Empowering*, 575–86, for a detailed discussion.

99. Dunn, *Romans 1–8*, 477. See Gieniusz, *Suffering*, 213, for a similar view.

100. Cf. Jewett, *Romans*, 522.

do experience a real sense of weakness as vulnerable human beings and feel that the help of the divine Spirit is much needed.

The verb συναντιλαμβάνομαι is used in the ancient world to denote "join in helping" or "come to help."[101] It is used in the LXX to refer to people taking up a portion of someone's work.[102] The usage in Ps 88:22 LXX is particularly relevant to Rom 8:25. In the Psalm the verb refers to the sustaining work of YHWH's hand in assisting his people. Thus, Dunn rightly says that the term conveys an "image of the Spirit shouldering the burden which our weakness imposes on us."[103] In other words, there is a sense of God's solidarity in this way of assisting.[104] The audience would find it comforting to hear that the Spirit is assisting them in their vulnerability and that God is standing by them.

The Spirit-intercession in 8:26–27 has some remarkable resemblances to the Spirit-inspired *Abba*-cry in 8:15, and the Gethsemane-prayer on which it is based. The cry in 8:15 and the intercession in 8:26–27 both involve the Spirit. And the ἀσθενείᾳ and στεναγμοῖς in 8:26 reflect the type of prayer at Gethsemane, where Jesus is vulnerable and cries out to God in his weakness. Also, the κατὰ θεόν in 8:26 may reflect Jesus' prayer at Gethsemane, in that the prayer is about doing God's will.[105] The common thread between the *Abba*-cry and the Spirit-intercession seems to be their shared features with Jesus' prayer and the Spirit's aid during times of great emotional need, which is an experience that the audience can resonate with in their suffering. The letter's depiction of the Spirit-intercession, like the *Abba*-cry, gives comfort to the audience in their affliction.[106]

Hence, Rom 8:24–27 provides the audience with two important resources as they seek to fulfill their vocation to suffer with Christ. It encourages them to persevere in putting their hope in their future glorification, even though at the present time there are no visible signs of it. It also speaks of the Spirit's solidarity with them in their weakness and vulnerability, as

101. Cf. Dunn, *Romans 1–8*, 476.

102. See Exod 18:22; Num 11:17.

103. Dunn, *Romans 1–8*, 477. Both Dunn and Jewett, *Romans*, 521, find the usage in Ps 88:22 LXX helpful here. Cf. Gieniusz, *Suffering*, 218; against Cranfield, *Romans I-VIII*, 421.

104. Gieniusz, *Suffering*, 226–27, goes as far as suggesting a "kenosis" of the Spirit's intercession.

105. Interestingly, the συναντιλαμβάνομαι in Rom 8:26 sounds somewhat like the Spirit-human shared activity in 8:16, where the verb συμμαρτυρέω is used.

106. I am delighted to discover that Wu, "Spirit's Intercession," 13, sees a similar connection between Jesus' *Abba*-cry in Mark 14:36 and that in Rom 8:26–27. While commentators often mention Mark 14:36 in their analysis of Rom 8:15, it is uncommon for them to do so here in 8:26–27.

well as the Spirit-intercession that prays according to God's will. With these invigorating and comforting resources they can indeed share Paul's conviction that the sufferings of the present time do not thwart the glory that is to be revealed (8:18). They are assured that they are equipped to partake in God's plan of transforming the cosmos by participating in Christ's suffering and glory.

ROMANS 8:28-30

The important role of the subunit 8:28–30 cannot be underestimated. Indeed, Jewett says that it is the "climactic celebration of the glory to be manifested in the elect."[107] The subunit brings the pericope 8:18–30 to a close, and at the same time wraps up some of the themes that started in 5:1–11.[108] Our discussion so far has shown that the glory of God's children is a key theme in the pericope. In fact the terms δοξάζω and δόξα appear in 8:18, 21, 30, and not in 8:31–39, signaling that the subunit 8:28–30 concludes the pericope. But of course 5:2 has already said that believers boast in the hope of glory (ἐλπίδι τῆς δόξης). Since hope is a key theme in the current pericope, and ἐλπίς/ἐλπίζω do not appear again until 12:12, the current subunit marks the end of the theme of hope of glory. Likewise, the Spirit was mentioned in 5:5 and will not appear again in 8:31–39. The two major remaining themes that coexist in 5:1–11 and 8:31–39 are suffering and love, which we will explore in Chapter 7.

The terms πρόθεσις, προορίζω, κλητός, and καλέω in 8:28–30 indicate that God's purpose for those who are called is an important theme in the subunit. We have suggested that 8:18–30 serves to explicate how believers' vocation of participating in Christ works. More specifically, the pericope is about God's purpose in glorifying his children via their faithful identification with Christ's suffering. It seems, then, that the concluding subunit of the pericope will spell out God's purpose for his children. I will argue that v. 28 says that the Spirit works all things for good for the children of God, who have been called according to his purpose. This means that even groaning, hardship, and affliction are meant for good, and indeed they are part and parcel of God's call. This has been the purpose of God, ever since humanity came under the dominion of sin and death. God predetermined that he

107. Jewett, *Romans*, 508.

108. Here I arrive at something that is somewhat similar to Fee, *Empowering*, 590, who says this concerning Rom 8:28–30, "Paul brings closure to everything that has preceded since v. 17. As we suffer together with Christ in our present existence, we have the Spirit as the firstfruits of our certain future redemption . . . "

would send his Son to create a new humanity so that they may be God's image-bearers again to glorify him (8:29–30). As we will see, the composition of v. 30 constitutes a powerful rhetorical device that brings the audience to the climax of this part of the letter—that is, their glorification. With this, 8:28–30 brings home to the audience a strong message concerning God's purpose of glorifying them through the call for them to suffer with Christ.

Verse 28

In 8:28 Paul says that "we know" (οἴδαμεν) that the Spirit/God works all things together for the good of those who love God, those who are called according to his purpose. What is striking here for an audience familiar with suffering is the notion that there is something "good" regarding their existence in this age. We have found in our analysis that suffering is ultimately caused by evil cosmic forces. But as we will see, God can turn evil into good, and indeed suffering cannot thwart his purpose.

Given the call to suffer with Christ in 8:17 and the context of suffering throughout 8:18–27, this means that even suffering is within God's purpose.[109] The audience groans with creation as they live in a world subjected to futility and decay. But they know that one day they will inherit the cosmos with Christ, and with hope and the Spirit's assistance they can meet the challenge of enduring hardship and injustice at the present time.

Who/what is the subject of συνεργεῖ? That is, who/what performs the action? There are three options: the "all things" (πάντα), God, or the Spirit. This has been a matter of debate, and ultimately we cannot be absolutely sure. Although "all things" seems to be a more natural reading, there is evidence against this option. As Fee says, at least in Paul's letters, πάντα is never used "as the subject of an active verb," and "in the frequent instances where πάντα appears as the object of a personal verb, it almost always precedes the verb."[110] On the other hand, the case for understanding "God" or "the Spirit" as the subject is quite strong. Taking "God" as the subject has the textual support of P46, A, B, 81, where ὁ θεός is added after συνεργεῖ, even

109. As Witherington, *Romans*, 226–7, says, "With *panta* ('all things') Paul probably has particularly in mind the sufferings of the present age. Paul believes that God can use such things, weaving them into his plan for a person's life, using all things to a good end." See also Cranfield, *Romans I-VIII*, 428; Matera, *Romans*, 204.

110. Fee, *Empowering*, 588. And Jewett, *Romans*, 526, says, "While it seems more appropriate on substantive grounds to construe πάντα as an accusative of speciation, 'in all things,' it remains unclear why Paul did not provide a preposition such as κατα πάντα, which would have removed all possibility of ambiguity." E.g., Dunn, *Romans 1-8*, 431; Byrne, *Romans*, 271–72.

though this longer version was likely to have been added to clarify who the subject was thought to be.[111] Another argument for "God" being the subject is that it is the most recently mentioned personal pronoun in the text. The third option is to have "the Spirit" as the subject. Jewett thinks that this is most likely because this requires no change of subject from the end of v. 27.[112] Also, the Spirit has been the subject of two verbs with a συ-prefix. Verse 16 says that the Spirit bears witness together with the spirit of the Christ-community that they are children of God. And most recently, v. 26 says that the Spirit assists us in our weakness.[113] In light of these, then, both "God" and "the Spirit" are preferable to "all things." But the context seems to favor "the Spirit." The work of the Spirit *in the present life* of believers has been a prominent feature of Rom 8:1–16, 26–27. Most recently the Spirit is said to be interceding for the audience (8:27).[114] If it is the case, then the verb συνεργέω in 8:28 is another συ-compound in Rom 8 (together with συμμαρτυρέω in 8:16, and possibly συναντιλαμβάνομαι in 8:26) that speaks of a shared divine-human role in the face of adversity.[115] While God through his Spirit works all things for the audience's good, they also take part in this work by their active participation in Christ's suffering. Our discussion will proceed on the assumption that the Spirit is the subject here, with the understanding that "God" is also a likely option. The point is that in all the present sufferings and cosmic chaos, God and his Spirit are actively assisting and empowering his children to face the challenge.[116] Not only has the Spirit already set believers free from the cosmic powers of sin and death (8:2). The Spirit also continues to enable God's children to ensure that his triumph over evil will be consummated. For the audience, this functions as another comforting and invigorating assurance in their affliction.

111. Cf. Hultgren, *Romans*, 320, 326–27. Those who think that the subject is "God" include Gignilliat, "Working Together with Whom?" 511–14; Kruse, *Romans*, 354; Hultgren, *Romans*, 326–27.

112. Jewett, *Romans*, 527.

113. Fee, *Empowering*, 589; Jewett, *Romans*, 527.

114. Fee, *Empowering*, 589. If the Spirit is indeed the subject, then 8:28–30 contains the last reference to the Spirit's work in Romans 8 and indeed the whole of Romans 5–8.

115. Cf. Jewett, *Romans*, 527. This applies whether the subject is "God" or "the Spirit."

116. The often observed proto-trinitarian theology of Rom 8 means that it is ultimately unnecessary to choose between "God" and "the Spirit" to be the subject here. (As mentioned, Fee, "Christology and Pneumatology," 218–25, provides a helpful discussion about the potential trinitarian expressions in Rom 8.) Also, even if we take "all things" as the subject, it cannot mean that they work "naturally" for the good of God's children, but that ultimately the Creator God is in control.

The phrase εἰς ἀγαθόν requires some discussion. Gieniusz helpfully draws us to Gen 50:20 LXX, where Joseph says to his brothers, "You deliberated against me for evil, but God deliberated concerning me for good (εἰς ἀγαθά) . . ."[117] This is an apt parallel to Rom 8:28, where the Spirit works all things—including sufferings—for the good of believers. Even though hardships are not good, they can be part of God's saving purpose for something "good." Likewise, YHWH says in Jeremiah that he has sent away Israel to the land of the Chaldeans for good (εἰς ἀγαθά); he will fix his eyes on them for good (εἰς ἀγαθά) and restore the land to them (24:5, 6 LXX).[118] Like the texts in Genesis and Jeremiah, Rom 8:28 speaks of the good that can come out of affliction and oppression. That is, God intends something for the good of those who love him, as the Spirit (or God) works all things together in the midst of their sufferings.[119]

Romans 8:28 says that those who love God are τοῖς κατὰ πρόθεσιν κλητοῖς. The adjective κλητός has been used in the salutation section to refer to Paul the apostle (1:1) and the audience themselves (1:6, 7).[120] The term πρόθεσις appears in both 8:28 and 9:11. It will be used in 9:11 to refer to God's purpose of election (ἐκλογὴν πρόθεσις τοῦ θεοῦ) for Israel and the remnant in chapters 9–11.[121] But here in 8:28, as it will become clear in v. 29, the πρόθεσις seems to refer to God's plan and determination for a restored humanity to be conformed to the image of the Son.[122]

In sum, 8:28 speaks to a people who love God and are called by God according to his purpose. God's Spirit is working all things together so that the groaning and pain of their present suffering—including that resulting from the decay of creation—are ultimately for their good. This does not mean that suffering is in and of itself good. In fact, it is a manifestation of the

---

117. Gieniusz, *Suffering*, 263. See also Rodgers, "Text of Romans 8:28," 549–50; Kruse, *Romans*, 354.

118. Other relevant usages of "for good" in the LXX include Deut 30:9; Neh 2:18; cf. 5:19; Jdt 4:15; Ps 118:122 (maybe); Sir 11:12; 39:27.

119. Hommel, "Denen, die Gott Lieben," 126–9, argues that the source of Romans 8:28 is Plato's *Republic* (see *Resp.* 10.612e; 10.613a). That may be so. But we should note here that there is a rich scriptural tradition for the expression τοῖς ἀγαπῶσιν τὸν θεόν in Rom 8:28, even though it is rare in Paul. Cf. Gieniusz, *Suffering*, 259–60. In the Torah it is said that YHWH's love will be with those who love him (Exod 20:6; Deut 5:10; 7:9). The psalmists say that YHWH will deliver those who love him (Ps 69:5 LXX; 96:10 LXX). Interestingly, in Ps 68:36–37 LXX it is said that God will save Zion. His people will inherit (κληρονομέω) it and "those who love" (οἱ ἀγαπῶντες) his name will live in it.

120. The verb καλέω appears in Rom 9:7, 12, 24, 25, 26, and they are the "remnant" in 9:27.

121. The term ἐκλογή is used in Rom 9:11; 11:5, 7, 28 to refer to Israel/the remnant.

122. Cf. Kruse, *Romans*, 355; Wright, *Romans*, 601.

powers of sin and death. But God is capable of turning evil into good. How this works will be explained in the next verse.

Verse 29

The mention of the conformity with God's Son (υἱός) in 8:29 is highly significant for the audience, for throughout 8:14–17, 18–30 they have been hearing that they themselves are God's children (υἱοί/τέκνα). This is especially so given the prominent notion of participation in Christ in the pivotal passage of 8:14–17. I will argue that 8:29 speaks of God's predetermined plan of calling believers to participate in Christ's suffering and glory, and that this involves a process of being conformed to the Son's image, in anticipation that they will become God's vice-regents ruling over the cosmos.

The ὅτι indicates that vv. 29–30 explains and elaborates on God's purpose in 8:28.[123] The verbs προγινώσκω and προορίζω,[124] despite modern theological interest in the terms, reflect the foreknowledge and election of God that Paul would take for granted, given the letter's affirmation of the important role of Israel's Scripture in his gospel. The fact that YHWH has the prerogative and power to decide and know in advance is assumed in the Scripture (see Gen 18:19; Jer 1:5; Amos 3:2).[125] In view of this, the point of 8:29a is quite simple: conformation to the Son's image has long been God's predetermined purpose.

The terms εἰκών and δοξάζω/δόξα in 8:29, 30 also occur in 1:21, 23, where human beings exchanged the glory of the immortal God for images resembling mortal human beings or animals. As mentioned in Chapter 5, this apparent reference to idolatry reflects the notion that the images of idols display the attributes of the associated deities.[126] Having been made in the Creator God's image, Adamic humanity is supposed to display his glory. As Ps 8:6 LXX says, the Lord crowned humans with δόξῃ καὶ τιμῇ. Idolatrous

123. The ὅτι most likely means that Rom 8:29–30 explains not just the last few words of 8:28 but the entire verse. See Jewett, *Romans*, 528; Cranfield, *Romans I-VIII*, 431.

124. The προορίζω will appear again in Rom 8:30, and the προγινώσκω in 11:2 (where it will be applied to Israel).

125. Cf. Byrne, *Romans*, 272; Jewett, *Romans*, 528; Cranfield, *Romans I-VIII*, 482; Hultgren, *Romans*, 328.

126. See our discussion of the meaning of "glory" in our analysis of Rom 8:17 in Chapter 5, where we looked at the images of Jupiter, Minerva and Ra. Here, the comments by Walton, *Ancient Near*, 212, are particularly useful. He says that "in both Egypt and Mesopotamia an idol contained the image of the deity. This allowed the image to possess the attributes of the deity, function as mediator of worship to the deity, and serve as indicator of the presence of the deity."

behavior happens when humans fail to reflect God's glory and worship the images of idols. By contrast, when their lives exhibit his glory, they reflect the image of God. Therefore, scholars rightly think that the εἰκών in 8:29 reflects the notion in Jewish thought and ancient worldviews, that human beings bear God's image and display his glory.[127] That is, image-bearers (most often kings and rulers) are representatives of the identity of the deities with the role and responsibility to carry out divinely ordained roles and works. Jewett succinctly puts it this way,

> The idea of humans bearing the image of God in Gen 1:27; Ps 8:6–7; and Sir 17:2–4 was derived from ancient kingship ideology, in which the ruler was thought to represent divine sovereignty and glory. Paul joins the OT tradition of democratizing this ideology by extending the restoration of sovereignty and glory to all those conforming to Christ's image.[128]

As argued before, the vocation of the children of God is that they may display God's glory again by identifying with Christ's suffering and glory. In view of this, the statement in 8:29 concerning being conformed to the image of the Son would be about exhibiting the glory of the Son by participating in him.

The adjective σύμμορφος is a rare word. It occurs only in one other place in the New Testament, namely, Phil 3:21. The cognate verb συμμορφίζω appears only in Phil 3:10. Neither of these words can be found in the LXX and are very rare in classical and Hellenistic Greek.[129] The rarity, as Gieniusz suggests, invites us to take seriously the components of the term, namely, σύν and μορφή.[130] That is, like the συ-compounds in 8:17, there is a strong sense of participation in Christ here in 8:29,[131] especially given the fact that in both 8:17 and 8:29 the two parties involved are believers and Christ.[132] Also, the use of the adjective (σύμμορφος) with the genitive (τῆς εἰκόνος)

---

127. See Dunn, *Romans 1–8*, 483; Byrne, *Romans*, 272–3. As Gieniusz, *Suffering*, 268, says, one can compare "with the Old Testament idea of God's image in which Adam was created and which he shares with his progeny."

128. Jewett, *Romans*, 529. Dunn, *Romans 1–8*, 483, notes that the notion of humans being God's image is not an exclusive Jewish thought, but says (rightly) that the prominent Adamic theme throughout Rom 5–8 suggests strongly that the Jewish background is in view in Rom 8:29.

129. Gieniusz, *Suffering*, 269; W. Grundmann, "σύν–μετά," 7.787.

130. Gieniusz, *Suffering*, 269.

131. Thus, Dunn, *Romans 1–8*, 483, rightly says that the συ-prefix here harks back to 8:17. Cf. Byrne, *Romans*, 270; Moo, *Romans*, 534n151; Gorman, "Treatise on Theosis," 26–27.

132. This is not always the case for other συ-compounds in Romans.

suggests that the term carries a substantival force.[133] This indicates that the conformity that the term stands for is not simply a general likeness or similarity in form.[134] Rather, it is about participation in Christ's existence, or "his way of being," as Byrne puts it.[135] Given the fact that Rom 3:26 and 5:12–21 speak of the loss of glory of humanity and humans being under the dominion of sin and death, conformity to the Son's image may be viewed as the transformation of God's image-bearers. That is, believers bear God's image by means of becoming sharers of the Son's identity and way of life, and this includes sharing in both Christ's suffering and glorification.[136] Commentators have called this a "process of transformation," in which believers cooperate with the Spirit to model their lives after Jesus in the present,[137] with the hope of sharing in his resurrection and hence the full realization of their υἱοθεσία at the renewal of creation.[138]

Fee rightly suggests that the term πρωτότοκος implies that Christ is the messianic Davidic Son of God.[139] Within the scriptural symbolic universe of Paul and his audience, the term may point to YHWH's relationship with Israel (Exod 4:22, 23). But in Ps 89:20, 26–27 (88:21, 27–28 LXX) "first-born" specifically refers to the Davidic figure, who would be the highest king on earth.[140] Commentators on this Psalm recognize the references in 89:19–37 to the Davidic promises found in 2 Sam 7:10–15, with Ps 89:28

133. Cf. Byrne, *Romans*, 272.

134. Gieniusz, *Suffering*, 269.

135. Byrne, *Romans*, 272. Campbell, *Union*, 232, cautions that "being conformed to the image of Christ cannot refer to quite the same reality as union with Christ himself," but he affirms that it refers to "conformity of believers to the pattern and narrative of Christ." I think "participating in Christ" and "conforming to the pattern of Christ" are suitable expressions for our purposes.

136. Cf. 2 Cor 3:18; Hiebert, "Romans 8:28–29," 180–82; Gieniusz, *Suffering*, 270–71; Jewett, *Romans*, 529. Dunn, *Romans 1–8*, 483, says specifically that the conformity includes the sharing of Christ's suffering, as mentioned in 8:11, 15–17.

137. Jewett, *Romans*, 528–9. See also Dunn, *Romans 1–8*, 483. Cf. Horrell, *Greening Paul*, 83. Against Kruse, *Romans*, 356, who thinks that it refers to the final resurrection. Gorman, "Treatise on Theosis," 26, is right to say that "conformity to Christ is both present and future." Gorman helpfully brings the texts in Rom 8:3–4, 17, 21, and 29, together, and draws several helpful theological conclusions (26–27).

138. In addition, Dunn, *Romans 1–8*, 484, rightly says that Paul's view of history is not cyclic and hence not a return to the original state of creation. Rather, it is about "moving toward an intended higher end, not simply returning to the beginning." We will say more about Rom 8:29 when we take a look at the echo of Genesis in Rom 8:18–30.

139. Fee, *Pauline Christology*, 250–51. Cf. Hultgren, *Romans*, 329. The general messianic sense of πρωτότοκος is also noted by Byrne, *Romans*, 273.

140. Cf. Hultgren, *Romans*, 329.

(88:29 LXX) explicitly mentioning the covenant.[141] Interestingly, υἱός and πρωτότοκος appear together in Rom 8:29. The audience has heard the first reference to the Son in 1:3–4, where it says that Christ is the Son of God and σπέρμα of David (1:3–4). That is, Christ is God's Son and simultaneously David's physical descendant (κατὰ σάρκα), who, according to Jewish messianic expectation, is the coming Davidic king. Putting these together, the letter in fact says that Christ carries a dual identity, namely, being God's Son and the Davidic king at the same time. This king is, of course, not only the king of Israel, but the entire cosmos. Accordingly, his image represents the identity of the Creator God himself. Since believers, as God's children, are to be conformed to his image, the πολλοῖς ἀδελφοῖς would refer to the formation of a *royal family*, with Christ as the firstborn and believers as his many siblings. They are indeed co-heirs of God (8:17). Together they will be God's vice-regents on earth, representing him within the cosmos.

In short, 8:29 speaks of God's predetermined plan of calling believers to participate in a process of transformation, in which they identify with Christ by modeling after his suffering and death.[142] In this way a large royal family of God is formed, and God's program of transforming humanity and renewing creation is being completed in this process.[143] The audience, then, is invited to consider a rather radical notion. Slaves, former war-captives, and the socioeconomically poor, belong to a royal family. Their call to suffer is in fact a call to participate in God's predetermined purpose.[144]

---

141. Broyles, *Psalms*, 357; Mays, *Psalms*, 285–87; Goldingay, *Psalms* 42–89, 677–81. Cf. Grogan, *Psalms*, 156.

142. Jackson, *New Creation*, 155–6, succinctly traces a similar movement from Rom 8:17 to 8:30, noting the significance of "image" along the way. Likewise, Wright, *Paul*, 438–42, examines Gen 1:28; 5:3; Rom 1:18–25; 3:23; 5:2; 8:17, 18, 21, 29, 30; 1 Cor 15:42–49; 2 Cor 4:4; Col 1:15; 3:9–11, and says that "[w]e have been Adam-image people; now we are to be Messiah-image people reflecting the image of the one who is himself the reflection of the invisible God" (439). Not surprisingly for Wright—given his emphasis on covenantal faithfulness—he sees that believers are "Messiah-image people," which is a matter that our analysis does not focus on, since our primary texts are found in Rom 5 and 8 (where Israel is not explicitly mentioned; but note our discussion of Davidic royal family in Rom 8:29).

143. Space limitations do not allow us to study the related matters in other Pauline letters. But see the brief survey by Matera, "Conformed to the image," 104–10, who examines the texts in 1 Cor 15; 2 Cor 4:7–5:10; Rom 8, and Phil 3.

144. In my analysis of Rom 5–8 so far, I have tried to work through the complex interconnected relationships between suffering, glory, image-bearing, the work of Christ and the Spirit, and the already-not-yet character of Paul's thinking. Not surprising, Wright. *Paul*, 440, also does that in his study of Rom 5–8. I am in broad terms in agreement with him when he says, "'Being conformed to the image of the son,' as in Romans 8.29, summarizes importantly *both* the present vocation of suffering, as in 8.17, and the promise of 'glory,' the theme which binds together 8.17 with 8.18, 8.21 and 8.30." But,

Verse 30

The repeated use of τούτους and καί in 8:30 constitutes a powerful rhetorical device designed to capture the audience's attention.[145] The chain appearances of τούτους καί progressively shifts the subject matter from God's predetermined purpose (signified by the προώρισεν) to the glorification of believers (see the ἐδόξασεν), which aptly fulfills the subunit's function of bringing Paul's discussion to a climactic end. The fact that the chain τούτους καί leads to the ἐδόξασεν, and that ἐδόξασεν is in fact the final word in the text here is highly significant. On the one hand, the audience is prompted to recognize the importance of their glorification in the current pericope. On the other hand, it also harks back to the δοξάζω/δόξα/συνδοξάζω in 5:2; 8:17, 18, 21, making "glory" a high point of the argument in Rom 5-8.[146]

With another προορίζω, 8:30 points back to the message in v. 29. God has decided in advance that the new humanity should be conformed to the image of his Son. But it is not only that God has predetermined that they undergo a process of transformation, he has also called them (note the repeated τούτους). The verb καλέω here recalls the adjective κλητός in 8:28 (cf. 1:1, 6, 7).[147] The audience has been called for a purpose, and the Spirit works all things together for them against all odds. The verb δικαιόω harks back to the beginning of the entire section in Rom 5-8 (5:1, 9), which is, in turn, based on the dense passage in 3:21-26. Right standing with God through Christ is crucial to the formation of a new humanity. Justification/ vindication is required because Adamic humanity falls short of the *glory* of God. The implicit notion is that those whom God justified/vindicated he also *glorified*.

The aorist ἐδόξασεν is troublesome for commentators who believe that the term here only refers to the glory at resurrection. This view will have to take the aorist "glorified" as anticipatory—that is, the aorist implies the certainty of glorification because salvation has already taken place.[148] But, as Jewett says, this would "require the final verb, 'glorified,' in the climactic sequence to be taken in a different sense from the four prior aorists, which

---

as we will see below, I think there is a significant *present dimension* when Paul speaks of the glorification of believers in 8:20.

145. Cf. Heil, *Romans*, 92.

146. Again, note that in Rom 5-8 the language of "glory" stops at 8:30.

147. Cf. Dunn, *Romans 1-8*, 485.

148. See Dunn, *Romans 1-8*, 485-86; Gieniusz, *Suffering*, 279-80. See also Jewett, *Romans*, 530, and Gieniusz, *Suffering*, 279-80, for discussions on the different options.

is problematic."[149] It seems that, as not a few scholars believe,[150] it is better to think that the glorification has already begun, and that it is a process moving forward to the final and full glorification at the resurrection. On the one hand, the children of God will fully display the glory of God (as he originally intended in the beginning) when the cosmos is renewed (cf. 8:21). On the other hand, they can display a measure of his glory as they live in the overlap of the ages. Throughout our discussion of the current pericope, we have seen how the notion of participation in Christ's suffering and glory in 8:17 works in the present life of believers. It seems that the process of glorification implied in 8:30 is best understood in terms of sharing in Christ's suffering and the display of his glory in this present life. As the children of God participate in Christ here and now, they, at least in some measure, display the glory of God. This process will be consummated at their resurrection.[151]

This process of glorification (8:30) and transformation (into the Son's image; 8:29) would be a radical notion in imperial Rome, given the type of people in Paul's audience. According to the prevailing worldview, glory was not assigned to those living with socioeconomic hardship and religio-political injustice. Glory, for example, was not an attribute of war-captives, slaves or the homeless. Nor was it particularly glorious to be poor or belong to the lower parts of the social hierarchy. But the audience heard that their present sufferings were actually an integral part of God's purpose in transforming his image-bearers and renewing the whole creation.

Our analysis of the text of Rom 8:18–30 is not complete without considering the underlying reference to the primordial stories in Genesis. This is the matter we will explore now, before we conclude our findings for the pericope.

---

149. Jewett, *Romans*, 530.

150. See Jewett, *Romans*, 530; Byrne, *Romans*, 270; cf. Kasemann, *Romans*, 245; Cranfield, *Romans I-VIII*, 433; Fee, *Pauline Christology*, 251n33.

151. At this point it is worth mentioning 2 Cor 3:18, which conveys a remarkably similar message as Rom 8:29–30. (See the key words in both places: εἰκών, μεταμορφόω, πνεῦμα, and δόξα.) My—rather rigid—translation of 2 Cor 3:18 goes like this: "And we all, with unveiled faces reflecting the glory of the Lord, are being transformed (μεταμορφούμεθα) into the same image from glory to glory, just as from the Lord, the Spirit." Here, Paul says that believers are being transformed by the Spirit into the image of the Lord and reflect his glory.

THE REVERSAL OF THE ADAMIC STORY IN GENESIS

Almost without exception commentators think that Genesis, especially 3:17–19, is alluded to in Rom 8:18–30.[152] But there is no uniform view regarding the extent to which Genesis influences the letter. In the following we will, however, discover that Genesis plays a highly significant role in assisting the audience to understand their vocation of suffering with Christ.[153] We will first examine the thematic and verbal links between Genesis and the letter, and then study the similarities between the narrative structure of Genesis and that of Rom 5–8. After that we will investigate the ways in which the scriptural primeval history provides additional resources for the audience to understand Rom 8:18–30. I will argue that Genesis substantially reinforces the notion that the audience is part of a new humanity whose role is to partake in God's intention to restore and transform a humanity bound by sin and death.[154] Importantly, Genesis lends support to our proposal that the believers' participation in Christ's suffering and glory is essential for the renewal of the whole creation.

Thematic and Verbal Links

Our study on the thematic and verbal links between Genesis and Romans will roughly follow the order of their appearance in our present pericope.[155] There are six links for consideration.

---

152. See discussion below for references to those commentators.

153. Grappe, "Qui me délivrera," 472–92, recognizes that Paul regularly refers to Adam throughout Rom 5–8. The article carefully examines the possible allusion to Adam in Rom 7:24 and 8:2 (with reference to Adam's dead body in *4 Ezra* 3:4–5). But surprisingly, Grappe does not have much to say about the links with Adam/Genesis in Rom 8:17, 18–30, except what commentators commonly mention (489–90).

154. Elliott, "Creation," 152, thinks that Genesis is not reflected in Rom 8 because Adam is not mentioned and that the terms used by Paul in Rom 8 is not found in Gen 1–3. I, however, think that the cumulative evidence below is sufficient to suggest otherwise.

155. At this point I should mention again that our focus is how might the text of Romans have evoked Gen 1–3. As mentioned before, Gen 1–3 consists of different accounts of primeval history (coming from different traditions and sources). We have limited access to how the audience in Rome might have read Gen 1–3. The approach I take here is simply to examine intertextual and thematic links between Gen 1–3 and Romans. This, in my view, is a reasonable way to detect how Gen 1–3 might have been a resource for the audience to understand Rom 8. There are other attempts to read Paul's mention of Adam/creation in light of Gen 1–3 and other Jewish texts. See, for example, Pate, "Genesis 1–3," 3–25. My sense is that any study like that—unless it is in the form of a highly sophisticated monograph—is unlikely to comprehensively capture

First, we note the explicit language of Adam and creation in Rom 5:12–21 and 8:18–30.[156] The audience has already encountered several pointers to Genesis before they come to 8:18–30. Our discussion in Chapter 3 suggested that Genesis would be evoked in Rom 5:12–21, on the basis of the clear intertextual links and similar narrative structures between the two texts. Since Rom 8:18–30 is very much an integral part of the argument that started in 5:1–21, and since κτίσις constitutes a key theme in 8:18–30, it is likely that Genesis continues to play a role behind the text. Also, as we found in the pivotal passage 8:14–17, the language of "child/son/Son" may bring to mind the primordial accounts in Genesis, where Adamic humanity is understood to be God's children created through his "breath." Since 8:18–30 is an extended elaboration of 8:14–17, its mention of κτίσις may point the audience to the Genesis narrative.

Second, there are linkages between the curse on the earth in Gen 3 and the futility and decay of creation in Rom 8. Most scholars think that the curse on the earth (γῆ) in Gen 3:17–19 is the background for the ματαιότης in Rom 8:20.[157] Sometimes the φθορά in 8:21 is also considered to be alluding to the same Scripture.[158] The basic thematic link is quite clear. In Genesis the earth was cursed; and, in Romans, creation was subjected to futility and the bondage of decay. Also, according to Genesis, humans have to labor and toil because the earth will yield thorns and thistles (3:17, 18). The earth was originally created to sustain life and allow humans to flourish. But now its functional capacity has degraded, and humans suffer accordingly. Quite clearly, then, the Gen 3 curse on the earth has consequences for human life. A similar picture is found in Rom 8:20–21. The decay of creation causes human suffering. The material creation is no longer a safe place. There are famines, earthquakes, and storms, and they are ultimately caused by the

the complexity of the interrelationships between the many scriptural texts and Paul's letters.

156. Note that Rom 5:12–21 and 8:18–30 are the second and second last pericope of Rom 5–8 respectively, and that 5:1–21 and 8:18–39 bracket Rom 5–8.

157. This includes scholars from Cranfield, *Romans I-VIII*, 413, to, more recently, Adams, *Constructing*, 178–79; Hahne, *Corruption*, 189; White, "Paul's Cosomology," 98n35; Jewett, *Romans*, 513. (Again, it should be noted that Gen 3 and Rom 8 do not say that creation is inherently evil.)

158. Hahne, *Corruption*, 195.

cosmic forces of sin and death.[159] Just as the curse on the earth in Gen 3 affects human wellbeing, so does the decay of creation harm humanity.[160]

Third, the hope in Rom 8:20 may alert the audience to Gen 3:15. Hahne suggests that the ἐφ᾽ ἐλπίδι in the letter may echo Gen 3:15 thematically.[161] While the curses in Gen 3:14–19 paint a gloomy future for both the serpent and Adamic humanity, there is a glimpse of hope in 3:15. The verse speaks of the enmity between the serpent's offspring and that of the woman, implying that the serpent's evil scheme will be met with an opponent. The highly symbolic text seems to represent the ongoing struggle between evil powers and humanity, with the latter eventually triumphing over the former.[162] I

159. Scholars like Horrell, *Greening Paul*, 75, raise a valid point that Gen 3:17 only refers to the negative effects of Adam's disobedience on specific elements of creation, rather than the entire (non-human) creation. But Horrell, Hunt, and Southgate continue to say,

> Nonetheless, without denying that the action of Adam is, for Paul, a fundamental point from which corruption and death enter the created order, it is worth considering the possibility that—given only a brief and allusive reference to the enslavement of the whole κτίσις to φθορά—what Paul has in view here is a broader allusion to the unfolding story of 1–11, in which corruption affects all flesh.

In my view, the curses in Gen 3 consist of highly symbolic language and should be treated accordingly. What is clear from both Gen 3 and Rom 5:12–13 is the widespread consequences of Adam's trespass across the entire cosmos. Also, since creation is not inherently evil, the call by modern scholars to care for the environment is valid.

160. There are two other possible (indirect) linkages between the curse in 3 and Rom 8. First, there are intertextual links between Rom 8:20, Ecclesiastes and Genesis, via the term ματαιότης. As mentioned, the word ματαιότης appears frequently in Ecclesiastes. Interestingly, Eccl 3:19–20 seems to echo Genesis. (See, e.g., Crenshaw, *Ecclesiastes*, 104; Murphy, *Ecclesiastes*, 37; cf. Brown, *Ecclesiastes*, 47.) In Gen 2:7; 3:19 Adam is said to have been made from the dust (χοῦς) of the earth, and that following his disobedience he will have to labor in pain until he returns to the earth. Likewise, Eccl 3:17–20 shows the type of futility that Adamic humanity experiences. The destinies of a human and an animal are the same, for they will both return to dust (3:20) and hence all things are absurd and futile (3:19). These intertextual links provide additional pointers for the audience to detect Genesis in Rom 8:20. Second, Jewett, *Romans*, 516, alerts us to another possible link between Romans 8:22 and 3:17–18, via Job 31:38–40. In Job 31:38 Job protests to God regarding his innocence and says, "if any time the earth (γῆ) groaned (ἐστέναξεν) over me . . . then let nettle come forth instead of wheat." It seems that Job is contrasting himself with Adam in terms of their relationship with the earth. While in Gen 3:17–18 the earth is cursed as a result of Adam's trespass, Job claims his innocence using his relationship with the earth as an example.

161. Hahne, *Corruption*, 192–93. Cf. Jackson, *New Creation*, 158.

162. As Wenham, *Genesis 1–15*, 80, says, "Once admitted that the serpent symbolizes sin, death, and the power of evil, it becomes much more likely that the curse envisages a long struggle between good and evil, with mankind eventually triumphing." Cf. Hartley, *Genesis*, 69, who also thinks that Gen 3:15 speaks of humans' ultimate triumph

have suggested previously that the ἐφ᾽ ἐλπίδι in Rom 8:20 most likely connects with the ὑπετάγη, implying that God subjected creation to futility in view of the hope of their future liberation when God's children are glorified. This hope seems to echo the ray of hope found in Gen 3:15.[163] Despite the futile outlook of creation, there is hope for the future because of the eagerly expected revelation of the children of God.

Fourth, the τῶν τέκνων τοῦ θεοῦ in Rom 8:21, like the references to God's children in 8:14–16, may recall Adam's filial relationship with God in Genesis. We have explored this in our discussion in Chapter 5, and discovered that the γένεσις, γεννάω, and εἰκών in Gen 5:1, 3 indicate that Adam is God's son. Likewise, believers are God's "sons" as members of his new humanity. While the identity of Adamic humanity is defined by Adam, a believer's identity is found in Christ. Whereas Adam's disobedience opened the door for sin and death to reign in the cosmos, the unveiling of the glory of God's children will be the pathway through which the final triumph over evil will take place (Rom 8:19–23).

Fifth, the verbs συστενάζω and συνωδίνω in Rom 8:22 may echo the στεναγμός and λύπη in Gen 3:16.[164] As mentioned, ὠδίνω and ὠδίν are used in Jer 4:31 and 22:23 LXX to refer to the travail of childbirth (metaphorically), and in both verses the language of groaning (στεναγμός; καταστενάζω) is also employed. Thus, the συστενάζει καὶ συνωδίνει in Rom 8:22 paints a picture of severe groaning and the birth pangs of creation. This picture can also be found in Gen 3:16, which says that God will multiply the woman's pains and groaning (τὰς λύπας . . . καὶ τὸν στεναγμόν), and in pain she will give birth to children (ἐν λύπαις τέξῃ τέκνα). The curse here is not applied to the earth or creation, but it is an integral part of the curses resulting from Adam's disobedience. In fact, later when Lamech named Noah in Gen 5:29, he did so in the hope that the Lord would bring release to humans from the labor and pain (ἀπὸ τῶν ἔργων . . . καὶ ἀπὸ τῶν λυπῶν) that exist on the earth (γῆ) that God had cursed. Here the same language of pain is used to refer to the hardship Adamic humanity has to live with. If we take into account the fact that humankind and creation are inseparable (according to ancient worldviews), then it is likely that Gen 3:16 is evoked in Rom 8:22.

Sixth, the εἰκών of the Son in Rom 8:29 very likely evokes Gen 1:26–27; 3:1–19; 5:1, 3, where Adam was God's son and humankind was created in

over the "forces of evil."

163. Genesis 3:15 would not have appeared to its original readers to be a prophecy concerning Jesus. Nevertheless, it might have been thought to allude to the deliverance from evil through Israel or Israel's Messiah. See 1 Chron 17:10–14 and Pahl, *Beginning*, 43.

164. Cf. Hahne, *Corruption*, 204; Tsumura, "OT Background," 620–21.

the likeness and image of God.[165] Here we can recall two of our previous findings to assist our analysis. The first is our discussion regarding the filial relationship that Adam had with God. According to Gen 1:26–27; 5:1, 3, Adam was God's son because he was created in his image. Our discussion has found that believers are God's children in the manner of Adam, except that their identify is now found in Christ (Rom 8:14–17). Since Adam is a τύπος of the one to come (Rom 5:14), namely, Christ, it follows that Christ bears God's image because he is God's Son. In light of this, it is very likely that Gen 1:26–27 and 5:1, 3 are evoked in Rom 8:29. Believers' conformity with the Son's image is indeed about the new humanity's modeling after Christ's pattern. Secondly, we recall that the believers' glorification concerns the transformation of humanity after Adamic humanity's failure to bear God's image. We have found in our analysis of 8:17 that Adamic humanity falls short of God's glory even though as God's image-bearers they are supposed to display his glory.[166] Instead, they engage in idolatrous behavior by worshipping the images of idols. In light of this, believers' conformity with the εἰκών of the Son in Rom 8:29 may evoke not only Gen 1:26–27; 5:1, 3 (texts that speak of Adam's image-bearing) but also Adam's loss of glory at his disobedience in 3:1–19. That is, the evocation takes place because Rom 8:29 paints a picture of the image-bearing of a new humanity that effectively reverses the tragic consequences of Adamic humanity's disobedience in Gen 3. The language of δοξάζω/δόξα in Rom 8:18, 21, 30 reinforces this. As argued before, 8:18–30 speaks of the unveiling of the glory of believers as they fulfill their vocation to suffer with Christ, and that their image-bearing is an integral part of their transformation into the image of the Son. It seems that 8:18–30 echoes Gen 3 via a theme that spells out God's project of restoring that which was lost in Adamic humanity's failed image-bearing.

In addition to these thematic and linguistic links between Genesis and the letter, the evocation of Genesis in Rom 8:18–30 is reinforced by the similar narrative structures between the story of Gen 1–3 and that of God's restored humanity in Christ. To these narrative structures we now turn.

---

165. Many commentators refer to Gen 1:26–27 when they interpret Rom 8:29, even though it may not be their emphasis. See Jewett, *Romans*, 529; Byrne, *Romans*, 272–73; Cranfield, *Romans I-VIII*, 432; Dunn, *Romans 1–8*, 483.

166. See our discussion on Rom 8:17 in Chapter 5 regarding the shared glorification with Christ.

Story of Adamic Humanity and That of Humanity in Christ

In Chapter 3 we compared the underlying narrative structure of Adam in Gen 1–3 and that of Adamic humanity in Rom 5–8, and we discovered significant similarities between them. At the time we noted that more data would be available later. As we are now at the end of the analysis of 8:18–30, it is time to revisit the comparison. Since there is a focus on creation in Rom 8, we will first take a closer look at the creation account in Genesis before outlining the underlying narrative structure of Gen 1–3.

A growing number of scholars today think that the good creation depicted in Genesis constitutes a cosmic temple of God.[167] If the cosmos is God's temple, then the fact that humans were made in his image is highly significant, because images of deities are prominently found in ancient temples. In Isa 66:1 YHWH declares that heaven is his throne and the earth is his footstool, and asks, "What is the house which you would build for me?" Since the preceding passage is about the new creation (65:17–25), 66:1 paints a picture of creation being YHWH's house—that is, his temple, or palace—consisting of his throne and footstool. There are texts that speak of YHWH/God setting the foundations and pillars of the heavens and earth (2 Sam 22:8, 16; Job 9:6; Pss 18:15; 75:3; 102:25; Amos 9:6; Zech 12:1), and describe how he stretched out the heavens like a canopy or a tent (Isa 40:22; 42:5; Jer 10:12; 32:17; Zech 12:1). These texts, with their architectural metaphors, portray the Creator God as the "master builder" of creation.[168] Indeed, Philo says that the "whole universe must be regarded as the highest and in truth the holy temple of God. As sanctuary it has the heaven, the most holy part of substance of existing things . . ." (De Spec. Leg. 1.66). With further evidence from Israel's Scripture and ancient Near Eastern traditions, Watts affirms that the cosmos is regarded as the Creator's temple-palace and that Adam and Eve were installed in it as his image.[169] Watts says,

> Just as YHWH sits enthroned in his cosmic temple, so too humanity images him, reigning between his knees as it were in

---

167. See Weinfeld, "Sabbath, Temple," 501–12; Levenson, Creation, 78–99; Watts, "New Creational Restoration," 15–37; Morrow, "Creation," 1–13. See especially the extensive treatment on the topic in Walton, Genesis 1, 122–92.

168. I borrow the apt phrase "master builder" from Watts, "New Creational Restoration," 18–19, who provides dozens of examples of Scripture using architectural language for God's creation.

169. Watts, "New Creational Restoration," 18–22. Note that the Hebrew היכל stands for both temple and palace.

the smaller temple-palace of the earth and functioning as his vice-regents.[170]

Watts is not alone here. Walton, for example, argues that, by reading Genesis in the context of ancient Near Eastern temple building, the temple in the Hebrew Bible is "much more than just the hub of the cosmos that sometimes represents the whole; it is the entire cosmos."[171] Walton agrees with Levenson's conclusion,

> The world which the Temple incarnates in a tangible way is not the world of history but the world of creation, the world not as it is but as it was meant to be and as it was on the first Sabbath.[172]

Walton also argues that kings were usually seen as representing the image of God. Kings were thought to have been imbued with the image of the deities and that was the source of their power and prerogative.[173] Indeed, according to Walton, "The image of God did the work of God on the earth."[174] Likewise, Beale says that Adam, being in God's image, was to serve as a priest-king in the Edenic sanctuary, and humans were to "reflect God's kingship by being his vice-regents on earth."[175]

This view of Genesis helps us to construct the story of creation. The good creation is God's cosmic temple in which the first humans dwelt. The role of Adamic humanity as God's image-bearers was to act as his vice-regents on earth, because humans were to be the Creator's representatives in his cosmic temple. By implication, creation was to sustain life and provide a safe place for humanity to flourish. If both humans and creation fulfilled their roles according to God's design, then the cosmos would be a place that displayed the glory of the Creator. But in Gen 3 the story takes a turn for the worse, for God's representatives on earth disobeyed him when the serpent tempted them. Since humans and the rest of the cosmos are bound up together, the serpent's scheme successfully brought curses on humans and the earth alike.[176] Since God's image-bearers failed to represent their Creator as

---

170. Watts, "New Creational Restoration," 21.

171. Walton, Genesis 1, 192. Cf. Walton, Lost World, 75–86.

172. Levenson, "Temple and the World," 297.

173. Walton, Ancient Near, 212.

174. Ibid., 212.

175. Beale, Temple, 81. And Pahl, Beginning, 36, says that the cosmos "is God's good creation, the temple-like sacred space for God's presence."

176. As Watts, "New Creational Restoration," 22, says, "Creation too is bound up in this and suffers as a consequence of human rebellion (Gen 3.17–18). The temple-palace and the bearer of the image fall together into ruin."

vice-regents, creation is no longer able to fulfill its role in sustaining life and providing a safe place for humans to dwell. At the same time there is enmity between humanity and the evil forces (metaphorically represented by the offspring of the serpent). The cosmos is no longer what it used to be.

In Chapter 3 we constructed the narrative structure of Adamic humanity in Romans. It bears resemblances to Adam's story in Genesis. We also briefly sketched the story of God's new humanity. Now we can provide more details of this story using the findings from our analysis of Rom 5–8. The story begins with the formation of a new humanity through the death and life of Christ (5:12–21). Believers, as members of this humanity, are to participate in Christ, the Son of God. They have been crucified with Christ and raised with him (6:1–11). Their story continues with the Spirit's leading, through which they have become children of God and co-heirs with Christ (8:14–17). They are called to identify with Christ in his suffering, with the purpose (and result) of being glorified with him (8:17). Their identification with Christ consists of a process of transformation, in which their present sufferings are visible signs of their image-bearing. In other words, they are living out the story when they patiently endure their trials and pain. As they do so, they display God's glory, with the sure hope of the eschatological redemption of their bodies. At the resurrection, they will be vindicated and their glorification will be fully realized. At the same time creation will be renewed and set free from futility and decay. Finally God's children will, together with Christ, inherit the cosmos. All along the story of the restored humanity has been anticipating this climactic act of divine drama, and the audience is invited to realize that their lives are an integral part in the unfolding of this story.[177]

It is true that there are details in the story of believers in Rom 5–8 that do not have exact counterparts in the story of Adam in Gen 1–3. For example, God's rest on the seventh day and the one-flesh-ness between a man and a woman have no parallels in Romans (Gen 2:2–3, 23–24). But the two stories have essentially the same actors (i.e., humanity, creation, and anti-God powers), and the basic narrative structure of the letter matches that of Genesis—though the storylines unfold in reverse order of each other. While Adam's failed image-bearing opened the door for persistent evil in

---

177. Adams, "Paul's Story of God," 26–34, sketches a somewhat similar storyline regarding God and his creation, with believers participating in the story. Adams' primary interest, however, is whether such a narrative can be constructed from Romans, rather than whether/how the Genesis accounts can help Paul's audience to understand the purpose of their suffering. Also, Horrell, *Greening Paul*, 71–85, present a narrative approach to Rom 8:19–23. Their concern, however, is primarily about the story of creation rather than the story of a new humanity.

the cosmos and a curse on the earth, believers' image-bearing in conformity to Christ exhibits God's triumph over evil and will eventually lead to the renewal of the whole creation. While Adam's disobedience led to the suffering of humanity and the groaning of creation, the present groaning of believers in their faithful participation in Christ will lead to their resurrection and the liberation of creation from bondage to decay. The tragic storyline of Gen 1–3 is matched with the hopeful storyline of Rom 5–8. The downward spiral of the fate of humans and the rest of creation in Genesis is matched with the eager expectation of the glory of a new humanity and renewal of creation. The absurdity and futility of creation and the associated pain and suffering of humans are matched by the *purposeful suffering* of believers as they share in Christ's suffering.[178] What is noteworthy here is, of course, the fact that suffering is a key connection between these stories.

Significance of the Evocation

The thematic and verbal links between Genesis and Romans, as well as their shared narrative structures, indicate strongly the evocation of Genesis in the letter. The Genesis backdrop is invaluable in that it enriches the audience's understanding of God's purpose in allowing them to suffer. First, the predetermined purpose of God and his call of believers in 8:28–30 can be traced back to primordial history when Adam succumbed to the serpent's snare. While Gen 1–3 itself does not explain how God was going to rescue Adamic humanity, reading Romans with Genesis in mind provides a view of God's predetermined purpose in calling believers to participate in his program of cosmic renewal.

Second, Genesis helps the audience to better understand their vocation. Our analysis of Rom 8:18–30 has shown that there is interdependency between the liberation of creation and the believers' faithful response to the call to suffer with Christ. The former cannot take place without the latter. Following the Genesis account it makes it clearer that this is indeed the case. Creation suffers because of the inability of Adamic humanity to bear God's

---

178. Wright, *Paul*, 475–94, especially 487–89, discusses a somewhat similar story ("The Outer Story: God and Creation"), although my approach here is very different from Wright's. In Wright's own words, "If the creator has made a good world, and if this power we call death, and the corruption and decay that lead to it and from it, are threatening to thwart the creator's plans, only a victory over corruption and death itself will restore things as they should be. *Only so, on other words, will the narrative grammar of the largest 'story' of all come out right*" (489; emphasis original). In my view, what is lacking in Wright's discussion is a stronger recognition of the place of the believer's vocation to suffer with Christ.

image and glorify him in the way they should. But God's restored humanity is being conformed to the image of his Son by sharing in his suffering. Empowered by the Spirit, believers can truly bear God's image and act as his vice-regents. In doing so they display God's glory; and hence creation once again fulfills its role in sustaining life and facilitating the flourishing of humankind.

Third, just as Adam reigned with God as vice-regent, so do the children of God, who are to reign as co-heirs with Christ. The story of Genesis portrays Adam as God's son, who is his representative image on earth. Likewise, as God's Spirit-led children, believers are God's representatives in the world, and function as members of his royal family (as in Rom 8:29) to reign over the cosmos. Despite the present trials and suffering, they are God's children, and possess all the privileges of being his heirs. Genesis affirms their identity in that they are the rightful heirs of God's cosmic temple.[179]

Fourth, the Genesis story provides a narrative reading of Rom 5–8 through which the audience discovers their place in the divine drama. The text of the letter directs the audience to locate themselves within the narrative trajectory of the story. From the outset, their story is about participating in Christ's crucifixion and life (5:12–21; 6:1–11). The story continues to include sharing in Christ's suffering and in the process being transformed so that their lives can, at least in some measure, display God's glory. The story will reach a climax at the final renewal of creation. The good creation in Genesis provides a picture of what it would be like at the climax of this story. The cosmic temple-palace in Genesis is a source of hope for the audience as it provides a clear picture of a place of delight and safety, in which the audience reigns with Christ. It is a world without chaos, for it is God's cosmic temple. It is an orderly cosmos. It is the place where their story will be consummated—and continue on as they and creation fulfill their roles in the cosmos.

In a profound sense, all of the above aspects share an underlying paradox, which presents tensions that the Genesis narrative does not resolve. The paradox is that glory is preceded by suffering; and the righteous have to suffer. It is God's predetermined purpose that the new people of God endure suffering at the present time, rather than avoid or escape from it. The

179. Here I might mention the findings of Kirk with respect to the relationship between sonship, image-bearing, and the rule of believers over creation. It seems that Kirk and I have independently arrived at similar conclusions. While his investigation focuses on the resurrection, my analysis primarily concerns suffering. Kirk, *Unlocking*, 149, says, "The interconnections between sonship, image-bearing, rule, and the ruled creation going the way of its ruler, help tie together various threads in Romans 8. There, where the restoration of glory in the resurrection is couched in terms of conformity to the image of Christ, the whole creation finds itself included in the work of redemption."

renewal of creation and the final resurrection of believers are contingent on their suffering. But if they are truly God's children, and God's representatives on earth, why should they suffer? If by the Spirit's leading they live a righteous life, if they are no longer under condemnation, and if the Spirit has already brought about their υἱοθεσία, why should they suffer in order to set creation free from its bondage? Unlike Adam, believers are in fact innocent sufferers. Genesis does not resolve the tension but rather heightens it, because in Genesis the curses operate on the principle of retributive justice. In contrast, believers suffer as righteous sufferers. It seems that the only explanation for the paradox is that the reversal of the effects of Adam's disobedience is centered upon the Christ-story. Just as Christ suffered and died for humanity in order to defeat the powers of sin and death and be vindicated at his resurrection, so his followers suffer so as to be glorified with him. Their call to participate in Christ is the reason for the paradox, for the Christ-story itself bears that paradoxical nature. The consequence of this is the eschatological tension of the already-not-yet life of believers, where suffering is inevitable as they live in the overlap of the ages.

AN ALTERNATIVE NARRATIVE TO ROME'S GOLDEN AGE

In Chapter 3 we said that the daily reality of suffering in the lives of the audience was incompatible with Rome's propaganda of peace and security, and that Rom 5:1–21 provided the audience with an alternative narrative of peace to that of the *pax Romana*. Likewise, 8:18–30 provides an alternative story to the rhetoric of the Golden Age in Rome.

Virgil speaks of the birth of a messianic figure in his *Fourth Eclogue*, through which a glorious age will come about. In this Golden Age, not only will there be justice; the reign of Saturn (a major Roman god of agriculture and harvest) will also return. The land will produce its bounty, and the cattle will no longer fear the lions. In Virgil's *Aeneid*, an explicit link is made between Augustus and the return of the Golden Age that was once ruled by Saturn (*Aen.* 6.789–794).[180] The *Ara Pacis Augustae* was commissioned on the fourth of July 13 BCE on the return of Augustus from his

180. Virgil says, "And this in truth is he whom you so often hear promised you, Augustus Caesar, son of a god, who will again establish a golden age in Latium amid fields once ruled by Saturn; he will advance his empire beyond the Garamants and Indians to a land which lies beyond our stars, beyond the path of year and sun, where sky-bearing Atlas wheels on his shoulders the blazing star-studded sphere . . . " (*Aen.* 6.789–794) Cf. Jewett, "Corruption," 27. For further discussion on Virgil's works on Rome's imperialist cosmology, see Punt, "Negotiating Creation," 2–3.

military campaigns. The East Wall is what is commonly called the Tellus Panel, and is well-preserved today. Tellus (or Tellus Mater) is the Roman goddess of Mother Earth. Tellus is quite possibly the central figure on the Panel, although one cannot be certain.[181] At any rate, the altar and the Tellus Panel symbolize peace, prosperity, and fertility, which in turn represent the blessings of the deities on the Augustan reign.[182] A similar theme remains alive in poetry and the civic cult during the reign of Nero. Commenting on Calpurnius Siculus' *Eclogue* (1:33–99), Jewett says,

> Nero's reign brings peace that is blessed by the gods. His magical "victory" allegedly restores nature to its original state in the primeval Age of Saturn . . . when the earth brought forth its harvest without the use of the plow.[183]

It is unlikely that the readers of Romans shared the peace and prosperity of this so-called Golden Age. Given the highly hierarchical nature of Roman society, it is most likely that the minority elites who benefited substantially from the prosperity—a prosperity brought about by the military successes of successive emperors and their brutal rule. For the majority of the audience, the notion of a Golden Age would not have made much sense—at least existentially—given the socioeconomic hardship and religio-political oppression they faced.

Romans, however, provided a counter-cultural narrative for the audience in Rome.[184] Instead of a Golden Age brought about by Caesar the "son of the deified," whose victory had returned the primeval state of nature, the Creator God sent his Son to defeat evil in the cosmos. More than that, the audience had joined his royal family of God's children. Despite the suffering they experienced at the moment, they exhibited God's glory and would eventually reign with him and bring about the ultimate cosmic renewal. Through this, they engaged in a process of transformation in which the tragic primordial story of Genesis was reversed, setting in motion a new

---

181. The exact identity of this central figure is subject to debate. Tellus, Italia, Venus, and Pax have all been suggested. See Zanker, *Power of Images*, 175. But according to Jewett, "Corruption," 29, "The feminine figure of Tellus (Mater) combines features of Venus, Ceres, and Cybele, whose depiction and surroundings imply a supernatural world in which plants are larger than life and animals live in peace with one another."

182. See also Jackson, *New Creation*, 66–67, regarding the imperial ideology symbolized by the *Ara Pacis*.

183. Jewett, "Corruption," 31. See also Jackson, *New Creation*, 74–75.

184. See also the brief discussions of Elliott, "Creation," 153–54; Jackson, *New Creation*, 168–9..

beginning for a renewed cosmos. This alternative narrative offered the audience an invigorating hope in times of need.[185]

CONCLUSION

In his study on Paul's cosmological language, Edward Adams says that Paul's purpose in Rom 8:18–30 is "to legitimate the sufferings of his readers."[186] He goes on to say that suffering is an integral and necessary stage in the cosmic process that will culminate in the freedom of God's children.[187] I have arrived at a somewhat similar conclusion, except that my inquiry is not so much about Paul's cosmology, but rather the audience's reception of his letter given their suffering and affliction in Rome. I have argued that suffering is an integral and essential part of God's purpose of transforming his cosmos. God's plan of restoration includes renewing the whole creation, and believers' faithfulness in their participation in Christ is an indispensable part of this project. To conclude our analysis we will summarize our key findings and propose some theological conclusions from our study.

Romans 8:18–30 wraps up the theme of hope of glory in affliction which commenced in 5:1–11, where the letter presented to the audience its first reference to suffering and exhorted them to persevere in their hardship. Now in 8:18 the audience hears a thesis statement from Paul, which states that the present sufferings do not thwart the glory to be revealed. We have found that suffering has value, even though it is not pleasant. Just as the suffering and atoning death of Christ have immense value, so does the suffering of believers because they suffer *with* Christ. For the audience, their affliction is the pathway to their glorification. Since their destiny is interlocked with that of creation, their suffering is worthwhile because it is the avenue through which creation will be freed from its bondage to decay. Famine, earthquakes, and plagues will no longer be a threat to the wellbeing of humans. No wonder the pericope 8:18–30 reaches its mid-point climax in v. 23, which speaks of believers' resurrection and the anticipated full realization of their υἱοθεσία. The body, the final stronghold of sin and death, will be redeemed, and the believers' glory will be unveiled, which will in

---

185. Punt, "Negotiating Creation," 7, provides an insightful postcolonial reading of Rom 8:18–30. Punt seems to think that the text should not be viewed as simply a challenge or opposition to the Roman Empire. Rather, the "contrast between imperial discourse and Pauline thinking should not overrun the ambiguity typical of uneven power situations."

186. Adams, *Constructing*, 183.

187. Ibid., 183. Adams refers to Gager, "Functional Diversity," 330, here.

turn lead to the renewal of the whole creation. Because suffering is essential for the renewal of creation, resources are made available for believers to face their trials. In the face of the socioeconomic hardship and religio-political injustice, the audience is encouraged to put their hope in God, even though there are no visible signs of this glory at the present time. The Spirit is also there to intercede for them according to God's will.

The concluding statements in 8:28–30 affirm that God turns suffering into good. God's plan was predetermined, and because of that Paul declares that believers have been saved and justified. The audience has been called so that God's purpose of renewing the creation may be fulfilled. Part of their call is that they will partake in a process of transformation in which they display God's glory in their daily suffering, in expectation of their final glorification.

Central to this is the notion of participating in Christ, which is encapsulated in v. 29. Believers are being conformed to the image of the Son, who is the firstborn of the royal family of God. Here the story of Christ, the story of God's new humanity, and the Genesis narrative intersect. Adam was created to bear God's image and reign with him as his son. But Adamic humanity failed to fulfill the role of being God's vice-regents over the cosmos. Consequently the cosmos is in chaos, and suffering is inevitable due to the dominion of the anti-God powers of sin and death. But the death and resurrection of God's Son have brought reconciliation (Rom 5:9). Through the Son's suffering and atoning death, God has triumphed over sin and death. By the Spirit's empowerment, the new humanity walks in his ways and is being conformed to the image of the Son. Once again humans display his glory, and (paradoxically) this takes place as they share in Christ's suffering.

In our discussion we have encountered the notion of the suffering righteous. Rom 8:18–23 bears a resemblance to the eschatological language found in Daniel, where God's people are called to be faithful in their suffering, believing that God will eventually vindicate and deliver them from their adversaries. We have also discovered that creation was subjected to futility through no fault of its own, which is similar to the experience of an innocent sufferer. This subjection inevitably causes pain to humans, for their existence is interlocked with that of creation. But believers are not under condemnation (8:1) and are empowered by the Spirit to walk in God's ways (8:3–8). They have been saved and justified. Yet they suffer. The notion of the suffering righteous will be vital to our study of 8:31–39, which will affirm that no one can bring any charge against God's children. The assurance is that nothing can separate them from the love of God. These themes will be key topics in the next chapter.

7

Participating in the Triumph of God

INTRODUCTION

Romans 8:31–39 is a majestic pericope that celebrates the fact that in the midst of suffering believers "triumph with surpassing victory" (ὑπερνικάω) through the God who loves them (8:37). As Jewett suggests, this pericope addresses the audience's deepest concern of shame—of being (relatively or absolutely) powerless sufferers who live with socioeconomic injustice—by affirming that they are loved and valued.[1] The affliction-list in 8:35 and the clear reference to suffering in the scriptural citation of 8:36 make this pericope highly significant for the audience. The sufferings enumerated and described in these verses would strike a chord with an audience familiar with sorrow and pain.

Romans 8:31–39 is, as it will be argued, the second half of the climactic conclusion to 8:1–39 as well as to 5:1—8:39. On the one hand, it continues to discuss the themes of the believers' vocation to suffer and their glorification with Christ. On the other hand, it wraps up the themes of God's love and affliction that commenced in 5:1–11—the two themes that 8:18–30 either does not cover or has not finished discussing. The current pericope also harks back to 5:12–21, in its use of the language of condemnation (5:16, 18; 8:34). Indeed, 8:31–39 concludes the letter's discussion in Rom 5–8 regarding God's purpose of transforming the cosmos.

---

1. Jewett, *Romans*, 536.

More specifically, we will discover that 8:31–34 affirms the fact that the believers' suffering is not the result of God's punishment in accordance with the principle of retributive justice. The climax of the pericope's argument is found in 8:35–37, where the audience would identify with the items in the affliction-list and be encouraged to hear that nothing can separate them from the love of Christ. Indeed, they triumph gloriously in their sufferings. This victory in Christ, as we will find, provides the audience with an understanding of suffering that is wide in scope and rich in purpose because it consists of the believers' participation in God's triumph over evil. The pericope finishes with an emphatic assertion that no cosmic forces—which are the ultimate causes of suffering—can separate believers from the love of God. The citation of Ps 44:22 in Rom 8:36 highlights the fact that believers suffer as righteous sufferers, for they are as innocent sheep being led to slaughter. We will discover that there is profound meaning and purpose in suffering as righteous sufferers. Apart from this scriptural citation, I will propose that there is significant evidence suggesting that the Third and Fourth Isaianic Servant Songs are evoked in Rom 8:31–39. These texts provide the audience with additional resources for understanding their shared identity with Christ and God's purpose in suffering.

Our findings will show that the function of the pericope goes beyond assuring the audience of God's abiding love in affliction. I will suggest that the pericope shows that in their suffering believers find themselves identifying with *the* righteous sufferer, namely, Christ himself, whom God did not spare but handed him over to death, so that death might be defeated (8:32). It is in identifying with Christ's innocent suffering that the children of God partake in God's triumph over evil.

AN APT AND CLIMACTIC CONCLUSION

Romans 8:31–39 is the second half of the climactic conclusion to both 8:1–39 and 5:1—8:39.[2] The fact that 8:31–39 concludes Rom 8 can be shown by the various thematic connections. Both 8:1–13 and 8:31–34 speak of believers' right standing with God and/or their righteous life pattern. We have already found in Chapter 4 that this is the case with 8:1–13. In our current pericope the terms κατακρίνω, ἐγκαλέω, and δικαιόω point to believers' right standing with God. Indeed, the κατακρίνω in 8:34 echoes the κατάκριμα/κατακρίνω in 8:1, 3, linking the pericope to the start of the argument in Rom 8. The discussion of suffering in 8:35–39 harks back to the vocation of believers

---

2. As mentioned in Chapter Six, Rom 8:18–30 is the first half. See also Jewett, *Romans*, 535; Harvey, *Listening*, 125–26.

to suffer with Christ in 8:17, and is a continuation of the exposition on the purpose of suffering in 8:18–30.

The many links to 5:1–21 point to the fact that 8:31–39 concludes the argument of Rom 5–8. We have already shown that 8:18–30 concludes the themes of hope, glory, and (partially) affliction in 5:1–11. Now 8:31–39 continues to explain why believers can boast in their afflictions (5:3). It emphatically speaks of God's abiding love in times of trouble and pain (8:35–39), which 5:5 briefly touched on, but without elaboration. The Son is mentioned in both 5:10 and 8:32, which constitute two of only four references to God's Son in 5:1—8:39. In 5:10 the death of the Son refers to his work of reconciliation, and 8:32 speaks of God's not sparing his Son in order to accomplish his restorative program for humanity. The κατακρίνω in 8:34 echoes the κατάκριμα in 5:16, 18. The death and resurrection of Christ are mentioned in 8:34 and throughout 5:12–21. Sin and death are cosmic powers that entered the cosmos, according to 5:12, 13, and 8:38–39 says that no cosmic forces can separate believers from Christ's love. These suggest that the current pericope harks back to 5:12–21. No one can condemn God's people, because Christ has defeated the powers of sin and death. Finally, the confessional phrase διὰ τοῦ κυρίου ἡμῶν Ἰησοῦ Χριστοῦ (with minor variations) can be found in 5:1, 11, 21; 6:23; 7:25, and 8:39, but nowhere else in Romans. This rhetorical marker is a further indication that 8:31–39 functions as a conclusion to Rom 8 as well as 5–8. In short, the pericope brings to an end the argument of 5:1—8:39, which is about God's restorative plan for humanity and the cosmos.[3] For an audience living with affliction and adversity, the pericope brings together the materials concerning suffering and God's abiding love, and places them in the context of their call to identify with Christ's suffering.

There are three subunits in 8:31–39, namely, 8:31–34, 8:35–37, and 8:38–39. The rhetorical questions in 8:31–34 assure the audience that God is on their side; and that despite hardship they enjoy a right standing with God. The subunit 8:35–37, as I will argue, plays a pivotal role in the pericope. It asserts that nothing—not even the sufferings in the affliction-list—can separate believers from God's love. Paul then cites an authoritative text from Israel's Scripture to state that believers are suffering like sheep to be slaughtered for the sake of Christ. It is in light of this claim that the letter declares that believers triumph with surpassing victory in their suffering. The

---

3. As mentioned in Chapter 3, Rom 5–8 is a distinct section in Romans, but it is not disconnected from the rest of the letter. While I do not think that 8:31–39 is primarily designed to prepare for the argument in Rom 9–11, the pericope probably has a rhetorical effect in securing the audience's agreement with Paul's argument so far, thus paving the way for the subject matter in the following section. See Kruse, *Romans*, 359.

subunit 8:38–39 rounds up the pericope with the assurance that no cosmic powers can separate believers from Christ's love.

ROMANS 8:31–34

The rhetorical question, τί οὖν ἐροῦμεν, in the opening verse of 8:31–34 provides a smooth transition from the previous pericope to the current one. It does so in a way that alerts the audience to the significance of the forthcoming subject matter in relation to what has already been said.[4] In light of the above discussion regarding the thematic and verbal links between the current pericope and the previous ones, the πρὸς ταῦτα most likely refers to the materials that started in 5:1, especially the argument concerning God's work of overturning the effects of Adam's disobedience and the believers' vocation of sharing in Christ's suffering.[5] Given the proximity to 8:18–30, the πρὸς ταῦτα would also specifically refer to God's purpose for his children to partake in the process of transformation, in which they display his glory. An integral part of this is of course the final renewal of creation, at which God's children will act as his vice-regents in his cosmic temple. So, it is "in view of these things" that the audience is invited to consider "what then shall we say?" In fact, for an audience familiar with affliction and pain, the πρὸς ταῦτα would most likely include τὰ παθήματα τοῦ νῦν καιροῦ in the thesis statement of 8:18. That is, existentially the audience would probably identify the πρὸς ταῦτα with the day-to-day pain and oppression they face in Rome before the final renewal.

In 8:31–34, Paul follows up his initial question, τί οὖν ἐροῦμεν, with a series of rhetorical questions (noting especially the interrogative τίς in 8:31, 33, 34, 35) and statements. Like the chain composition in v. 30, the repeated questions in 8:31–34, 35, carry strong rhetorical power, resembling a rising crescendo that draws maximum attention from the audience. I will argue that this subunit invites the audience to see that their suffering is not the result of God's punishment in terms of his retributive justice. Instead, their suffering is decidedly within the purpose of God. The subunit also speaks of God's triumph in the cosmic conflict against evil, as well as the assured

---

4. The same question τί οὖν ἐροῦμεν appears in Rom 4:1; 6:1; 7:7. In the words of Jewett, *Romans*, 535, the rhetorical question conveys the discourse's "processibility," "leading the hearer from the previous argument to this peroration in a smooth manner without any hint of censure."

5. Against Dunn, *Romans 1–8*, 499, who suggests that 8:31–39 rounds off the whole argument from 1:18. As Jewett, *Romans*, 535, says, such proposition is "too wide ranging." Cf. Kasemann, *Romans*, 246; Moo, *Romans*, 539; Hultgren, *Romans*, 336.

vindication of believers in their suffering. We will now study the subunit in detail.

Verses 31–32

The phrase εἰ ὁ θεὸς ὑπὲρ ἡμῶν, τίς καθ' ἡμῶν in 8:31 expresses a sense of confident trust in God. The ὑπέρ-κατά construction highlights two distinctive aspects of God's solidarity and protection, namely, the fact that God is on the side of believers, and that no-one can be against them.[6] Several commentators helpfully note that 8:31 reflects the claim in a number of Psalms that YHWH is on the side of the suffering righteous and hence they have nothing to fear (e.g., Pss 22:4 LXX; 55:12 LXX; 117:6–7 LXX).[7] This affirmation would encourage the audience. *In view of* their present sufferings in Rome (cf. 8:18), including the socioeconomic hardship and religio-political oppression, they are invited to consider what it means to have God on their side. That is, "If God is for them, who can be against them?" Like the psalmists, they have nothing to fear.

But *who/what* are against God's people? The audience might have thought of the perpetrators of religio-political and social injustices. Also, the cosmic powers of sin and death might have come to mind. Since Paul does not specify who is against them, we can only speculate. But the rhetorical effect of the question gives the audience a sense of confident trust in the Creator God, who has supreme power in the cosmos.

Paul says in v. 32 that God did not spare his own Son but handed him over for all.[8] The verb παραδίδωμι has been used in 4:25 to refer to the hand-

---

6. See Mark 9:40 for a similar ὑπέρ-κατά construction in the Greek.

7. Dunn, *Romans 1–8*, 500; Cranfield, *Romans I-VIII*, 435; Byrne, *Romans*, 279.

8. Commentators such as Dunn, *Romans 1–8*, 501, and Byrne, *Romans*, 275–76, have suggested that the τοῦ ἰδίου υἱοῦ οὐκ ἐφείσατο in Rom 8:32 alludes to the (near) sacrifice of Isaac by Abraham in Gen 22:16. Likewise, Campbell, "Story of Jesus," 113–6, believes that the story of Abraham and Isaac in Gen 22 informs Paul of the story of Jesus and God's love. And Lincicum, "Genesis," 109, says that Paul "describes God's giving of his own son with echoes of Abraham's willingness to sacrifice Isaac." The echo of Gen 22 is possible, but not without problems. The thematic difference between the two passages is significant. Genesis 22 is about *Abraham's* faith/faithfulness to be tested by God. Rom 8:32 is about *God's own* initiative of handing his own Son over. Although Genesis has been the main scriptural resource for Rom 5–8, all the references to Genesis derive from the primordial history of Gen 1–11 (or 1–3; 5, more specifically) and concern the story of humanity. See Jewett, *Romans*, 537, for a detailed discussion. For a discussion of opposing views, see Gaventa, "Interpreting," 128–30; cf. Kasemann, *Romans*, 247–48. I will not examine this (possible) allusion because it is hard to determine whether the audience would find Gen 22 to be a valuable resource for their understanding of suffering. But this can certainly be a useful future research topic.

ing over of Christ to death for humans' trespasses.[9] In light of the mention of Christ's death in 8:34 and the crucial role of his death in the reversal of Adam's trespass in 5:12–21, it is most likely that Christ's death is in view in 8:32, and that it refers to God's sending his Son to die for Adamic humanity so as to rescue them from the dominion of sin and death.[10] Also, 8:32 has one of only four references to the Son in Rom 5–8. In 5:10, it is said that through the Son's death there is reconciliation. In 8:3, God sent his Son to die an atoning death. It is, therefore, also likely that 8:32 alludes to both of these—that is, God's reconciling of humanity through the Son *and* the Son's atoning death.[11] Both are integral parts of God's restorative project.

But how does God defeat the cosmic powers of sin and death through Christ's death? I find Gaventa's proposal useful.[12] Gaventa notes that the παραδίδωμι refers to "the turning over of someone or something to a third party, often in a situation of conflict."[13] In the LXX, the term frequently refers to God's handing over a people or territory (Israel or otherwise) to another power or agent.[14] Interestingly, the term is used in 1 Cor 5:5 to refer to the handing over of a man to Satan for the destruction of the flesh.[15] No matter how this should be interpreted, it suggests that among the earliest Christians there was a notion of cosmic conflict in which Satan played a role and that someone might be "handed over" to the domain of Satan.[16] The cosmic conflict between God/Jesus and Satan/the devil is of course often mentioned in the New Testament (e.g., Eph 4:27; 1 Tim 3:6, 7; Heb 2:14; 1 John 3:8; Rev 12:9, 12), including the testing of Jesus by the devil in the Gospels (Mark 1:12–13; Matt 4:1–11; Luke 4:1–13). Indeed, in Rom 16:20 Paul

---

9. The use of παραδίδωμι in Isa 53 and the possible allusion to Isaiah in Rom 8:32 are recognized by commentators. See, for instance, Moo, *Romans*, 540n19. We will discuss this later.

10. Cf. Dunn, *Romans 1–8*, 500–501.

11. See our discussion on reconciliation and Christ's atoning death in our analysis of Rom 5:1–11 and 8:3 in Chapter 3 and Chapter 4. Our analysis of 8:3 also discusses the relationship between reconciliation and Christ's atoning death.

12. Gaventa, "Interpreting," 130–34.

13. Ibid., 131. Gaventa goes on to say that the term refers "to the act of handing someone or something over into the custody of another or to surrender in a military context . . . in a variety of sources, both biblical and non-biblical" (131–2).

14. Examples are numerous. See Exod 23:32; Lev 26:25; Num 21:3, 34; Deut 2:24, 30; Josh 2:24; 6:2, 16; 2 Kgs 21:14; 2 Chr 6:36.

15. Other Pauline references to Satan include 1 Cor 7:5; 2 Cor 2:11; 11:14, 12:7; 1 Thess 2:18; cf. 2 Thess 2:9; 1 Tim 1:20; 5:15.

16. Most likely in 1 Cor 5:5 Paul is speaking of the ultimate triumph of God for the salvation of the person. See Fee, *First Epistle to the Corinthians*, 213; Ciampa and Rosner, *First Letter to the Corinthians*, 207–9; Collins, *First Corinthians*, 212.

says that God will crush Satan (that is, the "adversary") under the believers' feet.[17] If, as discussed in Chapter 3, God has defeated sin and death by handing over his Son, then it is possible that 8:32 refers to the handing over of Christ to the powers of sin and death, and to the idea that these powers were overcome when Christ was raised from the dead.[18] Thus, Gaventa's proposal below seems plausible.

> [I]t is not sufficient to describe God's handing over only as a loving, sacrificial act, a gracious giving up; it is also an event in the ongoing struggle between God and anti-god powers. God brings to an end the "handing over" of humanity to Sin and Death by means of another handing over, this time of God's Son.[19]

The τὰ πάντα in 8:32 most likely refers to the cosmos that believers will inherit as co-heirs with Christ (8:17, 19–23).[20] This is reinforced by the σὺν αὐτῷ, for it seems to reflect the motif of participation in Christ found in 8:17 (where three συ-compounds are used). That is, believers will participate in the reign of God's Son. In light of these, the rhetorical question would sound like this (to the audience): If God did not spare his own Son but handed him over for them, then will he not also, together *with him*, graciously give them the renewed cosmos (God's cosmic temple) in which they will reign as God's vice-regents?[21] Given the fact that sin and death are the ultimate cosmic forces behind suffering, 8:32 provides the audience with the widest possible scope of assurance. God has defeated evil by handing his Son over to the cosmic powers. The implication is that he will also give his children all things. If they are to rule over creation, what/who can be against them?

---

17. Rom 16:20 most likely reflects the Jewish apocalyptic belief that Satan/the devil is the adversary of God and his people. See Dunn, *Romans 1–8*, 905; Jewett, *Romans*, 994–95; Byrne, *Romans*, 458. For further discussions concerning cosmic conflicts, see Bell, *Deliver us from Evil*, 1–114, 230–86, for a discussion on the devil and demons in the OT, the NT, and in the exorcisms of Jesus, as well as the redemption from Satan through participation in Christ; and Wright, *Origin of Evil Spirits*, 138–90, regarding the Book of Watchers in *1 Enoch* 1–36 and the reception of the Watcher tradition in the Dead Sea Scrolls.

18. The letter, however, does not give us any information regarding what exactly happened when Christ was handed over. The picture of an angry God punishing his Son for the sins of others (found in some popular preaching today) is absent.

19. Gaventa, "Interpreting," 136. (Emphasis original)

20. Dunn, *Romans 1–8*, 502; Jewett, *Romans*, 538; Byrne, *Romans*, 276; cf. Jervis, *At the Heart of the Gospel*, 106; Kruse, *Romans*, 360–61. Against Moo, *Romans*, 541.

21. Thus, Dunn, *Romans 1–8*, 509–10, rightly recognizes the cosmic dimension of the τὰ πάντα in Rom 8:32.

Verse 33

The rhetorical question in 8:33 asks, "Who will bring any charge against God's elect?"[22] As we will see, this question assures the audience that God will vindicate them as they faithfully endure suffering.

The verb ἐγκαλέω is probably a forensic term (see Acts 19:38, 40; 23:28, 29; 26:2, 7).[23] While the future ἐγκαλέσει suggests that it refers to the final judgment at God's tribunal, Jewett alerts us that "[n]owhere else in the OT, the NT, or associated literature is this verb employed in connection with eschatological judgment."[24] It seems better, then, to understand the ἐγκαλέσει to refer to a charge or accusation against someone in a (cosmic) court at any point in time. An associated question is: Who is the accuser? While the rhetorical nature of the question suggests that the identification of the accuser is not vital, Scriptures like Job 1–2 and Zech 3:1–2 suggest that Satan is a likely candidate.[25] Given the cosmological language in 8:38–39,[26] it makes sense to consider the charge in 8:33 an accusation by some kind of evil cosmic figure, who accuses believers in the manner of the Satan in Job and Zechariah, where the righteous are accused.

But, as discussed above, 8:31 has said God is on the side of the suffering righteous. No wonder 8:33 states that it is God who justifies, and hence no accusation can be successfully made against God's people. The adjective ἐκλεκτός recalls the adjective κλητός in 8:28 and the verb καλέω in 8:30, as well as the προγινώσκω and προορίζω in 8:29. As argued before, 8:28–30 is about God's purpose for his children, to be conformed to the Son's image, so that their suffering may be part of the process of transformation that displays his glory. Accordingly, the charge against God's children is invalid precisely because their present sufferings are in fact within his plan for his elect.

---

22. I note that the compact expressions in Rom 8:33–34 allow for different ways to place the punctuations. Here I follow the majority of scholars and put the question marks after the *first* θεοῦ and the κατακρινῶν only. See Dunn, *Romans 1–8*, 496–97; Byrne, *Romans*, 279; Moo, *Romans*, 537; Cranfield, *Romans I-VIII*, 434; Witherington, *Romans*, 222; Kruse, *Romans*, 361n406; against Jewett, *Romans*, 531.

23. The verb appears nowhere else in the NT.

24. Jewett, *Romans*, 539.

25. See Dunn, *Romans 1–8*, 502; Cranfield, *Romans I-VIII*, 438n3. Along with Kruse, *Romans*, 361, I think the view of Parlier, "La folle justice de Dieu," 105–6, that God is both the accuser and justifier is unlikely, given that Rom 8:31–32 clearly says that God is on the side of his people.

26. See Gaventa, "Neither," 273–75, for a detailed discussion on the presence of anti-God cosmic powers found in Rom 8:31–39.

The implication of the above is that the audience's suffering is not the result of God's judgment in accordance with the principle of retributive justice. Instead, believers' sufferings should be considered as an integral part of their vocation to suffer with Christ. Viewing it this way, God's justification can be understood to mean his vindication of righteous sufferers.[27] In other words, since God has defeated evil through his Son's death and resurrection, believers will inherit the cosmos and will be vindicated by God because their suffering is nothing short of a faithful fulfillment of their call to participate in Christ.

Verse 34

Romans 8:34 starts with the rhetorical question: Who is to condemn? The verb κατακρίνω recalls the κατάκριμα in 8:1, and 5:16, 18. As discussed above, this suggests that 8:31–39 harks back to God's intention of restoring humanity explicated in 5:12–21 and elaborated in 8:1–30. According to 5:12–21, through Christ's death and life, God's new humanity is no longer under condemnation. In view of 8:1–13, this is because of Christ's atoning death and the empowerment of the Spirit. No wonder 8:34 points to the death and resurrection of Christ, in response to the rhetorical question.

Paul goes on to say that the exalted Christ is at the right hand of God. This is widely thought to be an echo of Ps 110:1 (109:1 LXX).[28] As mentioned in Chapter 6, kings in the ancient world were considered to be vice-regents of deities. Since Ps 110:1 speaks of the rule of Israel's king, the image of Christ being at God's right hand points to his role as God's vice-regent.[29] This exalted status indicates that God has totally vindicated the Son after his suffering and death, and that God's plan to defeat evil has truly succeeded. We have found in our discussion of 8:29 that *the Son* is the Davidic king who is gathering a royal family. We have also seen in 8:32 that *together with the Son* God will give believers all things, so that they may reign as vice-regents over his creation. Here the imagery in 8:34 would help to assure the audience that indeed they will reign with Christ the king. Just as the Son suffered and is now vindicated and glorified, so do the children of God suffer and will be vindicated.

---

27. The present active participle δικαιῶν in Rom 8:33 indicates the ongoing nature of justification/vindication. Cf. Dunn, *Romans 1–8*, 503.

28. Cf. Fee, *Pauline Christology*, 255; Dunn, *Romans 1–8*, 503–4; Jewett, *Romans*, 542; Kruse, *Romans*, 362; Hultgren, *Romans*, 339; Keesmaat, "Psalms in Romans," 152.

29. See Dunn, *Romans 1–8*, 504. Cf. Jewett, *Romans*, 542.

The intercession of the exalted Christ in 8:34 recalls that of the Spirit in 8:27.[30] As in 8:27, a suffering people need intercession as a resource when they face hardships in imperial Rome. Since the exalted Christ is also the one who suffered and died in the first place, his intercession here may recall that of the "suffering righteous" in Job 42:8–10 and Isa 53:12 (MT only).[31] That is, Christ's prayers are effective, like those of Job and the Isaianic Servant, for they themselves are righteous. So, with the exalted vice-regent of God interceding for believers, and since they will reign with this messianic king, who is to condemn them?

In sum, 8:31–34 implies that believers' suffering is not the result of God's punishment, given the fact that the rhetorical questions are ineffective in accusing or condemning believers. Instead, their suffering is decidedly within the purpose of God, for they are fulfilling their vocation to identify with Christ. The subunit is distinctively christological. Through Christ, God has triumphed in the cosmic conflict against anti-God powers, which will result in the vindication of believers and their eventual reign as his vice-regents. Thus, through a series of rhetorical questions, 8:31–34 urges the audience to realize the implication of the Son's work for their present situation. Despite the trials and adversities they face, they can be rest assured of God's purpose in their suffering. Heil puts it well,

> Paul eloquently elevates his readers to the pinnacle of complete
> certainty and absolute assurance regarding their hope for future
> triumph over present distress.[32]

ROMANS 8:35–37

For an audience familiar with suffering, 8:35–37 is a very important passage. The rhetorical questions in v. 35, together with those in 8:31–34, produce a cumulative rhetorical effect to persuade the audience that even suffering cannot separate them from Christ's love. The affliction-list, posing as a series of rhetorical questions, heightens emotion through the enumeration of tribulations and trials that the audience would be familiar with. The citation of a Scripture in 8:36, as will be argued, functions as an authoritative voice stating that suffering is not only something commonly shared by the followers of Christ, but also an experience with a special purpose. The passage finishes with an exuberant note that turns suffering on its head. Even though

---

30. The verb ἐντυγχάνω is used in both 8:27 and 34.

31. See Dunn, *Romans 1–8*, 504.

32. Heil, *Romans*, 94.

suffering is in itself not pleasant, it is the pathway to the surpassing triumph of believers. The whole subunit presupposes the christocentric character of 8:31–34, and is wrapped in the belief that nothing can separate believers from the *love of Christ* (8:35), which is a theme that started in 5:5 and finds its climax in 8:35–39.

Verse 35

The first rhetorical question in 8:35 asks, "Who will separate us from the love of Christ?" The χωρίζω here is set in contrast to the σύν in 8:32. The rhetorical question in v. 32 implies that God's children will inherit God's creation *with Christ*.[33] Here in 8:35 the question will lead to the affirmation in v. 37 (and later in 8:38–39) that nothing will *separate* them from the love *of Christ*. Given the prominent theme of participation in Christ that is signified by the four συ-compounds in 8:17, 29, the χωρίζω in 8:35 (and 8:39) is an apt language that speaks of the outworking of a life shaped by a shared identity with Christ. The vocation of sharing in Christ's suffering leads to God's abiding love. The terms ἀγάπη and ἀγαπάω occur six times in Rom 5–8, and *only* in 5:1–11 and 8:31–39 (5:5, 8; 8:28, 35, 37, 39),[34] which suggests that 8:35–37 and 38–39 round up the theme of love that started in the beginning of the section. For an audience living in a hierarchical society like Rome, being loved by a deity would go beyond an emotional feeling (though in itself it is an important aspect of love). Being loved by God would include a strong element of being valued and honored, which was something rarely experienced by those at the lower levels of the social pyramid. The rhetorical question, then, is an important one, since it implies that everyone, regardless of their status, can experience God's love.

The affliction-list poses itself as a set of rhetorical questions, and it will surely capture the attention of its hearers.[35] The list is not meant to be exhaustive,[36] given the discrepancies between this and similar lists in Paul as well as extra-biblical materials.[37] A broad range of afflictions is covered

33. A similar observation is briefly made by Dunn, *Romans 1–8*, 504.

34. And they do not appear in Rom 1–4.

35. Hultgren, *Romans*, 339, notes the rhetorical power of the list.

36. It does not mean that the items in the list appear to the audience as random or arbitrary.

37. For studies of hardship-catalogues in Greco-Roman and Jewish literatures, see Hodgson, "Tribulation Lists," 59–80; Fitzgerald, *Cracks*, 47–116. Other affliction-lists in Paul can be found in 1 Cor 4:8–13; 2 Cor 1:3–11; 4:7–12; 6:3–10; 11:23–33; 12:10; Phil 3:12. See Jewett, *Romans*, 543–46, for a very thorough survey of the affliction-list here in Paul (and extra-biblical sources). Cf. Gorman, *Cruciformity*, 286–87; Dunn, *Romans*

in the list, with physical deprivation (λιμός, γυμνότης), political punishment (διωγμός, μάχαιρα), and the more generalized sufferings (θλῖψις, στενοχωρία, κίνδυνος) included.[38] All the items in the list, except μάχαιρα, can be found in other letters in the undisputed Pauline corpus, indicating that Paul would have had firsthand experience with various items and that he expects his audience to experience (or potentially experience) at least some of them. However, since our interest is how the audience would have understood suffering, our discussion will proceed primarily from the perspective of the audience (and what they may perceive as experiences that they share with the apostle), rather than Paul's own experience in particular.

The terms θλῖψις, στενοχωρία, and κίνδυνος seem to refer to suffering in a generic manner. The first two appear to be general terms for affliction or suffering.[39] The audience would easily identify with these terms, given their socioeconomic hardships. They might also be aware that Paul shared similar trials in his apostolic ministry. The κίνδυνος refers to threatening circum-stances and can be translated as "danger" or "peril."[40] Former war-captives would have experienced perilous situations, as their lives were threatened by Roman soldiers on the way to Rome. Jewish believers who were expelled from Rome following the Edict of Claudia would understand all three terms, for their relocation was to avoid danger and in itself a hardship.

The terms λιμός and γυμνότης refer to hunger and nakedness (or lack of clothing) respectively.[41] The λιμός may be caused by a general famine that affects everyone in a geographical area, or the lack of food due to economic depravity, especially in an urban setting like Rome. The γυμνότης may also denote poverty, since one visible sign of poverty is a lack of clothing.[42] The audience might have heard from other sources that Paul had these expe-

---

1–8, 504–5. Jewett's listing of other sevenfold Jewish and Greco-Roman catalogues is helpful. It seems that Paul and his audience might have been familiar with the use of sevenfold affliction-lists, which, in turn, reinforces the rhetorical force of Rom 8:36.

38. I roughly follow the categorization by Gorman, *Cruciformity*, 286–87, here. The fact that there are seven items may point to the Hebraic symbol of divine completeness, especially given the allusion to the creation story throughout Rom 5–8, where God rested on the seventh day after creating the world. If the Hebraic symbolism is in view, then one may say that even the sufferings in the affliction-list are divinely ordained.

39. BDAG, 362, 766. Some consider στενοχωρία as "extreme affliction" or "dire ca-lamity." (See Thayer, *Lexicon*, 587). Bertram, "στένος, στενοχωρία, στενοχωρέω," 7:607, says that θλῖψις and στενοχωρία are hard to differentiate in Paul.

40. BDAG, 432.

41. The term λιμός can denote famine or hunger, and has been used to denote the famine under Claudius (see BDAG, 475; cf. Acts 11:28).

42. LNSM, 49.23. It (γυμνότης) can also denote "destitution, lack of sufficient cloth-ing" (BDAG, 168).

riences (e.g. 1 Cor 4:11). As discussed in Chapter 2, the audience would have experienced these types of suffering due to their general social and economic conditions. Jewish believers returning to Rome after Claudius' expulsion might have become poor, because the cost of forced relocation would have been high. Slaves would know what poverty and hunger were like, either before or during their slavery.[43]

The term διωγμός most likely refers to socio-political or religious persecution, or even systemic harassment against a social/racial group in an organized manner.[44] The word μάχαιρα refers to a relatively short sword (or dagger) for cutting or stabbing.[45] It is often used to refer to an execution by the authority in a religio-political context (Acts 12:2; Heb 11:34, 37; Rev 13:10).[46] Former war-captives and those enslaved as a result of wars would know what persecution meant—and indeed the threat of the Roman sword,[47] as well as the injustice associated with it. Jewish believers affected by Claudius's Edict would have had firsthand experience of such persecution and injustice.[48] The imperial cult would also be a potential threat for the audience, knowing that at some stage their allegiance to Christ might be a cause for religious persecution in the future.[49]

Hence, the audience would most probably find themselves identifying with at least some of the items in the affliction-list in Rom 8:35, or else they would have known people in the Christ-community facing those trials. Rhetorically, the consecutive mention of the terms would heighten the emotional impact on the audience, for sufferings are all too familiar to them and/or their loved ones.

We should note that the pair θλῖψις and στενοχωρία appear at the leading, and hence, prominent, position in the list. The pair appears in Deut 28:53, 55, 57; Isa 8:22; 30:6, and in fact can be found in Rom 2:9. In 2:9 Paul says that there will be θλῖψις and στενοχωρία for those who do evil, which is clearly an elaboration of the citation of Ps 62:12/Prov 24:12 in Rom 2:6—which, in turn, says that God will repay everyone according to their

43. It was in the interest of the master to feed their slaves. But not all masters had economic resources in abundance, and not all them were always kind to their slaves.

44. LNSM, 39.45. Cf. BDAG, 201.

45. LNSM, 6.33.

46. BDAG, 496. Note that μάχαιρα appears again in Rom 13:4, where it most likely denotes the sword used by Roman authorities.

47. Cf. Pobee, *Persecution*, 5.

48. Cf. Keesmaat, "Psalms in Romans and Galatians," 150.

49. No matter how one understands Rom 13:1–7, v. 4 implies that the Roman sword (μάχαιρα) would be a reason for people to fear (φοβέω) if they had done wrong against the authority.

deeds. In Deut 28:53, 55, 57, θλῖψις and στενοχωρία are the result of the curses on Israel for unfaithfulness. Thus, one common usage of these terms refers to the punishment by God according to his retributive justice. The logic of the argument in Rom 8:35, however, is that θλῖψις and στενοχωρία cannot separate believers from Christ's love, which defies the convention of retributive justice. Likewise, the λιμός and μάχαιρα occur frequently in Jeremiah and Ezekiel, the majority of which concern the exile of Israel and God's punishment for disobedience.[50] The γυμνότης is found in Deut 28:48, again in the context of Israel's unfaithfulness. Like θλῖψις and στενοχωρία, the term can denote God's punishment. But Rom 8 denies such an idea and proposes that the suffering of the audience is undeserved, as the following verse demonstrates.[51]

Verse 36

Scholars have suggested various reasons for the citation of Ps 44:22 (43:23 LXX) in Rom 8:36.[52] For example, Cranfield says that its function is to "show that the tribulations which face Christians are nothing new or unexpected, but have all along been characteristic of the life of God's people."[53] Byrne says that it "gives an accurate account of Christian existence at the present time."[54] Jewett thinks that the citation is to convey the fact that believers' sufferings are for Christ's sake.[55] Moo says that 8:36 is "something of an interruption in the flow of thought" and that suggests that Paul is "concerned to show that the sufferings experienced by Christians should occasion no surprise."[56] All of these are valid, but do not, I believe, capture the significance of the

---

50. These two terms occur over fifty-eight times in Jeremiah and over forty-eight times in Ezekiel.

51. Deriving primarily from his study of the hardship-catalogues in 1 and 2 Corinthians, Fitzgerald, *Cracks*, 207, says that Paul is familiar with the traditions of the sage, and his use of these traditions and hardship-catalogues is "informed by OT traditions about the afflicted righteous man and suffering prophet, and it is transformed by his fixation on the cross of Christ." We will find that aspects of Fitzgerald's statement are similar to our findings in the forthcoming analysis. See also Kleinknecht, *Der leidende Gerechtfertigte*, 346, 355, who thinks that the affliction-list in Rom 8:35 is in line with the Jewish tradition of the suffering just.

52. The scriptural citation is signified by the γέγραπται. The fact that the cited text is from Ps 43:23 LXX is rarely disputed.

53. Cranfield, *Romans I-VIII*, 440. Cf. Moo, *Romans*, 543–44.

54. Byrne, *Romans*, 277.

55. Jewett, *Romans*, 548.

56. Moo, *Romans*, 543–44.

citation in its entirety. In my view, the citation has at least two important rhetorical functions.

First, the citation is strategically located at the end of a series of rhetorical questions in 8:31–35 and just before the triumphant claim in v. 37.[57] This suggests that it serves to answer these questions and sets the stage for what follows. More specifically, the citation responds to the questions in 8:35 and affirms that no suffering can separate believers from Christ's love. It also shows that their suffering is that of the suffering righteous (see below); hence they can truly be victorious in their suffering (hence the claim in v. 37). Second, the citation provides an authoritative scriptural proof that believers' suffering is for the sake of Christ and hence they are fulfilling God's purpose. In our analysis below we will discuss the role of the Scripture in 8:31–39 in detail, including the citation of Ps 44:22. Suffice it to say now that the citation is no random proof-text, and that it provides a substantial extra resource for the audience to understand the purpose of their suffering.[58] In addition, the image of a lamb being led to slaughter may allude to the Servant in Isa 53:7.

Some observations on the text of Rom 8:36 itself need to be made for the present discussion. The emphatic position of the ἕνεκεν σοῦ highlights the fact that believers suffer for Christ's sake.[59] This would likely provide a sense of purpose for the suffering that believers endure. The ὅλην τὴν ἡμέραν

57. See Stewart, "Cry of Victory," 40–44, for a comprehensive discussion of the "rhetoric of participation" in Rom 8:31–39, especially in relation to the citation in 8:36. Aspects of what Stewart covers are mentioned in my exegesis, although my study is independent of Stewart's work.

58. Cf. Gorman, Cruciformity, 307. I am delighted to read the essay by Stewart, "Cry of Victory," 25–46. Although the approach taken by Stewart is different from mine, we have arrived at similar conclusions. The following quotations highlight some key points made by Stewart, which, as we will see, are similar to my findings.

> [D]eath has become a way of identifying with the crucified messiah. Furthermore, the immediate context of Rom 8:28–30 is a clear statement of participation. . . . Paul's view of suffering and his reading of Ps 44 have been conformed to the narrative pattern of Jesus' cross and resurrection (44–45).

> Paradoxically, it is precisely because believers participate in Christ's suffering and death that they suffer innocently . . . As lament, this psalm [Ps 44] vocalizes the real pain and difficulty of suffering and sacrifice; however, as an announcement of victory, this psalm becomes a hopeful reminder of Jesus' resurrection and the believer's eventual participation at the parousia (45).

59. A good point mentioned by Jewett, Romans, 548. Like Jewett, I take the σοῦ to refer to Christ (hence "for Christ's sake"), given the use of Χριστός in 8:34 and 35, as well as the strong notion of participation in Christ in 8:17.

implies the intensity of their distress and pain.[60] The ὡς πρόβατα σφαγῆς highlights the fact that the suffering of believers is undeserved. Just as innocent sheep being led to slaughter, believers suffer as righteous sufferers, which is a notion that has emerged in our discussions on 8:31–34, and indeed in 8:17, 18–30. In short, 8:36 shows that believers are suffering *for the sake of Christ* as righteous sufferers.[61]

Verse 37

The subunit ends with a celebratory claim: "but in all these we triumph in glorious victory" (ἀλλ᾿ ἐν τούτοις πᾶσιν ὑπερνικῶμεν). The τούτοις πᾶσιν suggests that 8:37 is the ultimate answer to all the rhetorical questions since 8:31. Despite any charge against them, despite any condemnation, and despite the sufferings in the affliction-list, believers can be confident that they have victory. The term ὑπερνικάω in itself denotes a super-victory over one's adversaries.[62] In context, it most likely refers to the surpassing victory of believers over adversity and oppression. The present tense indicates that this victory is being achieved at the present time. For the audience in Rome, this victory would not be about defeating their oppressors physically, overcoming the perpetrators of injustice socio-politically, or becoming upwardly mobile in the social hierarchy. The economically poor would most likely remain poor and stay at the lower end of the social ladder. It is very unlikely that former war-captives had the power to even the score with the oppressive Romans. Few slaves had the resources to obtain their freedom (although some did). Nor did they normally have the power to oppose an abusive owner. Rather, in the context of suffering in Rome, their victory would be about participating in the process of transformation. They displayed God's glory by faithfully persevering in suffering (8:17, 18, 24–25, 28–30).[63] They might experience hunger, poverty, persecution, the

---

60. As Byrne, *Romans*, 280, says the ὅλην τὴν ἡμέραν highlights "the unrelenting nature of the trials."

61. As Dunn, *Romans 1–8*, 505–6, points out, the same Psalm is used in later Rabbinic literature to refer to the Maccabean martyrs. (Cf. Byrne, *Romans*, 280.) The death of the martyrs is of course considered to be righteous suffering. Isaiah 53:7 also echoes the same Psalm, and we will discuss the Fourth Isaianic Servant Song in detail. See also Gorman, *Cruciformity*, 307–8.

62. See Jewett, *Romans*, 548–9; cf. Dunn, *Romans 1–8*, 506; Seifrid, "Romans," 637. These commentators also note the parallels from Stoicism in Epictetus, where those who are trained philosophically must triumph in their trials. Likewise, Hultgren, *Romans*, 340, thinks that the term denotes "glorious victory" or "complete victory."

63. As Jewett, *Romans*, 549, says, "it is a victory currently visible in the lives of the

oppressive Roman sword, peril, and affliction of all kinds; but, since they were fulfilling God's call to participate in Christ's suffering, they were in fact victorious.[64]

The surpassing victory is possible "through him who loved us" (διὰ τοῦ ἀγαπήσαντος ἡμᾶς). The ἀγαπάω recalls the ἀγάπη at the start of the subunit (8:35). Who/what can separate believers from the love of Christ? Even though they are like sheep being led to slaughter, the love of Christ will see them through. This theme of God's abiding love in Christ is at the center of the argument throughout 8:35–39.

In sum, the subunit 8:35–37 plays a pivotal role within the pericope 8:31–39. The enumeration of suffering in the affliction-list resonates with the daily experiences of the audience and elicits a heightened emotional response. This is reinforced by the powerful rhetorical force of the questions throughout 8:31–34, 35. But with the celebratory claim of super-victory the letter affirms the value of their co-suffering with Christ. In all this, God's abiding love is the basis of their assurance. In the meantime, the scriptural citation places believers' experience in the category of righteous suffering. We will return to this citation to discuss its significance in detail.

ROMANS 8:38–39

The γάρ in 8:38 indicates that the subunit 8:38–39 elaborates on the celebratory claim in 8:37, and it does so with the perfect passive πέπεισμαι, which underlines "Paul's complete certainty" of his conviction that nothing can separate believers from God's love in Christ (8:39).[65] The letter lists ten factors that threaten to dissociate believers from God's love. The last factor, τις κτίσις, as our discussion will explain, fittingly declares that nothing in the created order can be a real threat. Rhetorically, the τις κτίσις constitutes an apt response to the questions initiated by the interrogative τίς in 8:31, 33, 34, and 35. The audience is invited to share the conviction of Paul that they are safe and secure in God. This love is of course *in Christ Jesus*, given the christological character of the pericope. And with the rhetorical marker ἐν

---

suffering saints." The present tense of the verb ὑπερνικῶμεν is another indication that the glorification of believers is already set in motion and not restricted to the future resurrection.

64. This type of victory is set in sharp contrast to that of imperial Rome. That is, victory is not through military might or oppressive rule. See the discussion by Keesmaat, "Psalms in Romans and Galatians," 351–52, on the subversive nature of the letter's claim. Cf. Jewett, *Romans*, 549–50.

65. Dunn, *Romans 1–8*, 506.

Χριστῷ Ἰησοῦ τῷ κυρίῳ ἡμῶν, the subunit closes the pericope 8:31–39 as well as the entire section in Rom 5–8.

It is not easy to determine the exact nature of the ten threats listed in 8:38–39,[66] but it is clear that at least some of the items refer to cosmic powers.[67] As is often observed, eight of them appear in pairs (θάνατος/ζωή, ἄγγελος/ἀρχή, ἐνίστημι/μέλλω, ὕψωμα/βάθος) and two individually (δύναμις, κτίσις).[68] Our interest lies in not so much identifying the exact meaning of each item in the list, but those that cause harm and affliction. Since cosmic forces ultimately lie behind suffering, we will pay special attention to the items pertaining to cosmic powers.[69]

Many scholars, rightly, think that the ἄγγελοι refers to demonic or fallen angels.[70] It has been suggested that the ἀρχαί may denote cosmic forces or political rulers. But given its association with ἄγγελοι in 8:38, many commentators think that ἀρχαί refers to superhuman forces.[71] Yet since ancient cosmological worldviews see a closely interconnected universe, where cosmic powers and socio-political systems are inseparable, the ἀρχαί probably refers to both the cosmic forces and the political rulers/principalities who reign on earth and have the power to threaten the well-being of believers.[72] The term δυνάμεις appears in the list as a stand-alone item (rather than being in a pair). It most likely stands for supernatural beings or spiritual powers, as the term is commonly used in this way in the New

66. For detailed discussions, see Jewett, Romans, 550–54; Adams, Constructing, 184–5; Carr, Angels and Principalities, 112–4; Wink, Naming the Powers, 47–50. As we will see, our conclusion disagrees with Carr's view that Rom 8:38–39 has "no reference to the hostile spiritual or astral world" (114). Our analysis of the entire section 8:31–39 goes against such a view. Cf. Hultgren, Romans, 341n388.

67. Jewett, Romans, 550; Hultgren, Romans, 340–42. Cf. Gaventa, "Neither," 274.

68. Also, we note that some manuscripts add ἐξουσίαι to the list in Rom 8:38–39, and some move the δυνάμεις back before the ἐνεστῶτα. But we have followed the majority view in neglecting these. See Jewett, Romans, 532; Dunn, Romans 1–8, 497.

69. Although θάνατος is a cosmic power in Rom 5:12–21, it is unlikely to be the case in Rom 8:38 because of its clear association with ζωή in the same verse. The ζωή is clearly a positive term in 5:12–21, as opposed to its usage in 8:38. It is best to view the pair θάνατος and ζωή as what a life of suffering constitutes. That is, whether we live or die, nothing in this life can separate us from God's love. See Dunn, Romans 1–8, 506–7; Byrne, Romans, 280.

70. See Jewett, Romans, 551–52; Dunn, Romans 1–8, 507. Cf. 1 Cor 6:3; 2 Cor 11:14; 12:7.

71. See the discussion by Jewett, Romans, 552.

72. Cf. Dunn, Romans 1–8, 507. In addition, see BDAG, 112, which says, "Also of angelic and demonic powers, since they were thought of as having a political organization."

Testament and Jewish literature.[73] The ὕψωμα and the βάθος are recognized astrological terms.[74] As Adams says, the pair probably refers to "the celestial powers which were believed to control the destinies of human beings."[75] As we can see, according to ancient cosmology, all of the items discussed above have the power to harm believers and cause pain and hardship. Given this background, the rhetorical construction in 8:38–39 with the repeated οὔτε invites the audience to realize that indeed nothing has the power (note the δύναμαι in 8:39) to separate them from God's love, for the evil powers that cause harm cannot thwart their super-victory.

The list of threats finishes with the τις κτίσις ἑτέρα. Adams is right to say that this expression denotes "any other creature,"[76] although it could also refer to any other cosmic factor not included in the other nine items.[77] The exact meaning of the expression is, in the final analysis, hard to determine. But what is clear is that it serves to convey to the audience that no "possible menaces,"[78] including any cosmic forces, are able to separate them from God's love. Thus, the subunit fittingly rounds off the argument in Rom 5–8. Sin and death entered the cosmos. Adamic humanity has been subject to their dominion, and so suffering is inevitable. But through Christ a new humanity has been formed. Their vocation is to participate in God's restorative purpose through their faithful suffering. In the process of glorification, God's love assures their absolute safety.

Thus, the pericope 8:31–39 majestically concludes 8:1–39 as well as 5:1—8:39 by affirming that there is no condemnation against believers, and that there is no cosmic power or anyone/anything that can separate them from God's love. They are indeed super-victors, even though they are suffering. Their victory has the widest possible scope, for it includes inheriting the whole creation and is at the center of God's triumph over evil.[79]

73. Matt 24:29; 1 Cor 15:24; Ps 102:21 LXX; *1 Enoch* 82:8. See also Jewett, *Romans*, 553; Dunn, *Romans 1–8*, 507; Adams, *Constructing*, 184–85.

74. Dunn, *Romans 1–8*, 508; Byrne, *Romans*, 281; Wink, *Naming the Powers*, 49; BDAG, 851. See *1 Enoch* 18:3, 11.

75. Adams, *Constructing*, 185.

76. Ibid. See also Dunn, *Romans 1–8*, 508.

77. Jewett, *Romans*, 554.

78. As Adams, *Constructing*, 185, says, "The phrase τις κτίσις ἑτέρα is added to make the point that all possible menaces to the believer are comprehended within God's creative and providential purposes: even the hostile spiritual powers are placed within the orb of the created order." See also Hultgren, *Romans*, 342.

79. At this point, as we move towards the end of our analysis of Rom 5–8, I should briefly mention the current scholarly debate on Pauline soteriology, especially in relation to Rom 5–8. Pauline scholars would be aware of the discussion between, for example, N. T. Wright, Douglas Campbell, and Michael Gorman. While Wright

THE USE OF PS 44:22 IN ROM 8:36

We said in our discussion above that the citation of Ps 44:22 in Rom 8:36 is employed as part of the rhetorical strategy of the letter to affirm that nothing can separate believers from Christ's love. We also mentioned that the cited text indicates that the suffering of believers likens to that of an innocent sufferer, and that they suffer *for the sake of Christ*. In the following we will first look at the relevance of the Psalm to the experience of those who suffer. Then we will examine the Psalm and its intertextual links with Romans. I will suggest that the citation will not appear to the audience as a random proof-text. We will also look at the psalmist's emphasis on the innocent suffering of God's people and protests to God about why they have to suffer. I will argue that the letter guides the audience to read the Psalm eschatologically in accordance with God's program of restoring humanity, which defies the retributive logic embedded in the psalmist's thinking. I will propose that the Psalm provides the audience with resources that significantly enrich their understanding and affirm the purpose of their suffering.

Romans 8:36 quotes Ps 43:23 LXX verbatim, which in turn follows Ps 44:23 MT very closely.[80] In fact, the LXX by and large follows the MT for the whole Psalm. Our analysis will use the LXX text unless otherwise stated (although generally I will follow the verse numbering of the NRSV for ease of reference).

The Lament Psalm and the Audience's Situation

The Psalm contains images that reflect the suffering of the audience in imperial Rome. The pictures of being pursued and scattered by the enemy (44:10, 11), and of being a byword and laughingstock among the nations (44:13), would likely be something that the audience could relate to. Former

---

emphasizes God's covenantal-faithfulness, Campbell reads Paul within an apocalyptic-participatory framework. And Gorman puts emphasis on the notion of theosis. (See Wright, *Paul*, 1007–1032; Campbell, *Deliverance*, 62–72; Gorman, *Inhabiting*, 40–104.) It is beyond the scope of our study to discuss the issues within the debate. But I think each of these scholars makes valuable contributions to our understanding of Paul. It seems that the findings of our study agree with different aspects of what these scholars advocate. This is not surprising, because each of these scholars alerts us to different aspects of Paul's thinking. The fact that our study is primarily on Rom 5–8 means that the works of Gorman and Campbell are particularly useful, because Wright's notion of covenantal faithfulness requires in-depth analysis of Rom 4 (Abraham) and Rom 9–11 (Israel).

80. Cf. Seifrid, "Romans," 636. Paul's omission of the opening causal ὅτι is insignificant.

war-captives of Roman conquests and their descendants would know what it meant to be foreigners in Rome under subjugation. The Psalm would also be particularly relevant to Jews like Prisca and Aquila, who probably had returned to Rome after being expelled as a result of Claudius's edict. The language of shame, disgrace, reproach, embarrassment, and poverty (44:9, 13, 15, 24) is likely to evoke an emotional response from those at the bottom of the social and economic hierarchy, especially in a culture obsessed with honor and shame.[81] The slaves, the chronically sick, the degraded, and the homeless would understand the shame and abasement in their daily life, even though their daily experience might not be directly related to defeat in battle.[82] For the ancients, overcoming adversity depended on whether one's gods were powerful enough. For those who experienced hardship and injustice in Rome, they might wonder whether the Creator God would deliver them from the anti-God powers that caused their tribulations. But in 44:1–8 the psalmist speaks of God's deliverance in past battles, which demonstrates his power over foreign gods. In short, for an audience familiar with pain and distress, the Psalm would be a fitting hymn and prayer, making the citation highly pertinent and appropriate.

Intertextual Links and Reading the Psalm Eschatologically in Light of Christ's Coming

The considerable number of verbal and thematic links between Ps 44 and Rom 5–8 shows that the reference to the Psalm is no random citation. But before listing the links, a few words about the structure and message of the Psalm are needed. The Psalm is a prayer that laments a battle defeat, with images of God's people being killed and scattered (44:10, 11, 19, 22).[83] It presents a helpful resource for those living with oppression and deprivation. The language of disgrace and dispersion in 44:10–11 would evoke

81. The term πτωχεία is found in Ps 43:25 LXX but there is no equivalent Hebrew in the MT.

82. My findings here are somewhat similar to the analysis of Keesmaat, "Psalms in Romans and Galatians," 149–50, although not without substantial differences. Keesmaat places a lot of emphasis on the oppression of the Empire, and interprets Rom 8 and the use of Ps 44 accordingly. I agree that the socio-political oppression of imperial Rome is a very significant contributor of the hardships faced by Paul's audience. But my focus is on how the audience would have understood the text of Rom 8 and its use of Ps 44. Keesmaat does pay close attention to the rhetorical strategy of the text. But at times I am not sure whether her emphasis on Roman imperialism overly dominates her interpretation.

83. See Broyles, *Psalms*, 201; Craigie and Tate, *Psalms 1–50*, 332.

the imagery of exile.[84] The Assyrian and Babylonian invasions are possible candidates for the historical background of the Psalm. But in the centuries leading up to Paul's time, the Jews would have used the Psalm as a lament during times of recurring battle defeats and dispersions.[85]

The Psalm has four subunits, namely, 44:1–8, 44:9–16, 44:17–22, and 44:23–26. Psalm 44:1–8 recalls how in the days of old God saved Israel and led them to victories. Instead of Israel being scattered by their enemies, the nations were driven away from their land. Verses 9–16 repeatedly speak of God's abandonment and the shame of defeat (during the Second Temple period), with an increasing sense of gloom as the unit progresses. In vv. 17–22 the psalmist boldly claims that the people have been faithful to God, strongly implying that their suffering is unjust. As Goldingay says,

> Given that God would be able to know what has been going on, God knows (the psalm implies) that Israel has been guilty of no such unfaithfulness. So people are not suffering because of their own actions but because of God.[86]

In Ps 44:23–26 the speaker cries out to God and urges him to act and redeem them. The basis of this emotional plea is that his people have been faithful.

There are substantial verbal and thematic correspondences between the Psalm and Rom 5–8. This suggests that the audience would find the citation fitting, although not without a touch of irony. The following chart shows the key words that can be found in both Rom 5–8 and Ps 43 LXX. These key words reflect both linguistic and thematic parallels.

Key word(s)	Psalm LXX (using LXX verse numbering)	Romans
δεξιά	43:4	8:34
σῴζω, σωτηρία	43:4, 7, 8 (σῴζω); 43:5 (σωτηρία)	5:9, 10; 8:24 (σῴζω)
ἐλπίζω, ἐλπίς	43:7 (ἐλπίζω)	8:24, 25 (ἐλπίζω); 5:2, 4, 5; 8:20, 24 (ἐλπίς)
θλίβω, θλῖψις	43:8, 25 (θλίβω)	5:3; 8:35 (θλῖψις)

84. As Goldingay, *Psalms 42–89, 42–43*, says concerning Psalm 44:10–11, "This is not merely a matter of defeat and loss but of massacre and exile." Cf. Clifford, *Psalm 1–72*, 219.

85. Cf. Broyles, *Psalms*, 201; Clifford, *Psalm 1–72*, 219; Craigie and Tate, *Psalms 1–50*, 332–33.

86. Goldingay, *Psalms 42–89*, 47.

κληρονομέω, κληρονόμος, συγκληρονόμος	43:4 (κληρονομέω)	8:17 (κληρονόμος and συγκληρονόμος)
καταισχύνω	43:8, 10	5:5
καρδία	43:19, 22	5:5; 8:27

There are significant shared usages of terms relating to suffering, hope, and salvation/deliverance (θλίβω/θλῖψις, ἐλπίζω/ἐλπίς, and σώζω/σωτηρία) between the Psalm and Rom 5–8. Both the Psalm and the letter speak of the inheritance of God's people, and both refer to the searching of the heart. Note that almost all of these terms are found in Rom 5:1–11 and 8:18–39, which are the pericopes that bracket 5:1—8:39 and where suffering is the main focus.[87] Again, these highlight the fact that the citation would not have appeared to the audience as a random proof-text. Indeed, the content of the Psalm may be evoked in the mind of the audience. It does not mean that the audience would recall every detail of Ps 44, but that the relevant topics and language are evoked and become useful resources for them to understand how the citation functions in Romans.

But not all of the shared themes and vocabulary would make sense to the audience, because of their eschatological setting; that is, in view of the fact that Christ has already come. The Psalm looks back to events in Israel's past and looks forward to future redemption and deliverance from their present suffering. For Paul's audience, however, Christ's work has already effected salvation and reconciliation (5:9, 10; 8:24). Yet they are suffering at present and still await God's deliverance from their trials (8:18–30).

In other words, while Ps 44 speaks of God's salvation *in the past* and the hope that Israel used to have, Romans speaks of God's *present* deliverance (from sin and death) for his people and the hope associated with it. The psalmist speaks of Israel's inheriting the land in *the days of old* (Ps 44:1), but Romans talks about God's people's inheritance in Christ *at the present time* (Rom 8:17). The speaker in the Psalm can only recall the *past* deliverance by God's right hand and the light of his face (Ps 44:3),[88] but Romans says that Christ is at the right hand of God *now* and is interceding for them (Rom 8:34). The Psalm says that God has put his people to shame (Ps 44:7, 9), but the letter says that its audience needs not be ashamed (καταισχύνω) in their

---

87. Keesmaat, "Psalms in Romans and Galatians," 150, goes as far as saying that the Psalm "has extensive parallels with Romans 8."

88. The right hand and right arm in Ps 44:3 (Ps 43:4 LXX) symbolize God's delight in his people. See, e.g. Goldingay, *Psalms 42–89*, 39.

present sufferings (Rom 5:5).[89] In the Psalm the speaker says that the God who searches the heart would know that they have not worshipped a foreign god (Ps 44:21–22). (If they had, they would have broken the covenant—which has just been mentioned in 44:18). But in Rom 8:26–27 the searching of the heart is about assisting believers in their weakness and that the Spirit may intercede for them.[90]

So, the shared vocabulary between Ps 44 and Rom 5–8 provide clear linkages between them via the themes of hope, suffering, salvation/deliverance, shame, and inheritance. But the audience needs to read Ps 44 eschatologically after the coming of Christ. That is, while the Psalm laments the inaction of God in their distress, recalls his past salvation, and pleads with him to act according to the covenant, the eschatological people of God in Romans already experience God's salvation and are already heirs of God's promise because God has acted by sending his Son to accomplish his project of renewing the cosmos. Yet at the same time trials and hardship are still inevitable for God's new humanity. They share Israel's experience in Ps 44 of innocent suffering. That is, as they wait eagerly for the full realization of their glory, they still experience hardship and affliction.

In short, the citation of Ps 44:22 in Rom 8:36 would not have appeared to the audience as a random proof-text. The verbal and thematic links would have prompted the audience to recognize the message and content of the Psalm itself, making it a useful resource for them to understand the letter. At the same time, the audience would have found that the Psalm only makes sense if they read it eschatologically. We will examine the implication of this later in our discussion.

Innocent Suffering with No Need to Protest

There are two features of the Psalm that are commonly detected, namely, the psalmist's claim of undeserved suffering and the tone of protest. Or, to put the two features together, the Psalm asks God why he allows his people

---

89. The above includes references to Rom 5–8 only. More can be said here if we include other references. For example, the psalmist speaks of Israel being humbled by their enemy (Ps 44:19, 25), which, in the context of a battle defeat and the apparent abandonment by God, would refer not only to the loss of national pride but also to the humble circumstances of the war-captives. Romans, however, says that believers should associate with the lowly (Rom 12:16), which include the slaves, war-captives, and their descendants. Likewise, Ps 44 says that God has sold Israel without honor (Ps 43:13 LXX). Many in imperial Rome would have experienced a similar kind of shame. But Romans asks its audience to honor one another in the community (Rom 2:7, 10; 12:10).

90. The bestowal of the Spirit is of course an eschatological event.

to suffer for no fault of their own? As we will find, studying these questions enhances our understanding of the interaction between the Psalm and Romans. Here we will discuss the two features one by one.

First, Ps 44 clearly speaks of the notion of undeserved suffering.[91] The Psalm defies any suggestion that Israel's suffering fits into the Deuteronomistic pattern, which says that Israel would suffer defeat in battle and YHWH's desertion if they failed to keep his covenant (Deut 27:11–26; 28:25—29:1). Since this pattern forms the basis for the warning of the prophets against disobedience,[92] the Psalm also resists the notion that the present battle defeat is a result of their idolatry and rebellion. Instead of saying that Israel is defeated in battle because of their disobedience, the psalmist claims that they have not done any wrong against the covenant or forgotten the name of their God (Ps 44:17, 20).[93] Israel's suffering is not a result of punishment or retribution for idolatry (as the prophets would have said), for they did not spread their hands to a foreign god (Ps 44:20). Thus, the Psalm is decidedly about the suffering of the righteous, who seek to serve God in faithfulness. This feature of Ps 44, as mentioned, fits in well with the situation of Paul's audience, which has been exhorted to suffer *with* Christ. Their sufferings are not a result of disobedience, but rather fidelity to God.[94]

Second, Ps 44 is a psalm of protest. Scholars note that it is more than a lament psalm. Broyles says that the speaker of the Psalm claims that "not only are the people innocent, God is guilty of cruel betrayal," and that it expresses "utter disappointment in God."[95] Indeed, Goldingay detects elements of protest throughout the entire Psalm.[96] The protest of the psalmist is supported by the claim of Israel's fidelity to the covenant and the seeming lack of a corresponding response from God. Here Rom-Shiloni's analysis is particularly helpful. Rom-Shiloni compares Ps 44 with Jer 18:13–17. In Jeremiah YHWH says that his people have *forgotten* him and as a result he will scatter them before the enemy. Psalm 44, however, says that God's people

---

91. As Grogan, *Psalms*, 98, says, it is a Job-like experience. Cf. Broyles, *Psalms*, 203; Rom-Shiloni, "Psalm 44," 698; Craigie and Tate, *Psalms 1–50*, 335; Mays, *Psalms*, 176.

92. Jeremiah 18:12–17 is a good example in which idolatry would lead to defeat in battle.

93. Rom-Shiloni, "Protest," 690–93, argues that the terminology of "forget" in Ps 44:18–20, 21–23, is covenantal terminology.

94. Jewett, *Romans*, 548, may well be right to think that the citation is used to counter the alternative claim that if they were genuinely righteous and filled with the Spirit, then they should be blessed with success and prosperity, rather than suffering.

95. Broyles, *Psalms*, 203–4.

96. Goldingay, *Psalms 42–89*, 38–49.

have not *forgotten* him, and yet he has scattered them among the nations.[97] Rom-Shiloni also refers to other Scriptures (Pss 42:10; 74:19; 77:10; Lam 5:20) that, like Ps 44, express God's people's feeling of desertion and neglect, and "call on God not to forget his obedient servants/people and not to withdraw from the long-standing covenant (Pss 74:20; 89:50; also the communal lament in Jer 14:19–22)."[98] In short, Ps 44 is no mere lament psalm, but a protest against God's apparent unjust treatment of those who are faithful to him. This feature of the Psalm, however, is absent in Rom 8:31–39. There is in fact no hint of protest throughout Rom 5–8.[99] For the psalmist, the reason for the protest is that according to the principle of retributive justice, they should not be suffering. Yet, as our exegesis has shown, the suffering of believers does not operate in accordance with such a principle. Instead, their suffering is an integral part of participating in Christ. At this point, the christological character of 8:31–39 comes to the fore. Since the believers' vocation is to identify with Christ, their present suffering is *for his sake*. Because Christ is central to their vocation, there is no need for protest.

The Cited Verse Itself

We will soon summarize our findings regarding the citation of the Psalm in Rom 8:36. But before that we should take a close look at the components of the cited verse itself, and see how they assist believers to read Paul's letter. For easy reference the cited text in Rom 8:36 is shown here.

ἕνεκεν σοῦ θανατούμεθα ὅλην τὴν ἡμέραν ἐλογίσθημεν ὡς πρόβατα σφαγῆς

The immediate context of Ps 44:22 is clearly the innocence of God's people. They have not worshipped other gods (44:20). God could search their hearts and find fidelity rather than idolatry (44:21). In light of this, the speaker says that it is for the sake of God that they are put to death all day long and being counted as "sheep of slaughter" (πρόβατα σφαγῆς). As mentioned above, the ἕνεκεν σοῦ stands in the emphatic position, which indicates to the letter's audience that their suffering is for the sake of Christ—just as the psalmist says that the people suffer for God's sake. Also, the expression

---

97. Rom-Shiloni, "Protest," 691–93.

98. Ibid., 693.

99. Parlier, "Justice," 108–9, makes a valid suggestion that Rom 8:35, 36, may answer the psalmist's complaint about the people's suffering (by pointing to God's love displayed in Christ's undeserved suffering for his people). But it should be noted that the text of Romans itself does not complain about suffering.

ὅλην τὴν ἡμέραν is commonly used in the Psalter to paint a vivid picture of the intense suffering of the sufferers (Pss 25:5; 38:6, 12; 52:1; 56:1, 2, 5; 73:14; 86:3; 88:9, 17; 102:8).[100] In fact, in 44:15 the speaker says that ὅλην τὴν ἡμέραν his/her "shame" (ἐντροπή) is before him/her. This intense depiction of suffering suggests that the expression reinforces the heightened emotions already triggered by the affliction-list in Rom 8:35.

The ὡς πρόβατα σφαγῆς is an image often found in Israel's Scripture. There seems to be three main usages. First, it refers to YHWH's judgment on the nations' rebellion, such as the judgment on Edom in Isa 34:6 and against Babylon in Jer 51:40. The immediate context of Ps 44:22 shows clearly that this usage is not in view. Second, it is used as a metaphor for the suffering of the righteous. For example, in Jer 11:19 it is used in relation to the prophet's own suffering despite his innocence and faithful service to YHWH. Importantly, this image of undeserved suffering already exists in Ps 44:11 to illustrate the innocence of God's people. This use of imagery is also found in Ps 44:22 and Rom 8:36.[101] It reinforces what we suggested in the exegesis on Rom 8:35–37 above. That is, the imagery signifies the fact that the believers' suffering is not the result of God's punishment, but rather reflects their vocation to suffer with Christ.[102]

The third usage of ὡς πρόβατα σφαγῆς is the picture of sheep or lambs being slaughtered as an offering to YHWH. This is, for example, found in the purification rituals in Leviticus and the offerings by Hezekiah and Josiah when they celebrated the Passover.[103] This imagery *cannot apply to believers here*, for so far Romans has not said that they are offered to God as a sacrifice.[104] Having said that, this usage may be a pointer to the Fourth Isaianic Servant Song, where the Servant is like a sheep being led to the slaughter (Isa 53:7). In our discussion below I will investigate the possibility that the imagery in the citation of Ps 44:22 prompts the audience of Romans to consider their shared identity with Christ as co-sufferers.[105]

100. See Seifrid, "Romans," 637.

101. As Seifrid, "Romans," 637, says, "Here it is solely because of God, who hides himself, that his people suffer, and not because of their guilt." Seifrid, however, does not use the same line of argument as I have used. He is making a general observation on the text.

102. Thus, Jewett, *Romans*, 548, rightly says that the citation demonstrates the community's solidarity with Christ.

103. The sheep/lambs are used as a guilt offering or burnt offering for the purification of lepers and leprous houses in Lev 14:13, 25; and as an offering to YHWH in 2 Chr 18:2 (by Jehoshaphat and Ahab); 30:15, 17 (by Hezekiah); 35:1, 6, 11 (by Josiah).

104. Believers' lives being a sacrifice/offering (θυσία) is found in Rom 12:1, not in Rom 8.

105. Cf. Hays, *Echoes*, 62–63; Byrne, *Romans*, 277; Seifrid, "Romans," 637.

Usages and Functions of the Citation

In the above analysis we have found that the citation is not arbitrary, and would not appear as a random proof-text to the audience. It seems that the letter guides the audience to an eschatological reading of Ps 44, whereby God's restorative project provides a christocentric framework for them to understand the quotation. Psalm 44:22 serves as an affirmation that believers are righteous sufferers. Yet there is no hint of the psalmist's protest to God, and so the Psalm's embedded assumption of retributive justice is avoided. This is not surprising, given the fact that the letter's argument does not operate on the principle of retributive justice but in accordance with God's restorative program. Believers' sufferings are an integral part of God's plan to transform the cosmos, and hence are visible signs of the faithful performance of their vocation. They suffer because they are participating in Christ—and hence they suffer *for the sake of Christ*. The purpose of their suffering is to display God's glory and be God's vice-regents over his creation, and because of this purpose their affliction has profound value.[106]

In other words, the scriptural citation in Rom 8:36 *functions* as an authoritative assurance that believers are indeed righteous sufferers when they faithfully participate in Christ. On the one hand, the argument of Rom 5–8 and the letter's rhetorical strategy in 8:31–39 implicitly overturn the Psalm's assumptions concerning retributive justice. On the other hand, the Psalm's passionate voice of innocent suffering clearly affirms the letter's argument concerning the audience's place in God's purpose. It is on this basis that the following verse in Romans (8:37) can speak of a surpassing victory in the midst of severe suffering.[107] With its strategic location within the sub-

---

106. Cf. Hays, *Echoes*, 58, who says, "The point is not that 'righteous people have always suffered like this'; rather, Paul's point in Rom 8:35–36 is that Scripture prophesies suffering as the lot of those (i.e., himself and his readers) who live in the eschatological interval between Christ's resurrection and the ultimate redemption of the world." I would like to add that the renewal of creation is part of the purpose of the present sufferings.

107. Keesmaat, "Psalms in Romans and Galatians," 152, thinks that Paul asserts God's presence in the midst of Roman oppression. She says,

> The whole dynamic of this passage rejects the traditional categories about who is victor and who is conquered. The messiah who died and was raised is the one in the position of authority at the right hand of God, and those who suffer are the ones who are—not conquered—but more than, indeed above, the conquerors. Paul is rejecting the imperial categories here of victory, categories beloved by both Israel and Rome, and is replacing them with the category of suffering love.

I think Keesmaat's insights are commendable. My hesitation to entirely embrace her argument is her strong emphasis on reading Romans in (anti-) imperial categories.

unit 8:35–37—after the affliction-list and before the confident triumphant cry—the citation emphatically assures the audience that they are indeed participants of God's triumph in spite of their affliction.

ISAIANIC SERVANT SONGS AND THE IDENTITY OF BELIEVERS

In his well-known *Echoes of Scripture in the Letters of Paul*, Richard Hays discusses the echoes of Isa 40–55 in Rom 8:18–39, and suggests that there is an intertextual echo of Isa 53:7 in the citation of Ps 44:22 in Rom 8:36.[108] In fact, commentators commonly detect verbal and thematic links with the Third and Fourth Servant Songs in various parts of Rom 5–8,[109] but few, if any, provide a detailed discussion. In the following we will discuss these in detail. We will first survey the factors that make the evocation of the Songs likely. We will then examine four texts in Rom 5–8 that may alert the audience to the Servant Songs.[110] More specifically, I will argue that there are evidences of the Fourth Song (Isa 52:13–53:12) being echoed in Rom 5:1–21, 8:3, and 8:31–34, and that the Servant refers to Christ in those places. The primary pattern in these echoes is that the Servant/Christ is handed over to die for others as an innocent sufferer. I will also argue that there are considerable links between the Third Song (Isa 50:4–11) and Rom 8:31–34, where the Servant seems to refer to believers. The pattern here is that the Servant and believers are both righteous sufferers. But, unlike the Fourth Song, there are no sacrificial overtones. Finally, I will argue that the Fourth Song is likely to be evoked in the citation of Ps 44:22 in Rom 8:36.[111] The imagery here is that the Servant suffers like an innocent lamb being led to slaughter, which

---

It is one thing to say that the letter implies a radical (non-violent) way to respond to imperial violence in Rome. But it is another thing to say that everyone who is suffering from socioeconomic hardship and religious oppression reads the text through the lens of imperial categories. Also, not all sufferings endured by Paul's audience are entirely the result of imperial oppression. They are caused by a combination of socioeconomic realities, religious, and racial tensions, as well as political oppression.

108. Hays, *Echoes*, 57–63.

109. See below.

110. The four Servant Songs are generally recognized to be Isa 42:1–9; 49:1–13; 50:4–11; and 52:13—53:12, although some prefer the shorter versions of the first three (42:1–4; 49:1–6; 50:4–9).

111. Those who have found significant connections between the Isaianic Servant Songs and Rom 5:1–11; 8:31–39, include: Shum, *Paul's Use*, 193–202; Seifrid, "Romans," 633–37; Kleinknecht, *Der leidende Gerechtfertigte*, 347–56; Wilk, *Die Bedeutung des Jesajabuches*, 280–84, 285–86, 395, 398–99. None of them provide the type of detailed treatment that we provide below.

is the experience of the psalmist as well as that of believers. We will examine how these echoes and patterns interact, forming an intriguing possibility for the audience to consider their merged identity with Christ in light of the life pattern of the Servant. I will propose that the Servant Songs provide yet another layer of scriptural voice to affirm the audience of their vocation and purpose in following Christ's way of life.

Factors Contributing to Evocation

In a moment we will examine specific texts in Rom 5–8 where the Servant Songs may be evoked.[112] But before that we will first look at three factors that contribute to the possibility of the evocation. First, the Songs, especially the Fourth Song, are used among the earliest Christians and in the Gospels, and it is likely that Paul's audience would be familiar with them. For example, Isa 42:1–4 is found in Matt 12:18–21, and Isa 53:4 LXX in Matt 8:17.[113] Both identify Jesus as the Servant, with the former clearly making Jesus the Spirit-anointed Servant, who would proclaim justice to the peoples. Isaiah 53:12 is cited by Jesus in Luke 22:37, and Isa 53:7, 8 are used by Philip in Acts 8:32–33.[114] Isaiah 53:10–11 is probably alluded to in the account of the last supper in Matt 26:28; Mark 14:24.[115] Again, all of these identify Jesus as the Servant.[116]

Second, there are over eighteen clear references to Isaiah in Romans, including two from the Fourth Servant Songs (Isa 52:15 in Rom 15:21; Isa

112. Critical scholarship widely treats Isa 40–55 as Deutero-Isaiah, and 56–66 as Trito-Isaiah. I, however, avoid using these terms. It is not because they are invalid, but that I am aware of the fact I am investigating how the audience would have understood Romans. Since the letter refers to different parts of Isaiah with the term "Isaiah" (e.g., Rom 9:27/Isa 10:22–23; Rom 15:12/Isa 11:10; Rom 10:16/Isa 53:1; Rom 10:20/Isa 65:1), I think it is better to stick with the same convention. The audience would not be concerned about the authorship and dating of the Isaianic texts.

113. Matt 8:17 follows the LXX version of Isa 53:4.

114. Acts 8:32–33 follows the LXX text of Isa 53:7, 8.

115. See, for example, Stein, "Last Supper," 448; Hagner, *Matthew 14–28*, 773; Nolland, *Matthew*, 1080. See Watts, *Isaiah's*, 356–60, for a detailed discussion on the allusion to Isa 53 in Mark 14:24. Cf. Boring, *Mark*, 391. The other passage that may allude to Isa 53 is Mark 10:45. Cf. Watts, *Isaiah's*, 270–86.

116. I note that Hooker, *Jesus and the Servant*, 80–83, 84, 101–2, 106, raises questions about whether the passages I cited above really identify Jesus as the Servant. Space limitations disallow me from discussing the issues in detail. But see Watts, *Isaiah's*, 277–84, 357–58, for a detailed engagement with Hooker. See also France, *Matthew*, 321–22, 471–72; Green, *Luke*, 775–76, who affirm that the passages I cited above do identify Jesus as the Servant.

53:1 in Rom 10:16),[117] and two very close to it (Isa 52:5 in Rom 2:24; Isa 52:7 in Rom 10:15).[118] The frequent citations suggest that Isaiah, including the Songs, was an important part of Israel's Scripture among early Christians and that the audience in Rome might be aware of its significance.[119]

Third, there are verbal and thematic links between the Servant Songs and Romans as a whole. For example, the following terms refer to the attributes and roles of the Servant: δικαιοσύνη/δικαιόω, κρίσις/κρίμα/κρίνω, ἔθνος, ἐλπίς/ἐλπίζω, σώζω/σωτηρία, and πνεῦμα.[120] Notably YHWH will anoint the Servant with his Spirit, and the Servant will establish justice in the nations (42:1, 4). Likewise, Romans says that Jesus is the anointed king and descendant of David (1:1–4; cf. the "Spirit of Christ" in 8:9). In Isa 49:13 the LXX says that the hills will be filled with δικαιοσύνη because of the blessings that come with the Servant, and of course the gospel in Romans is about the δικαιοσύνη θεοῦ (1:16–17). The Songs speak of the hope of the Gentiles (42:1, 4, 6, 9), and Romans has much to say about the Jew-Gentile community in Christ (e.g., 1:16–17; 15:7–13; and throughout Rom 1–4, 12–15).[121]

The above suggests that the audience would already have a degree of awareness of the Servant Songs. As we proceed to examine the specific passages in Rom 5–8 that echo the Songs, a few words concerning the text of Isaianic Servant Songs are in order. Among the over seventeen citations of Isaiah in Romans, about seven of them follow the LXX more closely than the MT. Only one of them follows both the LXX and the MT closely. The

117. Although Isa 52:15 and 53:1 (cited in Rom 15:21 and 10:16 respectively) are in the Servant Songs, they are not directly relevant to our specific investigation here concerning suffering. For a concise discussion, see Evans, "Isaiah 53," 159–62.

118. See Appendix E for the list of references to Isaiah in Romans.

119. For a good overview on the use of Isaiah in the rest of Romans, see Wagner, "Isaiah in Romans," 129, and Shum, *Paul's Use*, 258–64.

120. References to these Greek terms can be found in Isa 42:1, 3–6; 49:1, 4, 6–8, 13; 50:8; 51:4–8, 52:15; 53:8, 11 (all are LXX references). Only the references in the Servant Songs are listed here. There are about 350 occurrences in Isaiah altogether.

121. Also, both the Servant Songs and Romans use key words that speak of (or allude to) *slavery, deliverance, and hope*. These include terms like δεσμωτήριον/δεσμός, διασπείρω/διασπορά, ἔρημος, παρακαλέω/παράκλησις, εὐφροσύνη, εἰρηνεύω/εἰρήνη, ἔλεος, δικαιοσύνη/δικαιόω, δόξα/δοξάζω. (There are 310 occurrences of these Greek terms in Isaiah. In the Servant Songs they appear in Isa 42:6–8; 49:3, 5–6, 8–10, 13; 50:8; 52:13–14; 53:2, 5, 11 [all LXX].) For instance, the Servant Songs speak of the deliverance of Israel (42:7) and the return of the exiles (49:5–7, 12). YHWH will comfort the sick and lowly among the exiles as they return (49:10, 13). In Rom 5–8 Paul speaks of God's deliverance for those under the slavery of sin, death and the law, and later the letter talks about God's comfort and urges the community to comfort one another (12:8; 15:4, 5). The Songs say that the Servant will be justified/vindicated (50:8), and be glorified exceedingly (52:13). And of course Romans has much to say about the justification/vindication and glorification of God's people.

rest of them contain variations of both the LXX and the MT.[122] In light of this, the LXX seems to be the best available version of Scripture for our discussion below, and we will refer to the MT only when necessary.[123] As we will see, the two Songs that Rom 5–8 echoes are the Third and Fourth Servant Songs. While the LXX follows the MT quite closely in the Third Song, there are some discrepancies between the MT and the LXX for the Fourth Songs. But, unless otherwise stated, those discrepancies are not significant for our purposes, because they generally do not affect the specific shared themes and messages between Romans and the Fourth Song. (See Appendix F for a discussion on the discrepancies between the MT and LXX.[124])

The Fourth Servant Song and Rom 5:1–21

In his careful study on Paul's use of Isaiah in Romans, Shum convincingly proposes several echoes of the Fourth Servant Song in Rom 5:6, 8, 19, and possibly 5:1.[125] In the following I will show that there are correspondences between the Servant in Isa 53 and Christ in Rom 5.[126] The main points of contact are found in the language of παραδίδωμι, πολύς, εἰρήνη, and the δικ-word group, and the fact that both Christ and the Servant were handed over to die for others so that there may be peace and justification/vindication. What we will not find is that there is an exact match between the two life patterns of Christ and the Servant in every detail (which is notably the case in the use of the Song in Matt 8:14–17; 12:15–21).[127] Instead, Christ and the

122. See Appendix E for the list of citations, and which citations follow the LXX/MT.

123. As mentioned in Chapter 1, the reality is that we do not know which version(s) of Scripture the audience in Rome used. Fortunately, our analysis will depend on the cumulative evidence available to us, without overreliance on any one piece of information. Hence, the LXX (as we have it today) should be quite sufficient for our investigation.

124. See David A. Sapp, "Isaiah 53," 189–92, for a detailed comparison between the Qumran variant textual readings, the MT and the LXX. The variants between the Hebrew texts seem to be of no major significance for our purposes. As for the differences between the LXX and the Hebrew texts, we will highlight them when needed.

125. Shum, *Paul's Use*, 189–200. Shum also shows that Rom 4:25 alludes to Isa 53:6, 12.

126. See Appendix G for a table listing the details of the possible links between Rom 5 and the Fourth Song.

127. The citation of Isa 53:4 LXX in Matt 8:17 refers to the Servant's taking up our infirmities. The context of Matt 8:14–17 is the many healings Jesus performs. Jesus is taken as the Servant-figure for one particular characteristic of the Servant, namely, through him there is healing. Some of the details concerning the Servant in the citation of Isa 42:1–4 in Matt 12:15–21 cannot be found in Jesus' life—e.g., he will not cry out and no one will hear his voice in the streets. The point of Matt 12:15–21 seems to be

Servant share the same core storyline, in which they die as innocent sufferers for the sake of others. Here I will list the most relevant verses of the Song for ease of reference.

Isaiah 53:5 αὐτὸς δὲ ἐτραυματίσθη διὰ τὰς ἀνομίας ἡμῶν καὶ μεμαλάκισται διὰ τὰς ἁμαρτίας ἡμῶν· **παιδεία εἰρήνης** ἡμῶν ἐπ' αὐτόν, τῷ μώλωπι αὐτοῦ ἡμεῖς ἰάθημεν.

Isaiah 53:8 ἐν τῇ ταπεινώσει ἡ κρίσις αὐτοῦ ἤρθη· τὴν γενεὰν αὐτοῦ τίς διηγήσεται; ὅτι **αἴρεται ἀπὸ τῆς γῆς** ἡ ζωὴ αὐτοῦ, ἀπὸ **τῶν ἀνομιῶν** τοῦ λαοῦ μου ἤχθη εἰς **θάνατον**.

Isaiah 53:11 ἀπὸ τοῦ πόνου τῆς ψυχῆς αὐτοῦ, δεῖξαι αὐτῷ φῶς καὶ πλάσαι τῇ συνέσει, **δικαιῶσαι δίκαιον** εὖ δουλεύοντα **πολλοῖς**, καὶ τὰς ἁμαρτίας αὐτῶν αὐτὸς ἀνοίσει.

The links between Isa 53:8 and Rom 5:6, 8 seem strong.[128] Both verses in the letter speak of Christ's dying for sinners/the godless, and Isa 53:8 says that the Servant is taken away from the earth and led to death on account of the lawless.[129] Thus, in both cases the Servant/Christ dies for others as a sacrificial act rather than because of his own sins. The πολλοί and δίκαιοι in Rom 5:19 echo the πολλοῖς as well as the δικαιῶσαι and δίκαιον in Isa 53:11.[130] In the letter it is said that through Christ's obedience—that is, through his death—*many* will be made *righteous*. Isaiah 53:11–12 speaks of the *vindication* of the Servant, the *righteous one*, who serves as a servant to *many*. He bears their sins and is given over to death for them. In both cases, Christ/the Servant dies for many, even though the persons being justified/vindicated are different.

In addition, the εἰρήνη in Rom 5:1 appears in Isa 53:5. Rom 5:1 says that believers have been justified and have peace with God, which, in the context of 5:1–11, refers to the reconciliation that Christ's death has accomplished (5:9, 19, 11). In Isa 53:5 it is said that the Servant was wounded and weakened because of people's lawlessness, and upon him was their "discipline of peace" (παιδεία εἰρήνης). Although the peace spoken of in the letter and the Song are somewhat different, there is a sense that through the sacrificial act

---

simply that Jesus is God's chosen Servant according to the prophet.

128. Shum, *Paul's Use*, 196; Byrne, *Romans*, 171.

129. The MT says that the Servant was cut off and stricken for the transgression of people.

130. See Evans, "Isaiah," 161, for a discussion of the links between Rom 5:19 and Isa 53:11.

of Christ/the Servant peace is attained/cultivated.[131] Interestingly, Rom 4:25 also seems to echo Isa 53:6, 11, 12, with the παραδίδωμι and the διχ-words appearing in both the letter and the Isaianic texts.[132] In both cases, Christ/ the Servant is handed over to death for the sins/trespasses of sinners. Even though Rom 4:25 is outside the section 5:1—8:39, it is the verse just before the section and its message of justification and Christ's death is found in 5:1—11.

Admittedly, the other details concerning Christ and the Servant do not match exactly. But the storylines of Christ and the Servant are similar. Indeed, their stories share similar actors, namely, God, Christ/the Servant, and people who have sinned (or under the bondage of sin). In both cases Christ/ the Servant is an innocent sufferer, who died not because of his own sins but the sins of others. And God is the one who handed over Christ/the Servant to death. Hence, the audience of Rom 5:1–21 is invited to understand the Servant christologically. In the context of the Song itself, the "many" that the Servant died for would primarily be understood to refer to exilic Israel.[133] But in Romans the "many" refers to God's new humanity. This means that the Song has to be read eschatologically as well. The coming of Christ is not only for the blessings of ethnic Israelites, but for all humanity.

The Fourth Servant Song and Rom 8:3

Our discussion has shown that there are possible links between Rom 5:1, 6, 8, 19 and the Fourth Servant Song, in that both Christ and the Servant suffered and were handed over by God to die for others. Embedded in Rom 5:1–21 is the first reference to the Son (5:9) in the section 5:1—8:39, whose death is instrumental to the reconciliation of humanity. If the Son's death and vocation are similar to that of the Servant, then we should take a good look at the atoning death of the Son in Rom 8:3, which is the second reference to God's Son in 5:1—8:39.

There are evidences of thematic links between Rom 8:3 and the Fourth Servant Song.[134] First, both texts share the theme of Christ/the Servant

131. Rom 5:1 also echoes Isa 53:11 MT (but not the LXX). In both cases justification is accomplished through Christ/the Servant.

132. The δικαίωσις in Rom 4:25 resonates with the δικαιῶσαι and δίκαιον in Isa 53:11. Shum, *Paul's Use*, 189, goes as far as saying, "[t]hat Rom 4:25 alludes to Isa 53 seems beyond doubt." Scholars do often think that Paul is influenced by Isa 53. See, for instance, Dunn, *Romans 1–8*, 224–25; Byrne, *Romans*, 156; Evans, "Isaiah," 160–61.

133. But of course the Servant would be light to the nations too (Isa 49:6).

134. Perhaps because they are distracted by other pressing issues, commentators rarely see any links between Rom 8:3 and the Songs. See, for instance, Jewett, *Romans,*

giving his life over to those who are bound by sin. In Chapter 4, I argued that the περὶ ἁμαρτίας in Rom 8:3 carries the motif of atoning sacrifice in Israel's Scripture. This means that God sent his Son to die as an atoning sacrifice to bring about a new humanity through reconciliation.[135] The role of Christ here resembles that of the Servant. The notion that the Servant bears people's sins, and is handed over for sins, is found repeatedly in the Fourth Servant Song (53:4, 5, 6, 11, 12).[136] Therefore, Christ and the Servant share a similar vocation. Interestingly, the usages of the expression περὶ ἁμαρτίας in Rom 8:3 and Isa 53:10 LXX differ. In Romans it refers to the death of Christ as a sacrifice, but in the LXX it refers to the wicked who make an offering for themselves (not the Servant dying as a guilt offering [אשׁם], as the MT says).[137] This does not mean that the thematic link mentioned above is invalid, for the link is about Christ's/the Servant's giving up of his life, rather than the manner through which it has taken place. Having said that, the περὶ ἁμαρτίας may constitute a verbal link between the two texts, prompting the audience to consider the relevance of the Servant Song. Despite the fact that the one being offered is different (Christ versus a sacrificial lamb), in either case an offering is needed for those who have sinned.

482–4; Dunn, *Romans 1–8*, 419–22; Kruse, *Romans*, 325–30. Neither do Shum, *Paul's Use*, 200, Seifrid, "Romans," 633, and Kleinknecht, *Der leidende Gerechtfertigte*, 324–56.

135. As mentioned in Chapter 4, Rom 8:3 was written without the later theories of atonement in mind. The exact mechanism of how Christ's atoning death works is hard to determine from the text of Rom 8:3 alone.

136. In the MT the Servant is also said to bear people's iniquity (עון) and sin (חטא) (Isa 53:6, 11, 12).

137. Thus, the MT of the Fourth Song constitutes a stronger echo in Rom 8:3, because it says that the Servant is made a "guilt offering" (אשׁם). The atoning significance of the Hebrew version of Isa 53 is recognized by, for example, Sapp, "Isaiah 53," 188–89; Goldingay, *Isaiah*, 306–8. But there are those who are keen to deny all cultic overtones even in the Hebrew text. For example, Janowski, "He Bore Our Sins," 68–69, says that the cultic vocabulary is lacking in Isa 53:10 and indeed the rest of 52:13—53:12. He draws a distinction between חטאת and אשׁם, saying that the latter does not refer to trespass or transgression. Instead, it only refers to the consequence of transgression. As a result, the statement in Isa 53:10 is about the surrender of life as a means of "wiping out guilt." The Servant's role is, therefore, about "taking over the consequences of *others' actions*." Also, Hofius, "Fourth Servant Song," 168–75, makes a distinction between "exclusive place-taking" and "inclusive place-taking. The former refers to the "substitution or transference of guilt," and is about a taking of another's place that exempts or excludes the other party. The latter, however, is about Christ's taking the place of others in a way that still includes them as persons, thus "affecting their very being" (163). In my view, Isa 53:10 MT *supports* Paul's view on Christ's death, but the view of the MT does not have to be exactly the same as Paul's view. There is a sense of sacrificial death in Rom 8:3, but the way it works in Christ needs a comprehensive view of all the data in Paul's letter. Paul's use of περὶ ἁμαρτίας does not have to be narrowed down to one particular view of justification.

Second, I argued previously that the expression ἐν ὁμοιώματι σαρκὸς ἁμαρτίας in Rom 8:3 speaks of Christ's identification with humanity, sharing humans' frailty and vulnerability, though without sin. Also, implicit in 8:3 is that Christ died a humiliating death on the Roman cross.[138] Christ's experience with human frailty and humiliation is similar to that of the Servant in the Fourth Servant Song. The Servant grew up as a human child, and is familiar with pain, sickness, calamity, oppression, and humiliation (52:14; 53:2–5, 8). In fact, the First and Third Servant Songs also speak of the Servant's gentleness, innocence and suffering (42:3; 50:6).

With these two parallels, the audience is invited to consider Christ as a gentle innocent Servant-figure, who has given up his life for the sins of others. Again, the Servant is understood christologically.

The Fourth Servant Song and Rom 8:31–34

We have seen evidence that the Fourth Servant Song is echoed when the Son of God is mentioned in Rom 5:10 and 8:3. The only two remaining references to the Son in 5:1—8:39 are in 8:29 and 8:32.[139] Given the likelihood that the Fourth Song has been evoked in the two previous references to the Son, one wonders whether there are points of contact between 8:31–34 and the Song for the latter to be evoked?[140] In the following I will suggest that there are correspondences between the Song and Rom 8:32, 34.

The verb παραδίδωμι is found in both Rom 8:32 and Isa 53:6, 12. In the exegesis on 8:32 above I argued that the term refers to God's handing over his Son so as to defeat the cosmic powers of sin and death. That is, God's act of handing over his Son is more than a simple sacrificial act of love,[141] but also his way of releasing humans from sin's dominion. This corresponds to the handing over of the Servant for people's sins in Isa 53:6, 12.[142] The death

138. Of course this cannot be overplayed either, because it is not explicitly mentioned in the text of Rom 8:3.

139. I am referring to the four instances in Rom 5–8 where the υἱός denotes the Son of God.

140. The echo of the Fourth Servant Song in Rom 8:31–34 is rarely recognized by scholars. For instance. Shum, *Paul's Use*, 200, thinks that the echo of Isa 53:6 in Rom 8:32 is verbal only; and he does not mention the echo to Isa 53:12 in Rom 8:34. But see the brief treatment by Kleinknecht, *Der leidende Gerechtfertigte*, 344, 354, and the *very short* discussion by Wilk, *Die Bedeutung des Jesajabuches*, 398–99.

141. This is of course in itself true and important in the argument of the letter.

142. In fact, Isa 53:6 says that the Lord has handed the Servant over to those who are like sheep that "have been deceived/gone astray" (ἐπλανήθημεν). This remarkably sounds like the serpent's scheme of deceiving the first humans in Gen 3, upon which

of Christ is mentioned in Rom 8:34, which corresponds to the death of the Servant in Isa 53:8, 9, 12. Once again Christ and the Servant share a similar storyline, and once again there are three players, namely, God, the Son/the Servant, and those he died for. In Rom 8:31–34 we see God handing over his Son to die for humanity so that they may be set free from sin's bondage. In the Song God has handed over the Servant so that he may bear the sins of many. It is true that we do not find an exact match between the Servant in the Song and Christ in the letter in terms of the details of their life pattern. But there are parallels between their core stories. That is, they both suffer as innocent sufferers for the sake of others.

The Third Servant Song and Rom 8:31–34[143]

So far our analysis has found correspondences between the *Fourth* Servant Song and Romans, and that *Christ* is the Servant-figure. In the following we will see links between the *Third* Servant Song (Isa 50:4–11) and Rom 8:31–34,[144] and that it is the life pattern of believers that corresponds to that of the Servant.[145] I will suggest that the Servant plays a dual role in Rom 8:31–34, for his life is consistent with both Christ and his followers.

For the sake of easy referencing in our discussion, I list the most relevant verses of the Song here.

Isaiah 50:7 καὶ **κύριος βοηθός μου** ἐγενήθη, διὰ τοῦτο οὐκ ἐνετράπην, ἀλλὰ ἔθηκα τὸ πρόσωπόν μου ὡς στερεὰν πέτραν καὶ ἔγνων ὅτι **οὐ μὴ αἰσχυνθῶ**.

Isaiah 50:8 ὅτι ἐγγίζει **ὁ δικαιώσας** με **τίς** ὁ **κρινόμενός** μοι; ἀντιστήτω μοι ἅμα καὶ **τίς** ὁ **κρινόμενός** μοι; ἐγγισάτω μοι.

---

sin and death entered the cosmos and reign over Adamic humanity.

143. Significant discussions on the use of the Third Servant Song in Rom 8:31–34 can be found in Shum, *Paul's Use*, 200–2, and Seifrid, "Romans," 633–37; Wilk, *Die Bedeutung des Jesajabuches*, 280–84, 285–86.

144. The differences between the MT and the LXX seem to be minor in the third Servant Song. See Appendix H for my translations of Isa 50:8, 9 for easy comparison between the MT and LXX.

145. Commentators often recognize the possible links to the third Servant Song, but its significance is not emphasized. Even though Dunn, *Romans 1–8*, 503, says that it is "highly likely" that in Rom 8:33 Paul "echoes (deliberately or unconsciously)" Isa 53:8, he does not elaborate on its significance. Similarly, Byrne, *Romans*, 276, says, "The formulation appears to owe a good deal to a passage towards the end of the Third Servant Song (Isa 50:8–9a)." But Byrne does not elaborate further. Although Seifrid, "Romans," 633–36, mentions the Servant Song quite often, he does not elaborate as much as our discussion here. Cf. Witherington, *Romans*, 232; Jewett, *Romans*, 541.

Isaiah 50:9 ἰδοὺ **κύριος βοηθεῖ μοι·** τίς κακώσει με; ἰδοὺ πάντες
ὑμεῖς ὡς ἱμάτιον παλαιωθήσεσθε, καὶ ὡς σὴς καταφάγεται ὑμᾶς.

The Third Song and Rom 8:31–34 share the repeated use of τίς (Isa
50:8, 9, 10; Rom 8:31, 33, 34) and hence similar rhetorical strategies. They
also share the use of the verb δικαιόω (Isa 50:8; Rom 8:33). And the closely
related terms ἐγκαλέω, κατακρίνω, and κρίνω can be found in both texts
(Rom 8:31, 33, 34; Isa 50:8x2).[146] The shared vocabulary and rhetorical
strategy invite the audience to consider the Third Servant Song as an interpretive partner of the letter. Isaiah 50:6–7 lists the sufferings that the Servant
endures, such as scourges, blows on the cheeks, and the shame of spitting.
But in all these the Servant is not disobedient or rebellious (50:5). Since
the Servant has suffered unjustly, the Lord comes to his aid and because
of that he will not be put to shame (50:7). Importantly, the Lord vindicates
(δικαιόω) the Servant, and consequently no accusations can be made against
him (50:8–9). It is on the basis of the Servant's innocence and God's vindication that the rhetorical questions are asked. Who is the one who judges me
(53:8)? And who will harm me, since the Lord helps me (53:9)?

Likewise, as our exegesis above has shown, Rom 8:31–34 implies that
believers are righteous sufferers, for their sufferings are part and parcel of
their vocation to participate in Christ. They endure hardships for no fault
of their own. In fact, the slaves and former war-captives among the audience would probably have experienced scourges and the shame of being
hit or spat on, like the Servant. Thus, the rhetorical questions function as
affirmation of their innocent suffering and their fidelity to God. Who is to
condemn? If God is for them, who can be against them?

In other words, the Servant and those who are in Christ share similar
life patterns. Both are familiar with pain and sorrow, and their suffering is
not because of God's punishment in accordance with the principle of retributive justice. Indeed, they are both righteous sufferers. God is on their
side and no-one can judge or condemn them. In fact, God vindicates them.
It should be noted that, unlike the Fourth Servant Song, the Third Song does
not speak of the Servant being handed over for the sins of others. Likewise,
believers in Romans are not handed over for the sins of others. In
sum, for the audience, the Third Servant Song provides an extra resource
to assure them that they are indeed walking in God's purpose. Just like the
Servant, they are suffering because of their fidelity to God and that God will

---

146. Thus, Shum, *Paul's Use*, 201, says that we can claim that there is "an intertextual
link" between Rom 8:31–34 and Isa 50:8–9. Note also the "condemn" (ירשׁיע) in Isa 50:9
MT. Cf. Kleinknecht, *Der leidende Gerechtfertigte*, 343, 354, who says that the θεὸς ὁ
δικαιῶν in Rom 8:33 recalls Isa 50:8 (354).

vindicate them. The basis for their vocation is not that they will bear the sins of others, but that Christ has already broken the power of sin.

What should be noted at this point is how the Third and Fourth Servant Songs are both evoked in Rom 8:31–34. I suggest that together they provide the audience with a sense of their shared identity with Christ. Christ's life is patterned after the Servant, and so are the lives of believers. Hence, the believers' life pattern coheres with that of Christ via the Servant Songs. At the same time, Rom 8:14–17 has already explicated the merged identities between Christ and believers. And 8:18–30 has been an extended elaboration of what it means to participate in the suffering and glory of Christ. In light of these, the Servant Songs, I propose, would provide another layer of resource for the audience to understand their calling. That is, as *children of God*, their shared identity and life pattern with *the Son of God* have much to do with their shared vocation of suffering as righteous sufferers.

The difference between Christ and believers is that Christ was handed over to defeat the reign of sin and free humanity from its bondage, and believers are not. Instead, the believers' suffering is about their fidelity to God and their rule over creation as his renewed image-bearers. In all these, though, the Servant functions as a scriptural pattern of righteous suffering, a pattern that allows the audience to understand their own suffering and that of Christ's, as well as how they may share in his suffering.

The Fourth Servant Song and the Citation of Ps 44:22 in Rom 8:36

Our discussion has shown that there is considerable evidence of the Fourth Servant Song being evoked in the first and last chapters of Rom 5–8. On three occasions, namely, 5:1–21; 8:3; and most recently 8:31–34, Christ is the Servant-figure who acted as the righteous sufferer to defeat sin and death. We have also seen that the Third Servant Song is likely to have been evoked in 8:31–34, where believers are the Servant-figure. They suffer not because of their sins but their faithfulness. What is emerging is that the Servant has become a metonym (a substitute representative name) that represents Christ as well as believers by way of the various characteristics of the Servant in the Servant Songs. We may summarize the echoes of the Servant in our findings as below.

Romans passage	Isaianic Servant Song	The Servant corresponds to	Pattern of the Servant
5:1–21	Fourth Song	Christ	Was handed over to death because of the sins of others
8:3	Fourth Song	Christ	Gentle, humble, and righteous sufferer Was handed over to death because of the sins of others
8:31–34	Fourth Song	Christ	Was handed over to death because of the sins of others
8:31–34	Third Song	Believers	Suffers righteously because of fidelity God vindicates the Servant

In the following I will propose that the *Fourth* Servant Song is evoked in Rom 8:36 via Ps 44:22,[147] and this time it is the *believers* whose life pattern resembles that of the Servant. This will further enhance the sense of shared identity between Christ and believers.

As discussed, the citation of Ps 44:22 in Rom 8:36 places the suffering of believers in the category of innocent suffering. Also, the ἕνεκεν σοῦ in the emphatic position conveys the fact that believers' sufferings are christocentric. *For the sake of Christ,* they are like sheep destined for slaughter. It is this imagery that invites the audience to consider the Fourth Servant Song, where Isa 53:7 speaks of the Servant being led to slaughter.[148] In fact, the second half of the citation is very close to Isa 53:7b, with three matching key terms and the sheep-to-slaughter imagery.

Romans 8:36b ἐλογίσθημεν ὡς πρόβατα σφαγῆς

Psalm 43:23 LXX ἐλογίσθημεν ὡς πρόβατα σφαγῆς

Isaiah 53:7b LXX ὡς πρόβατον ἐπὶ σφαγὴν ἤχθη

147. The echoes of Isa 53:7 in Rom 8:36 deserve more attention than it is given. For example, in his detailed commentary, Jewett, *Romans*, 548, does not mention Isa 53:7 at all. Neither does Shum, *Paul's Use*, 201–2, in his otherwise superb study. Seifrid, "Romans," 636–37, only mentions it in passing, although he detects multiple echoes to the Servant Songs in Rom 8. Likewise, Dunn, *Romans 1–8*, 505–6, only mentions it briefly. Indeed, the latest commentaries by Kruse, *Romans*, 363, and Hultgren, *Romans*, 340, do not mention it at all.

148. Interestingly, Gorman, *Cruciformity*, 307–10, discusses Ps 44 and the Fourth Servant Song together when he examines the Jewish notion that God vindicates the persecuted righteous. Gorman notes that Rom 8:36 cites Ps 44:22, but does not elaborate on the connection with the Song.

The compact intertextual links between the three texts suggest that an echo of the Servant is very probable. Interestingly, another Scripture that shares a similar imagery of sheep being led to slaughter is found in Jer 11:19a LXX. But both Romans and Isaiah differ from Jeremiah in terms of vocabulary and sentence construction.[149] This means that it is more likely that the letter points to the Isaianic text and not Jeremiah.[150] The possibility of the evocation of the Song is also increased by the shared theme of innocent suffering between Ps 44, the Fourth Servant Song, and Rom 8:31–36, a theme that the sheep-to-slaughter imagery signifies.

In addition, the echo to the Song is greatly enhanced by the many possible echoes to the Servant throughout Rom 5–8. The frequent pointers to the Servant in the letter means that when the imagery of sheep-to-slaughter is read, the audience would be prompted to consider such a well-known Scripture among earliest Christians. Also, although so far the Fourth Song has been applied to Christ himself in the echoes, the audience has just been invited to see themselves as the Servant in 8:31–34 (via the Third Song). This, combined with the heightened emotion aroused by the affliction-list in the verse before, means that Isa 53:7 provides a fitting scriptural resource for the audience to identify with in their present sufferings. The combined effects of all these is that they find themselves sharing not just the sentiment of the psalmist but also the life pattern of the Servant. And in doing so, they are participating in Christ, because Christ's suffering is also patterned after that of the Servant.

It should be noted that the echo of the Fourth Song does not mean that there are substantial parallels between the life of believers and that of the Servant in this particular Song. Believers were not handed over for the sake of the lawless like the Servant, for example. Rather, as our discussion above suggests, the point of the citation is that believers' sufferings are for the sake of Christ and that they are the lot of the suffering righteous. In other words, the life pattern of believers and that of the Servant converge on one simple storyline, namely, that they suffer severely as innocent sufferers because of their fidelity to Christ/YHWH. We may now complete our table of the echoes of the Servant in Rom 5–8 as below (by adding a new row at the bottom of the last table).

---

149. Jeremiah 11:19a LXX: ὡς ἀρνίον ἄκακον ἀγόμενον τοῦ θύεσθαι (ἀρνίον, not πρόβατον; the verb θύω, not σφαγή). Thus, it is somewhat surprising that Grieb, *Story*, 82, mentions (very briefly) Jer 11:19 but not Isa 53:7.

150. Also, interestingly, Ps 44:23 MT uses a different word for "sheep" (צאן) from that in Isa 53:7 MT (שׂה). This suggests that the citation of the LXX serves as a vehicle to point the audience to Isa 53:7 LXX.

Romans passage	Isaianic Servant Song	The Servant corresponds to	Life pattern of the Servant
5:1–21	Fourth Song	Christ	Was handed over to death because of the sins of others
8:3	Fourth Song	Christ	Gentle, humble and innocent sufferer Was handed over to death because of the sins of others
8:31–34	Fourth Song	Christ	Was handed over to death because of the sins of others
8:31–34	Third Song	Believers	Suffers righteously because of fidelity to God God vindicates the Servant
8:36	Fourth Song	Believers	Suffers severely as innocent sheep because of fidelity to YHWH

The possible evocation of the Fourth Servant Song assists the audience to understand their suffering in three significant ways. First, it speaks of a different type of innocent suffering from that of Ps 44. The focus of the psalmist is that the people's suffering is undeserved and hence protest is warranted. The Servant, however, does not need to protest, even though his suffering is also undeserved. Rather, the Servant is vindicated because he willingly suffers. This view of suffering fits in well with the situation of believers, whose present afflictions are an integral part of their faithful participation in Christ in anticipation of God's vindication at the resurrection.

Second, since Christ is also the Servant-figure throughout Rom 5–8, once again the Servant plays a dual role. That is, the Servant is simultaneously applied to Christ and believers. Although what I am suggesting here is somewhat tentative, I do think that the dual-echo can take place in several ways. At one level, regardless of whether Christ is understood as the Servant in 8:36, the fact that Christ has been the Servant in Rom 5–8 and that the Servant is now applied to believers in 8:36 means that a dual-echo is happening within the context of 8:31–39. At another level, since the *Fourth* Servant Song is consistently echoed in Rom 5–8 to refer to Christ, the lamb in 8:36 may invoke the image of Christ being the Servant in the *Fourth* Song. Of course, the θανατούμεθα in 8:36 means that believers are in view. But what is inferred here seems to be that the innocent suffering of believers is like that of Christ *the* Servant. At yet another level, as mentioned before, the imagery of a sheep being led to slaughter often refers to an offering to God in Israel's Scripture. This in turn points to the sacrificial overtones signified by the περὶ ἁμαρτίας in Rom 8:3 (regardless of how or whether the Servant Song is evoked there). In light of this, although the "sheep" (note the plural πρόβατα) in 8:36 refers to believers, the audience might be reminded of Christ being the Servant-lamb. In view of this matrix of imageries and intertextual links, the audience is invited to see their lives in light of the life pattern of the Servant, while simultaneously viewing Christ as the suffering Servant. We may even say that Christ is *the* Suffering Servant, and by participating in him, believers themselves constitute a suffering community. In this way, their present sufferings in Christ take on a rich meaning and purpose, for they are the visible signs of their shared identity with the Son of God. It is because of this that *in their sufferings* they emerge as super-victors through him who loves them.

Third, the fact that the life pattern of the Servant is echoed by the life of both Christ and believers affirms what we have found in Rom 8:14–17 and 8:18–30 regarding the merged identities of Christ and the children of God. The Isaianic Servant helps believers to understand their identity and the purpose of their suffering. Just as Christ *the* righteous sufferer suffered in the manner of the Suffering Servant, so do those whose vocation is to identify with him and suffer in the way that the Servant does. Just as the Servant is vindicated because of his fidelity, so was Christ vindicated at his resurrection. In the same manner, believers will be vindicated at their resurrection.

As we finish our analysis of the possible echo to the Servant in Rom 8:36, we should not forget the role of the citation in Rom 8:36, which is to set the stage for the celebratory triumphal statement in 8:37. If Christ is *the* righteous sufferer who faithfully died to accomplish God's triumph over evil, then those who participate in him also partake in that triumph as they faithfully fulfill their vocation in Christ.

CONCLUSION

Romans 8:31–39 is the second part of the climactic conclusion to both 8:1–39 and 5:1—8:39. The rhetorical questions in 8:31–34, 35 pave the way for the affirmation in vv. 35–39 that nothing can separate believers from God's love, for their suffering is not the result of God's punishment according to the convention of retributive justice. The affliction-list in 8:35 heightens emotion among the audience as they find themselves identifying with the pain and trials in the list. The heightened emotion is met with the imagery of sheep destined to slaughter in 8:36, which highlights the fact that they are innocent sufferers. With a christological and eschatological reading of Ps 44:22 in Rom 8:36, the citation functions as an authoritative text that places believers' affliction squarely in the category of the suffering of the righteous. This is important for an audience familiar with hardship and pain. They need to be sure that their affliction is indeed part of their vocation and purpose (rather than God's punishment) and that their suffering is worthwhile. There is profound value in suffering because they suffer for the sake of Christ, with the purpose of participating in God's project of transforming the cosmos.

The fact that they suffer for Christ's sake means that they are identifying with *his* suffering (according to 8:14–17). As they do so, they find themselves displaying God's glory and are indeed participants of God's triumph over evil. Their shared identity with Christ is not only about their destiny to reign with God, but also the partaking of his triumph. This is why in all sufferings—including everything in the affliction-list—they "triumph with surpassing victory" (ὑπερνικάω) through the God who loves them (8:37). The pericope finishes with the assurance that nothing, not even cosmic forces, can dissociate them from the love of God. All of these are, of course, based on the fact that God did not spare his own Son but handed him over in order to destroy the powers of evil through Christ's death and resurrection (8:32, 34). In light of these, the letter provides the audience with an understanding of suffering that is wide in scope and rich in its purpose, for their affliction is an integral part of *God's* triumph, which includes the defeat of all evils in the cosmos.

At the same time the Servant Songs may be evoked through the cumulative signposts to the Servant in Rom 5–8. The evocation would serve to assure the audience that their suffering is indeed part and parcel of their shared identity with Christ. Just like the Servant, the audience suffers as righteous sufferers, modeling after Christ who is *the* Servant and *the* righteous sufferer. Finally, for the audience in imperial Rome, the notion of a super-victory would of course be rather radical. The supreme victor in Rome was Caesar, and he was victorious because it was perceived that the gods were on his side. But the letter claims a victory that is far-reaching in scope: partaking in God's cosmic victory. What is even more radical is that the victory of believers hinges on their faithful identification with Christ's suffering. That is, they are victorious because they are willing to suffer. Or to put it simply, they win by losing.

8

Overall Conclusion

A THEOLOGY OF SUFFERING

We started our inquiry with a socio-historical study and painted a general picture of the types of suffering the audience experienced in first-century Rome. We found that the audience was familiar with many forms of socioeconomic hardship and religio-political injustice. In our exegesis we asked how this audience would have understood Rom 5–8. We studied the pericopes in Rom 5 and 8 in detail, since these two chapters contain the most substantial references to suffering. We paid special attention to the rhetorical strategy of these texts. We also constructed the narratives that are embedded in the texts. We examined the citation of Ps 44:22 in Rom 8:36 closely, and explored other possible evocations of Israel's Scripture. We found that the primordial accounts in Genesis would most likely be evoked in Rom 5–8, which, in turn, would be a valuable resource for the audience. We also proposed that the Isaianic Servant Songs would have been evoked, which could be another significant resource for the audience. Throughout our exegesis we attempted to discover how the audience would have construed their theology of suffering—that is, their perspective of life and suffering developed as a result of interacting with the letter—and our findings were summarized at the end of our exegesis of each pericope.[1] Now it is

---

1. As mentioned in ch. 1, we do not use the term "theology" to denote a systematic account of faith and belief. Rather, "theology of suffering" refers to the audience's perspective on suffering in light of what they hear from the letter and their lived experience of pain and affliction.

time to put all our findings together and delineate a theology of suffering accordingly. The following is an outline of this theology.

First, suffering is the vocation of believers and is an integral part of God's purpose for humanity and creation. It does not mean that suffering is pleasant or in itself good. Rather, it means that suffering has a purpose, and that purpose is to share in Christ's glory. Suffering is part and parcel of God's predetermined plan to restore humanity and renew creation. As believers suffer, they are being transformed so that they may bear Christ's image and display God's glory.

Second, since suffering is the vocation of God's children, it defies the principle of retributive justice. Their suffering is not the result of God's punishment. Rather, suffering has educative value—and far more! The suffering of Christ-followers is like that of the suffering righteous, and is a visible sign of their faithfulness to God. They suffer with the assured hope that they will one day be vindicated, and that they will receive the cosmos as their inheritance. The ultimate purpose of their suffering is that they will be God's vice-regents, reigning over the cosmos as members of his royal family.

Third, the theology of suffering in Rom 5–8 is thoroughly christological and eschatological. Believers suffer *with* Christ, and they will be glorified *with* him. Just as Christ identified with humanity, and just as he suffered and died so as to break the powers of sin and death, so do believers identify with Christ and share in his suffering. Also, believers are God's children because they are led by the eschatological Spirit. As God's children, they are partakers of his eschatological blessings, and because of that they are heirs of God. Indeed, they are co-heirs with Christ, and precisely because of that, they are to suffer with him. The audience, then, are members of God's eschatological community, awaiting their resurrection and the consummation of their glorification.

Fourth, suffering is an integral part of participating in God's triumph. The ultimate cause of suffering is the powers of sin and death. These are evil forces that contend against God's purpose for humanity and creation. But God has triumphed over evil by sending his Son to die for humanity. By identifying with the Son's suffering and glory, the children of God also participate in his triumph. Thus, the purpose of their suffering has the widest scope and the most profound meaning, for their affliction and pain are part and parcel of God's triumph over evil.

Finally, the Scriptures bear witness to this theology. The eschatological character of the theology is affirmed by Jer 30–33 and Ezek 34–37, which anticipate God's deliverance and the outpouring of the Spirit. The primordial accounts in Genesis provide the underlying narrative framework for Adamic humanity and the entry of sin and death into the cosmos. Genesis, then, tells the audience why there are evil forces in the world, which cause suffering and pain for human beings. Genesis also provides the narrative framework behind the Christ-story and that of the new humanity in Christ, for the stories of Christ and the new people of God bear a similar pattern to the Adamic story, except that the events take place in reverse order. Both the story of Christ and that of his followers involve a call to faithful suffering to fulfill God's purpose. In addition, by providing an apt depiction of the suffering righteous, the Isaianic Servant Songs assist the audience to see Christ as *the* righteous sufferer, as well as the fact that believers are fellow partakers of righteous suffering.

CONCLUDING REFLECTIONS

I set out to ask how an audience familiar with socioeconomic hardship and religio-political injustice might have understood Rom 5 and 8. Arguably Paul would have known the daily reality faced by his audience in Rome and hence the impact of his letter on the Christ-followers in the house churches. I hope the above findings will make a contribution to Pauline scholarship. But I am aware that our study also has significant implications to the followers of Jesus today. Many in the non-western world are suffering from socioeconomic hardship. Indeed, not a few westerners live below the poverty line. Mission studies tell us that urban poverty is rapidly becoming a global issue, given the fast urbanization process around the world, and the associated widening gap between the rich and the poor. Poor living conditions, large numbers of migrant workers, and unjust socioeconomic systems are found in today's cities, not unlike what happened in ancient Rome. There are multiethnic impoverished urban neighborhoods in both western and non-western countries, just as there were in the Roman Empire. The present-day issue of human trafficking (recruitment and transportation of persons by means of threat or coercion) is not dissimilar to slavery in ancient Rome. If the findings in this book are correct, then the Jesus-followers in today's urban world will find Romans remarkably relevant and comforting. I hope this book can be a resource for them.

Appendix A

Key Greek Terms in Romans

THERE ARE THREE TABLES in this appendix. They concern the terminology of suffering in Romans, the distribution of key Greek terms across the letter, and the key words that denote filial relationship and inheritance.

TERMS RELATED TO SUFFERING

Terms clearly related to suffering	References	Terms related to suffering given the context of the passage	References
θλῖψις	2:9; 5:3 x2; 8:35; 12:12	ματαιότης	8:20
στενοχωρία	2:9; 8:35	ἀσθένεια	8:25
πάθημα	7:5; 8:18	σφαγή	8:36
συμπάσχω	8:17	κακός (Not all occurrences in Romans are counted. Only those referred to suffering are.)	12:17 x2; 12:21 x2
συστενάζω	8:22	ὀνειδισμός	15:3
συνωδίνω	8:22	θάνατος, ζωή, ἄγγελοι, ἀρχαί, ἐνεστῶτα, μέλλοντα, δυνάμεις, ὕψωμα, βάθος, "τις κτίσις ἑτέρα" (The ten items that cannot separate believers from Christ's love.)	8:38–39
στενάζω	8:23		
στεναγμός	8:26		
διωγμός	8:35		
λιμός	8:35		
γυμνότης	8:35		
κίνδυνος	8:35		

μάχαιρα	8:35		
λύπη	9:2		
Total number of occurrences	20 (16 in Rom 5–8)	Total number of occurrences	18 (13 in Rom 5–8)
Note that the δικ-words appear fifty-five times in Romans.			

OCCURRENCES OF KEY TERMS IN DIFFERENT SECTIONS OF ROMANS

	Occurrence in Rom 1–4	Occurrence in Rom 5–8	Occurrence in Rom 9–11	Occurrence in Rom 12–15	Occurrence in Rom 16
ζωή, ζάω	2	24	3	8	0
ἐλπίς, ελπιζω	2	9	0	6	0
λύπη, θλῖψις, στενοχωρία, διωγμός, λιμός, γυμνότης, κίνδυνος, μάχαιρα, πάθημα, συνωδίνω, συμπάσχω, στενάζω, στεναγμός, συστενάζω (words related to suffering and groaning)	2	16	1	2	0
θανατόω, θάνατος, νεκροω, νεκρός, νεκρωσις	5	34	3	1	0
ἁμαρτάνω, ἁμαρτία, ἁμάρτημα	8	46	1	1	0
βασιλεύω, κυριεύω	0	9	0	1	0

δοῦλος, δότης, δουλεία, δουλοω	1	10	0	0	0
ἐλεύθερος, ἐλευθερία, ἐλευθερόω	0	7	0	0	0
σῴζω, σωτηρία	1	3	8	1	0
αἷμα	2	1	0	0	0
ὀργή	6	3	2	3	0
δοξάζω, δόξα	7	5	5	3	1
πίστις, πιστεύω	34	3	14	10	1
δικαιοσύνη, δικαίωμα, δικαιόω, δικαίωσις	26	18	10	1	0
Χριστός	8	24	7	17	9
Ἀδάμ	0	2	0	0	0
εἷς to denote Adam or his act	0	About 12 (in 6 verses in 5:12–21)	0	0	0
Ἕλλην, ἔθνος, Ἰουδαῖος	22	0	12	10	2
πνεῦμα	3	23	2	6	0
ἀγαπάω, ἀγάπη	0	6	2	8	0

TERMS RELATED TO FILIAL RELATIONSHIP AND INHERITANCE

Greek term	Filial relationship highlighted by the Greek term	Number (and places) of occurrences in Rom 1–4	Number (and places) of occurrences in Rom 5–8	Number (and places) of occurrences in Rom 9–11	Number (and places) of occurrences in Rom 12–16
υἱός	*Christ as God's Son*	3 (1:3, 4, 9)	4 (5:10; 8:3, 29, 32)		
τέκνον/υἱός	*Christ-followers as God's children*		5 (8:14, 16, 17; 19, 21)		
τέκνον/υἱός	Israel as children of Abraham, the patriarchs, or God			7 (9:7, 8 [x3], 9, 26, 27)	
πατήρ	*God as Father of Christ*		1 (6:4)		
πατήρ (in "αββα ὁ πατήρ")	*God as Father of Christ-followers*		1 (8:15)		
πατήρ	As part of the confessional statement "our father" or "father of our Lord Jesus Christ"	1 (1:7)			1 (15:6)
πατήρ	Abraham/Isaac as father	5 (4:11, 12, 16, 17, 18)		1 (9:10)	
πατήρ	Israel's patriarchs			2 (9:5; 11:28)	1 (15:8)
κληρονόμος	Abraham and/or his descendants as heir/heirs	2 (4:13, 14)			

συγκληρονόμος	Christ as heir of God (as in being "co-heirs" of God)		1 (8:17)		
κληρονόμος, συγκληρονόμος	Christ-followers as heirs/co-heirs of God		3 (8:17)		
πρωτότοκος	Christ as firstborn		1 (8:29)		
υἱοθεσία	In reference to Christ-followers		2 (8:15, 23)		
υἱοθεσία	In reference to Israel			1 (9:4)	

Appendix B

Additional Information Regarding the Social Location of the Audience in Rome

SPACE LIMITATIONS DISALLOW US from discussing every matter in Chapter 2 (concerning the social location of the audience in Rome) in detail. This appendix serves to provide further information about life in ancient Rome.

SOCIAL LOCATION OF CERTAIN PEOPLE IN ROM 16

There have been scholarly discussions about the economic situation of a number of the people mentioned in Rom 16. Unfortunately they do not provide a lot of information about the socioeconomic situation of Paul's audience in Rome. Although Pheobe, Gaius, and Erastus (16:1–2, 23) might be relatively well-to-do, they did not live in Rome. At any rate, Longenecker and Friesen think that it is unlikely that any of them belonged to E1–E3 in Longenecker's economic scale in Chapter 2.[1] There are discussions around whether Prisca and Aquila (16:3–4) were relatively well-to-do. But again it is unlikely that they belonged to the elite class (E1–E3). The exact economic situation of the couple is subject to debate, although it may be somewhere between E4 and E6, depending on whether one thinks that their work was profitable.[2]

---

1. See Longenecker, *Remember*, 236–44; Friesen, "Poverty," 354–55.

2. See the diverse opinions of Lampe, *From Paul*, 191–95; Longenecker, *Remember*, 246–49; Friesen, "Poverty," 352–54; and Oakes, "Methodological," 33–34.

SOCIAL DIVISIONS

Gender inequality was another example of social distinction.[3] The generally low social status of women meant that they could potentially be exploited. It is true that, according to Garnsey and Saller, "Roman women enjoyed a legal independence in marriage that is quite remarkable by comparison with the position of women in many other traditional agrarian societies."[4] But it should be noted that this only applied to Roman citizens. From the second-century BCE a large portion of Rome's population were non-Romans. Indeed, Jeffers argues that many early Christ-followers were not citizens,[5] and hence most of their female members would not benefit from Roman law.[6] As Kroeger says, "Roman women were bound throughout their lives to a male protector or tutor . . . Ultimate power, known as *patria potestas*, lay in the hands of the family's father or grandfather."[7]

THE NUMBER OF PEOPLE KILLED OR ENSLAVED BY ROME

The Romans killed and enslaved tens of thousands of war-captives in their military campaigns. For example, in 177 BCE, 80,000 were killed or enslaved in Sardinia; in 167 BCE 150,000 were enslaved from Greece (Livy 45.34.5); and Julius Caesar took 53,000 of the Aduatuci in 57 BCE. Even though these figures were not necessarily accurately recorded, they do give us a indication of the scale of slavery that took place following Roman conquest.

ECONOMIC SITUATION OF THE JEWS IN ROME

There is evidence that there were at least eleven synagogues in Rome, out of which seven were in Transtiberinum, which was one of the economically

---

3. It is impossible to overstate the injustice caused by gender inequality. In fact, often gender and economic inequalities combined to cause extensive injustice.

4. Garnsey and Saller, *Roman Empire*, 131; cf. Kroeger, "Women," 1277.

5. According to Jeffers, *Conflicts*, 7, "most Roman Christians were freeborn aliens, slaves, or citizens of slave origin."

6. It is also true that certain opportunities for upward mobility existed for women in Roman cities, and that inscriptions show that some non-elite females were engaged in manufacture and commerce. But it must be noted that overall Greco-Roman culture regarded women as incapable of achieving the same level of intellectual ability as men. See Jeffers, *Greco-Roman*, 249–50.

7. Kroeger, "Women," 1277.

depressed areas in Rome.[8] Lampe thinks that people in Trastevere were among those with the lowest social status. It was extremely densely populated, with knackers and tanner operations spreading "a penetrating odor."[9] Using evidence from literary sources and inscriptions, Lampe proposes several "Jewish quarters" in Rome, where the Jews were likely to have lived. In particular, he affirms that there were Jewish settlements in Trastevere, between the Porta Collina, and the Porta Esquilina, and before the Porta Capena.[10] Also, using Rom 16 as his primary data, Lampe suggests that Jewish followers of Jesus in Rome consisted of about 15 percent of the house churches.[11] It is hard to know how reliable this estimate is, but it indicates that there was a minority group of Jews in the Roman congregations. And, like other Jews in Rome, they would be quite poor.

THE SLAVE POPULATION IN ROME/THE EMPIRE

There are diverse views regarding the number of slaves in Rome and the Empire. On the one hand, Rupprecht thinks that up to 85 to 90 percent of the population of Rome and Peninsula Italy in the first and second centuries BCE were slaves or of slave origin.[12] On the other hand, others suggest a lower range of 16.6 to 20 percent (of enslaved, excluding ex-slaves).[13] And then according to Bartchy, about one third of the Roman Empire were enslaved, in addition to many more of slave origin.[14] Watson, however, estimates that one quarter of the population in the Empire were slaves, and within Rome itself it might have been 25 to 40 percent.[15] For our purposes, it should be safe to use Watson's figures, for they stand somewhere in the middle of all the estimates.

8. See Jewett, *Romans*, 57; Jeffers, *Conflicts*, 10.

9. Lampe, *From Paul*, 50–52.

10. Ibid., 38–40.

11. Lampe, "Roman Christian," 224–25.

12. Rupprecht, "Slave," 881.

13. See Harrill, "Slavery," 1126.

14. Bartchy, "Slave, Slavery," 1098.

15. Watson, "Roman," 1002.

WAS SLAVERY A FORM OF MASS EMPLOYMENT?

For some time since the 1970s, scholars tended to think of slavery in the Greco-Roman world as a benign form of mass employment.[16] According to this view, slaves could be better off than poor free persons because of their guaranteed employment. Also, it is claimed that many were willing to sell themselves into slavery in order to seek social security or even to climb the social ladder. One influential proponent of this positive view is Bartchy. But Byron highlights the limitations of Bartchy's approach, for he relies heavily on the Roman legal texts. First, the primary source for the study of Roman law, *Digest of Justinian*, was not published until 533 BCE, which can only provide a general—and inherently incomplete—picture of the legal situation of early Imperial Rome. Second, legal codes can only provide inexact knowledge about the actual social practice. Byron also cautions against an over-reliance on philosophical and literary works. These works were often written by and for members of the aristocracy. It is not certain that moral philosophers' teaching sympathetic to alleviating the plight of the enslaved truly represented actual public opinion. Nor is it clear that it influenced the way slaves were treated.[17] Seneca paints a picture of the life of slaves in *Epistulae morales* Letter 47, which is aptly summarized by Harrill, "Seneca condemns 'harsh' punishment of slaves as injurious to the master's character but sees no problem with more moderate regular disciplining of one's slaves."[18]

16. Byron, "Background," 116.

17. See Ibid., 119, 131–32.

18. Harrill, "Slavery," 1125. The whole letter is about the treatment of slaves. For instance, *Ep.* 47.11 says, "I do not wish to involve myself in too large a question, and to discuss the treatment of slaves, towards whom we Romans are excessively haughty, cruel, and insulting." But, as Harrill notes, Seneca's concern was more about his Stoic ideals against arrogant masters, rather than the inhuman slave system itself.

Appendix C

The Meaning of κτίσις in Rom 8:19–22

In Chapter 6 we outlined the most common options identified by scholars for the meaning of κτίσις in Rom 8:19–22, which are: (a) human and non-human creation together; (b) non-human creation plus humans who are not in Christ; (c) non-human creation only. We concluded that the best option is (c), and that it is the near consensus in recent scholarship. Here we will provide a more detailed discussion on the matter.

We outlined in Chapter 6 the common reasons for the validity of option (c). But two objections can be raised against them. First, the first person plural στενάζομεν in 8:23 does not imply a distinction between human and non-human creation. Rather, it simply means that believers join the rest of creation in its groaning. That is, believers are members of creation, which includes the entire created order (human and non-human).[1] Second, the point of 8:20 is not so much about the "free will" of κτίσις, but the subjection by God.[2] Hence, the οὐχ ἑκοῦσα is not so much about autonomous human will.

My preference for option (c) is guided by several factors. The first is the usage of κτίσις in Paul's day. As mentioned in Chapter 6, Edward Adams' monograph provides a comprehensive study of the term.[3] It can refer to "act of creation" (e.g., Ps Sol 8:7), "creature/created thing" (e.g., Tob 8:5, 15), "non-human creation" (e.g., Wis 2:6; 5:17; 16:24; 19:6), or "created universe" (embracing heaven, earth, all humans, and indeed all creatures;

---

1. Cf. Gaventa, "Neither," 276–77, who says that "no clear distinction is made; the eagerness with which all of creation longs for the apocalypse of God's children does not preclude God's children themselves from being part of that same eager expectation."

2. Gaventa, "Neither," 276. Cf. Hultgren, *Romans*, 321. See also Gaventa, *Our Mother Saint Paul*, 53–55.

3. Adams, *Constructing*, 77–81.

e.g., Sir 49:16; 3 *Macc.* 2:2, 7; Jdt 16:14).[4] "Act of creation" and "creature" quite clearly do not fit into the context of Rom 8:19–23. The remaining two usages only apply to options (a) and (c) above, for option (b) would have been a very unusual alternative given this linguistic background.[5] Indeed, out of the fifteen occurrences of κτίσις in the NT outside Rom 8:19–23,[6] one can hardly argue for a usage that denotes "non-believers and non-human creation."

The second factor we might consider is what the audience would have thought. I have argued that the συστενάζει καὶ συνωδίνει in Rom 8:22 paints a very gloomy picture of suffering, and that for the audience it would be hard for them to think that, for instance, the perpetrators of injustice or the elite would suffer that way. In light of this, the κτίσις does not include (at least) certain human beings.

In light of the above, option (c) is preferred. It is (primarily) because, on linguistic grounds, κτίσις should be understood as *either* non-human creation *or* an all-encompassing term that includes all humans and the rest of the created order. At the same time, at least some humans would not be perceived by the audience as groaning and laboring in pain. It is in view of this that I see the στενάζομεν in 8:23 as a significant (third) factor to consider, a factor that scholars do take seriously.[7] The οὐ μόνον ... ἀλλὰ καί construction at the beginning of 8:23 suggests that there is some distinction between what applies to the κτίσις and the "we" in the στενάζομεν in 8:23. This, together with the other two factors, make (c) the preferred option.

---

4. The non-Jewish standard use of κτίσις denotes "founding" or "foundation." This is hardly applicable in Rom 8:19–23. See Adams, *Constructing*, 77, 176n102.

5. Adams, *Constructing*, 176.

6. The κτίσις is found in Mark 10:6; 13:19; 16:15; Rom 1:20, 25; 8:19–22, 39; 2 Cor 5:17; Gal 6:15; Col 1:15, 23; Heb 4:13; 9:11; 1 Pet 2:13; 2 Pet 3:4; Rev 3:14.

7. Adams, *Constructing*, 176; Hahne, *Corruption*, 180.

Appendix D

Parallels between Rom 8:18–30
and Jewish Literature

THIS APPENDIX CONSISTS OF a brief survey of some parallels between Rom 8:18–30 and Jewish writings. The findings will serve to affirm the validity of our exegesis of the pericope.

THE ESCHATOLOGICAL HOPE IN SUFFERING

In Chapter 2 we discussed the hope of the suffering righteous in Jewish apocalyptic literature and martyrdom theology, such as Dan 7–12 and 2 Macc 6:1–7:42.[1] Daniel 7, for example, speaks of the hope of God's final triumph over evil powers, which are embedded in the political and social ruling power structures of Babylon and Persia in Daniel's day. God's people are to remain steadfast as they wait for their God to deliver and vindicate the faithful (7:18, 25). Likewise, at their martyrdoms Eleazar and the seven brothers believe that their suffering will bring to an end the wrath of the Almighty (2 Macc 7:39). Romans 8:18–23 seems to speak of a similar eschatological hope. The social and political contexts of Daniel and 2 Maccabees are similar to that of the audience, in that hardships are often caused by socio-political injustice. Our analysis of Rom 8:18–30 suggests that the letter shares the same belief that God will vindicate the faithful. This belief, in turn, constitutes the hope of glory in severe trials. In addition, the cosmic dimension of suffering in Daniel is similar to our finding that Romans

---

1. Another example is 1QH 9:1–11. Dunn, *Romans 1–8*, 468–69, makes a similar observation and says, "The comparison of the suffering of the righteous with the glorious vindication which will be theirs is well established in Jewish thought prior to the time of Paul (see particularly Dan 7:7:17–27; Wis Sol 2–5; 2 Macc 7; 1 *Enoch* 102–4 . . .)."

speaks of sin and death as cosmic forces—powers that are the ultimate cause of suffering.

A CREATION THAT IS UNSAFE

Our analysis regarding the creation in Rom 8:19–23 is supported by Jewish apocalyptic writings such as *4 Ezra* and *2 Baruch*.[2] God's good creation no longer sustains life and is not always safe for humans, although it is not inherently evil. As *4 Ezra* 7:11 says, "For I [God] made the world for their [Israel's] sake, and when Adam transgressed my statutes, what has been made was judged." The result is that there will be toils, dangers, and hardships in this world (7:12). Then verse 14 says, "Therefore unless the living pass through the difficult and vain experiences, they can never receive those things that have been reserved for them." A scene of the final judgment is depicted in 7:26–44, at which the resurrection will take place and the righteous will be rewarded accordingly. And later in 7:88, 97–99, it is said that those who have served the Most High faithfully will be glorified and their face will shine like the sun. Similarly, *2 Bar.* 56:1–16 speaks of a creation that is full of affliction, illness, and labor after Adam's transgression. And 54:13–19 talks about the reward of the coming glory for the righteous, and torment for the unrighteous at God's judgment. These texts do not say that creation became inherently evil after Adam's disobedience. But they do indicate that it is no longer safe for humans to dwell.[3] They also suggest that humans need to live through hardship in order to receive what God originally intended for them through his good creation.[4] Both *4 Ezra* and *2 Baruch* are colored by the destruction of Jerusalem in 70 BCE, and the authors exhort ethnic Israelites to live righteously among the nations,

2. See Hahne, *Corruption*, 97–168, for a very detailed analysis on *4 Ezra* and *2 Baruch*, and Jewish apocalyptic literature in general. See also an earlier study by Gowan, "Fall and Redemption," 89–103. Gowan is right that apocalyptic literature does not directly speak of a fallen world that is in need of redemption as suggested by Gen 3:17 (101). But at the same time Gowan finds that human rebellion and the destruction of the whole earth are sometimes connected (100), even though the material creation is not considered to be in and of itself evil at all. Gowan also suggests that the renewed creation is to "provide blessings for righteous human beings in the new age," and the "transformation of nature in the last days is . . . simply a part of God's rich, new blessings for the righteous, when his rule over the whole cosmos becomes manifest" (100).

3. Cf. Hahne, *Corruption*, 113–14, 129–30; Gowan, " Fall and Redemption," 95–96, 100; Moo, "Cosmic," 79.

4. Cf. Hahne, *Corruption*, 113. Note, however, that *4 Ezra* 7:26–44 does not refer to the renewal of the non-human creation, but only the perishing of the corruptible and the resurrection of the righteous at the final judgment (see esp. 7:31, 37).

believing that the suffering righteous can put their hope in God's eschatological judgment. Romans seems to share a similar outlook. It speaks of the unsafe creation, and the hope of the faithful in their sufferings. But Romans does not share the ethnocentric character of the two Jewish apocalyptic books.[5] Also, as opposed to the emphasis on retributive justice in *4 Ezra* and *2 Baruch*, the focus of Rom 5–8 is God's restorative project, which depends on his gracious act in Christ. The letter clearly places an emphatic hope in the revelation of the glory of God's new humanity, whose faithful response to their calling to suffer with Christ will be instrumental in bringing about the renewal of creation.

THE HOPE OF RESURRECTION

It should be noted that, in Jewish literature, resurrection is often considered to be God's vindication of the suffering righteous when he restores his people.[6] Daniel 12:1–3 says that after a time of distress the righteous sufferers will awake from sleep and be rewarded with everlasting life. As mentioned above, *4 Ezra* 7:26–44 speaks of the final judgment and resurrection, where those who have faithfully endured suffering will be rewarded. Second Maccabees conveys a similar notion. At the martyrdom of her sons, the mother reminds them that it is the Creator God who shaped the beginning of humankind and devised the origin of all things (7:23). She then mentions the hope of resurrection in order to encourage them not to fear death (7:23, 28–29). As mentioned in Chapter 2, in Jewish thinking the hope of God's vindication and eschatological deliverance encourages sufferers to remain faithful in times of immense adversity. Resurrection is certainly an integral part of this hope.[7] Likewise, the resurrection in Rom 8:23 would provide hope for an audience suffering from socioeconomic hardship and systemic injustice in imperial Rome. The redemption of the body at the final renewal functions as an impetus to remain faithful in their vocation.

All of the above affirm our exegesis of Rom 8:18–30 in some ways. In fact, Daniel and 2 Maccabees may have been a resource for the audience to

---

5. As Adams, *Constructing*, 184, notes, Rom 8:19–22 draws on apocalyptic motifs, but it does not stimulate or sustain "social alienation or exclusiveness."

6. Kirk, *Unlocking*, 14–32, provides a good discussion on the functions of resurrection in early Judaism.

7. As Kirk, *Unlocking*, 31–32, says regarding this Jewish perspective, "At times, the theodicy question is squarely in view, with the injustices of this world finding adequate, sometimes *quid pro quo*, resolution in the resurrection. At times, resurrection answers an implicit question about justice by encouraging people to continue obeying God in hopeful trust of a coming day in which the world will be set to rights."

understand Romans, given the fact that these texts would have been important Jewish materials circulated among the early churches. While *4 Ezra* and *2 Baruch* were written after 70 BCE, they demonstrate how a suffering people would have applied their eschatological hope to their particular circumstances. The parallels between these writings and Romans support our analysis of how Paul's audience would have read the letter.

Appendix E
Lists of citations of Isaiah in Romans

THE FOLLOWING TABLES LIST the citations of Isaiah in Romans. Scholars do differ in terms of how the citations are identified, and the following is based on the work of Silva, Michel, Ellis, and Kock.[1] This list is not meant to be definitive, but is intended to provide a reasonably accurate picture of the use of Isaiah in Romans.

Cases where Paul follows closer to the LXX than the MT			
Rom 9:29	Isa 1:9	Rom 2:24	Isa 52:5
Rom 15:12	Isa 11:10	Rom 10:16	Isa 53:1
Rom 11:34	Isa 40:13	Rom 10:20–21	Isa 65:1–2
Rom 14:11	Isa 45:23 (and Isa 49:18?)		

Cases where Paul does not follow the LXX or the MT very closely			
Rom 9:33	Isa 8:14	Rom 11: 8	Isa 29:10
Rom 9:27–28	Isa 10:22–23	Rom 10:15	Isa 52:7
Rom 11:27b	Isa 27:9	Rom 11:26–27	Isa 59:20–21
Rom 9:33	Isa 28:16	Rom 3:15–17	Isa 59:7–8
Rom 10:11	Isa 28:16		

1. The citations in the tables are derived from Silva, "Old Testament in Paul," 631, which is in turn based on the works of O. Michel, *Paulus und seine Bibel* (Darmstadt: Wissenschaftliche Buchgesellschaft, 1929); Ellis, *Paul's Use of the Old Testament*; and Koch, *Die Schrift als Zeuge des Evangeliums*.

Cases where Paul follows both the LXX and the MT closely	
Rom 15:21	Isa 52:15

Debatable citation	
Rom 9:20	Isa 29:16 (45:9)

Note that there is no Isaianic citation in Romans that follows the MT closely but not the LXX.

Appendix F

The Differences between the MT and LXX Texts of the Fourth Isaianic Servant Song

THE FOLLOWING DISCUSSION WILL highlight the differences between the MT and LXX texts of the Fourth Isaianic Servant Song.[1] Since Isa 53:1–12 is the main text that Rom 5–8 refers to, it will be the focus of our discussion here.

Three significant differences between the MT and LXX can be identified. First, the LXX somewhat weakens the cultic motif in the MT by removing some of the language that clearly implies the death of the Servant. In Isa 53:4, instead of being stricken by God (signified by נגע [strike] and נכה [smite]), the LXX says that the Servant is in "trouble"/"toil" (πόνος) and under a "plague"/"calamity" (πληγή). In Isa 53:8, the MT says that the Servant is "cut off" (גזר) from the land of the living, while the LXX says that he is "taken up" ("take up"; αἴρω) from the earth. In addition, the MT says that the Servant was stricken ("strike"; נגע) for/by the transgression (פשע) of God's people. The LXX says that he was led ("lead"; ἄγω) to death by the lawlessness (ἀνομία) of the Lord's people. In Isa 53:10, the MT says that YHWH desires to "crush" (דכא) the Servant with pain, but the LXX says that he wants to "cleanse" (καθαρίζω) him from his plague. In Isa 53:12, the MT says that the Servant "laid bear" ("lay bear/empty"; ערה) himself to death. But the LXX uses a weaker verb "hand over" (παραδίδωμι).

We cannot be sure why the LXX translators translated the Hebrew this way. But *clearly the Servant was handed over and led to death*, although the LXX weakens the motif of cultic sacrifice. As a result, the LXX does not have the same strong cultic sense that the MT has for the Servant's death. Indeed, in Isa 53:10, the Servant is an offering for sin according to the MT, but the

---

1. I am indebted to the work of Sapp, "Isaiah 53," 173–84, here. Of course the discrepancies between the Hebrew and the Greek texts of Isa 53 can be detected independently. But Sapp's analysis is particularly insightful.

LXX says that it is the wicked who make an offering for themselves.[2] But having said all that, it is important to note that the Servant in the LXX was led to slaughter/death, as signified in 53:7, 8.

Second, the LXX puts greater emphasis on the fact that the Lord is on the side of the Servant because of his humble state, and he desires to rescue him. In Isa 53:8 MT, it is by "coercion/oppression" (עצר) that the Servant was taken away. But in the LXX it says that it is by "humiliation"/"humble state" (ταπείνωσις) that the Servant was taken away. In 53:10, the MT says that it is YHWH who makes an offering of the Servant's soul, but the LXX does not say anything about such action on the part of the Lord. The LXX says in 53:10c–11a that the Lord desires to take away the Servant's agony. Such a clear intention of removing the Servant's pain is absent in the MT. Thus, in Isa 53:8–11a there is a train of thought in LXX that the Lord intends to rescue the Servant because of his humility, which is absent in the MT.

Third, the LXX has a stronger sense of the Servant being the righteous sufferer and is vindicated accordingly. This is found in Isa 53:11. The LXX says that the Lord wishes "to vindicate a righteous one [ie., the Servant]" (δικαιῶσαι δίκαιον) as he serves well as a servant for many. The MT has "the righteous one, my servant, shall justify many" (צדיק עבדי לרבים ועונתם). Thus, in the LXX the "many" are not the object of justification, but beneficiaries of the Servant's service. And because of the righteous act of the Servant, he is vindicated (proved to be righteous).[3]

In sum, what we find in the MT is that it is the will of YHWH that the Servant, the righteous one, should justify many through his sacrificial death. On the other hand, in the LXX we find that the Servant serves many but is handed over to death. He is, however, vindicated as a humble righteous sufferer.

---

2. Note the second person plural δῶτε and the plural ὑμῶν in Isa 53:10 LXX.

3. Cf. Sapp, "Isaiah 53," 174–75.

Appendix G

Links between Rom 5:1–21
and the Fourth Servant Song

THIS TABLE HIGHLIGHTS THE similar themes between Rom 5:1–21 and the Fourth Servant Song.

SIMILAR THEMES BETWEEN ROM 5:1-21 AND THE FOURTH ISAIANIC SERVATN SONG

Romans	Themes	Isaiah LXX	Themes
5:1 Δικαιωθέντες οὖν ἐκ πίστεως εἰρήνην ἔχομεν πρὸς τὸν θεὸν διὰ τοῦ κυρίου ἡμῶν Ἰησοῦ Χριστοῦ	Justification of believers through Christ Peace with God	53:5 αὐτὸς δὲ ἐτραυματίσθη διὰ τὰς ἀνομίας ἡμῶν καὶ μεμαλάκισται διὰ τὰς ἁμαρτίας ἡμῶν· παιδεία εἰρήνης ἡμῶν ἐπ' αὐτόν, τῷ μώλωπι αὐτοῦ ἡμεῖς ἰάθημεν. 53:11 ἀπὸ τοῦ πόνου τῆς ψυχῆς αὐτοῦ, δεῖξαι αὐτῷ φῶς καὶ πλάσαι τῇ συνέσει, δικαιῶσαι δίκαιον εὖ δουλεύοντα πολλοῖς, καὶ τὰς ἁμαρτίας αὐτῶν αὐτὸς ἀνοίσει.	The Servant was wounded because of our lawlessness and weakened because of our sins He brings healing Upon him is the discipline (instruction) of our peace Vindication of the Servant (LXX only, not MT) The Servant bears sins (MT only: Justification of people)

5:6 Ἔτι γὰρ Χριστὸς ὄντων ἡμῶν ἀσθενῶν ἔτι κατὰ καιρὸν ὑπὲρ ἀσεβῶν ἀπέθανεν. 5:8 συνίστησιν δὲ τὴν ἑαυτοῦ ἀγάπην εἰς ἡμᾶς ὁ θεός, ὅτι ἔτι ἁμαρτωλῶν ὄντων ἡμῶν Χριστὸς ὑπὲρ ἡμῶν ἀπέθανεν.	Christ died for the ungodly and sinners	53:8 ἐν τῇ ταπεινώσει ἡ κρίσις αὐτοῦ ἤρθη· τὴν γενεὰν αὐτοῦ τίς διηγήσεται; ὅτι αἴρεται ἀπὸ τῆς γῆς ἡ ζωὴ αὐτοῦ, ἀπὸ τῶν ἀνομιῶν τοῦ λαοῦ μου ἤχθη εἰς θάνατον.	The Servant was taken away from the earth and led to death on account of people's lawlessness
5:19 ὥσπερ γὰρ διὰ τῆς παρακοῆς τοῦ ἑνὸς ἀνθρώπου ἁμαρτωλοὶ κατεστάθησαν οἱ πολλοί, οὕτως καὶ διὰ τῆς ὑπακοῆς τοῦ ἑνὸς δίκαιοι κατασταθήσονται οἱ πολλοί.	Many are made righteous through Christ's obedience, that is, his death	53:11 ἀπὸ τοῦ πόνου τῆς ψυχῆς αὐτοῦ, δεῖξαι αὐτῷ φῶς καὶ πλάσαι τῇ συνέσει, δικαιῶσαι δίκαιον εὖ δουλεύοντα πολλοῖς, καὶ τὰς ἁμαρτίας αὐτῶν αὐτὸς ἀνοίσει.	The vindication of the Servant, who is well subject to many and that he will bear their sins

Appendix H

Translations of Isa 50:8, 9

The differences between the MT and the LXX seem to be minor in the third Servant Song. Here are my translations for Isa 50:8, 9 for comparison between the MT and LXX.

TRANSLATIONS FOR ISA 50:8, 9

	Translation of the MT	Translation of the LXX
Isaiah 50:8	The one who justifies/vindicates me is near; who will contend with me? Let us stand up together. Who has a case against me [literally: "lord of my judgment"]? Let him/her come approach me.	Because he who justifies/vindicates me comes near; who is the one who judges me? Let him/her oppose me at once! And who is the one who judges me? Let him/her come near!
Isaiah 50:8	Behold, the sovereign YHWH will help me; who can condemn me? Behold, all of them will wear out like a garment; the moth will eat them up.	Behold, the Lord helps me; who will harm me? Behold, all of you will become old like a garment, just like a moth will devour you.

Bibliography

Adams, Edward. *Constructing the World: A Study in Paul's Cosmological Language.* London: T. & T. Clark, 2000.

———. "Paul's Story of God and Creation." In *The Narrative Dynamics in Paul,* edited by Bruce W. Longenecker, 19–43. London: Westminister John Knox, 2002.

Annaeus Lucanus, Marcus. *Pharsalia.* Translated by J. D. Duff. LCL 220. Cambridge, MA: Harvard University Press, 1928.

Atkins, Margaret, and Robin Osborne, eds. *Poverty in the Roman World.* Cambridge: Cambridge University Press, 2009.

Aune, David E. "Religion, Greco-Roman." In *DNTB,* edited by Craig A. Evans and Stanley E. Porter, 917–26. Leicester: IVP, 2000.

Balz, H. "φοβέω, φοβέομαι, φόβος, δέος." In *TDNT* 4:189–219.

Barclay, John M. G. *Pauline Churches and Diaspora Jews.* WUNT 1.275. Tübingen: Mohr Siebeck, 2007.

Bartchy, S. S. "Slave, Slavery." In *DLNTD,* edited by Ralph P. Martin and Peter H. Davids, 1098–1102. Leicester: IVP, 1997.

Beale, Greg K. *The Temple and the Church's Mission: A Biblical Theology of the Dwelling Place of God.* Leicester: Apollos, 2004.

Beker, J. Christiaan. *Paul the Apostle.* Philadelphia: Fortress, 1980.

———. *Suffering and Hope: The Biblical Vision and the Human Predicament.* Grand Rapids: Eerdmans, 1994.

———. "Suffering and Triumph in Paul's Letter to the Romans," *HBT* 7 (1985) 105–19.

———. "Vision of Hope for a Suffering World," *PSB* 3 (1994) 26–32.

Bell, Richard. *Deliver Us from Evil: Interpreting the Redemption from the Power of Satan in NT Theology.* WUNT 1.216. Tübingen: Mohr Siebeck, 2007.

Berger, Peter L. *The Sacred Canopy: Elements of a Sociological Theory of Religion.* Garden City, NY: Anchor, 1969.

Bertone, John A. *The Law of the Spirit.* Studies in Biblical Literature 86. New York: Peter Lang, 2005.

Bertram, Georg. "στένος, στενοχωρία, στενοχωρέω." In *TDNT* 7:604–8.

Black, C. Clifton. "Pauline Perspectives on Death in Romans 5–8." *JBL* 103.3 (1984) 413–33.

Blackwell, Ben C. "Immortal Glory and the Problem of Death in Romans 3.23." *JSNT* 32 (2010) 285–308.

Boring, M. Eugene. *Mark: A Commentary.* Louisville: Westminster John Knox, 2006.

Bowley, J. E. "Pax Romana." In *DNTB*, edited by Craig A. Evans and Stanley E. Porter, 771–75. Leicester: IVP, 2000.

Branick, Vincent P. "The Sinful Flesh of the Son of God (Rom. 8:3)." *CBQ* 47 (1985) 246–62.

Broyles, Craig C. *Psalms*. NIBC. Peabody, MA: Hendrickson, 1999.

Brueggemann, Walter. *Genesis: A Bible Commentary for Teaching and Preaching*. Atlanta, GA: John Knox, 1982.

———. *A Commentary on Jeremiah*. Grand Rapids: Eerdmans, 1998.

Burke, Trevor J. *Adopted into God's Family*. NSBT. Downers Grove, IL: IVP, 2006.

———. "Pauline Adoption: a Sociological Approach." *EvQ* 73 (2001) 119–34.

Burkert, Walter. *Greek Religion*. Cambridge: Harvard University Press, 1985.

———. *The Orientalizing Revolution*. Translated by Margaret Pinder. Cambridge: Harvard University Press, 1995.

Byrne, Brendan. *Romans*. Sacra Pagina 6. Collegeville: Liturgical, 1996.

———. *'Sons of God'—'Seed of Abraham': A Study of the Idea of the Sonship of God of all Christians against the Jewish Background*. AnBib 83. Rome: Biblical Institute, 1979.

Byron, John. "Paul and the Background of Slavery: The *Status Quaestionis* in New Testament Scholarship." *Currents in Biblical Research* 3.1 (2004) 116–39.

———. *Recent Research on Paul and Slavery* Sheffield: Sheffield University Press, 2008.

Calpurnius Siculus. "Ecologue IV." In *Minor Latin Poets*, vol. 1, translated by J. W. Duff and A. M. Duff. LCL 284. Cambridge, MA: Harvard University Press, 1934.

Campbell, Constantine R. *Paul and Union with Christ: An Exegetical and Theological Study*. Grand Rapids: Zondervan, 2012.

Campbell, Douglas A. *The Deliverance of God*. Grand Rapids: Eerdmans, 2009.

———. "The Story of Jesus in Romans and Galatians." In *The Narrative Dynamics in Paul*, edited by Bruce W. Longenecker, 97–124. London: Westminister John Knox, 2002.

Carr, Wesley. *Angels and Principalities: The Background, Meaning and Development of the Pauline Phrase hai archai kai hai exousiai*. SNTSMS 42. Cambridge: Cambridge University Press, 1981.

Charlesworth, James H. ed. *The Old Testament Pseudepigrapha*. 2 vols. Garden City, NY: Doubleday, 1983–85.

Christoffersson, Olle. *The Earnest Expectation of the Creature: The Flood-Tradition as Matrix of Romans 8:18–27*. Stockholm: Almqvist and Wiksell, 1990.

Ciampa, Roy E. and Brian S. Rosner. *The First Letter to the Corinthians*. PNTC. Grand Rapids: Eerdmans, 2010.

Cicero. *De Officiis*. Translated by Walter Miller. LCL 30. Cambridge, MA: Harvard University Press, 1913.

Clifford, Richard J. *Psalm 1–72*. AOTC. Nashville: Abingdon, 2002.

Cohick, Lynn H. *Women in the World of the Earliest Christians*. Grand Rapids: Baker, 2009.

Collins, Raymond F. *First Corinthians*. Sacra Pagina. Collegeville, MN: Liturgical, 2006.

Constantineanu, Corneliu. *The Social Significance of Reconciliation in Paul's Theology: Narrative Readings in Romans*. LNTS 421. London: T. & T. Clark, 2010.

Craigie, Peter C. and Marvin E. Tate. *Psalms 1–50*. WBC. Nashville: Thomas Nelson, 2004.

(1967)

 (1967)

Cranfield, C. E. B. *A Critical and Exegetical Commentary on the Epistle to the Romans: Introduction and Commentary on Romans I–VIII.* ICC. London: T. & T. Clark, (1975)

Crook, Zeba. "Honor, Shame, and Social Status Revisited." *JBL* 128 (2009) 591–611.

Croy, N. Clayton. *Endurance in Suffering.* SNTSMS 98. Cambridge: Cambridge University Press, 1998.

Das, Andrew. *Solving the Roman Debate.* Minneapolis: Fortress, 2007.

de Boer, Martinus C. *The Defeat of Death.* JSNTSup 22. Sheffield: Sheffield Academic, 1988.

Deissmann, A. *Light from the Ancient East.* London: Hodder & Stoughton, 1927.

deSilva, David A. "Honor and Shame." In *DNTB*, edited by Craig A. Evans and Stanley E. Porter, 518–22. Leicester: IVP, 2000.

———. "Ruler Cult." In *DNTB*, edited by Craig A. Evans and Stanley E. Porter, 1026–1030. Leicester: IVP, 2000.

Donfried, Karl P., ed. *The Romans Debate.* 2nd ed. Peabody: Hendrickson, 1991.

Drake, H. H. Williams III. Review of *Arguing with Scripture*, by Christopher D. Stanley. *Review of Biblical Literature*, January 2005. http://www.bookreviews.org/pdf/4228_4164.pdf.

Dunn, James D. G. *Christology.* London: SCM, 1989.

———. *Romans 1–8.* WBC 38A. Dallas: Word, 1988.

———. *Romans 9–16.* WBC 38B. Dallas: Word, 1988.

———. *The Theology of Paul the Apostle.* Grand Rapids: Eerdmans, 1998.

Eastman, Susan. "Whose Apocalypse? The Identity of the Sons of God in Romans 8:19." *JBL* 121 (2002) 263–77.

Edwards, R. B., et al. "Rome: Overview." In *DNTB*, edited by Craig A. Evans and Stanley E. Porter, 1010–18. Leicester: IVP, 2000.

Ehrensperger, Kathy. "Paul and the Authority of Scripture: A Feminist Perception." In *As it is Written: Studying Paul's Use of Scripture*, edited by Stanley E. Porter and Christopher D. Stanley, 291–319. Atlanta, GA: SBL, 2008.

Elliott, Neil. "The Anti-Imperial Message of the Cross." In *Paul and Empire*, edited by Richard A. Horsley, 167–83. Harrisburg, PA: Trinity, 1997.

———. "Creattion, Cosmos, and Conflict in Romans 8–9." In *Apocalyptic Paul: Cosmos and Anthropos in Romans 5–8*, edited by Beverley Roberts Gaventa, 131–56. Waco, TX: Balyor University Press, 2013.

———. *The Rhetoric of Romans: Argumentative Constraint and Strategy and Paul's Dialogue with Judaism.* JSNTSup 45. Sheffield: Sheffield Academic, 1990.

Elliott, Neil, and Mark Reasoner. *Documents and Images for the Study of Paul.* Minneapolis: Fortress, 2011.

Ellis, E. E. *Paul's Use of the Old Testament.* Edinburgh: Oliver & Boyd, 1957.

Enns, Peter. "Ecclesiastes 1: Book of Ecclesiastes." In *DOTWPW*, edited by Tremper III Longman and Peter Enns, 121–32. Leicester: IVP, 2008.

———. *Ecclesiastes*, THOTC. Grand Rapids: Eerdmans, 2011.

———. *The Evolution of Adam.* Grand Rapids: Brazos, 2012.

Esler, Philip F. *The First Christians in Their Social Worlds: Social-Scientific Approaches to New Testament Interpretation.* London: Routledge, 1994.

Evans, Craig. "Isaiah 53 in the Letters of Peter, Paul, Hebrews, and John." In *The Gospel According to Isaiah 53*, edited by Darrell L. Bock and Mitch Glaser, 145–70. Grand Rapids: Kregel, 2012.

灵
灵

Fatehi, Mehrdad. *The Spirit's Relation to the Risen Lord in Paul.* WUNT 2.128. Tübingen: Mohr Siebeck, 2000.

Fee, Gordon D. "Christology and Pneumatology in Romans 8:9–11—and Elsewhere: Some Reflections on Paul as a Trinitarian." In *To What End Exegesis?* Grand Rapids: Eerdmans, 2001.

———. *The First Epistle to the Corinthians.* NICNT. Grand Rapids: Eerdmans, 1987.

———. *God's Empowering Presence.* Peabody, MA: Hendrickson, 1994.

———. *Paul, the Spirit and the People of God.* Peabody, MA: Hendrickson, 1996.

———. *Pauline Christology.* Peabody, MA: Hendrickson, 2007.

Fish, Stanley. *Is There a Text in this Class? The Authority of the Interpretive Communities.* Cambridge: Harvard University Press, 1980.

Fisk, Bruce N. "Paul among the Storytellers: Reading Romans 11 in the Context of Rewritten Bible." In *Paul and Scripture: Extending the Conversation*, edited by Christopher D. Stanley, 55–94. Atlanta, GA: SBL, 2012.

———. "Synagogue Influence and Scriptural Knowledge among the Christians of Rome." In *As it is Written: Studying Paul's Use of Scripture*, edited by Stanley E. Porter and Christopher D. Stanley, 157–85. Atlanta, GA: SBL, 2008.

Fitzgerald, John T. *Cracks in an Earthern Vessel: An Examination of the Catalogues of Hardships in the Corinthian Correspondences.* Atlanta, GA: SBL, 1988.

Forman, Mark. *The Politics of Inheritance in Romans.* SNTSMS 148. Cambridge: Cambridge University Press, 2011.

Fowler, Robert M. *Let the Reader Understand: Reader-Response Criticism and the Gospel of Mark.* Minneapolis: Fortress, 1991.

———. "Reader-Response Criticism." In *Searching for Meaning*, edited by Paula Gooder, 127–29. London: SPCK, 2008.

France, R. T. *The Gospel of Matthew.* NICNT. Grand Rapids: Eerdmans, 2007.

Fredrickson, David E. "Paul, Hardships, and Suffering." In *Paul in the Greco-Roman World*, edited by J. Paul Sampley, 172–206. Harisburg, PA: Trinity, 2003.

Fretheim, Terence E. *Genesis.* NIB 1. Nashville: Abingdon, 1994.

Friesen, Steven. "Poverty in Pauline Studies: Beyond the So-Called New Consensus." *JSNT* 26 (2004) 323–61.

Ferguson, Everett. *Backgrounds of Early Christianity*, Grand Rapids: Eerdmans, 1993.

Gaius. *The Institutes of Gaiu.* Translated by W. M. Gordon and O. F. Robinson. London: Gerald Duckworth, 1988.

Gager, J. G., Jr. "Functional Diversity in Paul's Use of End-Time Language." *JBL* 89 (1970) 325–37.

Gamble, Harry Y. *Books and Readers in the Early Church: A History of Early Christian Texts.* New Haven, CT: Yale University Press, 1995.

Garnsey, Peter, and Richard Saller. *The Roman Empire: Economy, Society and Culture.* London: Gerald Duckworth, 1987.

Gaventa, Beverly Roberts. "The 'Glory of God' in Paul's Letter to the Romans." In *Interpretation and the Claims of the Text*, edited by Jason A. Whitlark, et al., 29–42. Waco, TX: Balyor University Press, 2014.

———. "Interpreting the Death of Jesus Apocalyptically: Reconsidering Romans 8:32." In *Jesus and Paul Reconnected*, edited by Todd D. Still, 125–45. Grand Rapids: Eerdmans, 2007.

———. "Neither Height nor Depth: Discerning the Cosmology of Romans." *SJT* 64 (2011) 265–78.

————. *Our Mother Saint Paul*. Louisville Westminster John Knox, 2007.

Georgi, Dieter. "God Turned Upside Down." In *Paul and Empire*, edited by Richard A. Horsley, 148–57. Harrisburg, PA: Trinity, 1997.

Gieniusz, Andrzej. *Romans 8:18–30—Suffering Does Not Thwart the Future Glory*. Atlanta, GA: Scholars, 1999.

Giesen, Heinz. "Befreiung des Gesetzes aus der Sklaverei der Sünde als Ermöglichung der Gesetzeserfüllung (Röm 8,1–4)." *BZ* 53 (2009) 179–211.

Gignilliat, Mark S. "Working Together with Whom?: Text-critical, Contextual, and Theological Analysis of συνεργεῖ in Romans 8,28." *Bib* 87 (2006) 511–15.

Gillman, Florence Morgan. "Another Look at Romans 8:3: 'In the Likeness of Sinful Flesh.'" *CBQ* 49 (1987) 597–604.

Glancy, Jennifer A. *Slavery in Early Christianity*. Oxford: Oxford University Press, 2002.

Goldingay, John. *Isaiah*. NIBC. Peabody, MA: Hendrickson, 2001.

————. *Psalms 42–89*. BCOT 2. Grand Rapids: Baker Academic, 2007.

Gordon, Arthur E. *Illustrated Introduction to Latin Epigraphy*. Los Angeles: University of California Press, 1983.

Gorman, Michael J. *Apostle of the Crucified Lord*. Grand Rapids: Eerdmans, 2004.

————. *Cruciformity: Paul's Narrative Spirituality of the Cross*. Grand Rapids: Eerdmans, 2001.

————. *Inhabiting the Cruciform God*. Grand Rapids: Eerdmann, 2009.

————. "Romans: The First Christian Treatise on Theosis." *JTI* 5 (2011) 13–34.

Gow, M. D. "Fall." In *DOTP*, edited by T. D. Alexander and D. W. Baker, 285–91. Leicester: IVP, 2003.

Gowan, Donald E. "The Fall and Redemption of the Material World in Apocalyptic Literature." *HBT* 7 (1985) 83–103.

Grappe, Christian. "Qui me délivrera de ce corps de mort? L'Esprit de vie! Romains 7,24 et 8,2 comme éléments de typologie adamique." *Biblica* 83 (2002) 472–92.

Green, Joel B. *1 Peter*. THNTC. Grand Rapids: Eerdmans, 2007.

————. "Gethsemane." In *DJG*, edited by Joel B. Green, et al., 265–68. Leicester: IVP, 1992.

————. *The Gospel of Luke*. NICNT. Grand Rapids: Eerdmans, 1997.

Greenspoon, Leonard. "By the Letter? Word for Word? Scriptural Citation in Paul." In *Paul and Scripture: Extending the Conversation*, edited by Christopher D. Stanley, 9–24. Atlanta, GA: SBL, 2012.

Grieb, A. Katherine. *The Story of Romans: A Narrative Defense of God's Righteousness*. Louisville: Westminster John Knox, 2002.

Grundmann, W. "σύν-μετά." In *TDNT* 7:766–97.

Grogan, Geoffrey W. *Psalms*. THOTC. Grand Rapids: Eerdmans, 2008.

Gunkel, Hermann. *Genesis*. Translated by Mark E. Biddle. Macon, GA: Mercer University Press, 1997.

Haacker, Klaus. *The Theology of Paul's Letter to the Romans*. Cambridge: Cambridge University Press, 2003.

Hagner, Donald A. *Matthew 14–28*. WBC. Nashville: Thomas Nelson, 1995.

Hahne, Harry Alan. *The Corruption and Redemption of Creation: Nature in Romans 8.19–22 and Jewish Apocalyptic Literature*. London: T. & T. Clark, 2006.

Harrill, J. A. "Slavery." In *DNTB*, edited by Craig A. Evans and Stanley E. Porter, 1124–27. Leicester: IVP, 2000.

Harris, William V. *Ancient Literacy*. Cambridge, MA: Harvard University Press, 1989.

Hartley, John E. *Genesis*. NIBC. Peabody, MA: Hendrickson, 2000.

Harvey, John D. *Listening to the Text: Oral Pattern in Paul's Letters*. Grand Rapids: Baker, 1998.

Hays, Richard B. *Echoes of Scripture in the Letters of Paul*. New Haven, CT: Yale University Press, 1989.

Heil, John Paul. *Paul's Letter to the Romans: A Reader-Response Commentary*. New York: Paulist, 1987.

Hiebert, D. Edmond. "Romans 8:28–29 and the Assurance of the Believer." *BSac* 148 (1991) 170–83.

Hodge, Caroline Johnson. *If Sons, Then Heirs*. Oxford: Oxford University Press, 2007.

Hodgson, Robert. "Paul the Apostle and First Century Tribulation Lists." *ZNW* 74 (1983) 59–80.

Hofius, Otfried. "The Fourth Servant Song in the New Testament Letters." In *The Suffering Servant: Isaiah 53 in Jewish and Christian Sources*, edited by Bernd Janowski and Peter Stuhlmacher, 163–88. Grand Rapids: Eerdmans, 2004.

Hommel, H. "Denen, die Gott Lieben: Erwägungen zu Römer 8:28." *ZNW* 80 (1989) 126–29.

Hooker, Morna D. *From Adam to Christ*. Cambridge: Cambridge University Press, 1990.

———. *Jesus and the Servant*. London: SPCK, 1959.

Horrell, David G. "A New Perspective on Paul? Rereading Paul in a Time of Ecological Crisis." *JSNT* 33 (2010) 3–30.

Horrell, David G., et al. *Greening Paul: Rereading the Apostle in a time of Ecological Crisis*. Waco, TX: Baylor University Press, 2010.

Horsley, Richard A. *Paul and Empire*. Harrisburg, PA: Trinity, 1997.

———. *Paul and the Roman Imperial Order*. Edited by Richard A. Horsley. Harrisburg, PA: Trinity, 2004.

———. "The Slave Systems of Classical Antiquity." In *Slavery in Text and Interpretation*, edited by A. D. Callahan, et al., 19–66. Semeia 83/84. Atlanta: Scholars, 1998

Horsley, Richard A., et al., eds. *Performing the Gospel: Orality, Memory, and Mark*. Minneapolis: Fortress, 2006.

Hultgren, Arland J. *Paul's Letter to the Romans*. Grand Rapids: Eerdmans, 2011.

Hurtado, Larry W. "Jesus' Divine Sonship in Paul's Epistle to the Romans." In *Romans and the People of God*, edited by Sven K. Soderlund and N. T. Wright, 217–33. Grand Rapids: Eerdmans, 1999.

Iser, Wolfgang. *The Act of Reading: A Theory of Aesthetic Response*. Baltimore: Johns Hopkins University Press, 1978.

———. *The Implied Reader: Patterns of Communication in Prose Fiction from Bunyan to Beckett*. Baltimore: Johns Hopkins University Press, 1974.

Jackson, T. Ryan. *New Creation in Paul's Letters: A Study of the Historical and Social Setting of a Pauline Concept*. WUNT 2.272. Tübingen: Mohr Siebeck, 2010.

Janowski, Bernd. "He Bore Our Sins: Isaiah 53 and the Drama of Taking Another's Place." In *The Suffering Servant: Isaiah 53 in Jewish and Christian Sources*, edited by Bernd Janowski and Peter Stuhlmacher, 48–74. Grand Rapids: Eerdmans, 2004.

Jeffers, James S. *Conflicts at Rome*. Minneapolis: Fortress, 1991.

———. *The Greco-Roman World of the New Testament Era*. Downers Grove, IL: IVP, 1999.

Jeremias, Joachim. *Abba: Studien zur neutestamentlichen Theologie und Zeitgeschichte.* Göttingen: Vandenhoeck & Ruprecht, 1966.

Jervis, L. Ann. *At the Heart of the Gospel: Suffering in the Earliest Christian Message.* Grand Rapids: Eerdmans, 2007.

Jewett, Robert. "The Corruption and Redemption of Creation." In *Paul and the Roman Imperial Order.* Edited by Richard A. Horsley, 25–46. Harrisburg: Trinity, 2004.

———. *Romans: A Commentary.* Hermeneia. Minneapolis: Fortress, 2007.

Johnson, Luke Timothy. *Reading Romans: A Literary and Theological Commentary.* Macon, GA: Smyth & Helwys, 2001.

Joshel, Sandra R. *Slavery in the Roman World.* Cambridge: Cambridge University Press, 2010.

Judge, E. A. "The Conflict of Educational Aims in New Testament Thought." *Journal of Christian Education* 9 (1966) 32–45.

Juvenal. *Juvenal: The Sixteen Satires.* Translated by P. Green. London: Penguin, 1974.

Kasemann, Ernst. *Commentary on Romans.* Translated by Goffrey W. Bromiley. Grand Rapids: Eerdmans, 1980.

Keck, Leander E. *Romans.* ANTC. Nashville: Abingdon, 2005.

Keener, Craig. *Romans.* NCC. Eugene, OR: Cascade, 2009.

Keesmaat, Sylvia C. *Paul and His Story: (Re)Interpreting the Exodus Tradition.* JSNTSup 181. Sheffield: Sheffield Academic, 1999.

———. "The Psalms in Romans and Galatians." In *The Psalms in the New Testament,* edited by Steve Moyise and Maarten J. J. Menken, 139–61. London: T. & T. Clark, 2004.

Kim, Mitchell. "Respect for Context and Authorial Intention: Setting the Epistemological Bar." In *Paul and Scripture: Extending the Conversation,* edited by Christopher D. Stanley, 115–29. Atlanta, GA: SBL, 2012.

Kim, Seyoon. "2 Cor. 5:11–21 and the Origin of Paul's Concept of "Reconciliation." *NovT* 34 (1997) 360–84.

Kirk, J. R. Daniel. "Reconsidering Dikaiōma in Romans 5:16." *JBL* 126 (2007) 787–92.

———. *Unlocking Romans: Resurrection and the Justification of God.* Grand Rapids: Eerdmans, 2008.

Kittel, G., and G. Friedrich, eds. *Theological Dictionary of the New Testament.* Translated by G. W. Bromiley. 10 vols. Grand Rapids: Eerdmans, 1964–1976.

Kleinknecht, Karl Theodor. *Der leidende Gerechtfertigte. Die alttestamentlich-judische Tradition vom "leidenden Gerechten" und ihre Rezeption bei Paulus.* WUNT 2.13. Tübingen: Mohr Siebeck, 1984.

Koch, Dietrich-Alex. *Die Schrift als Zeuge des Evangeliums. Untersuchungen zur Verwendung und zum Verständnis der Schrift bei Paulus.* BHT 69. Tübingen: J. C. B. Mohr, 1986.

Konsmo, Erik. *The Pauline Metaphors of the Holy Spirit.* Studies in Biblical Literature 130. New York: Peter Lang, 2010.

Kroeger, C. C. "Women in Greco-Roman World and Judaism." In *DNTB.* Edited by Craig A. Evans and Stanley E. Porter, 1276–280. Leicester: IVP, 2000.

Kruse, Colin. *Paul's Letter to the Romans.* PTNC. Grand Rapids: Eerdmans, 2012.

Lampe, Peter. *From Paul to Valentinus.* Translated by M. Steinhauser. Minneapolis: Fortress, 2003.

———. "The Roman Christian of Romans 16." in *The Romans Debate.* Edited by Karl P. Donfried. Peabody, MA: Hendrickson, 1991.

Lategan, Bernard C. "Coming to Grips with the Reader in Biblical Literature." In *Reader Perspectives on the New Testament*, edited by Edgar V. McKnight, 3–20. Atlanta, GA: Scholars, 1989.

Levenson, Jon D. *Creation and the Persistence of Evil: The Jewish Drama of Divine Omnipotence*. New York: Harper and Row, 1988.

———. "The Temple and the World." *JR* 64 (1984) 275–98.

Levison, John R. "Holy Spirit." In *DNTB*, edited by Craig A. Evans and Stanley E. Porter, 507–15. Leicester: IVP, 2000.

———. *The Spirit in First-century Judaism*. Leiden: J. E. Brill, 1997.

Lim, Kar Yong. *The Sufferings of Christ Are Abundant In Us: A Narrative Dynamics Investigation of Paul's Sufferings in 2 Corinthians*. LNTS. London: T. & T. Clark, 2009.

Lincicum, David. "Genesis in Paul." In *Genesis in the New Testament*, edited by Steve Moyise and Maarten J. J. Menken, 93–110. LNTS. London: T. & T. Clark, 2012.

———. Review of *Arguing with Scripture*, by Christopher D. Stanley. *JETS* 49 (2006) 429–31.

Longenecker, Bruce W. *Remember the Poor: Paul, Poverty, and the Greco-Roman World*. Grand Rapids: Eerdmans, 2010.

Longenecker, Bruce W., and Kelly D. Liebengood, eds. *Engaging Economics*. Grand Rapids: Eerdmans, 2009.

Longenecker, Richard N. "The Focus of Romans." In *Romans and the People of God*, edited by Sven K. Soderlund and N. T. Wright, 49–69. Grand Rapids: Eerdmans, 1999.

———. *Introducing Romans*. Grand Rapids: Eerdmans, 2011.

MacMullen, R. *Roman Social Relations*. New Haven, CT: Yale University Press, 1974.

Malina, Bruce J. *The New Testament World*. 3rd ed. Louisville: Westminster John Knox, 2001.

Malina, Bruce J., and John J. Pilch. *Social-Science Commentary on the Letters of Paul*. Minneapolis: Fortress, 2006.

Martin, Dale. *Slavery as Salvation*. New Haven: Yale University Press, 1990.

———. "Review Essay: Justin J. Meggitt—*Paul, Poverty and Survival*." *JSNT* 84 (2001) 51–64.

Martin, Ralph P. "Reconciliation: Romans 5:1–11." In *Romans and the People of God*, edited by Sven K. Soderlund and N. T. Wright, 36–48. Grand Rapids: Eerdmans, 1999.

Marshall, Christopher D. *Beyond Retribution*. Grand Rapids: Eerdmans, 2001.

Matera, Frank J. "Conformed to the Image of God's Own Son: The Goal of God's Redemptive Plan according to the Pauline Epistles." In *Interpretation and the Claims of the Text*, edited by Jason A. Whitlark, et al., 103–16. Waco, TX: Balyor University Press, 2014.

———. *Romans*. Paideia. Grand Rapids: Baker, 2010.

Matlock, R. Barry. "The Arrow and the Web: Critical Reflections on a Narrative Approach to Paul." In *The Narrative Dynamics in Paul*, edited by Bruce W. Longenecker, 44–57. London: Westminister John Knox, 2002.

Mays, James L. *Psalms*. Interpretation. Louisville: John Knox, 1994.

McKeown, James. *Genesis*. THOTC. Grand Rapids: Eerdmans, 2008.

McKnight, Edgar V. *Post-Modern Use of the Bible: The Emergence of Reader-Oriented Criticism*. Nashville: Abingdon, 1988.

Meeks, Wayne. *The First Urban Christians.* 2nd ed. New Haven, CT: Yale University Press, 2003.

Meggitt, Justin J. *Paul, Poverty and Survival.* Edinburgh: T. & T. Clark, 1998.

———. "Responses to Martin and Theissen." *JSNT* 84 (2001) 85–94.

Michel, O. *Paulus und seine Bibel.* Darmstadt: Wissenschaftliche Buchgesellschaft, 1929.

Michel, Otto. *Der Brief an die Römer.* 5th ed. Göttingen: Vandenhoeck & Ruprecht, 1978.

Morley, Neville. "The Poor in the City of Rome." In *Poverty in the Roman World,* edited by Margaret Atkins and Robin Osborne, 21–39. Cambridge: Cambridge University Press, 2009.

Moo, Douglas. *The Epistle to the Romans.* NICNT. Grand Rapids: Eerdmans, 1996.

Moo, Jonathan. "Romans 8.18–22 and Isaiah's Cosmic Covenent." *NTS* 54 (2008) 74–89.

Morris, Leon. *Romans.* Grand Rapids: Eerdmans, 1988.

Morrow, Jeff. "Creation as Temple-Building and Work as Liturgy in Genesis 1–3." *OCABS* 2 (2009) 1–13.

Moyise, Steve. "Intertextuality and the Study of the Old Testament in the New Testament." In *The Old Testament in the New Testament,* edited by Steve Moyise, 14–41. Sheffield: Sheffield Academic, 2000.

———. "Intertextuality, Historical Criticism and Deconstruction." In *The Intertextuality of the Epistles: Explorations of Theory and Practice,* edited by Thomas L. Brodie, et al., 24–34. Sheffield: Sheffield Phoenix, 2006.

———. *Paul and Scripture.* London: SPCK, 2010.

———. "Does Paul Respect the Context of His Quotations?" In *Paul and Scripture: Extending the Conversation,* edited by Christopher D. Stanley, 97–114. Atlanta, GA: SBL, 2012.

Nolland, John. *The Gospel of Matthew.* NIGTC. Grand Rapids: Eerdmans, 2005.

Oakes, Peter. "Methodological Issues in Using Economic Evidence in Interpretation of Early Christian Texts." In *Engaging Economics,* edited by Bruce W. Longenecker and Kelly D. Liebengood, 9–36. Grand Rapids: Eerdmans, 2009.

———. *Reading Romans in Pompeii.* London: SPCK, 2009.

Obeng, E. A. "Abba, Father: The Prayer of the Sons of God." *ExpTim* 99 (1988) 363–66.

Pahl, Michael W. *The Beginning and the End.* Eugene, OR: Cascade, 2011.

Parlier, Isabelle. "La folle justice de Dieu. Romains 8,31–39." *FoiVie* 91 (1992) 103–10.

Pate, C. Marvin. "Genesis 1–3: Creation and Adam in Context." *CTR* 10 (2013) 3–25.

Paulien, Jon. "Elusive Allusions in the Apocalypse." In *The Intertextuality of the Epistles: Explorations of Theory and Practice,* edited by Thomas L. Brodie, et al., 61–70. Sheffield: Sheffield Phoenix, 2006.

Paulsen, Henning. *Überlieferung und Auslegung in Römer 8.* WMANT 43. Neukirchen: Neukirchener Verlag, 1974.

Pearson, Brook W. R. "New Testament Literary Criticism." In *Handbook to Exegesis of the New Testament,* edited by Stanley E. Porter, 241–66. Leiden: Brill Academic, 2002.

Philo of Alexandria. *Philo.* 10 vols. Translated by F. H. Colson and G. H. Whitaker. LCL. Cambridge, MA: Harvard University Press, 1929–62.

Pobee, John S. *Persecution and Martyrdom in the Theology of Paul.* JSNTSup 6. Sheffield: JSOT, 1985.

Porter, Stanley E. "Paul's Concept of Reconciliation, Twice More." In *Paul and His Theology*, edited by Stanley E. Porter, 131–52. Boston: E. J. Brill, 2006.

Powers, Daniel G. *Salvation Through Participation*. Leuven: Peeters, 2001.

Punt, Jeremy. "Identity, Memory, and Scriptural Warrant: Arguing Paul's Case." In *Paul and Scripture: Extending the Conversation*, edited by Christopher D. Stanley, 25–53. Atlanta, GA: SBL, 2012.

———. "Negotiating creation in imperial times (Rom 8:18–30)." *HTS* 69 (2013) 1–8.

Rahlfs, Alfred, and Robert Hanhart, eds. *Septuaginta*. Rev. ed. Stuttgart: Deutsche Bibelgesellschaft, 2006.

Robbins, Vernon K. *Exploring the Texture of Texts: A Guide to Socio-Rhetorical Interpretation*. Valley Forge, PA: Trinity, 1996.

Rodgers, N. *The Roman World*. London: Hermes, 2005.

Rodgers, Peter R. "The Text of Romans 8:28." *JTS* 46 (1995) 547–50.

Rom-Shiloni, Dalit. "Psalm 44: The Powers of Protest." *CBQ* 70 (2008) 683–98.

Rupprecht, A. A. "Slave, Slavery." In *DPL*, edited by Gerald F. Hawthorne, et al., 881–83. Leicester: IVP, 1993.

Saggs, H. W. F. *Babylonians*. London: British Museum, 2000.

Sapp, David A. "The LXX, 1QIsa, and the MT Versions of Isaiah 53 and the Christian Doctrine of Atonement." In *Jesus and the Suffering Servant*, edited by W. H. Bellinger and William R. Farmer, 170–92. Harrisburg, PA: Trinity, 1998.

Schmidt, T. E. "Riches and Poverty." In *DPL*, edited by Gerald F. Hawthorne, Ralph P. Martin, and Daniel G. Reid, 826–27. Leicester: IVP, 1993.

Schreiner, Thomas R. *Romans*. BECNT. Grand Rapids: Baker, 1998.

Scott, James M. *Adoption as Sons of God*. WUNT 2.48. Tübingen: Mohr Siebeck, 1992.

———. "Adoption, Sonship." In *DPL*, edited by Gerald F. Hawthorne, et al., 15–18. Leicester: IVP, 1993.

Seifrid, Mark A. "Romans." In *Commentary on the New Testament Use of the Old Testament*, edited by Don A. Carson and Greg K. Beale, 607–94. Grand Rapids: Baker Academic, 2007.

Seneca. *Natural Questions*. Translated by Thomas H. Corcoran. LCL 450 and 457. Cambridge, MA: Harvard University Press, 1971–72.

Shum, Shiu-Lun. *Paul's Use of Isaiah in Romans*. WUNT 2.156. Tübingen: Mohr Siebeck, 2002.

Silva, Moises. "Old Testament in Paul." In *DPL*, edited by Gerald F. Hawthorne, et al., 630–42. Leicester: IVP, 1993.

Smith, Barry D. *Paul's Seven Explanations of the Suffering of the Righteous*. Studies in Biblical Literature 47. New York: Peter Lang, 2002.

Stamps, Dennis L. "Rhetorical and Narratological Criticism." In *Handbook to Exegesis of the New Testament*, edited by Stanley E. Porter, 219–40. Leiden: Brill Academic, 2002.

Stanley, Christopher D. *Arguing with Scripture: The Rhetoric of Quotations in the Letters of Paul*. London: T. & T. Clark, 2004.

———. "What We Learned—and What We Didn't." In *Paul and Scripture: Extending the Conversation*, edited by Christopher D. Stanley, 321–30. Atlanta, GA: SBL, 2012.

Stein, R. H. "Last Supper." In *DJG*, edited by Joel B. Green, et al., 444–50. Leicester: IVP, 1992.

[Handwritten annotations:]
stoic phylosophy
At Glasgow, supervised by John Barclay
Stewart James (1935), A man in Christ   NY: Harper
Stendahl, Krister — 196 ... 1877 Paul among Jews & Gentiles

Stewart, Tyler A. "The Cry of Victory: A Cruciform Reading of Psalm 44:22 in Romans 8:36." *JSPL* 3 (2013) 25–46.

Still, Todd D., and David G. Horrell. eds. *After the First Christians.* London: T. & T. Clark, 2009.

Still, Todd D. "Placing Pain in a Pauline Frame: Considering Suffering in Romans 5 and 8." In *Interpretation and the Claims of the Text*, edited by Jason A. Whitlark, et al., 73–88. Waco: Balyor University Press, 2014.

Stowers, Stanley K. *A Rereading of Romans: Justice, Jews, and Gentiles.* New Haven, CT: Yale University Press, 1997.

Strawn, B. A. "Pharaoh." In *DOTP*, edited by T. D. Alexander and D. W. Baker, 631–36. Leicester: IVP, 2003.

Stuart, Douglas. *Hosea-Jonah.* WBC 31. Waco, TX: Word 1987.

Suetonius. *The Lives of the Twelve Caesars.* 2 vols. Translated by J. C. Rolfe. LCL 31 and 38. Cambridge, MA: Harvard University Press, 1913.

Talbert, Charles H. *Learning Through Suffering.* Collegeville, MN: Liturgical, 1991.

———. *Romans.* SHBC. Macon, GA: Smyth & Helwys, 2002.

Tamez, Elsa. *The Amnesty of Grace: Justification by Faith From a Latin American Perspective.* Nashville: Abingdon, 1993.

Tannehill, Robert C. *The Shape of the Gospel.* Eugene, OR: Cascade, 2007.

Thayer, Joseph. *Thayer's Greek-English Lexicon of the New Testament.* Peabody, MA: Hendrickson, 1996.

Theissen, Gerd. "Social Conflicts in the Corinthian Community: Further Remarks on J. J. Meggitt, Paul, Poverty and Survival." *JSNT* 25 (2003) 371–91.

———. "The Social Structure of Pauline Communities: Some Critical Remarks on J. J. Meggitt, Paul, Poverty and Survival." *JSNT* 84 (2001) 65–84.

Thielman, Frank. *Paul and the Law.* Downers Grove, IL: IVP, 1994.

Tsang, Sam. "Are We 'Misreading' Paul?: Oral Phenomena and Their Implication for the Exegesis of Paul's Letters." *Oral Tradition* 24 (2009) 205–25.

Tsumura, D. T. "An OT Background to Rom 8.22." *NTS* 40 (1994) 620–21.

Vanhoozer, Kevin J. "The Reader in New Testament Interpretation." In *Hearing the New Testament*, edited by Joel B. Green, 259–88. Grand Rapids: Eerdmans, 2010.

Virgil. *Eclogues, Georgica, Aeneid.* 2 vols. Translated by H R. Fairclough. LCL 63 and 64. Cambridge, MA: Harvard University Press. 1916.

Wagner, J. Ross. *Heralds of the Good News*, Brill: Boston, 2003.

———. "The Heralds of Isaiah and the Mission of Paul." In *Jesus and the Suffering Servant*, edited by W. H. Bellinger and William R. Farmer, 193–222. Harrisburg, PA: Trinity, 1998.

———. "Isaiah in Romans and Galatians." In *Isaiah in the New Testament*, edited by Steve Moyise and Maarten J. J. Menken, 117–32. London: T. & T. Clark, 2005.

Walker, D. D. "Benefactor." In *DNTB*, edited by Craig A. Evans and Stanley E. Porter, 157–9. Leicester: IVP, 2000.

Wallace, Daniel. *Greek Grammar Beyond the Basics: An Exegetical Syntax of the New Testament.* Grand Rapids: Zondervan, 1996.

Walters, James C. "Paul, Adoption, and Inheritance." In *Paul in the Greco-Roman World*, edited by J. Paul Sampley, 42–76. Harrisburg, PA: Trinity, 2003.

Waltke, Bruce K. *Genesis.* Grand Rapids: Zondervan, 2001.

Walton, John H. *Ancient Near Eastern Thought and the Old Testament.* Nottingham: Apollos, 2007.

————. *Genesis 1 As Ancient Cosmology.* Winona Lake, IN: Eisenbrauns, 2011.

————. *The Lost World of Genesis One: Ancient Cosmology and the Origins Debate.* Downers Grove, IL: IVP, 2009.

Walton, John H., et al. *The IVP Bible Background Commenatry: Old Testament.* Downers Grove, IL: IVP, 2000.

Watson, D. F. "Roman Social Classes." In *DNTB*, edited by Craig Evans and Stanley E. Porter, 999–1004. Leicester: IVP, 2000.

Watson, Francis. "Is There a Story in These Texts?" In *Narrative Dynamics in Paul: A Critical Assessment*, edited by Bruce W. Longenecker, 231–40. Louisville: Westminster John Knox, 2002.

————. *Paul and the Hermeneutics of Faith.* London: T. & T. Clark, 2004.

Watts, Rikk E. "The New Exodus/New Creational Restoration of the Image of God: A Biblical–Theological Perspective on Salvation." In *What Does It Mean To Be Saved*, edited by John G. Jr. Stackhouse, 15–42. Grand Rapids: Baker, 2002.

Watts, Rikki E. *Isaiah's New Exodus in Mark.* Grand Rapids: Baker, 1997.

Wedderburn, A. J. M. *The Reasons for Romans.* SNTW. Edinburgh: T. & T. Clark, 1988.

Weinfeld, Moshe. "Sabbath, Temple and the Enthronement of the Lord." In *Mélanges bibliques et orientaux en l'honneur de M. Henri Cazelles*, edited by A. Caquot and M. Delcor, 501–12. Kevelaer: Verlag Butzon & Bercker, 1981.

Welborn, L. L. Review of *Remember the Poor*, by Bruce W. Longenecker. *Review of Biblical Literature*, July 2012. http://www.bookreviews.org/pdf/7899_9350.pdf.

Wenham, David. *Paul: Follower of Jesus or Founder of Christianity?* Grand Rapids: Eerdmans, 1995.

Wenham, G. J. *Genesis 1–15.* WBC 1. Waco, TX: Word, 1987.

White, Joel. "Paul's Cosmology: The Witness of Romans, 1 and 2 Corinthians, and Galatians." In *Cosmology and New Testament Theology*, edited by Jonathan T. Pennington and Sean M. McDonough, 90–106. London: T. & T. Clark, 2008.

Wilckens, Ulrich. *Der Brief an die Römer—Röm 6–11.* EKKNT 6. Zurich: Benziger, 1980.

Wilk, Florian. *Die Bedeutung des Jesajabuches für Paulus.* FRLANT 179. Göttingen: Vandenhoeck & Ruprecht, 1998.

Wink, Walter. *Naming the Powers.* Philadelphia: Fortress, 1984.

Witherington, Ben III. *Paul's Letter to the Romans: A Socio-Rhetorical Commentary.* Grand Rapids: Eerdmans, 2004.

Wolter, Michael. "Der Apostel und seine Gemeinden als Teilhaber am Leidensgeschick Jesu Christi: Beobachtungen zur paulinischen Leidenstheologie." *NTS* 36 (1990) 535–57.

Wright, Archie T. *The Origin of Evil Spirits: The Reception of Genesis 6.1–4 in Recent Literature.* WUNT 2.198. Tübingen: Mohr Siebeck, 2005.

Wright, Christopher J. H. *The Message of Ezekiel.* Leicester: IVP, 2001.

Wright, N. T. *The Climax of the Covenant.* Edinburgh: T. & T. Clark, 1991.

————. *The Letter to the Romans.* NIB X. Nashville: Abingdon, 2002.

————. "New Exodus, New Inheritance: The Narrative Structure of Romans 3–8." In *Romans and the People of God*, edited by Sven K. Soderlund and N. T. Wright, 26–35. Grand Rapids: Eerdmans, 1999.

————. "Paul and Caesar: A New Reading of Romans." In *A Royal Priesthood: The Use of the Bible Ethically and Politically*, edited by Craig Bartholemew, 173–93. Carlisle: Paternoster, 2002.

———. *Paul and the Faithfulness of God*. Minneapolis: Fortress, 2013.

———. *The Resurrection of the Son of God*. Minneapolis: Fortress, 2003.

Wu, Julie L. "The Spirit's Intercession in Romans 8:26–27." *ExpTim* 105 (1993) 13.

Wu, Siu Fung. "Practise Love and Follow Christ." *Transformation* 29 (2012) 62–72.

Yates, John W. *The Spirit and Creation in Paul*. WUNT 2.251. Tübingen: Mohr Siebeck, 2008.

Yeo, K. K. "Christ and the Earth in Pauline and Native American Understandings." In *Cross-cultural Paul: Journeys to Others, Journeys to Ourselves*, edited by Charles H. Cosgrove, et al., 179–218. Grand Rapids: Eerdmans, 2005.

Zanker, Paul. *The Power of Images in the Age of Augustus*. Ann Arbor, MI: University of Michigan Press 1990.

Ziesler, John A. "The Just Requirement of the Law (Romans 8:4)." *ABR* 35 (1987) 77–82.

Index of Ancient Sources

Jeremiah

Lamentations

Ezekiel

Index of Subjects

Index of Modern Authors